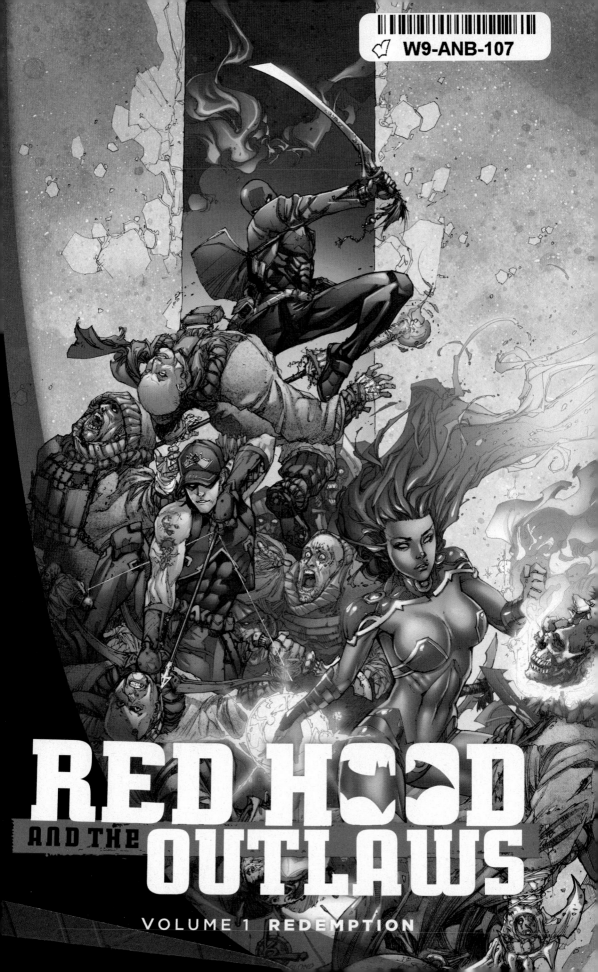

RED HOOD
AND THE OUTLAWS

VOLUME 1 REDEMPTION

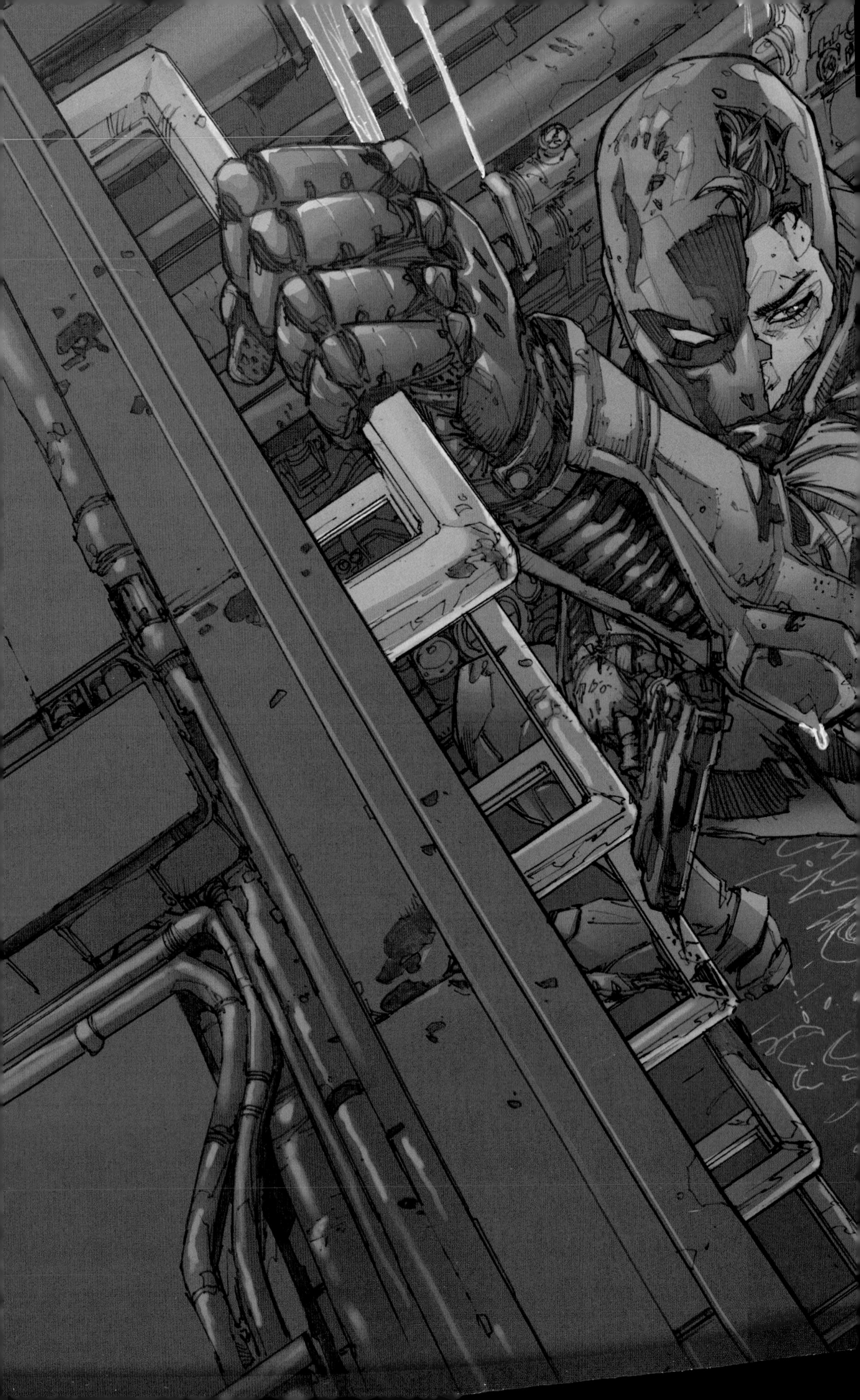

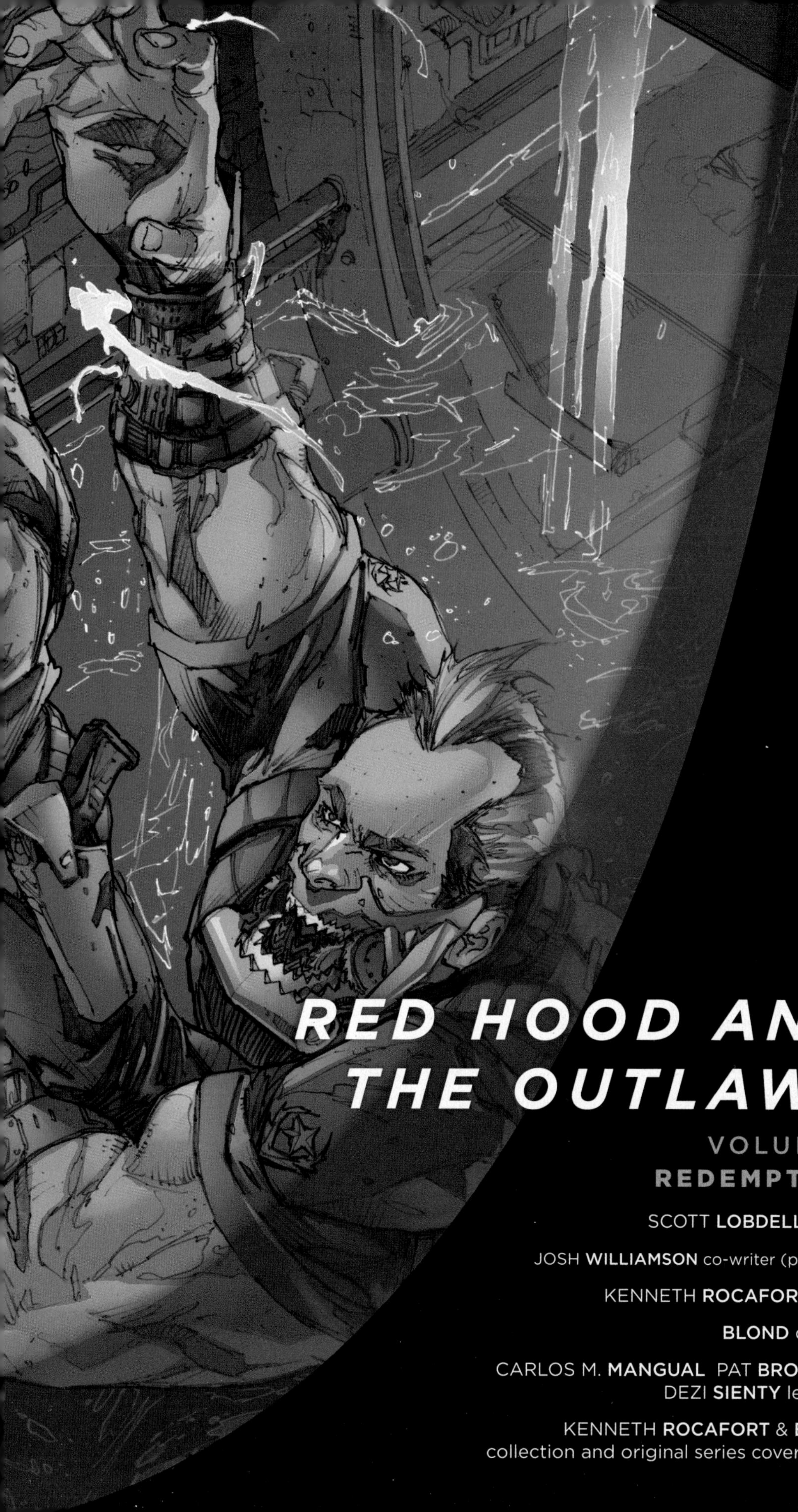

RED HOOD AND THE OUTLAWS

VOLUME 1
REDEMPTION

SCOTT **LOBDELL** writer

JOSH **WILLIAMSON** co-writer (part one)

KENNETH **ROCAFORT** artist

BLOND colorist

CARLOS M. **MANGUAL** PAT **BROSSEAU**
DEZI **SIENTY** letterers

KENNETH **ROCAFORT** & **BLOND**
collection and original series cover artists

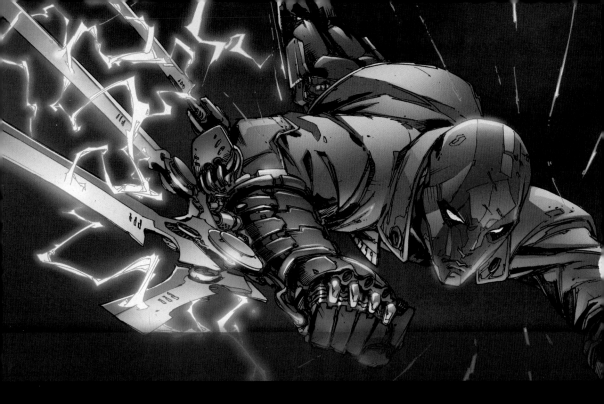

BOBBIE CHASE Editor – Original Series KATIE KUBERT Assistant Editor – Original Series
PETER HAMBOUSSI Editor ROBBIN BROSTERMAN Design Director – Books
ROBBIE BIEDERMAN Publication Design

BOB HARRAS Senior VP – Editor-in-Chief, DC Comics

DIANE NELSON President DAN DIDIO and JIM LEE Co-Publishers
GEOFF JOHNS Chief Creative Officer
JOHN ROOD Executive VP – Sales, Marketing & Business Development
AMY GENKINS Senior VP – Business & Legal Affairs NAIRI GARDINER Senior VP – Finance
JEFF BOISON VP – Publishing Planning MARK CHIARELLO VP – Art Direction & Design
JOHN CUNNINGHAM VP – Marketing TERRI CUNNINGHAM VP – Editorial Administration
ALISON GILL Senior VP – Manufacturing & Operations HANK KANALZ Senior VP – Vertigo & Integrated Publishing
JAY KOGAN VP – Business & Legal Affairs, Publishing JACK MAHAN VP – Business Affairs, Talent
NICK NAPOLITANO VP – Manufacturing Administration SUE POHJA VP – Book Sales
COURTNEY SIMMONS Senior VP – Publicity BOB WAYNE Senior VP – Sales

DC Comics, 1700 Broadway, New York, NY 10019
A Warner Bros. Entertainment Company.
Printed by Transcontinental Interglobe, Beauceville, QC, Canada. 11/1/13. Third Printing.

ISBN: 978-1-4012-3712-7

SUSTAINABLE FORESTRY INITIATIVE
Certified Chain of Custody
Promoting Sustainable Forestry
www.sfiprogram.org
SFI-00507
This Label only applies to the text section

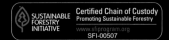

Library of Congress Cataloging-in-Publication Data

Lobdell, Scott.
Red Hood and the Outlaws volume 1 : redemption / Scott Lobdell, Kenneth Rocafort.
p. cm.
"Originally published in single magazine form in Red Hood and The Outlaws 1-7."
ISBN 978-1-4012-3712-7
1. Graphic novels. I. Rocafort, Kenneth. II. Title. III. Title: Redemption.
PN6728.R4385L63 2012
741.5'973—dc23
2012023700

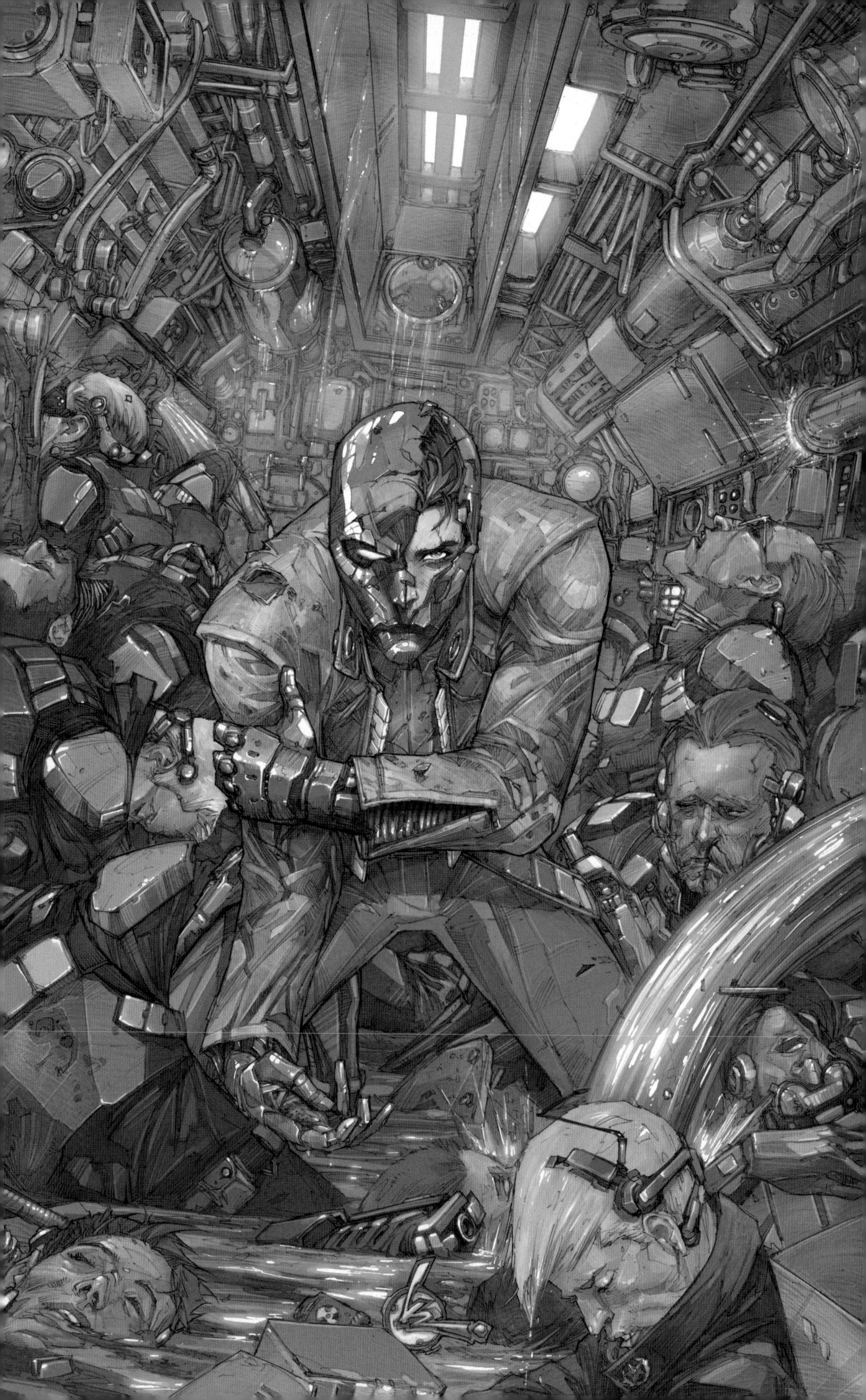

PENCILLER KENNETH ROCAFORT INKER PAGE# A2
TITLE RED HOOD AND THE OUTLAWS ISSUE # 6 MONTH INTERIORS

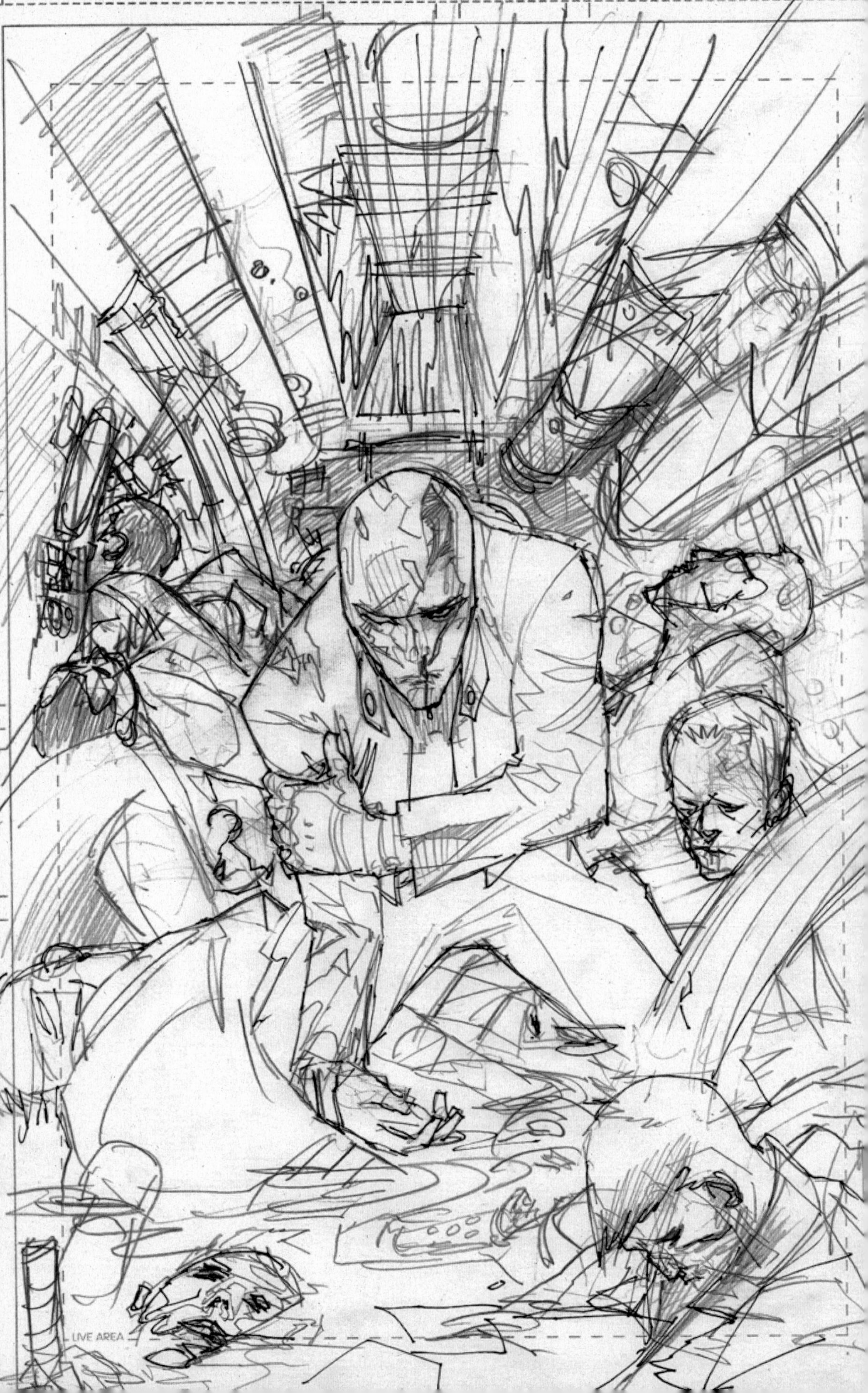
LIVE AREA

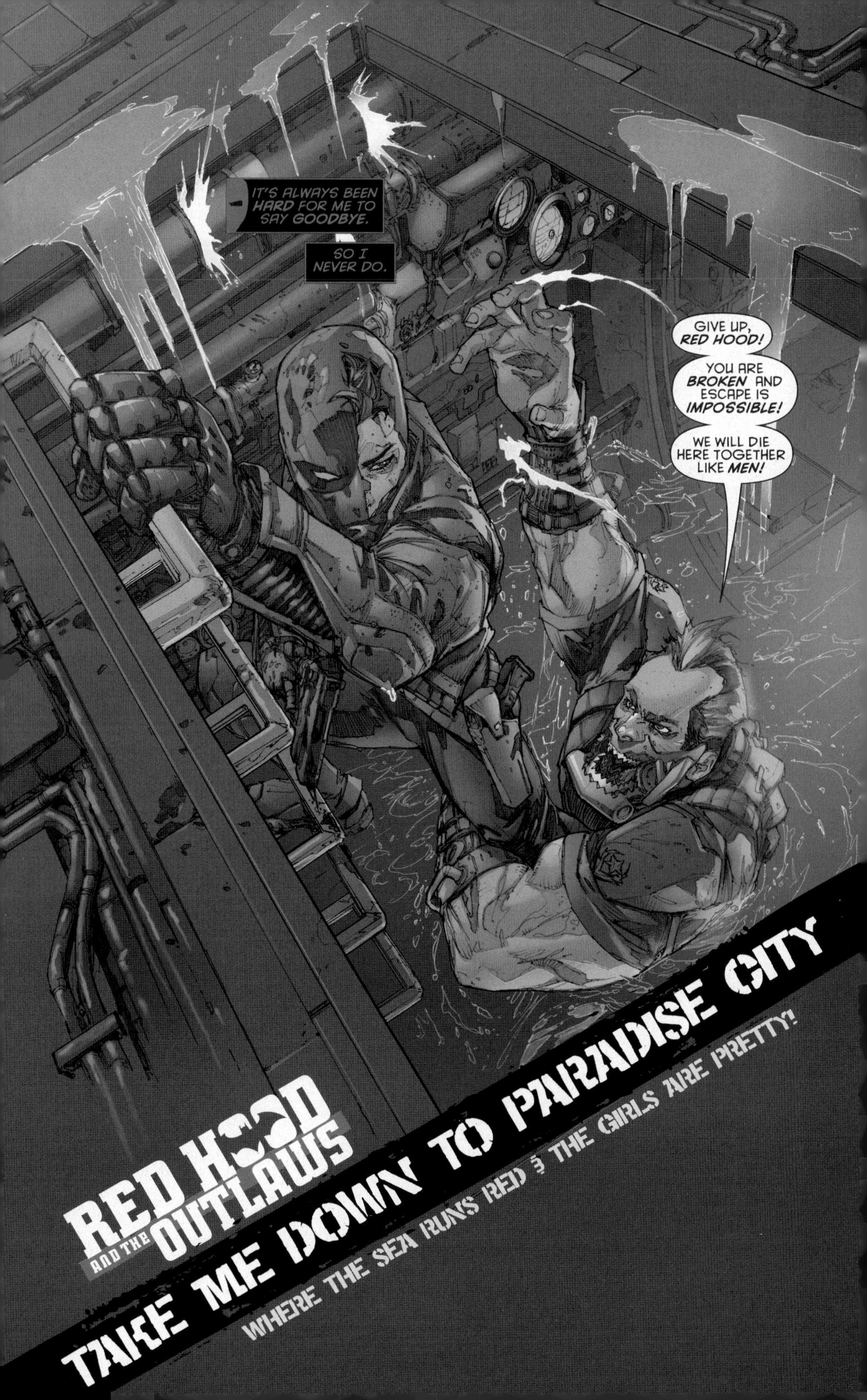
IT'S ALWAYS BEEN HARD FOR ME TO SAY GOODBYE.
SO I NEVER DO.
GIVE UP, RED HOOD!
YOU ARE BROKEN AND ESCAPE IS IMPOSSIBLE!
WE WILL DIE HERE TOGETHER LIKE MEN!
RED HOOD AND THE OUTLAWS
TAKE ME DOWN TO PARADISE CITY
WHERE THE SEA RUNS RED & THE GIRLS ARE PRETTY!

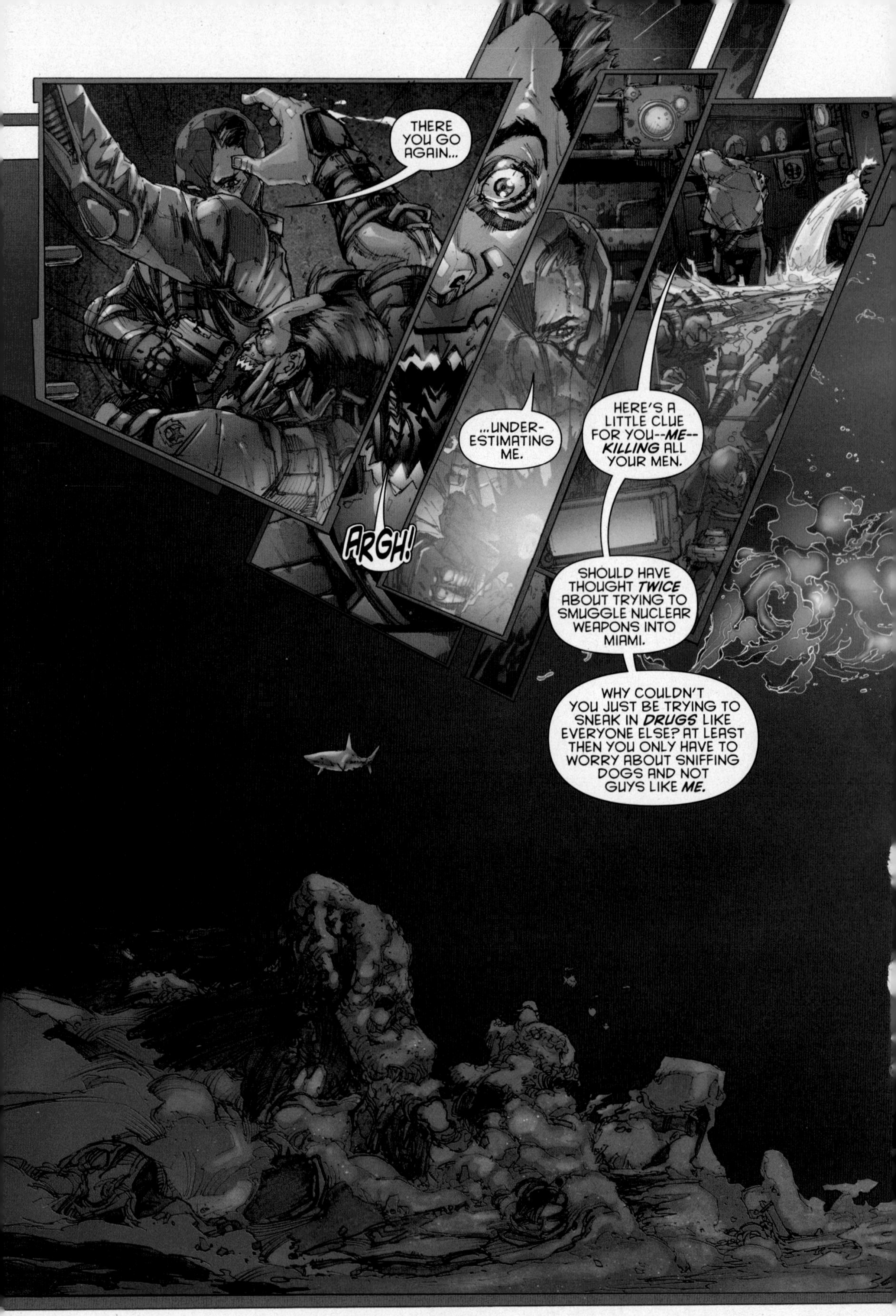
THERE YOU GO AGAIN...
...UNDER-ESTIMATING ME.
ARGH!
HERE'S A LITTLE CLUE FOR YOU--ME--KILLING ALL YOUR MEN.
SHOULD HAVE THOUGHT TWICE ABOUT TRYING TO SMUGGLE NUCLEAR WEAPONS INTO MIAMI.
WHY COULDN'T YOU JUST BE TRYING TO SNEAK IN DRUGS LIKE EVERYONE ELSE? AT LEAST THEN YOU ONLY HAVE TO WORRY ABOUT SNIFFING DOGS AND NOT GUYS LIKE ME.

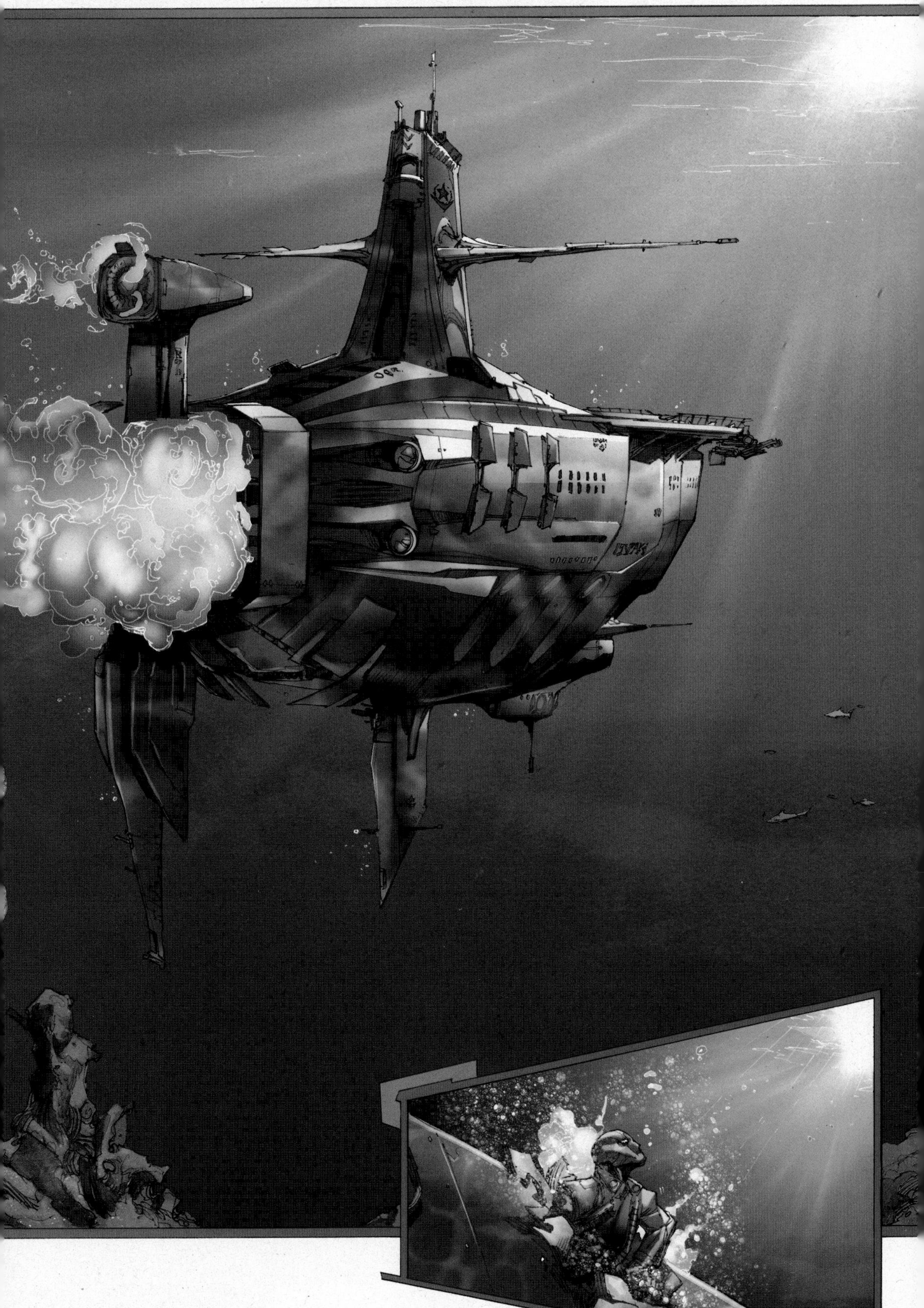

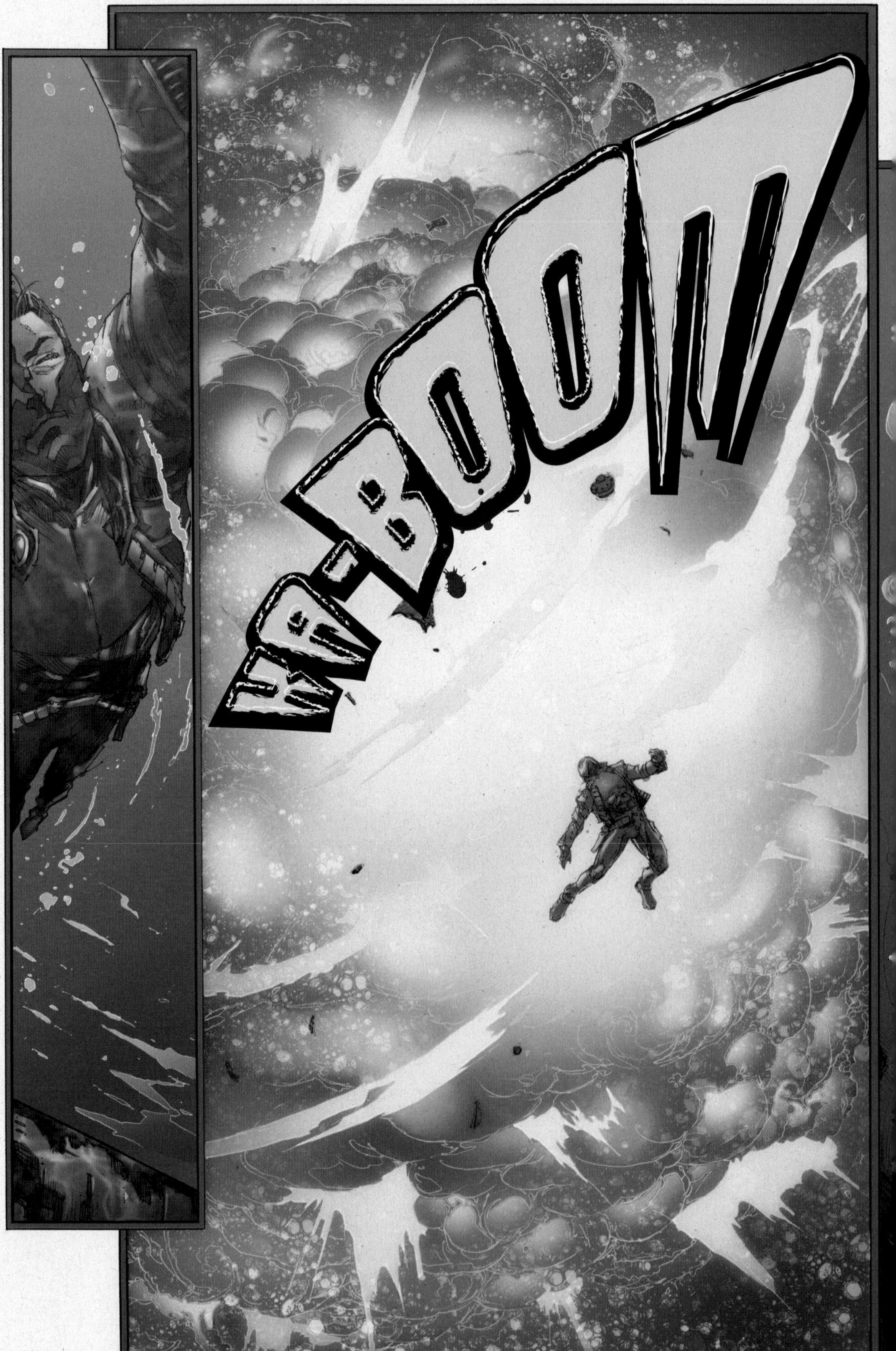
KA-BOOM

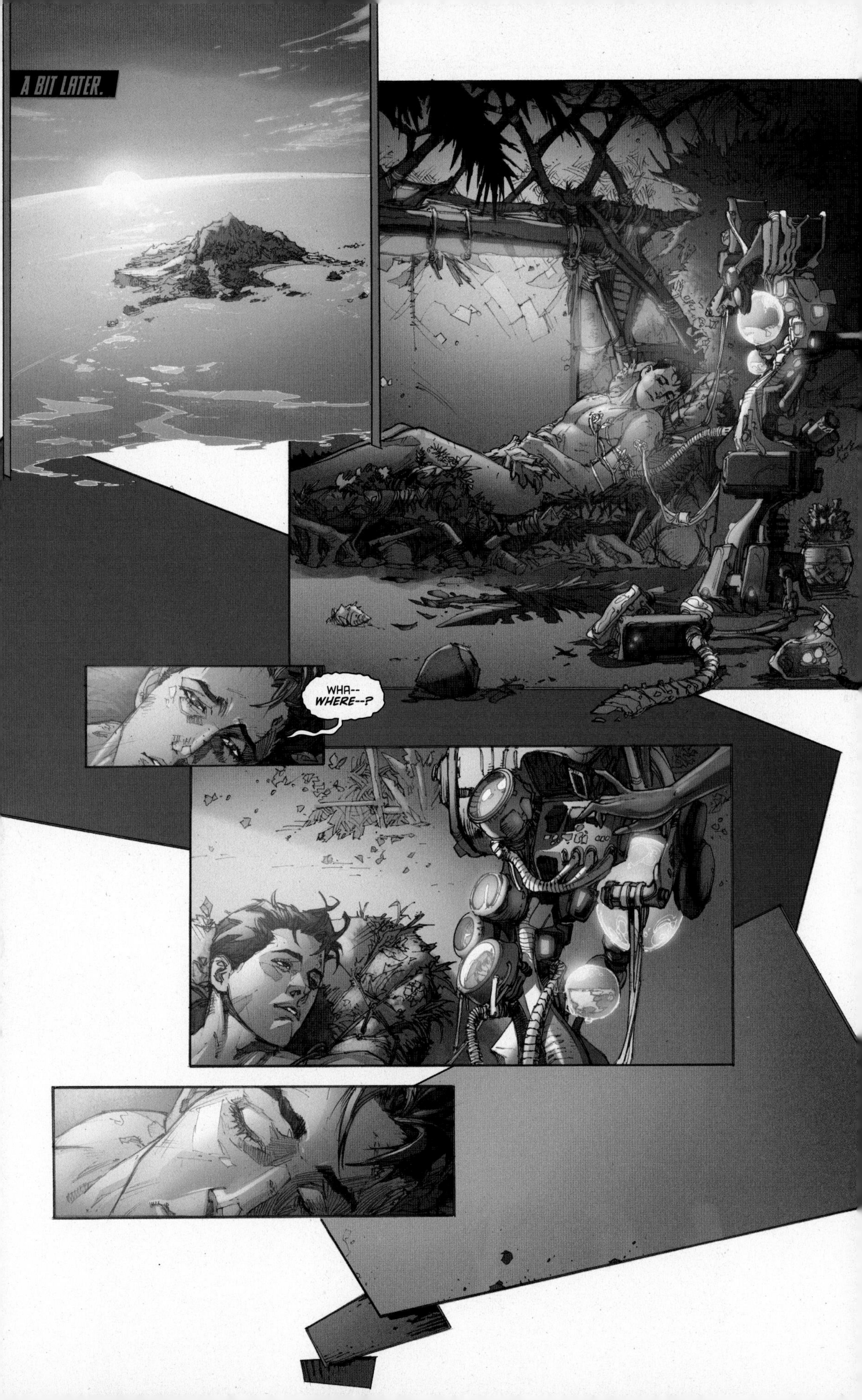
A BIT LATER.
WHA--
WHERE--?

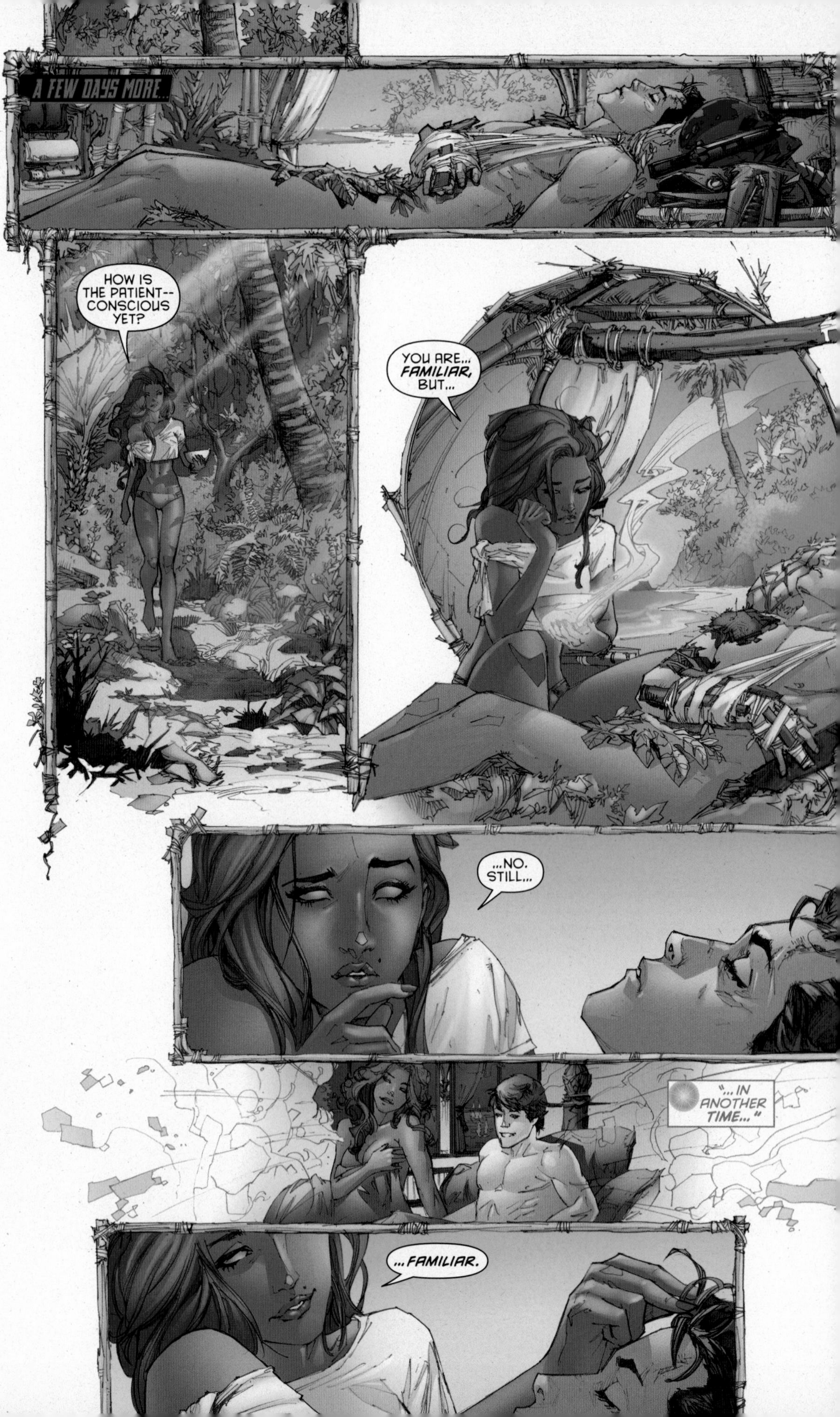
A FEW DAYS MORE...
HOW IS THE PATIENT-- CONSCIOUS YET?
YOU ARE... FAMILIAR, BUT...
...NO. STILL...
"...IN ANOTHER TIME..."
...FAMILIAR.

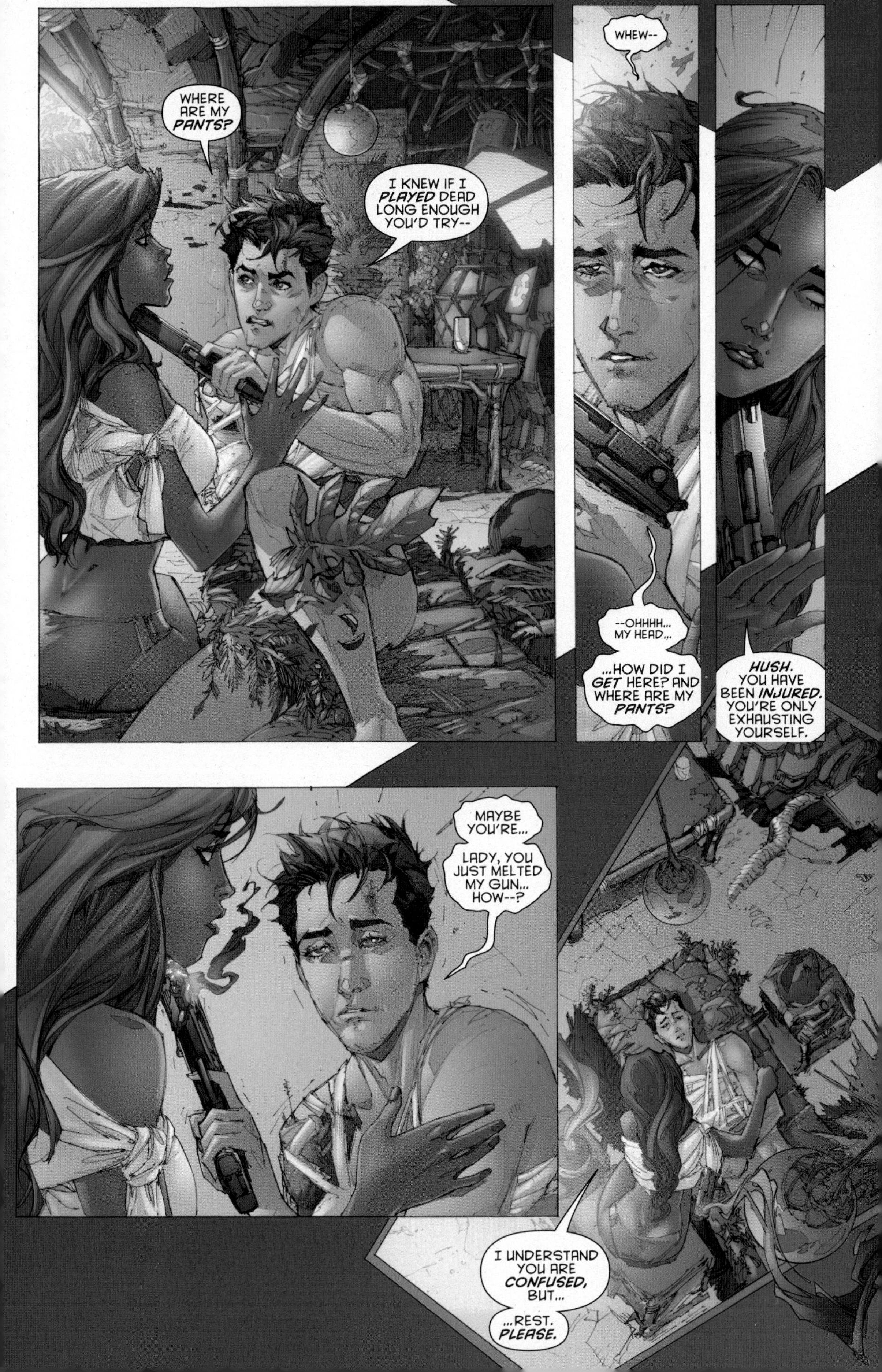

WHERE ARE MY *PANTS?*
I KNEW IF I *PLAYED* DEAD LONG ENOUGH YOU'D TRY--
WHEW--
--OHHHH... MY HEAD...
...HOW DID I *GET* HERE? AND WHERE ARE MY *PANTS?*
HUSH. YOU HAVE BEEN *INJURED.* YOU'RE ONLY EXHAUSTING YOURSELF.
MAYBE YOU'RE...
LADY, YOU JUST MELTED MY GUN... HOW--?
I UNDERSTAND YOU ARE *CONFUSED,* BUT...
...REST. *PLEASE.*

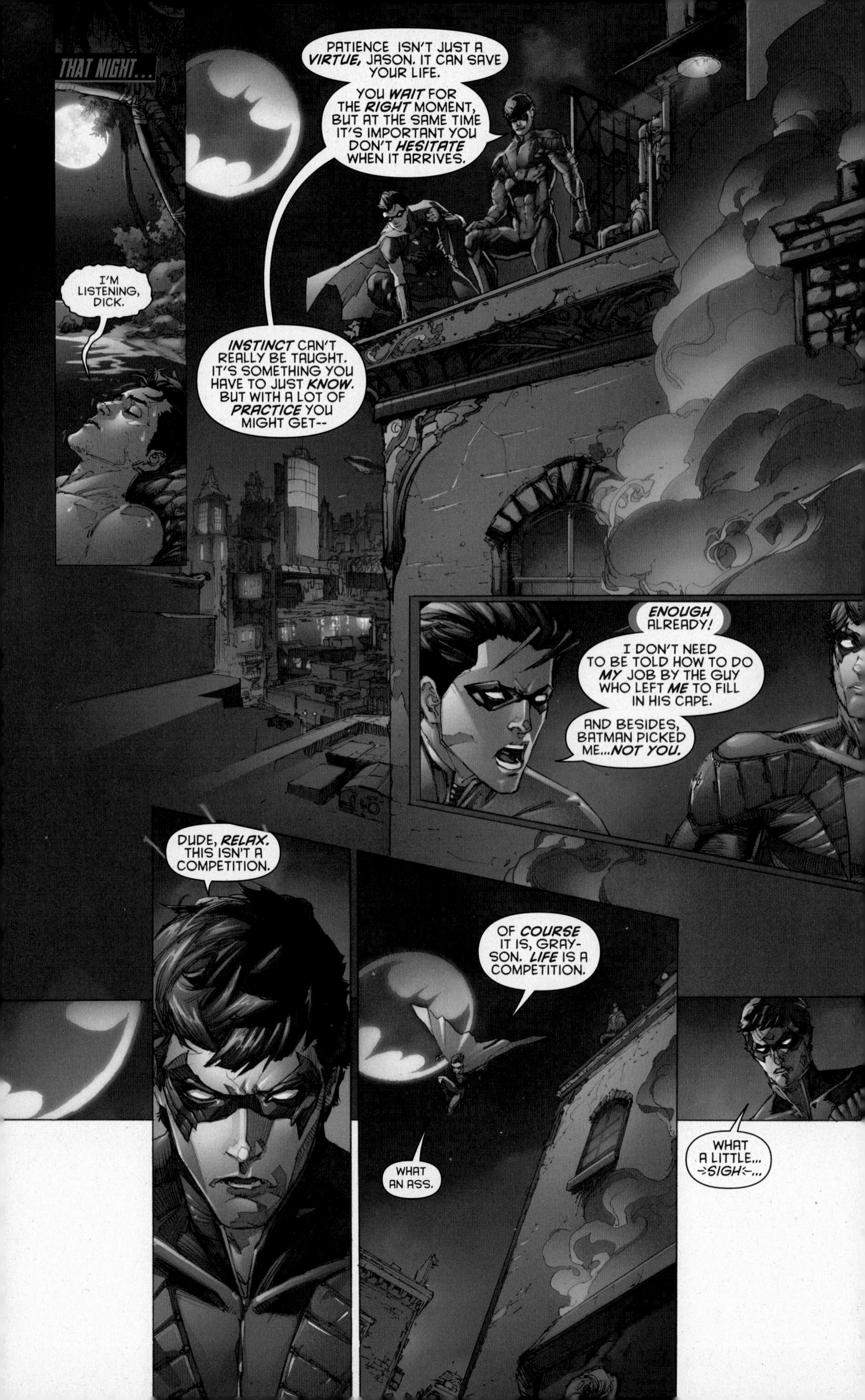
THAT NIGHT...
PATIENCE ISN'T JUST A VIRTUE, JASON. IT CAN SAVE YOUR LIFE.
YOU WAIT FOR THE RIGHT MOMENT, BUT AT THE SAME TIME IT'S IMPORTANT YOU DON'T HESITATE WHEN IT ARRIVES.
I'M LISTENING, DICK.
INSTINCT CAN'T REALLY BE TAUGHT. IT'S SOMETHING YOU HAVE TO JUST KNOW. BUT WITH A LOT OF PRACTICE YOU MIGHT GET--
ENOUGH ALREADY!
I DON'T NEED TO BE TOLD HOW TO DO MY JOB BY THE GUY WHO LEFT ME TO FILL IN HIS CAPE.
AND BESIDES, BATMAN PICKED ME...NOT YOU.
DUDE, RELAX. THIS ISN'T A COMPETITION.
OF COURSE IT IS, GRAYSON. LIFE IS A COMPETITION.
WHAT AN ASS.
WHAT A LITTLE... ~SIGH~...

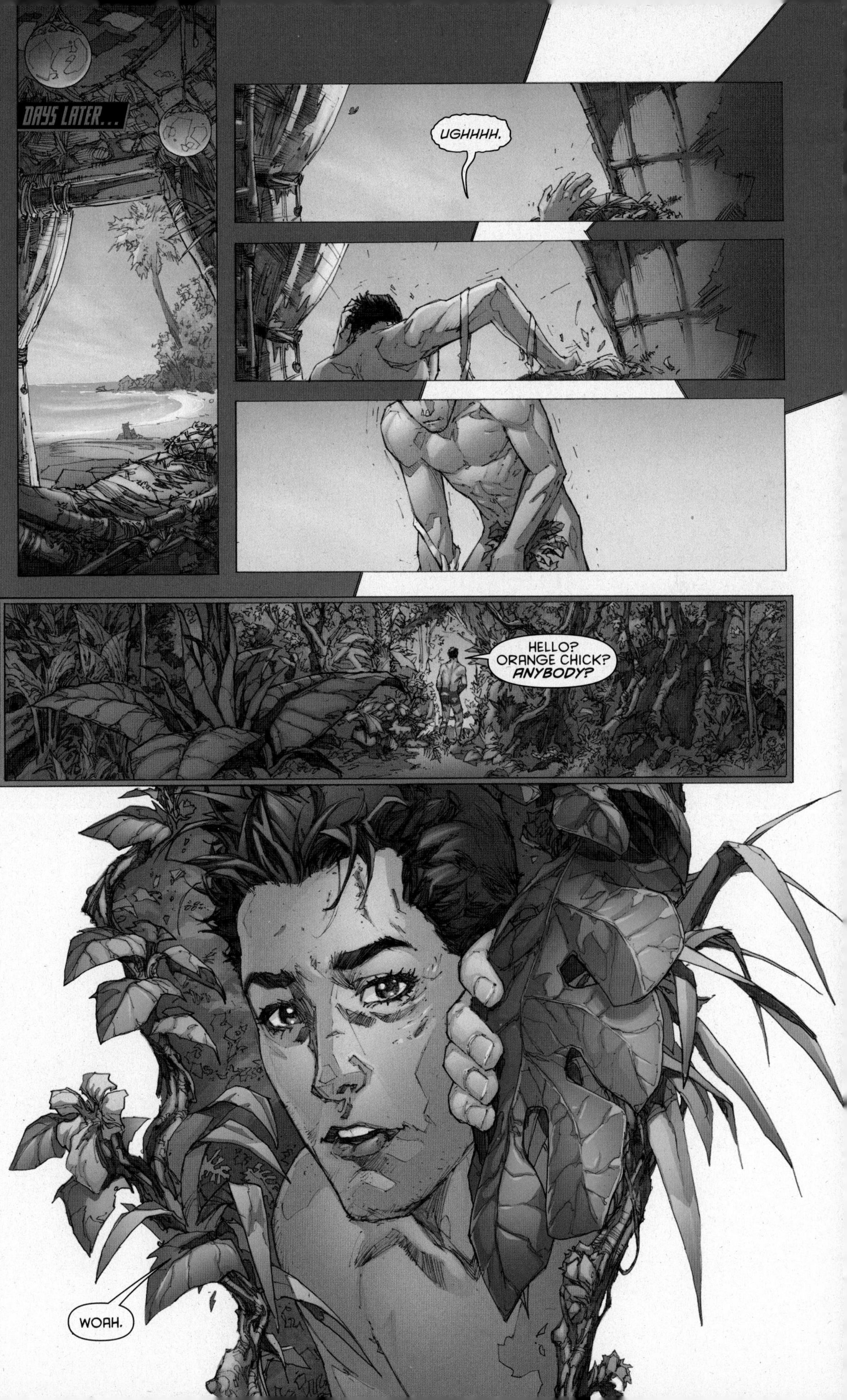
DAYS LATER...
UGHHHH.
HELLO?
ORANGE CHICK?
ANYBODY?
WOAH.

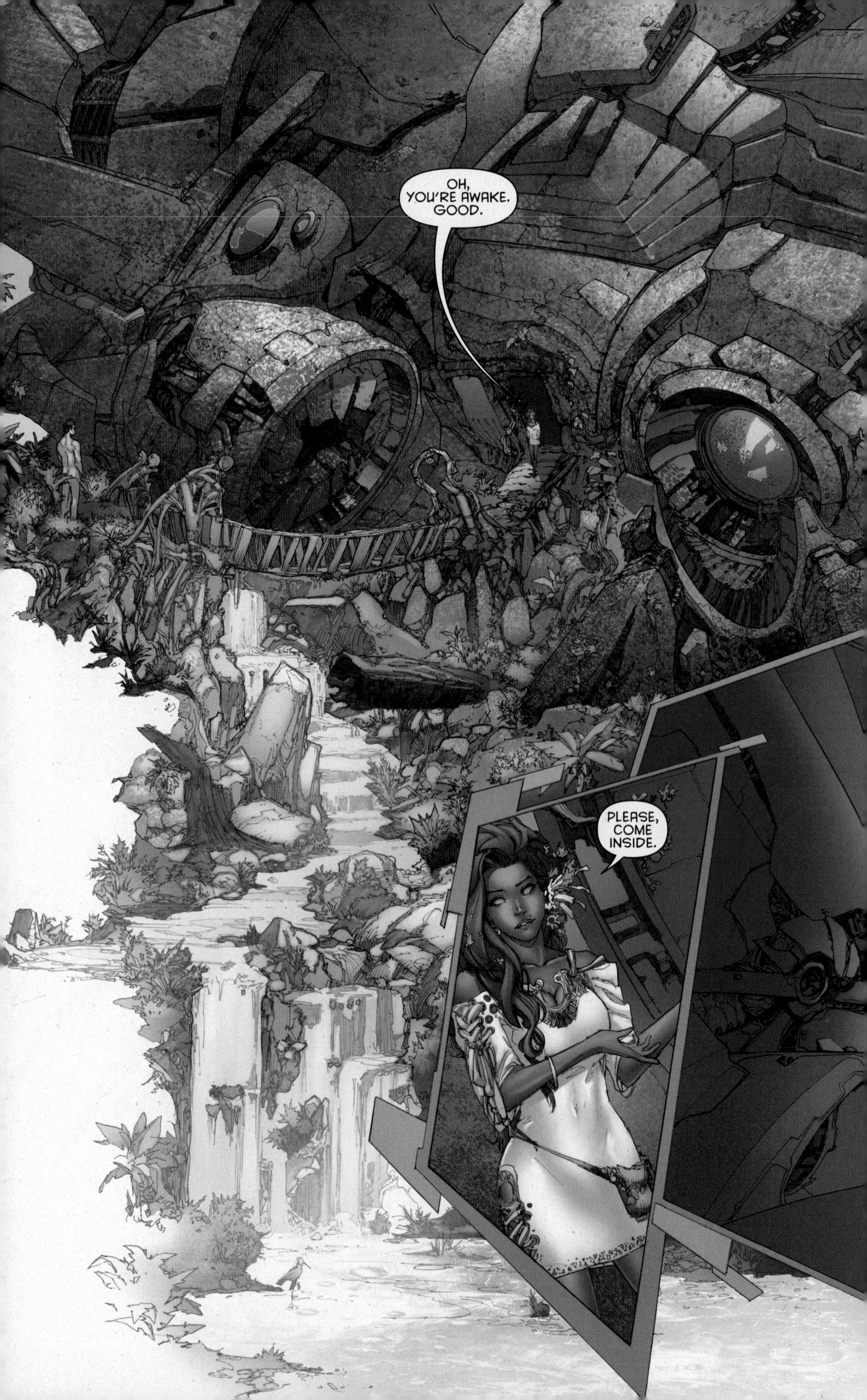
OH, YOU'RE AWAKE. GOOD.
PLEASE, COME INSIDE.

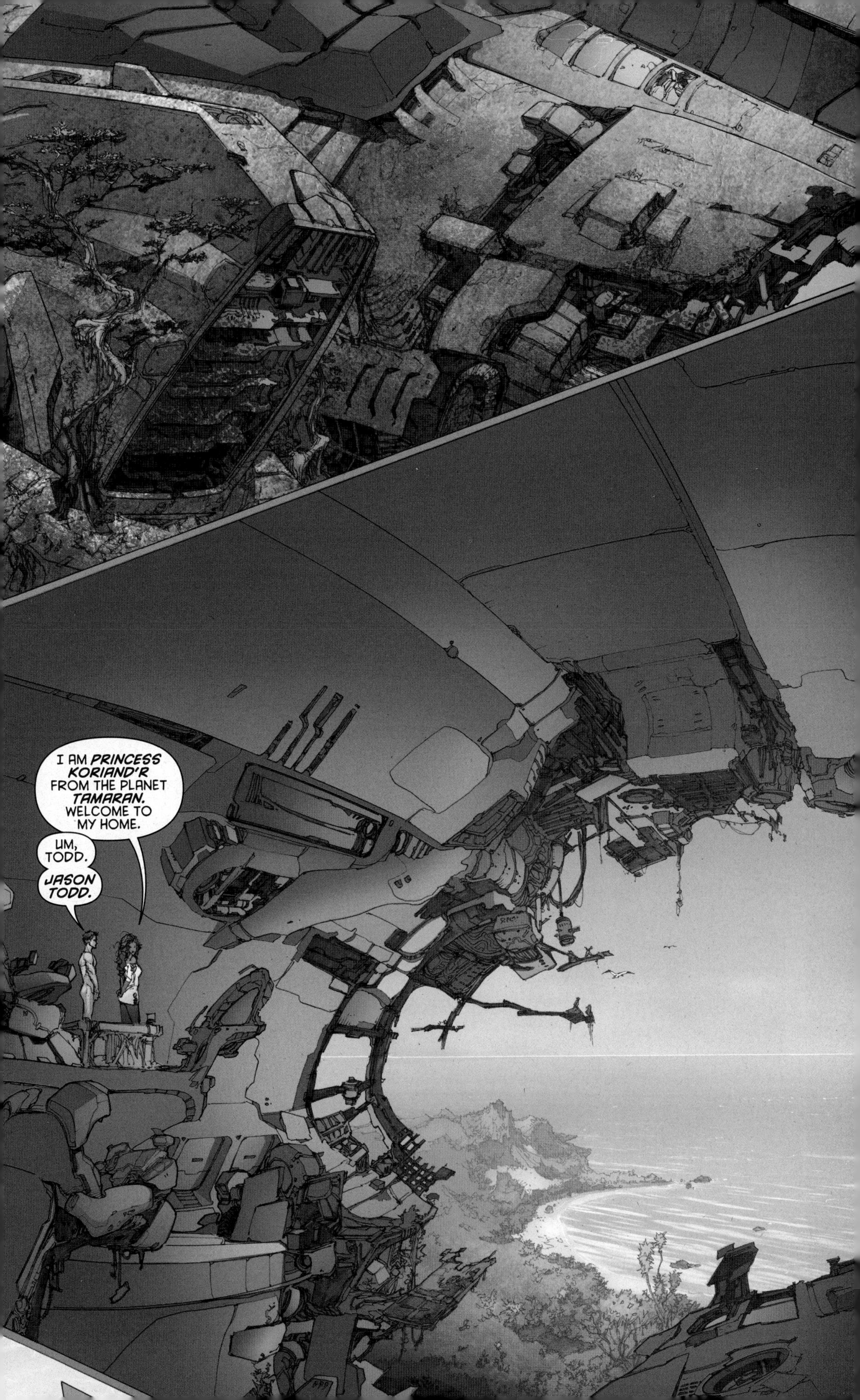
I AM PRINCESS KORIAND'R FROM THE PLANET TAMARAN. WELCOME TO MY HOME.
UM, TODD.
JASON TODD.

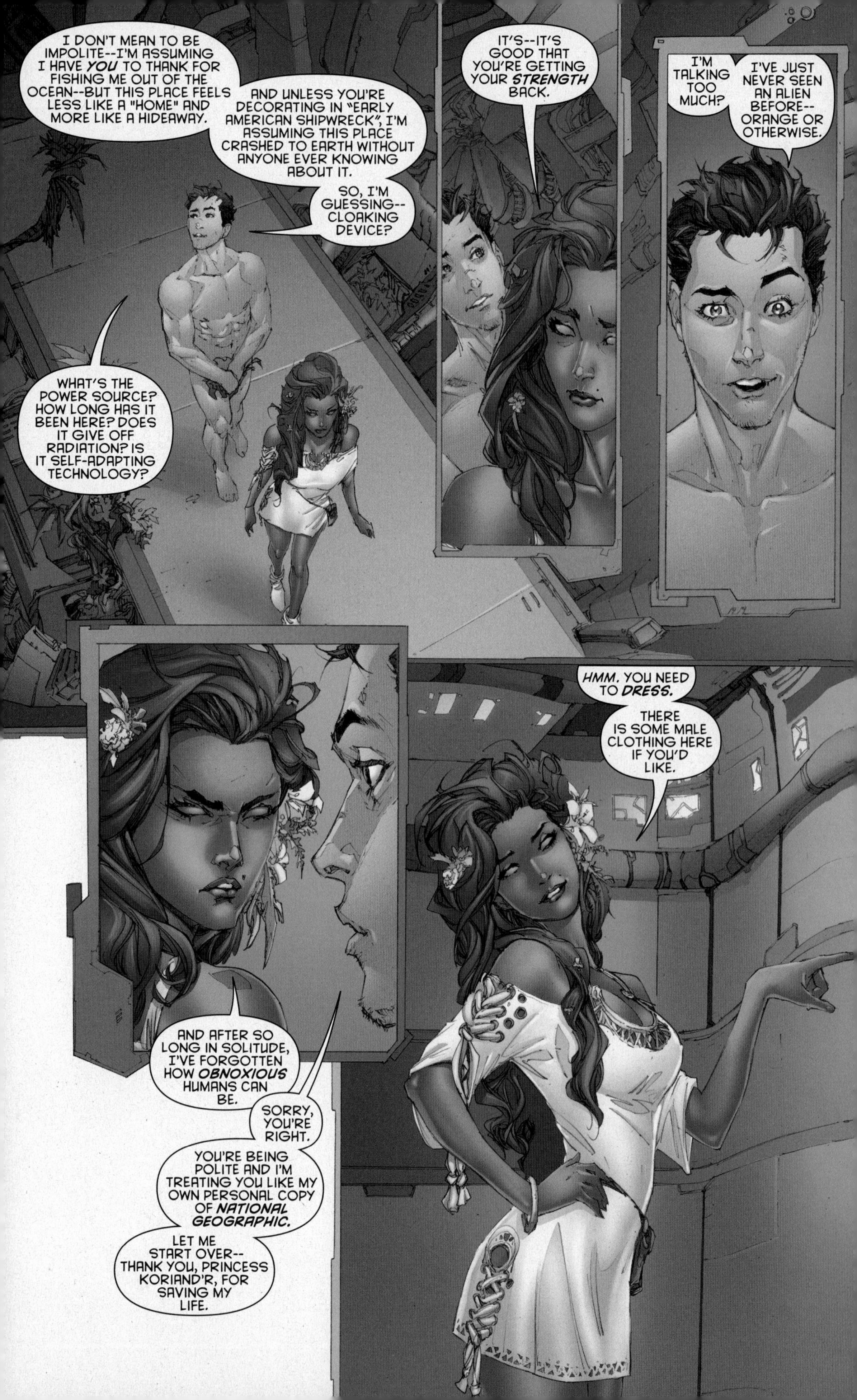
I DON'T MEAN TO BE IMPOLITE--I'M ASSUMING I HAVE *YOU* TO THANK FOR FISHING ME OUT OF THE OCEAN--BUT THIS PLACE FEELS LESS LIKE A "HOME" AND MORE LIKE A HIDEAWAY.
AND UNLESS YOU'RE DECORATING IN "EARLY AMERICAN SHIPWRECK", I'M ASSUMING THIS PLACE CRASHED TO EARTH WITHOUT ANYONE EVER KNOWING ABOUT IT.
SO, I'M GUESSING--CLOAKING DEVICE?
WHAT'S THE POWER SOURCE? HOW LONG HAS IT BEEN HERE? DOES IT GIVE OFF RADIATION? IS IT SELF-ADAPTING TECHNOLOGY?
IT'S--IT'S GOOD THAT YOU'RE GETTING YOUR *STRENGTH* BACK.
I'M TALKING TOO MUCH?
I'VE JUST NEVER SEEN AN ALIEN BEFORE--ORANGE OR OTHERWISE.
AND AFTER SO LONG IN SOLITUDE, I'VE FORGOTTEN HOW *OBNOXIOUS* HUMANS CAN BE.
SORRY, YOU'RE RIGHT.
YOU'RE BEING POLITE AND I'M TREATING YOU LIKE MY OWN PERSONAL COPY OF *NATIONAL GEOGRAPHIC.*
LET ME START OVER--THANK YOU, PRINCESS KORIAND'R, FOR SAVING MY LIFE.
HMM. YOU NEED TO *DRESS.*
THERE IS SOME MALE CLOTHING HERE IF YOU'D LIKE.

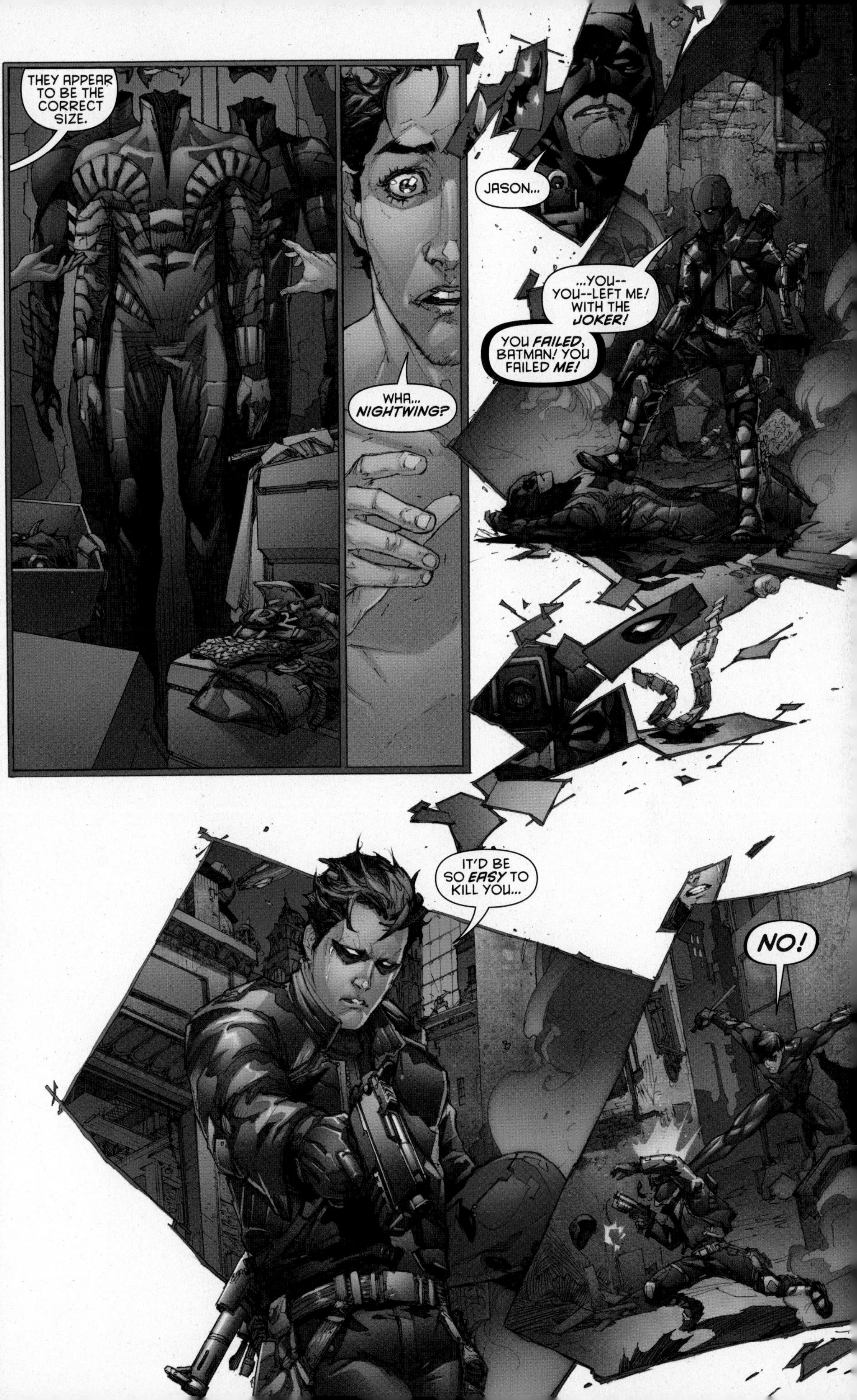
THEY APPEAR TO BE THE CORRECT SIZE.
WHA... NIGHTWING?
JASON...
...YOU-- YOU--LEFT ME! WITH THE JOKER!
YOU FAILED, BATMAN! YOU FAILED ME!
IT'D BE SO EASY TO KILL YOU...
NO!

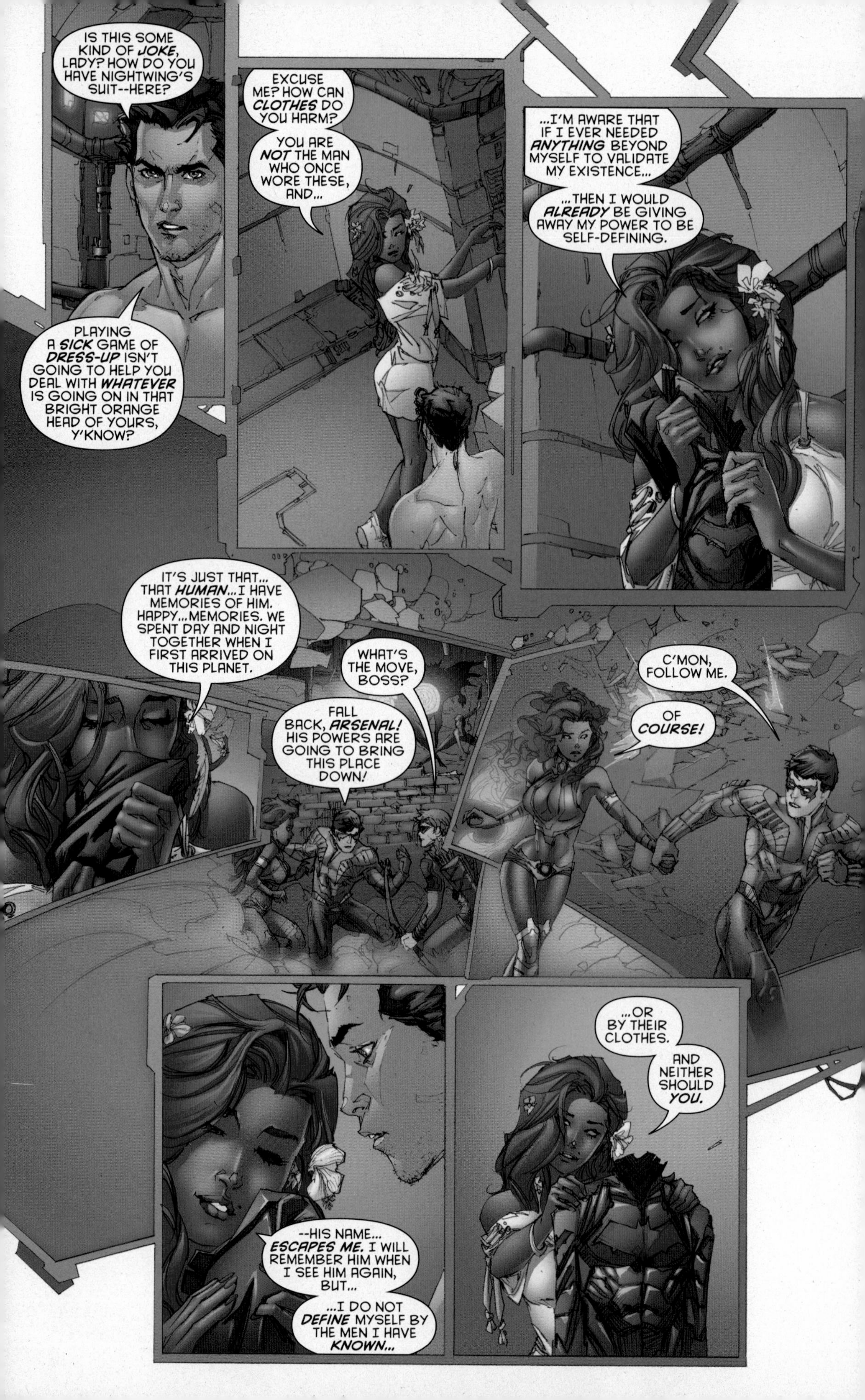
IS THIS SOME KIND OF JOKE, LADY? HOW DO YOU HAVE NIGHTWING'S SUIT--HERE?
PLAYING A SICK GAME OF DRESS-UP ISN'T GOING TO HELP YOU DEAL WITH WHATEVER IS GOING ON IN THAT BRIGHT ORANGE HEAD OF YOURS, Y'KNOW?
EXCUSE ME? HOW CAN CLOTHES DO YOU HARM?
YOU ARE NOT THE MAN WHO ONCE WORE THESE, AND...
...I'M AWARE THAT IF I EVER NEEDED ANYTHING BEYOND MYSELF TO VALIDATE MY EXISTENCE...
...THEN I WOULD ALREADY BE GIVING AWAY MY POWER TO BE SELF-DEFINING.
IT'S JUST THAT... THAT HUMAN... I HAVE MEMORIES OF HIM. HAPPY... MEMORIES. WE SPENT DAY AND NIGHT TOGETHER WHEN I FIRST ARRIVED ON THIS PLANET.
WHAT'S THE MOVE, BOSS?
FALL BACK, ARSENAL! HIS POWERS ARE GOING TO BRING THIS PLACE DOWN!
C'MON, FOLLOW ME.
OF COURSE!
--HIS NAME... ESCAPES ME. I WILL REMEMBER HIM WHEN I SEE HIM AGAIN, BUT...
...I DO NOT DEFINE MYSELF BY THE MEN I HAVE KNOWN...
...OR BY THEIR CLOTHES.
AND NEITHER SHOULD YOU.

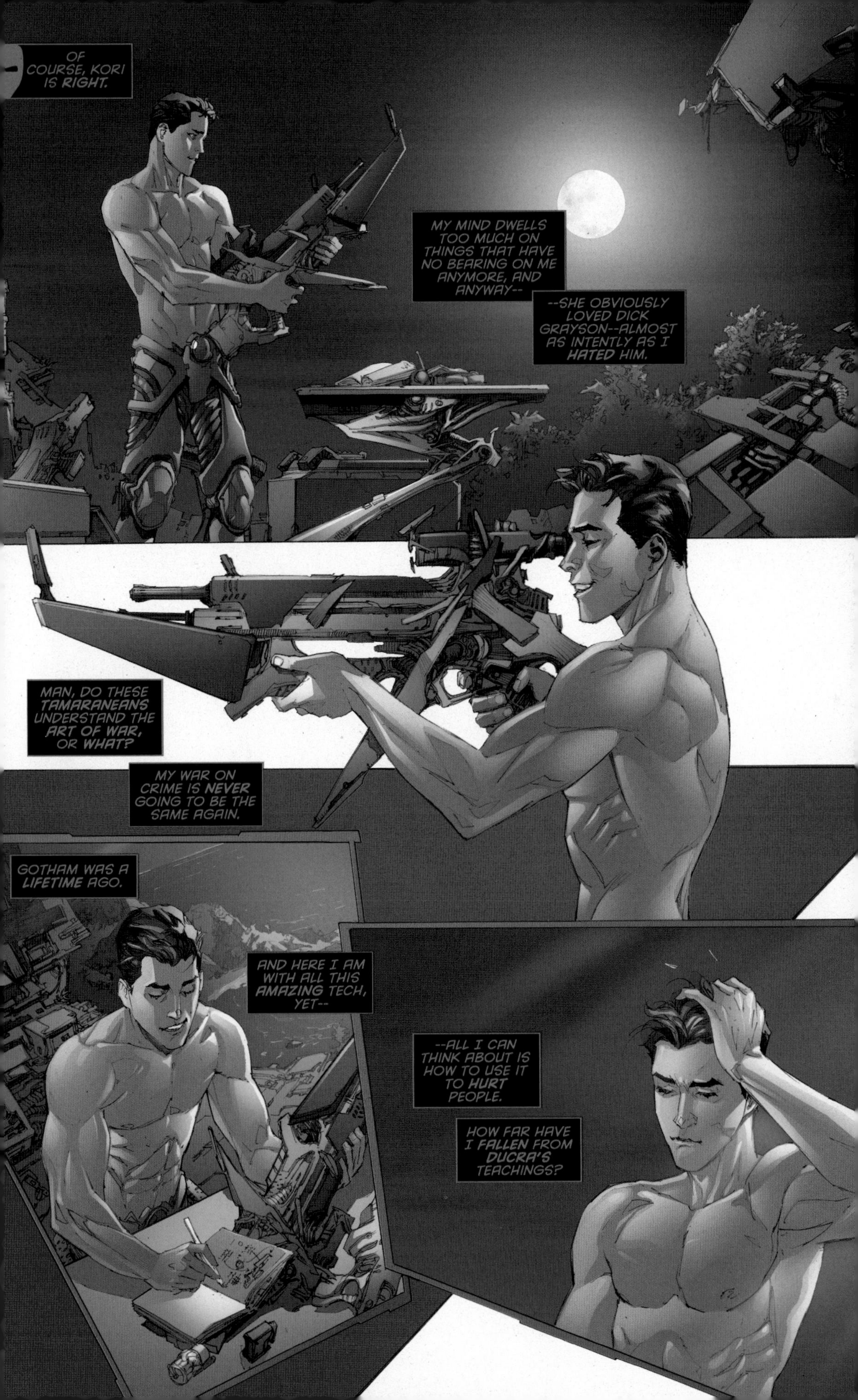
OF COURSE, KORI IS RIGHT.
MY MIND DWELLS TOO MUCH ON THINGS THAT HAVE NO BEARING ON ME ANYMORE, AND ANYWAY--
--SHE OBVIOUSLY LOVED DICK GRAYSON--ALMOST AS INTENTLY AS I HATED HIM.
MAN, DO THESE TAMARANEANS UNDERSTAND THE ART OF WAR, OR WHAT?
MY WAR ON CRIME IS NEVER GOING TO BE THE SAME AGAIN.
GOTHAM WAS A LIFETIME AGO.
AND HERE I AM WITH ALL THIS AMAZING TECH, YET--
--ALL I CAN THINK ABOUT IS HOW TO USE IT TO HURT PEOPLE.
HOW FAR HAVE I FALLEN FROM DUCRA'S TEACHINGS?

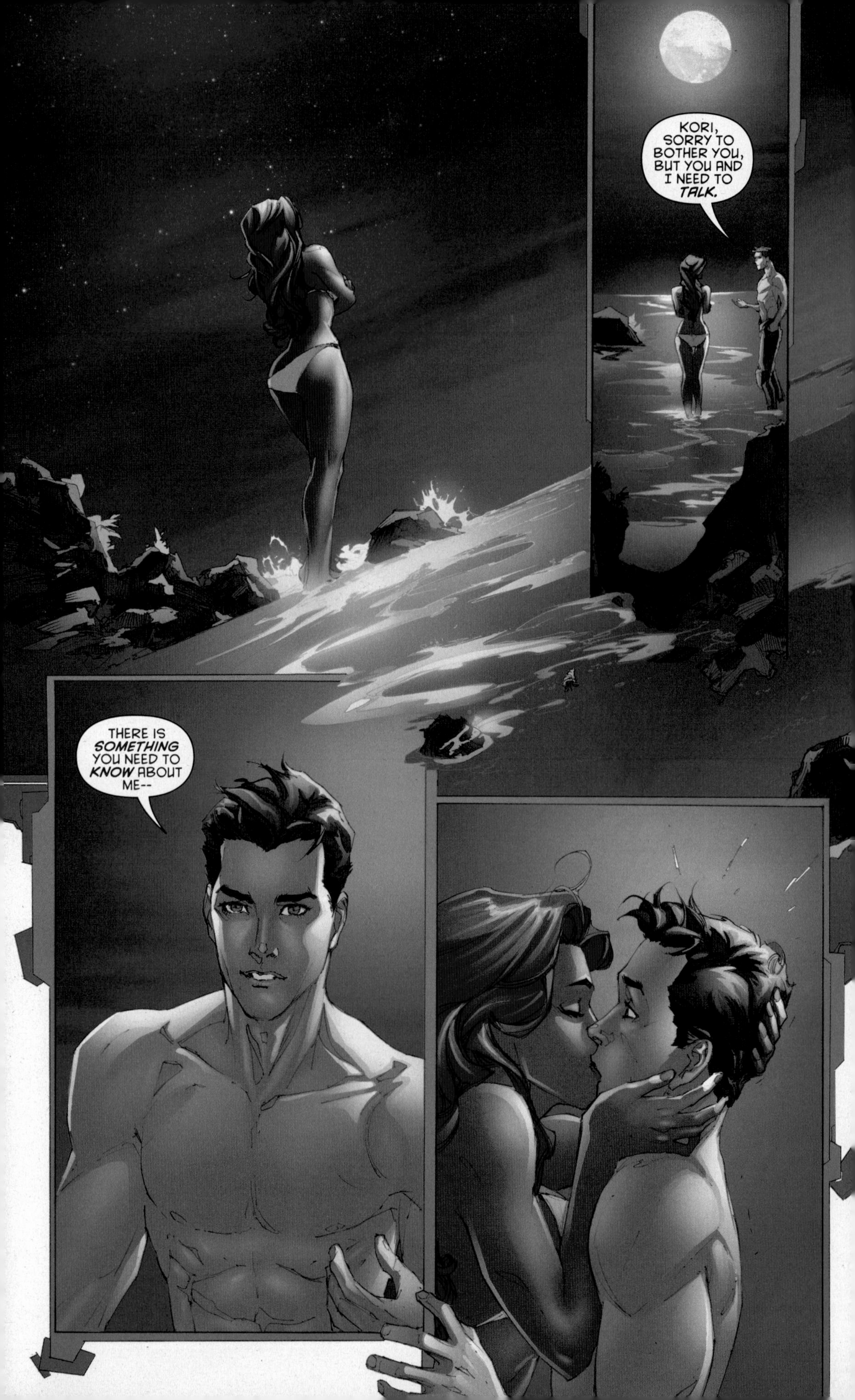
KORI, SORRY TO BOTHER YOU, BUT YOU AND I NEED TO *TALK.*
THERE IS *SOMETHING* YOU NEED TO *KNOW* ABOUT ME--

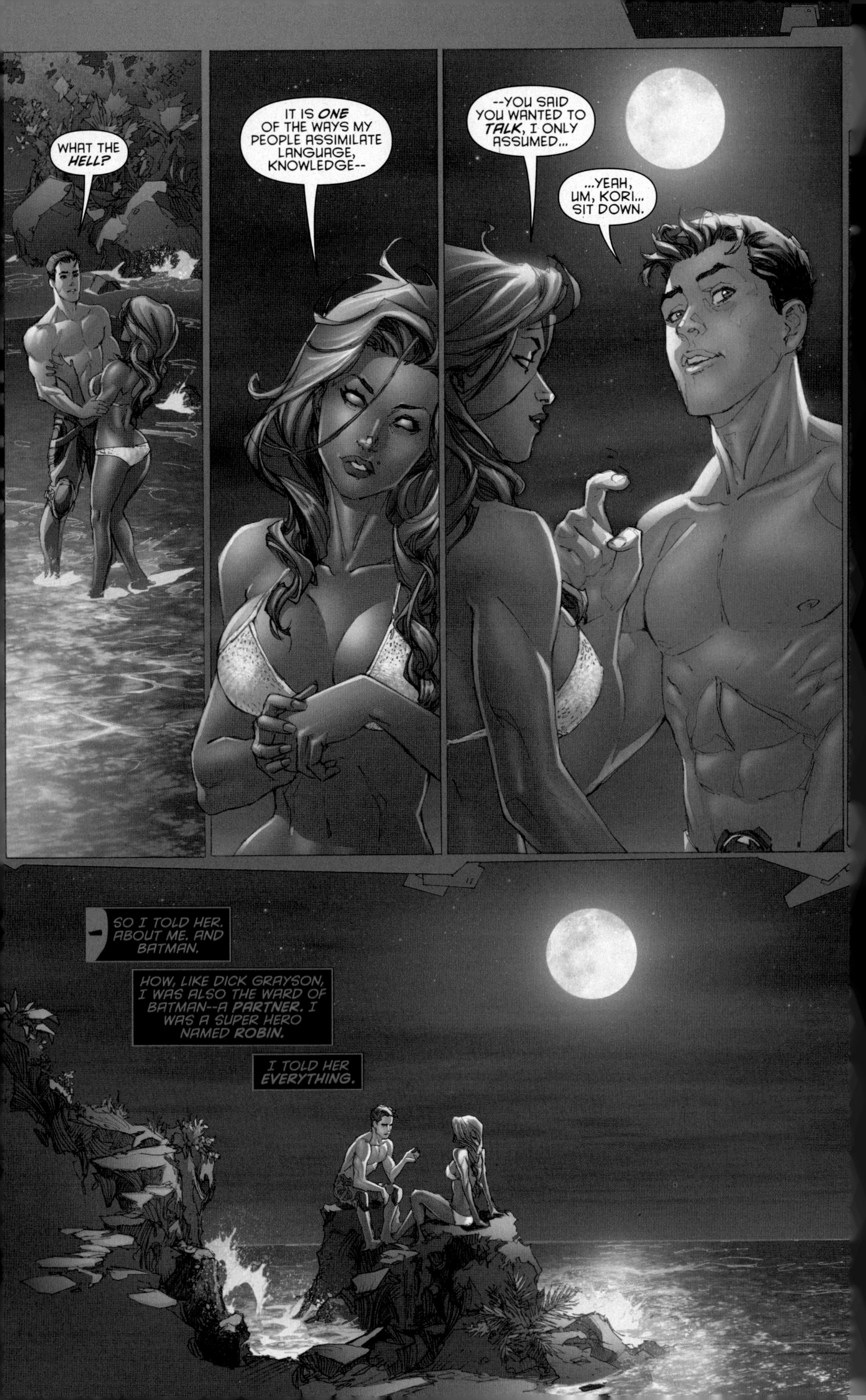
WHAT THE *HELL?*
IT IS *ONE* OF THE WAYS MY PEOPLE ASSIMILATE LANGUAGE, KNOWLEDGE--
--YOU SAID YOU WANTED TO *TALK*, I ONLY ASSUMED...
...YEAH, UM, KORI... SIT DOWN.
SO I TOLD HER. ABOUT ME. AND BATMAN.
HOW, LIKE DICK GRAYSON, I WAS ALSO THE WARD OF BATMAN--A PARTNER. I WAS A SUPER HERO NAMED *ROBIN*.
I TOLD HER *EVERYTHING*.

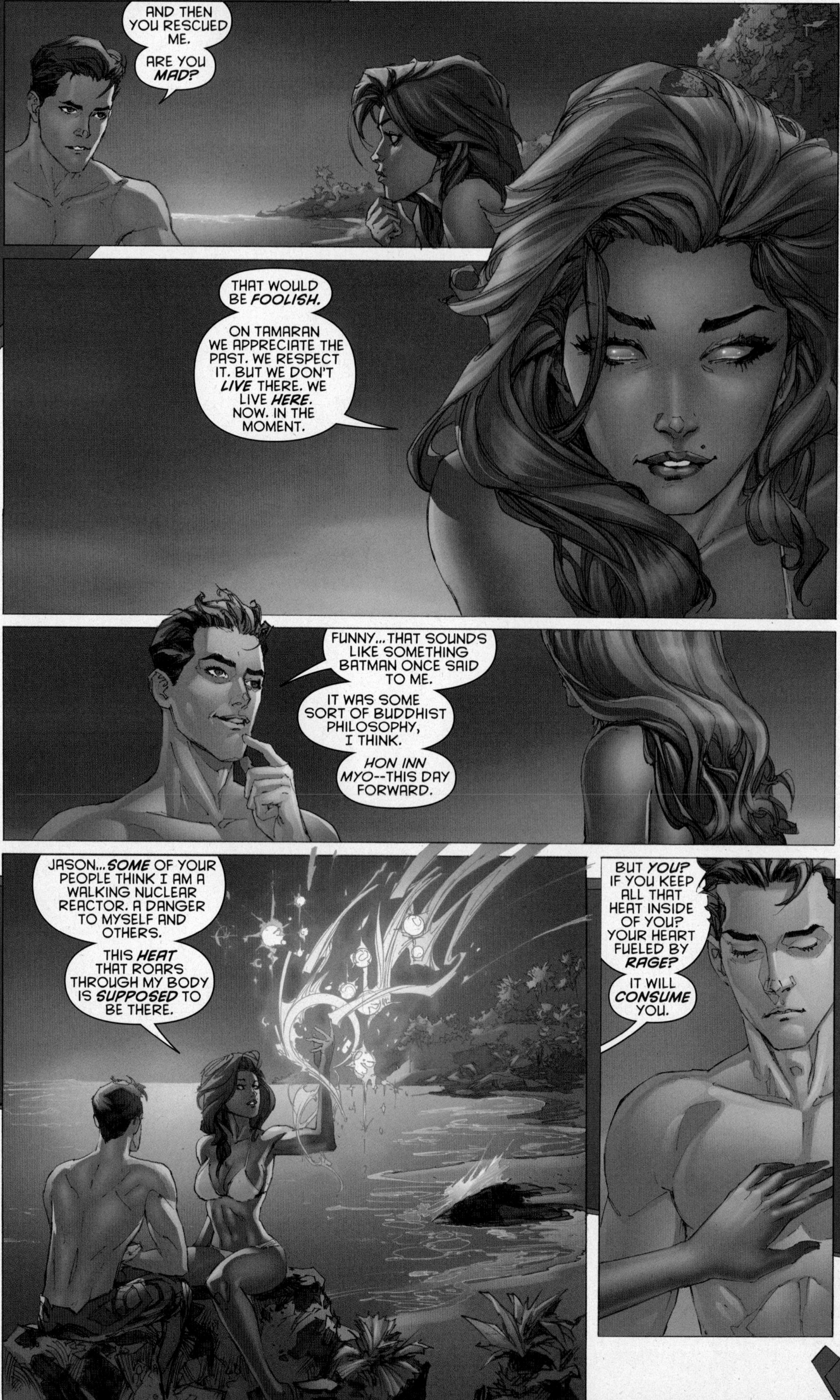

AND THEN YOU RESCUED ME.
ARE YOU *MAD?*
THAT WOULD BE *FOOLISH.*
ON TAMARAN WE APPRECIATE THE PAST. WE RESPECT IT. BUT WE DON'T *LIVE* THERE. WE LIVE *HERE.* NOW. IN THE MOMENT.
FUNNY... THAT SOUNDS LIKE SOMETHING BATMAN ONCE SAID TO ME.
IT WAS SOME SORT OF BUDDHIST PHILOSOPHY, I THINK.
HON INN MYO--THIS DAY FORWARD.
JASON... *SOME* OF YOUR PEOPLE THINK I AM A WALKING NUCLEAR REACTOR. A DANGER TO MYSELF AND OTHERS.
THIS *HEAT* THAT ROARS THROUGH MY BODY IS *SUPPOSED* TO BE THERE.
BUT *YOU?* IF YOU KEEP ALL THAT HEAT INSIDE OF YOU? YOUR HEART FUELED BY *RAGE?*
IT WILL *CONSUME* YOU.

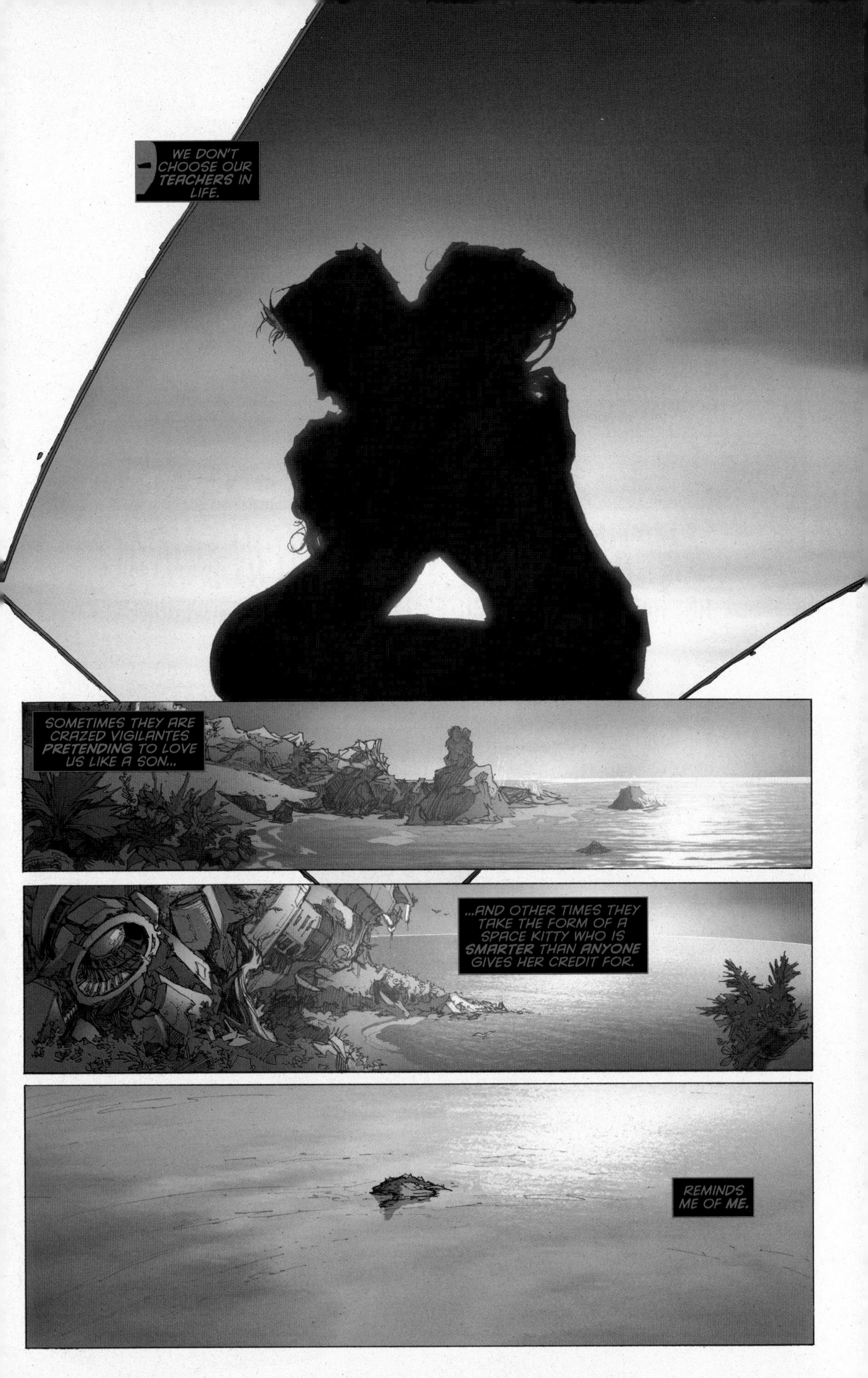
WE DON'T CHOOSE OUR TEACHERS IN LIFE.
SOMETIMES THEY ARE CRAZED VIGILANTES PRETENDING TO LOVE US LIKE A SON...
...AND OTHER TIMES THEY TAKE THE FORM OF A SPACE KITTY WHO IS SMARTER THAN ANYONE GIVES HER CREDIT FOR.
REMINDS ME OF ME.

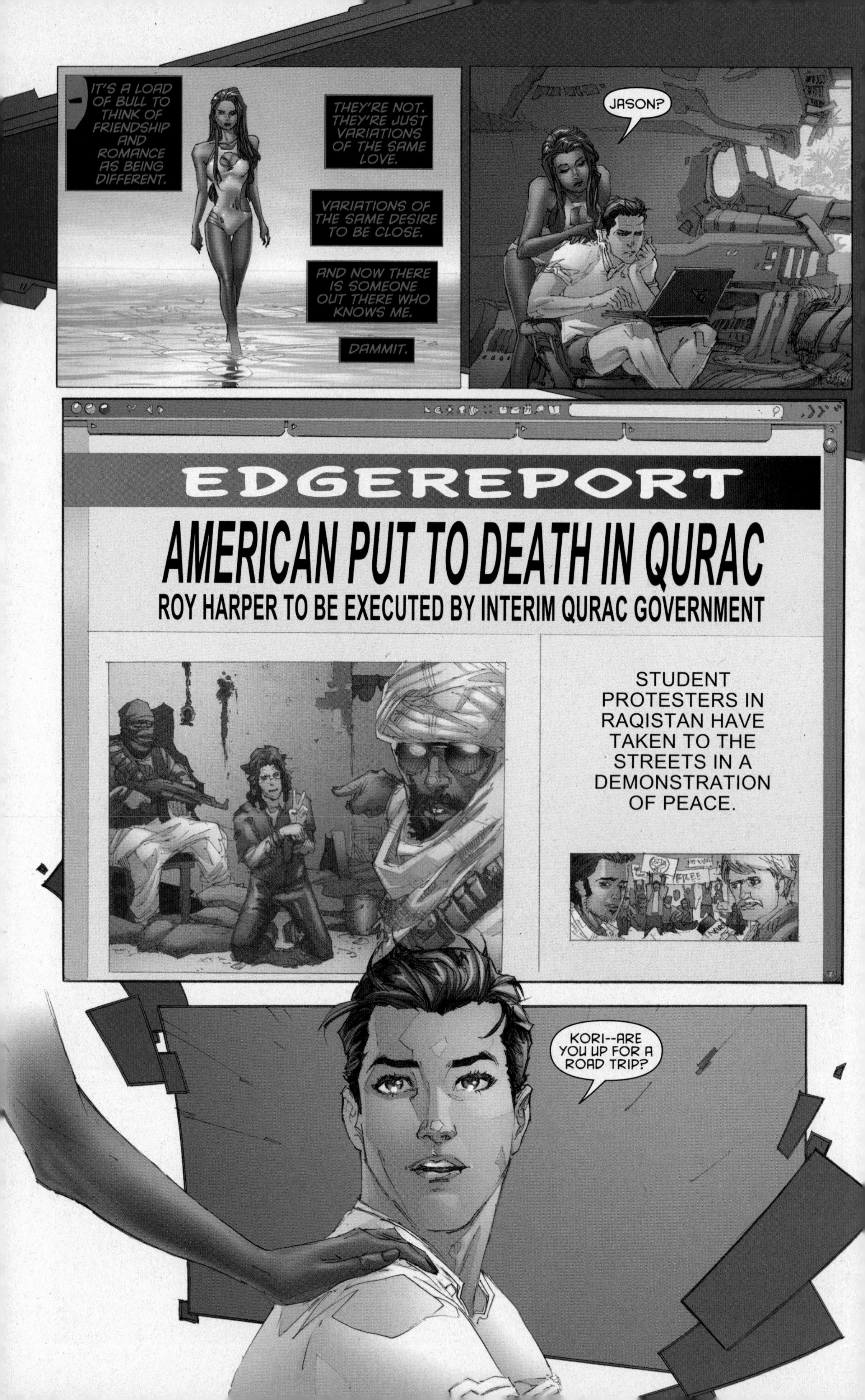

IT'S A LOAD OF BULL TO THINK OF FRIENDSHIP AND ROMANCE AS BEING DIFFERENT.
THEY'RE NOT. THEY'RE JUST VARIATIONS OF THE SAME LOVE.
VARIATIONS OF THE SAME DESIRE TO BE CLOSE.
AND NOW THERE IS SOMEONE OUT THERE WHO KNOWS ME.
DAMMIT.
JASON?
EDGEREPORT
AMERICAN PUT TO DEATH IN QURAC
ROY HARPER TO BE EXECUTED BY INTERIM QURAC GOVERNMENT
STUDENT PROTESTERS IN RAQISTAN HAVE TAKEN TO THE STREETS IN A DEMONSTRATION OF PEACE.
KORI--ARE YOU UP FOR A ROAD TRIP?

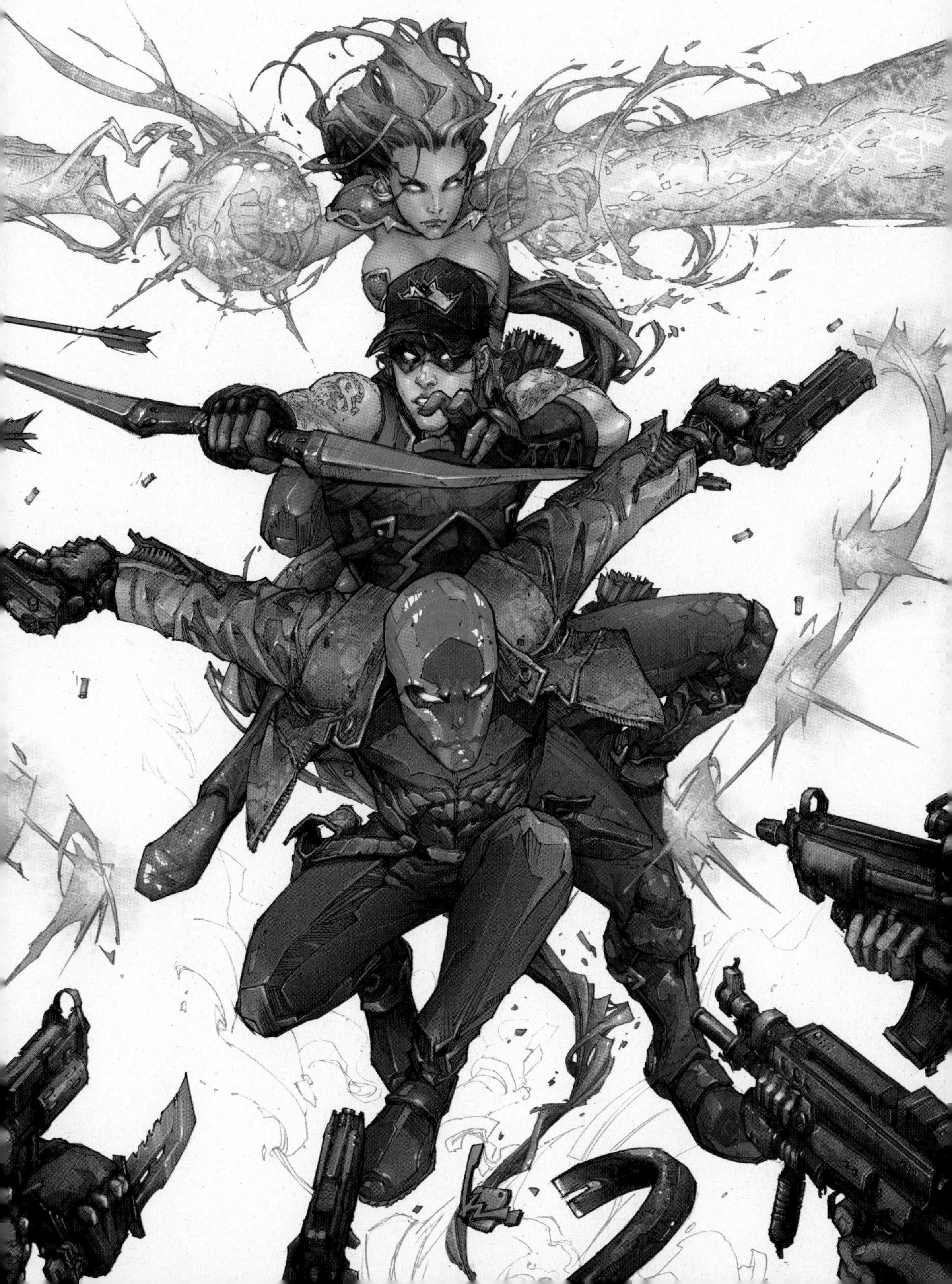

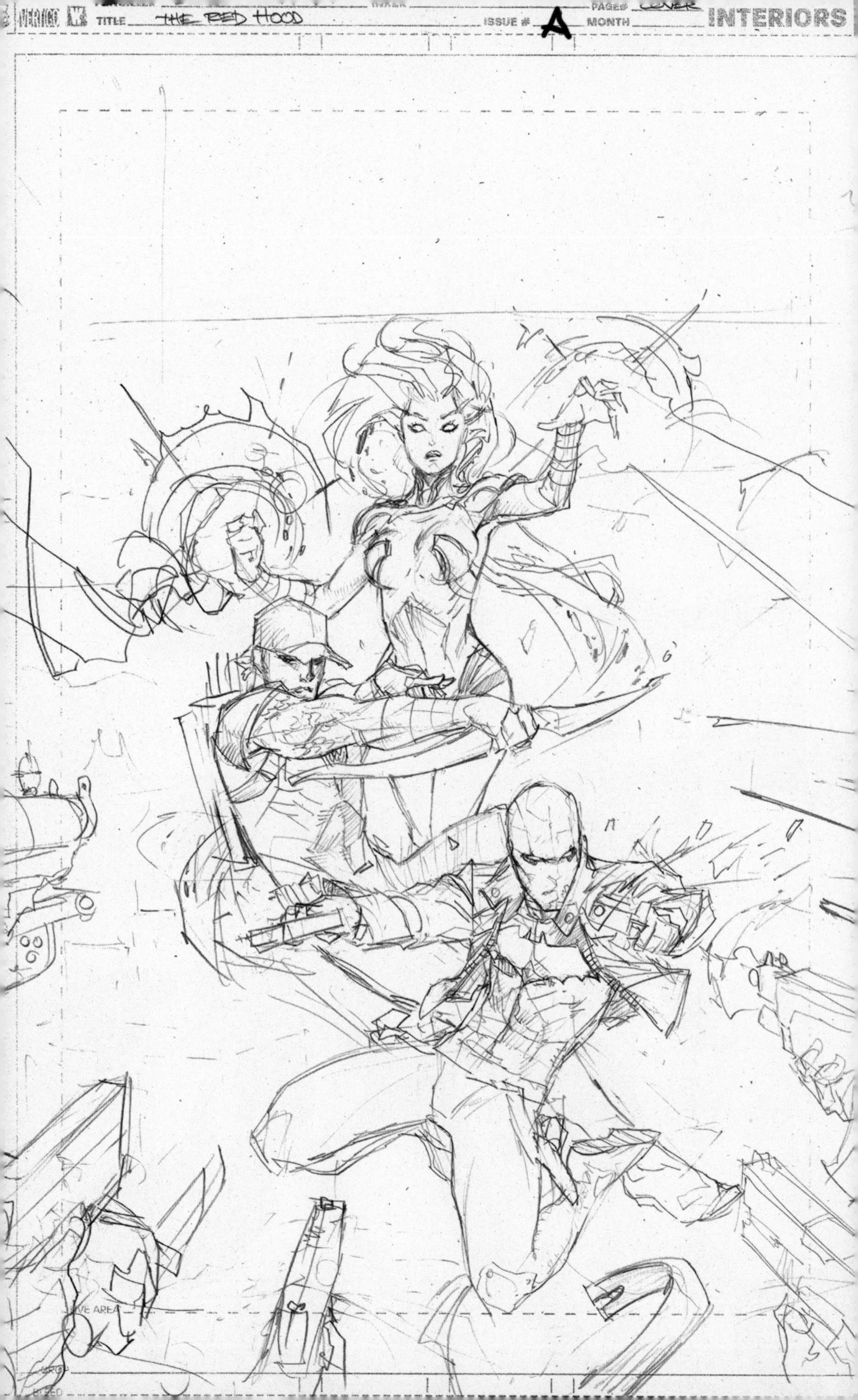
TITLE THE RED HOOD
ISSUE # A
PAGE# COVER
MONTH
INTERIORS

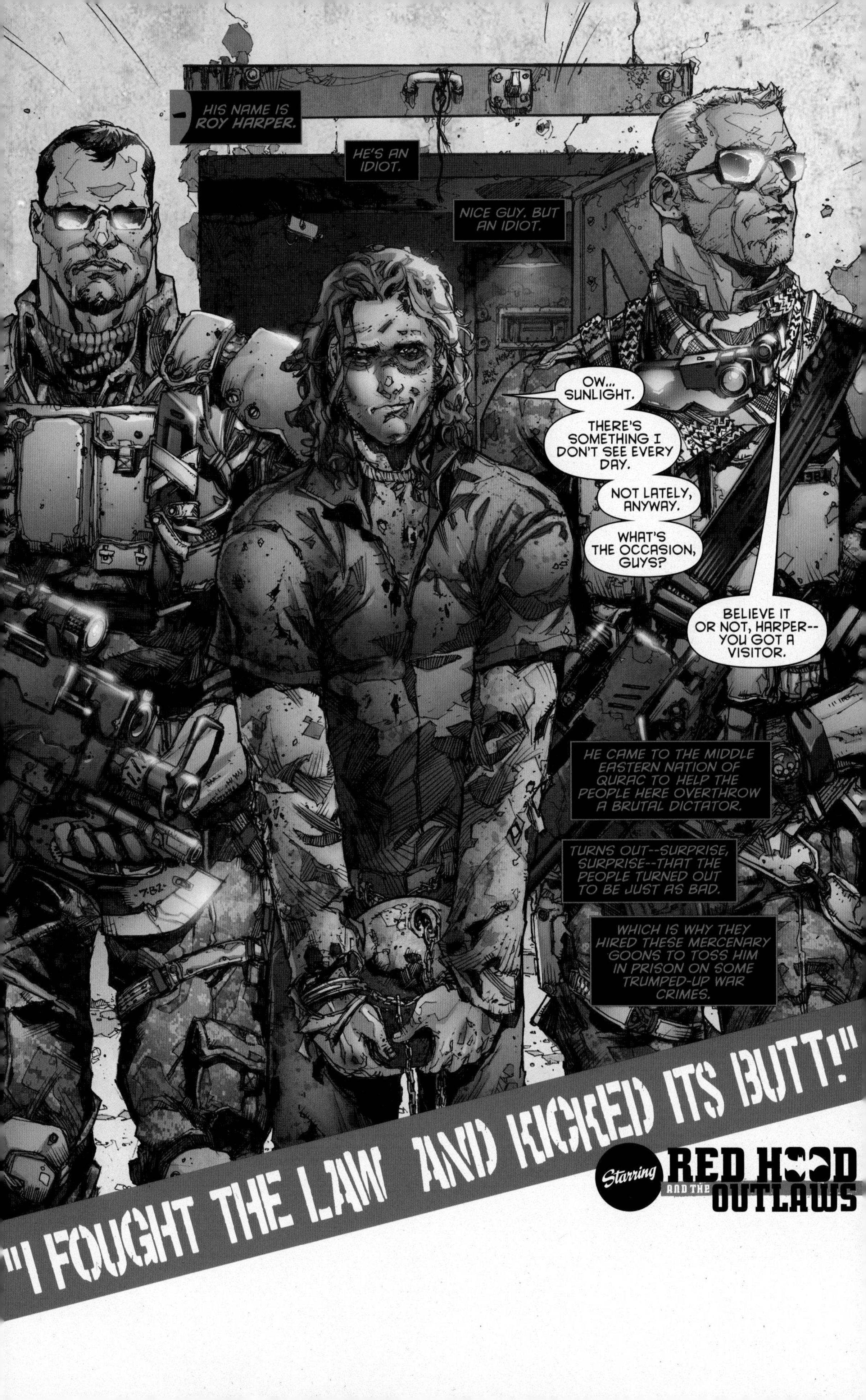
HIS NAME IS ROY HARPER.
HE'S AN IDIOT.
NICE GUY. BUT AN IDIOT.
OW... SUNLIGHT.
THERE'S SOMETHING I DON'T SEE EVERY DAY.
NOT LATELY, ANYWAY.
WHAT'S THE OCCASION, GUYS?
BELIEVE IT OR NOT, HARPER-- YOU GOT A VISITOR.
HE CAME TO THE MIDDLE EASTERN NATION OF QURAC TO HELP THE PEOPLE HERE OVERTHROW A BRUTAL DICTATOR.
TURNS OUT--SURPRISE, SURPRISE--THAT THE PEOPLE TURNED OUT TO BE JUST AS BAD.
WHICH IS WHY THEY HIRED THESE MERCENARY GOONS TO TOSS HIM IN PRISON ON SOME TRUMPED-UP WAR CRIMES.
"I FOUGHT THE LAW AND KICKED ITS BUTT!"
Starring RED HOOD AND THE OUTLAWS

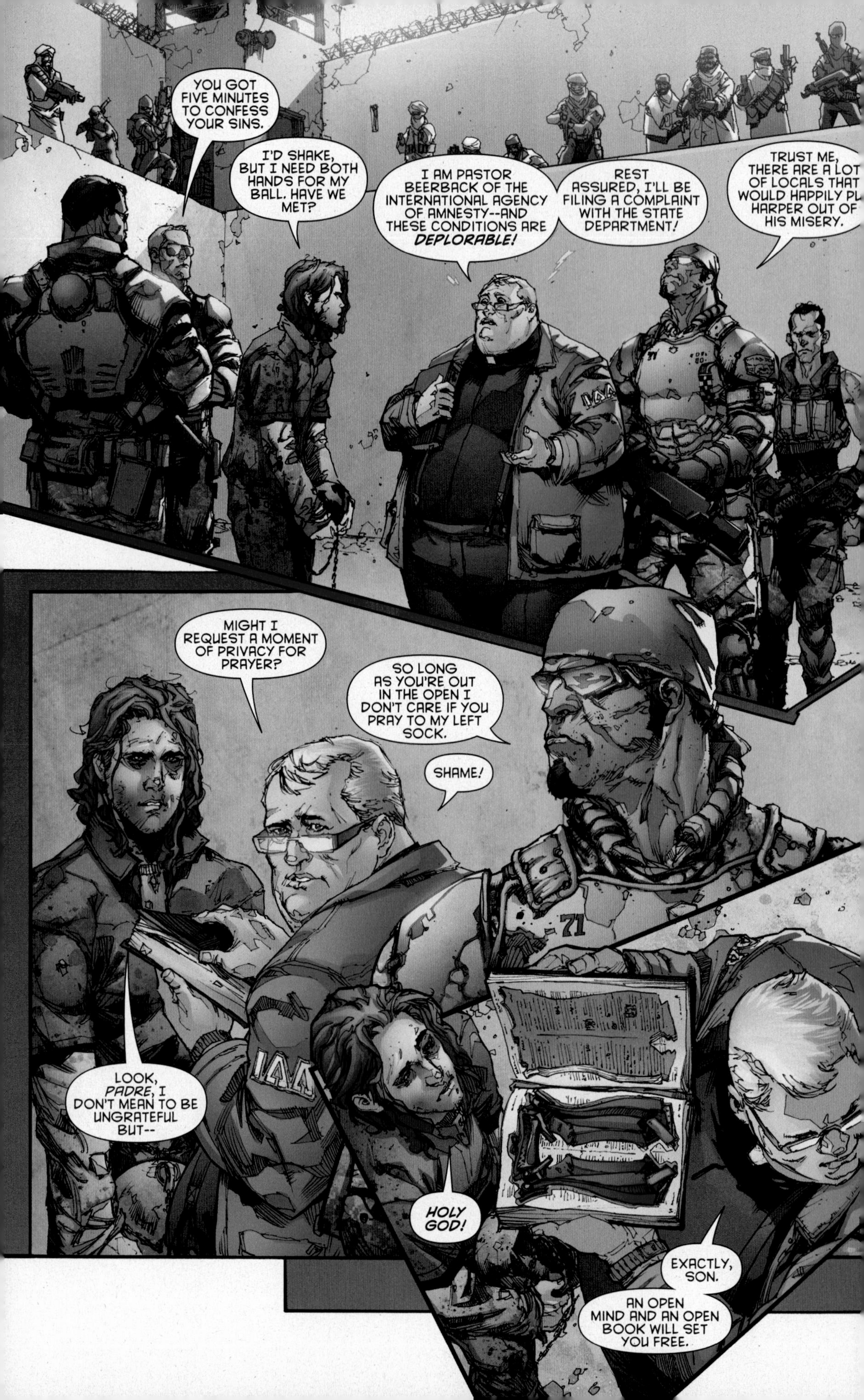
YOU GOT FIVE MINUTES TO CONFESS YOUR SINS.
I'D SHAKE, BUT I NEED BOTH HANDS FOR MY BALL. HAVE WE MET?
I AM PASTOR BEERBACK OF THE INTERNATIONAL AGENCY OF AMNESTY--AND THESE CONDITIONS ARE DEPLORABLE!
REST ASSURED, I'LL BE FILING A COMPLAINT WITH THE STATE DEPARTMENT!
TRUST ME, THERE ARE A LOT OF LOCALS THAT WOULD HAPPILY PU HARPER OUT OF HIS MISERY.
MIGHT I REQUEST A MOMENT OF PRIVACY FOR PRAYER?
SO LONG AS YOU'RE OUT IN THE OPEN I DON'T CARE IF YOU PRAY TO MY LEFT SOCK.
SHAME!
LOOK, PADRE, I DON'T MEAN TO BE UNGRATEFUL BUT--
HOLY GOD!
EXACTLY, SON.
AN OPEN MIND AND AN OPEN BOOK WILL SET YOU FREE.

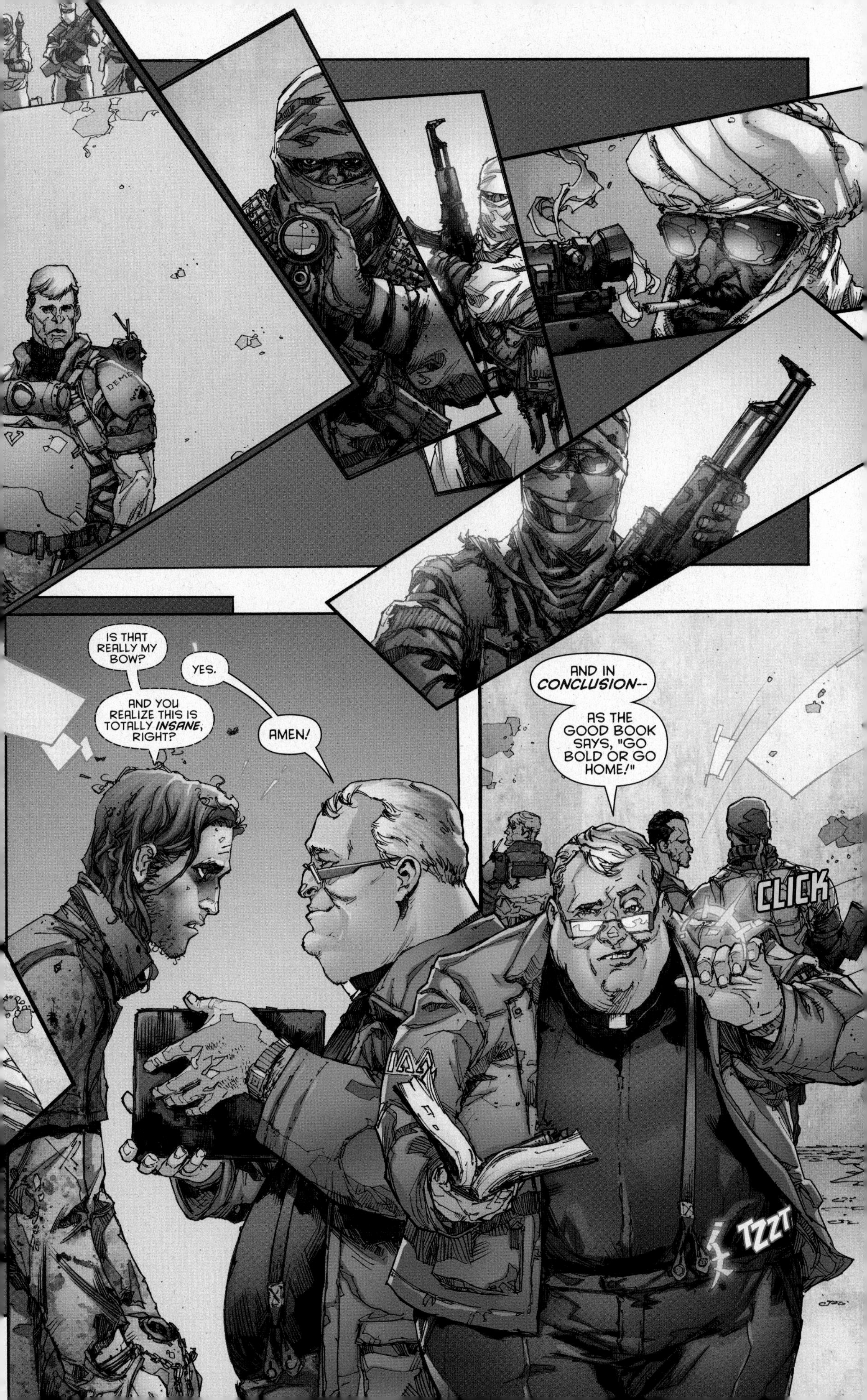
IS THAT REALLY MY BOW?
YES.
AND YOU REALIZE THIS IS TOTALLY INSANE, RIGHT?
AMEN!
AND IN CONCLUSION--
AS THE GOOD BOOK SAYS, "GO BOLD OR GO HOME!"
CLICK
TZZT

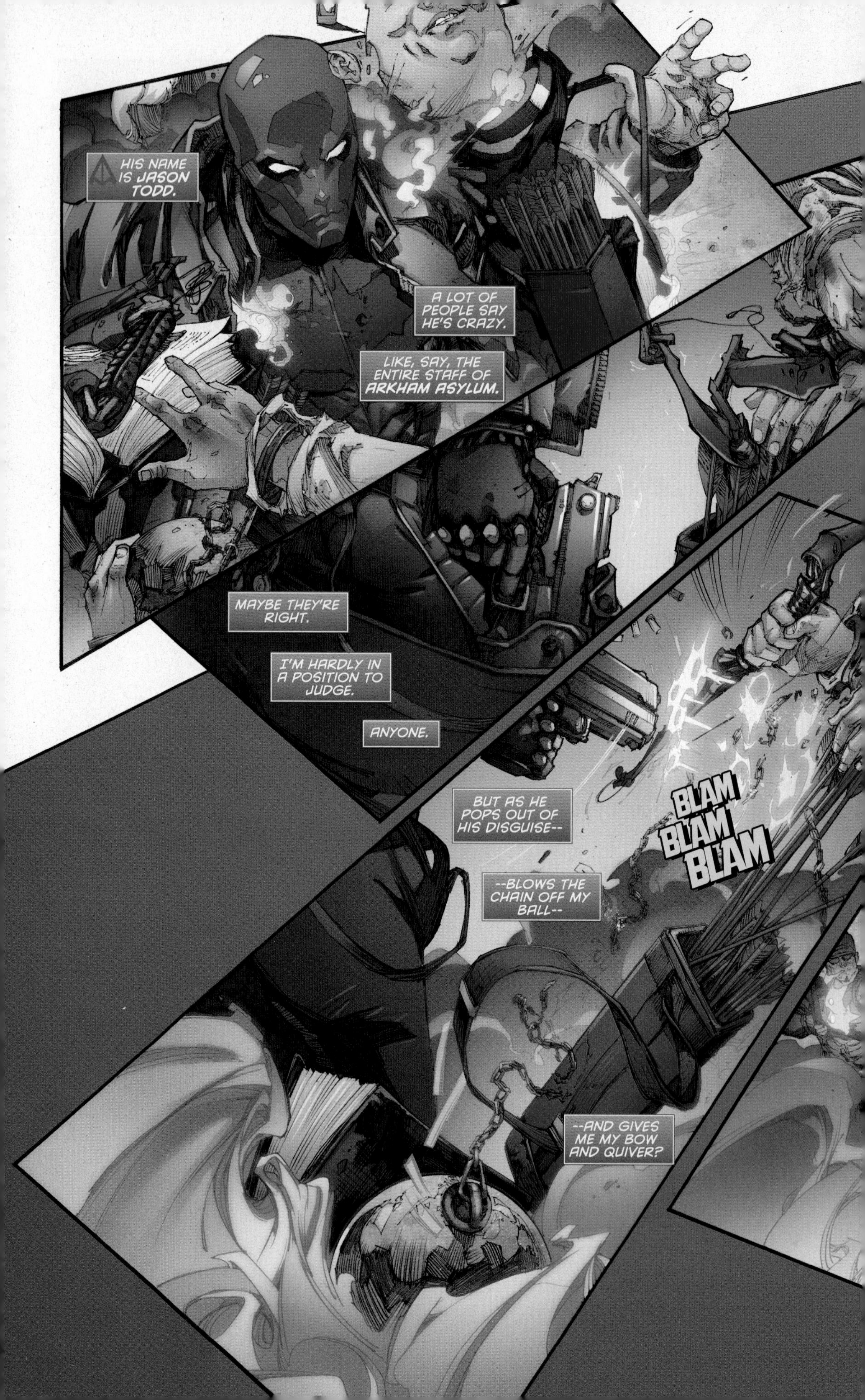
HIS NAME IS JASON TODD.
A LOT OF PEOPLE SAY HE'S CRAZY.
LIKE, SAY, THE ENTIRE STAFF OF ARKHAM ASYLUM.
MAYBE THEY'RE RIGHT.
I'M HARDLY IN A POSITION TO JUDGE.
ANYONE.
BUT AS HE POPS OUT OF HIS DISGUISE--
BLAM
BLAM
BLAM
--BLOWS THE CHAIN OFF MY BALL--
--AND GIVES ME MY BOW AND QUIVER?

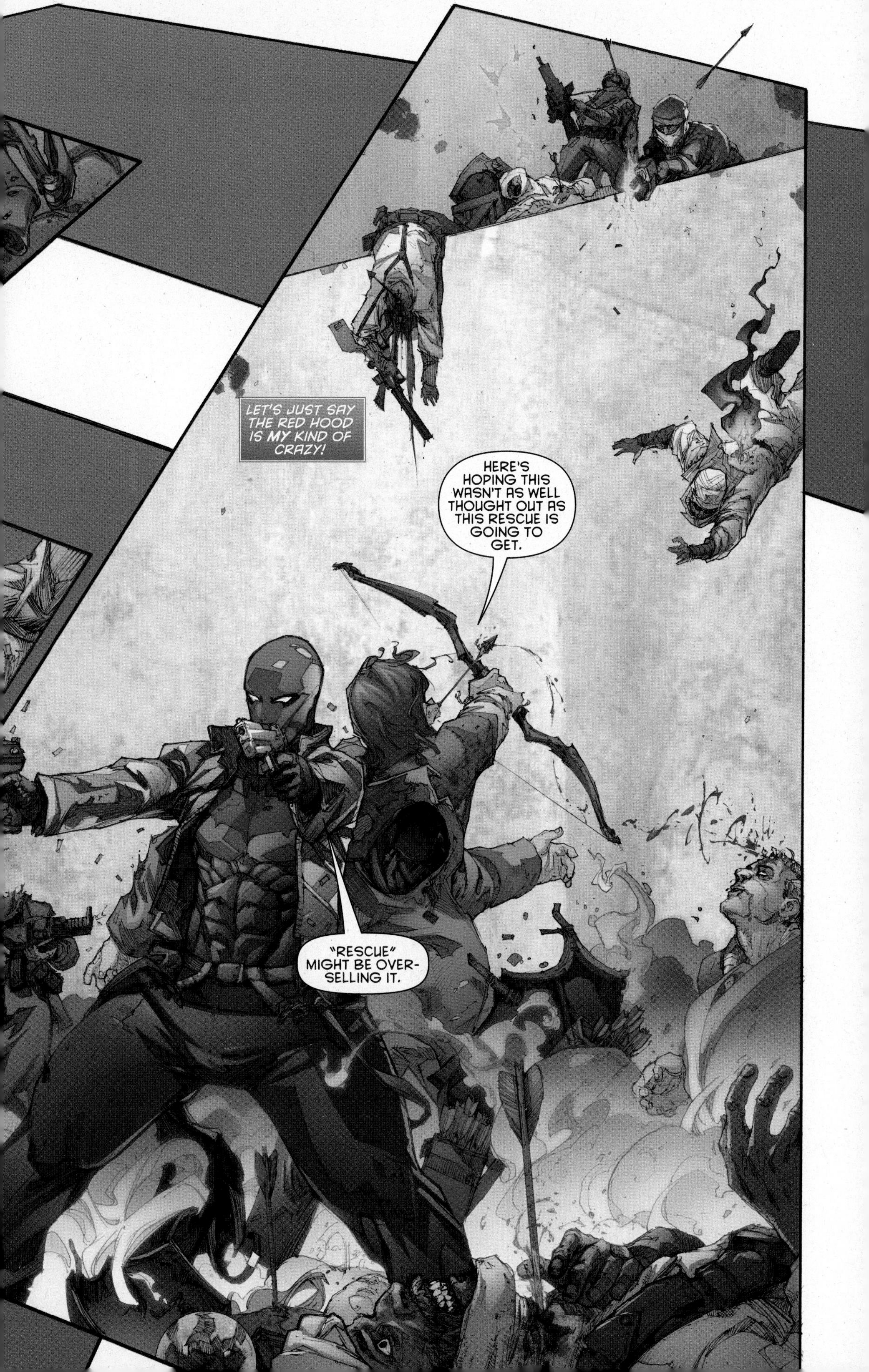
LET'S JUST SAY THE RED HOOD IS MY KIND OF CRAZY!
HERE'S HOPING THIS WASN'T AS WELL THOUGHT OUT AS THIS RESCUE IS GOING TO GET.
"RESCUE" MIGHT BE OVER-SELLING IT.

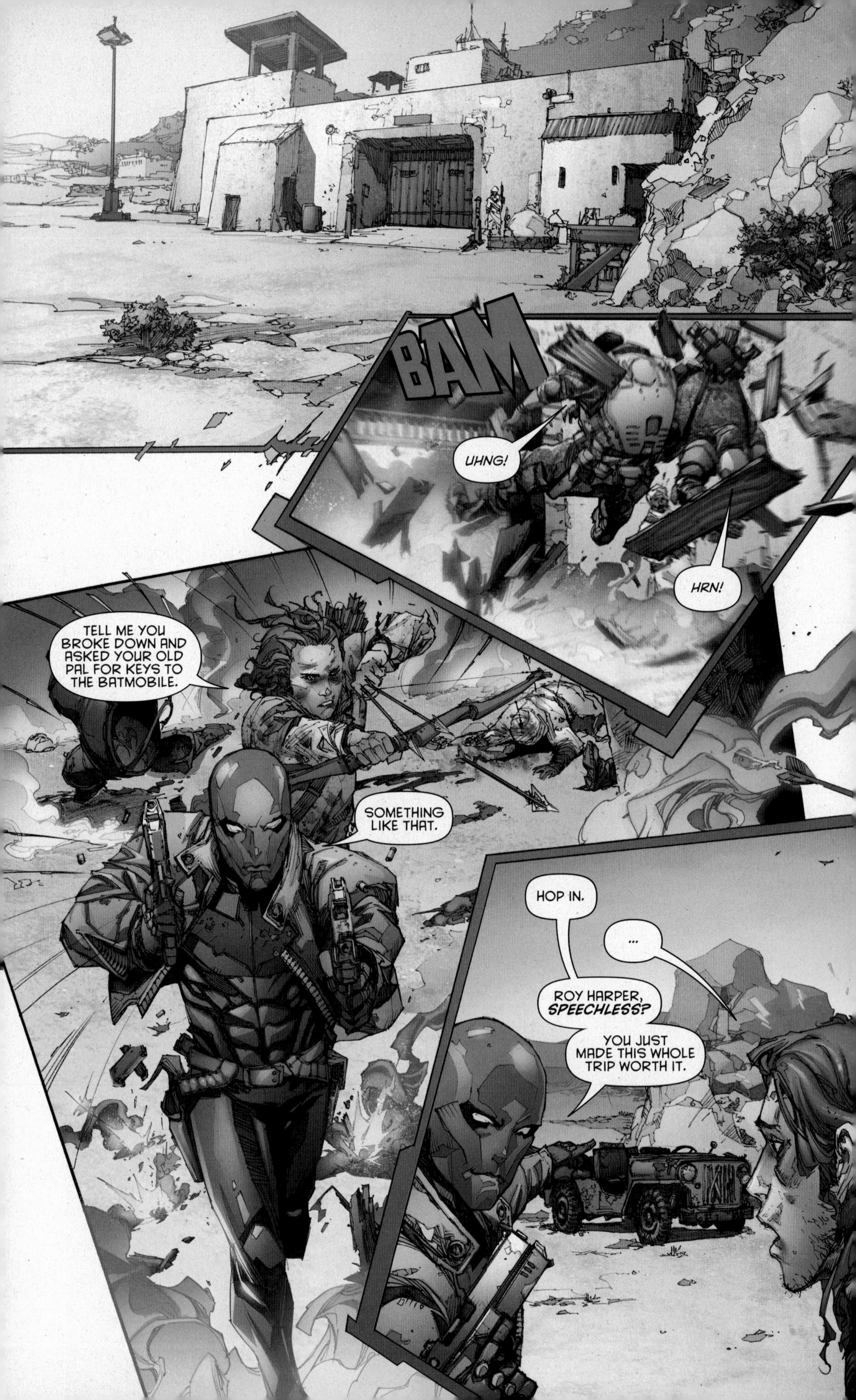
BAM
UHNG!
HRN!
TELL ME YOU BROKE DOWN AND ASKED YOUR OLD PAL FOR KEYS TO THE BATMOBILE.
SOMETHING LIKE THAT.
HOP IN.
...
ROY HARPER, *SPEECHLESS?*
YOU JUST MADE THIS WHOLE TRIP WORTH IT.

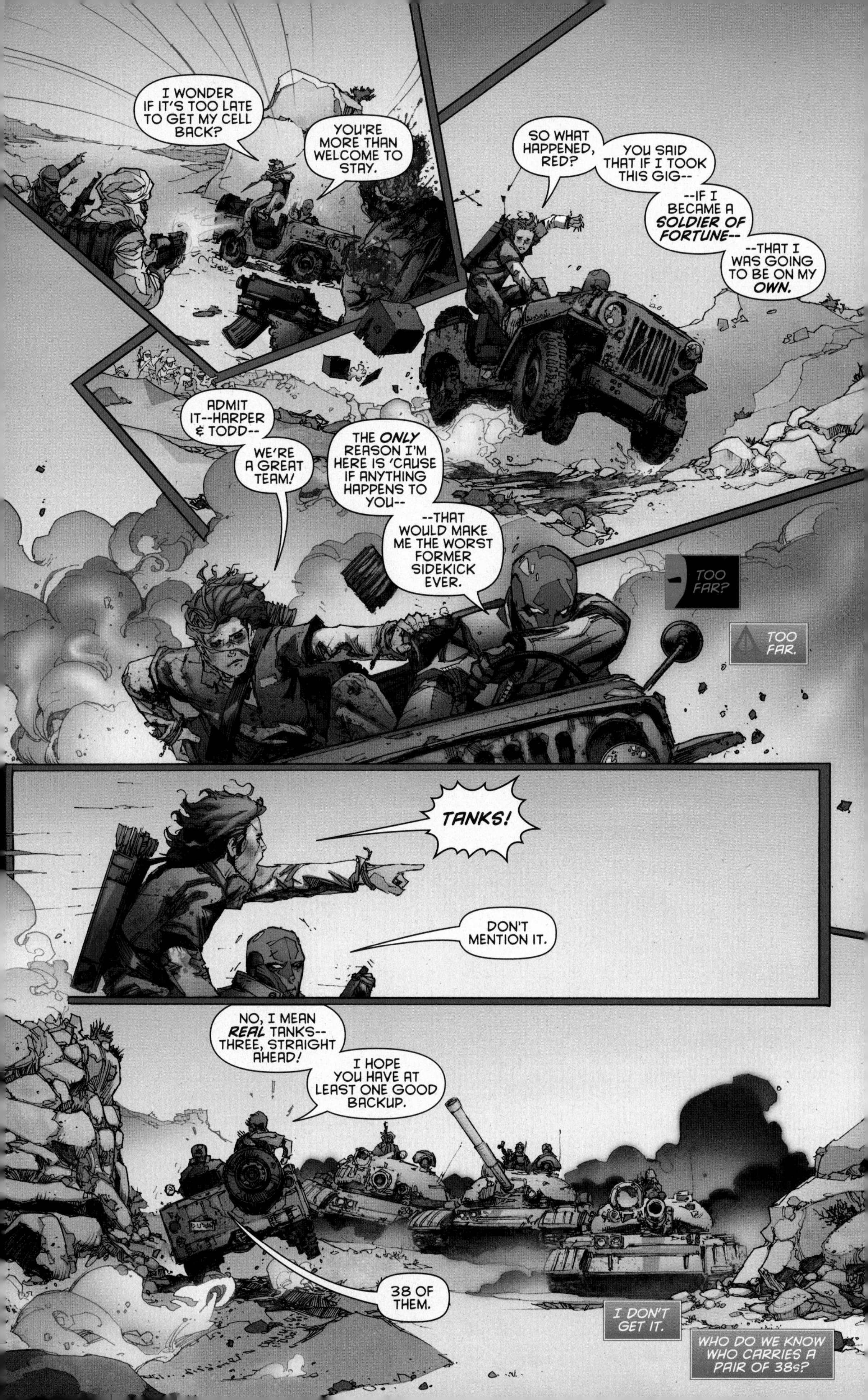
I WONDER IF IT'S TOO LATE TO GET MY CELL BACK?
YOU'RE MORE THAN WELCOME TO STAY.
SO WHAT HAPPENED, RED?
YOU SAID THAT IF I TOOK THIS GIG--
--IF I BECAME A SOLDIER OF FORTUNE--
--THAT I WAS GOING TO BE ON MY OWN.
ADMIT IT--HARPER & TODD--
WE'RE A GREAT TEAM!
THE ONLY REASON I'M HERE IS 'CAUSE IF ANYTHING HAPPENS TO YOU--
--THAT WOULD MAKE ME THE WORST FORMER SIDEKICK EVER.
TOO FAR?
TOO FAR.
TANKS!
DON'T MENTION IT.
NO, I MEAN REAL TANKS-- THREE, STRAIGHT AHEAD!
I HOPE YOU HAVE AT LEAST ONE GOOD BACKUP.
38 OF THEM.
I DON'T GET IT.
WHO DO WE KNOW WHO CARRIES A PAIR OF 38s?

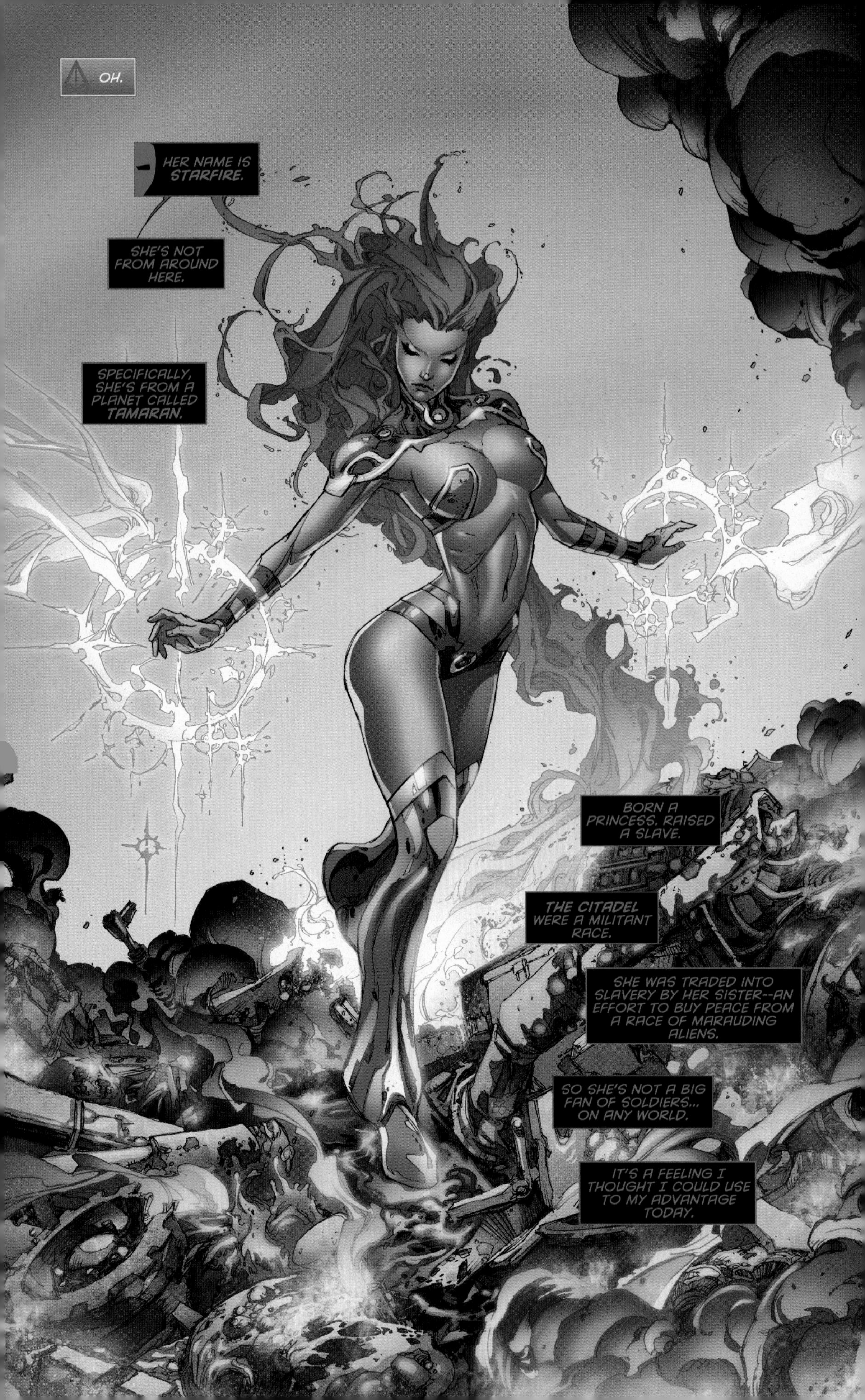
OH.
HER NAME IS STARFIRE.
SHE'S NOT FROM AROUND HERE.
SPECIFICALLY, SHE'S FROM A PLANET CALLED TAMARAN.
BORN A PRINCESS. RAISED A SLAVE.
THE CITADEL WERE A MILITANT RACE.
SHE WAS TRADED INTO SLAVERY BY HER SISTER--AN EFFORT TO BUY PEACE FROM A RACE OF MARAUDING ALIENS.
SO SHE'S NOT A BIG FAN OF SOLDIERS... ON ANY WORLD.
IT'S A FEELING I THOUGHT I COULD USE TO MY ADVANTAGE TODAY.

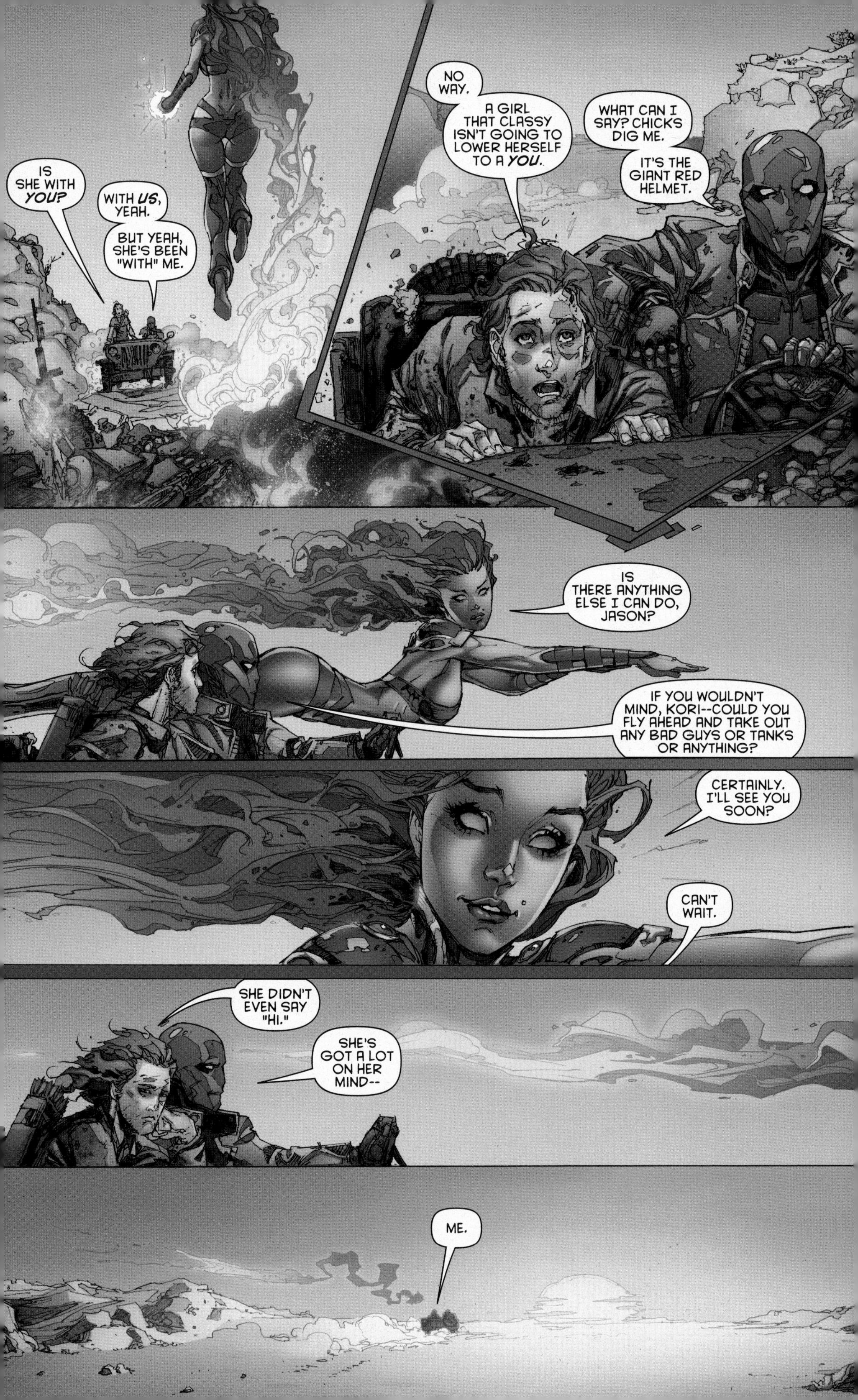
IS SHE WITH *YOU*?
WITH *US*, YEAH.
BUT YEAH, SHE'S BEEN "WITH" ME.
NO WAY.
A GIRL THAT CLASSY ISN'T GOING TO LOWER HERSELF TO A *YOU*.
WHAT CAN I SAY? CHICKS DIG ME.
IT'S THE GIANT RED HELMET.
IS THERE ANYTHING ELSE I CAN DO, JASON?
IF YOU WOULDN'T MIND, KORI--COULD YOU FLY AHEAD AND TAKE OUT ANY BAD GUYS OR TANKS OR ANYTHING?
CERTAINLY. I'LL SEE YOU SOON?
CAN'T WAIT.
SHE DIDN'T EVEN SAY "HI."
SHE'S GOT A LOT ON HER MIND--
ME.

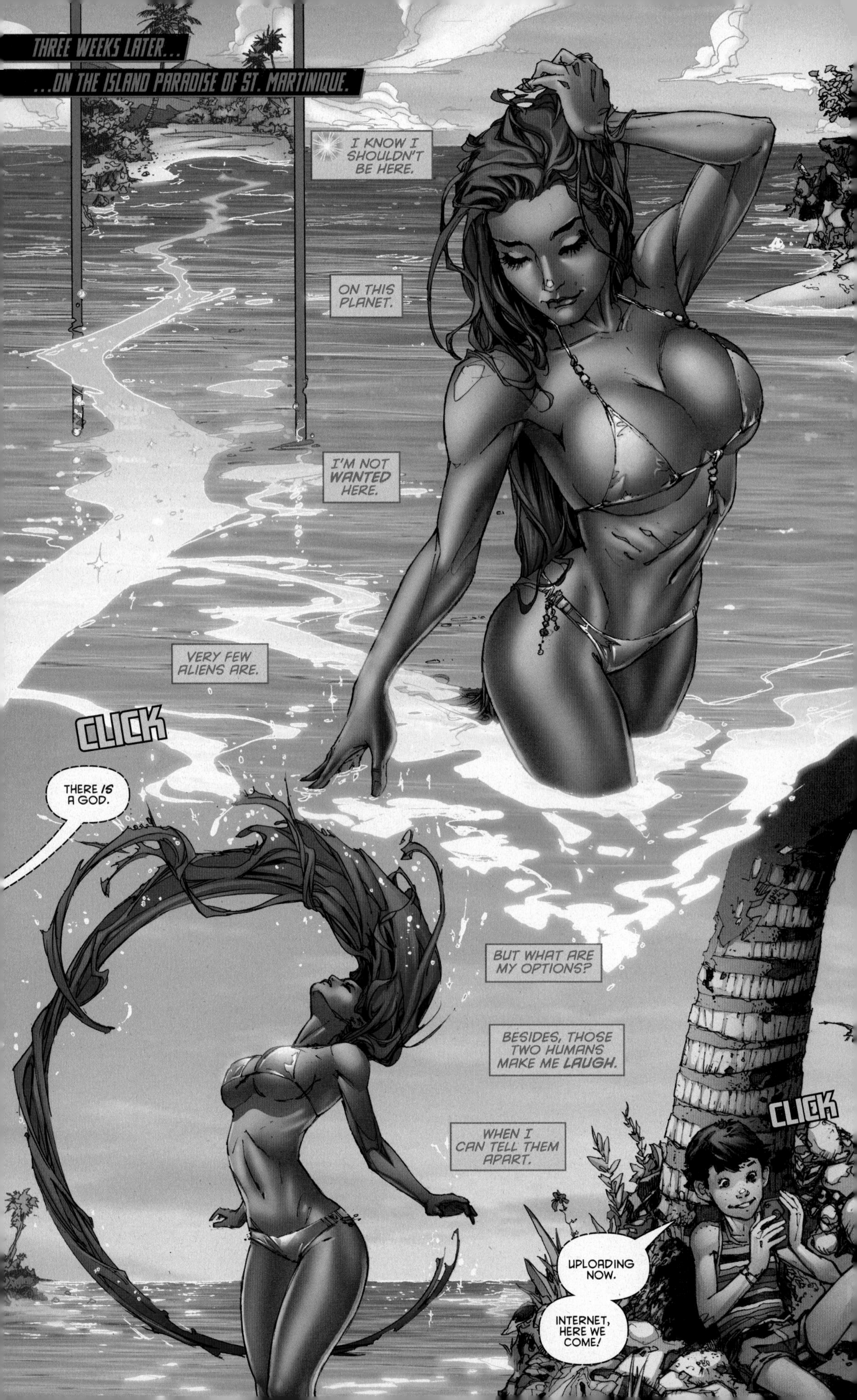
THREE WEEKS LATER...
...ON THE ISLAND PARADISE OF ST. MARTINIQUE.
I KNOW I SHOULDN'T BE HERE.
ON THIS PLANET.
I'M NOT WANTED HERE.
VERY FEW ALIENS ARE.
CLICK
THERE IS A GOD.
BUT WHAT ARE MY OPTIONS?
BESIDES, THOSE TWO HUMANS MAKE ME LAUGH.
WHEN I CAN TELL THEM APART.
CLICK
UPLOADING NOW.
INTERNET, HERE WE COME!

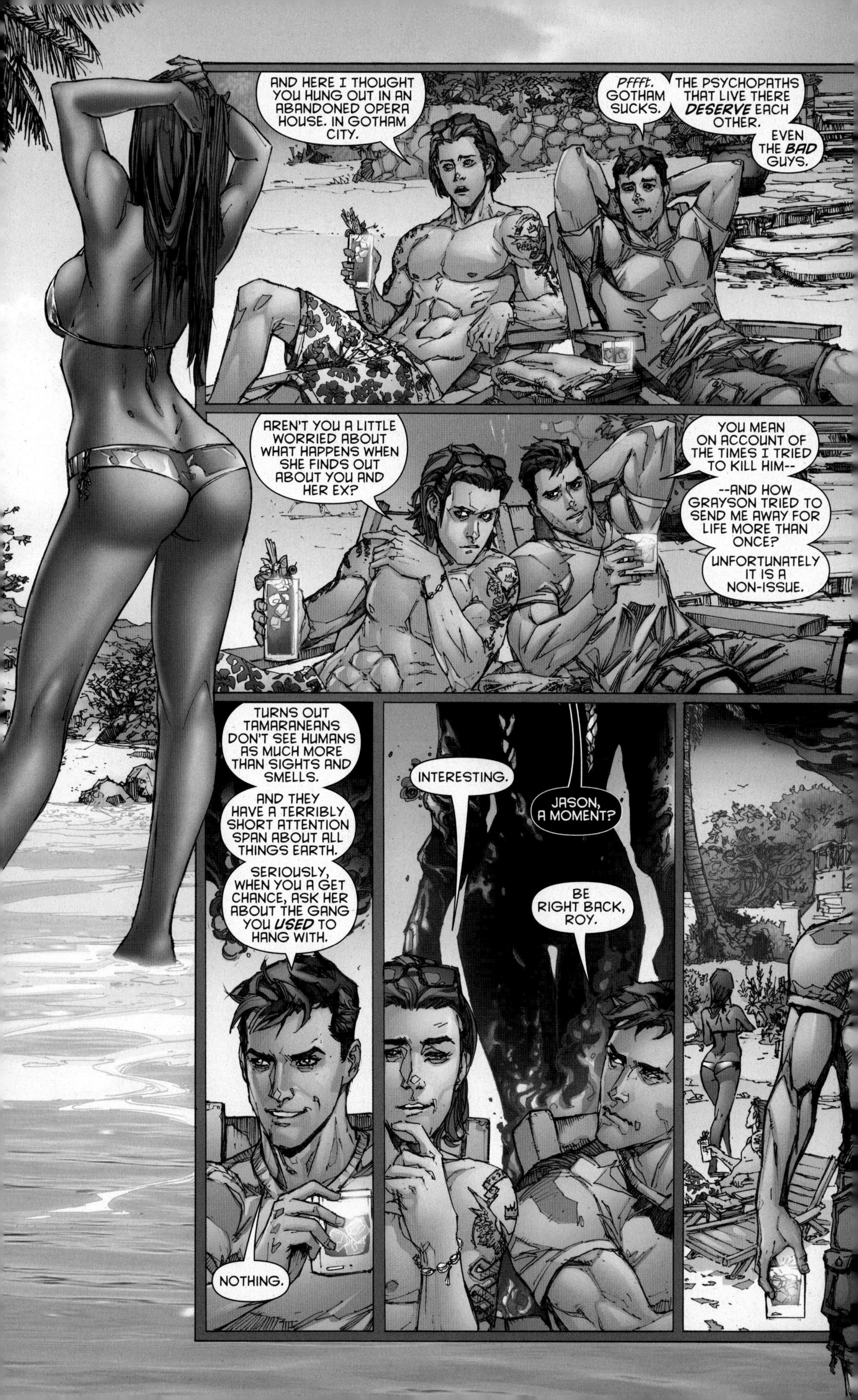

AND HERE I THOUGHT YOU HUNG OUT IN AN ABANDONED OPERA HOUSE. IN GOTHAM CITY.
Pfffft. GOTHAM SUCKS.
THE PSYCHOPATHS THAT LIVE THERE DESERVE EACH OTHER.
EVEN THE BAD GUYS.
AREN'T YOU A LITTLE WORRIED ABOUT WHAT HAPPENS WHEN SHE FINDS OUT ABOUT YOU AND HER EX?
YOU MEAN ON ACCOUNT OF THE TIMES I TRIED TO KILL HIM--
--AND HOW GRAYSON TRIED TO SEND ME AWAY FOR LIFE MORE THAN ONCE?
UNFORTUNATELY IT IS A NON-ISSUE.
TURNS OUT TAMARANEANS DON'T SEE HUMANS AS MUCH MORE THAN SIGHTS AND SMELLS.
AND THEY HAVE A TERRIBLY SHORT ATTENTION SPAN ABOUT ALL THINGS EARTH.
SERIOUSLY, WHEN YOU A GET CHANCE, ASK HER ABOUT THE GANG YOU USED TO HANG WITH.
NOTHING.
INTERESTING.
JASON, A MOMENT?
BE RIGHT BACK, ROY.

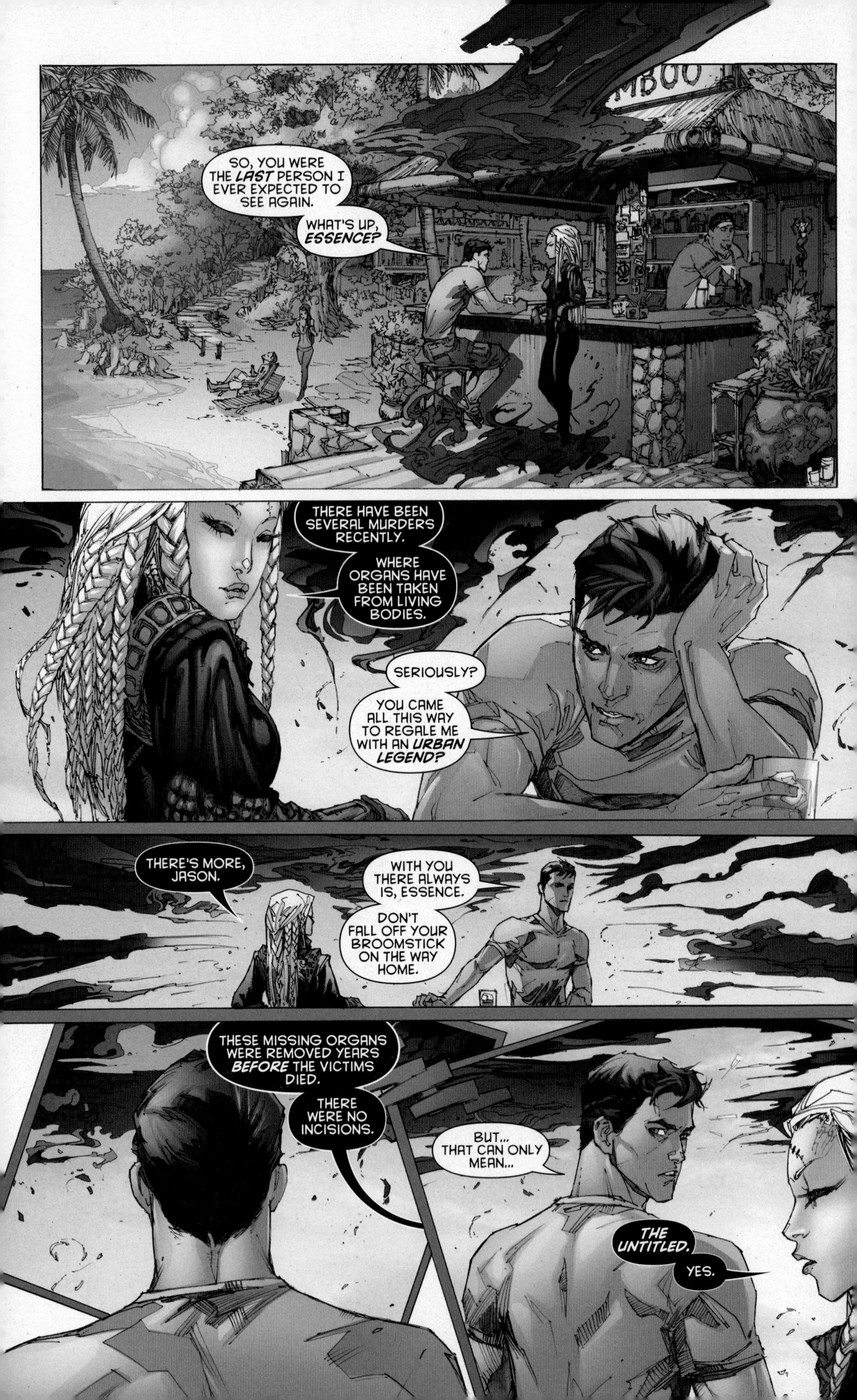
MBOO
SO, YOU WERE THE LAST PERSON I EVER EXPECTED TO SEE AGAIN.
WHAT'S UP, ESSENCE?
THERE HAVE BEEN SEVERAL MURDERS RECENTLY.
WHERE ORGANS HAVE BEEN TAKEN FROM LIVING BODIES.
SERIOUSLY?
YOU CAME ALL THIS WAY TO REGALE ME WITH AN URBAN LEGEND?
THERE'S MORE, JASON.
WITH YOU THERE ALWAYS IS, ESSENCE.
DON'T FALL OFF YOUR BROOMSTICK ON THE WAY HOME.
THESE MISSING ORGANS WERE REMOVED YEARS BEFORE THE VICTIMS DIED.
THERE WERE NO INCISIONS.
BUT... THAT CAN ONLY MEAN...
THE UNTITLED.
YES.

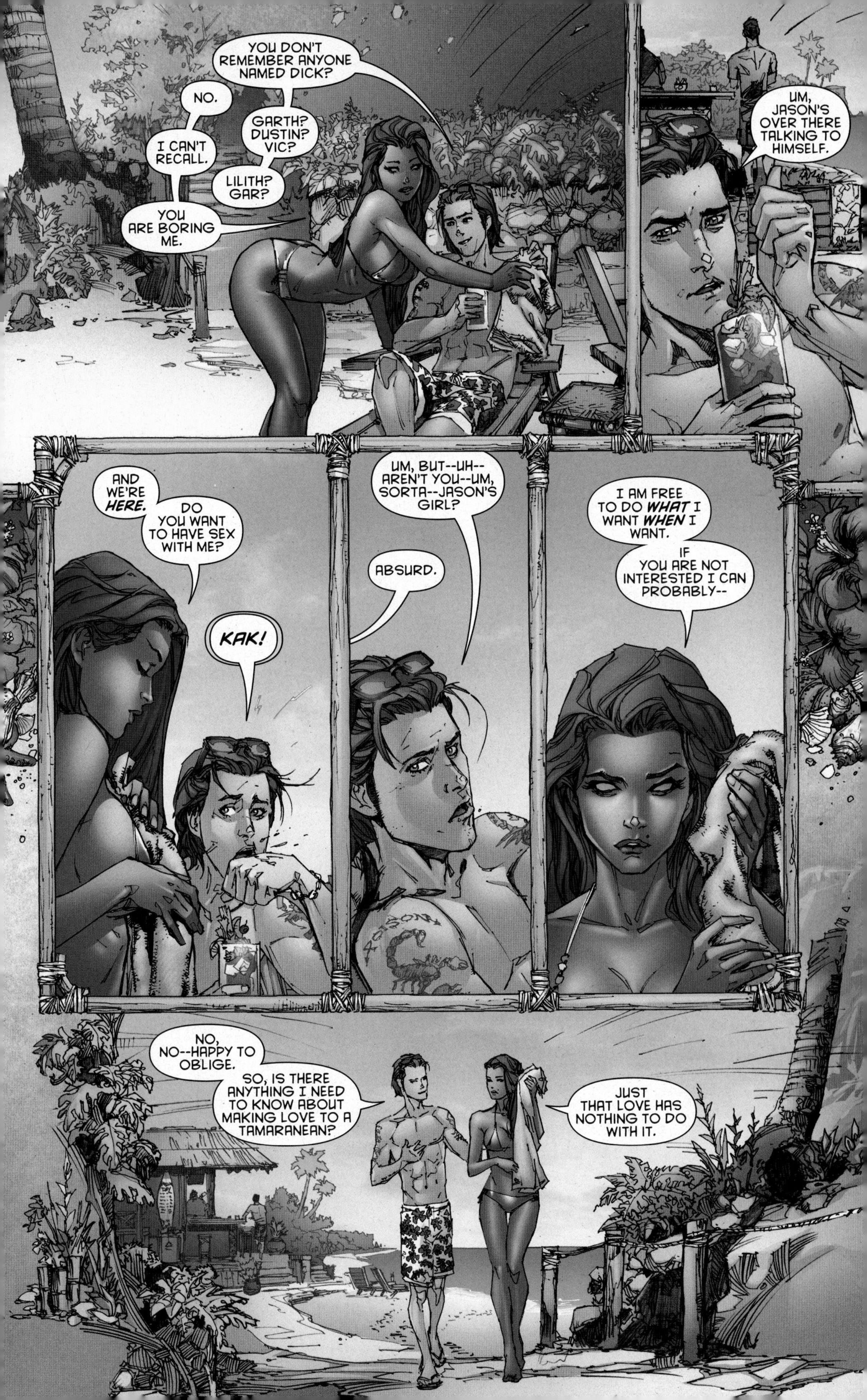
YOU DON'T REMEMBER ANYONE NAMED DICK?
NO.
GARTH? DUSTIN? VIC?
I CAN'T RECALL.
LILITH? GAR?
YOU ARE BORING ME.
UM, JASON'S OVER THERE TALKING TO HIMSELF.
AND WE'RE HERE.
DO YOU WANT TO HAVE SEX WITH ME?
KAK!
UM, BUT--UH--AREN'T YOU--UM, SORTA--JASON'S GIRL?
ABSURD.
I AM FREE TO DO WHAT I WANT WHEN I WANT.
IF YOU ARE NOT INTERESTED I CAN PROBABLY--
NO, NO--HAPPY TO OBLIGE.
SO, IS THERE ANYTHING I NEED TO KNOW ABOUT MAKING LOVE TO A TAMARANEAN?
JUST THAT LOVE HAS NOTHING TO DO WITH IT.

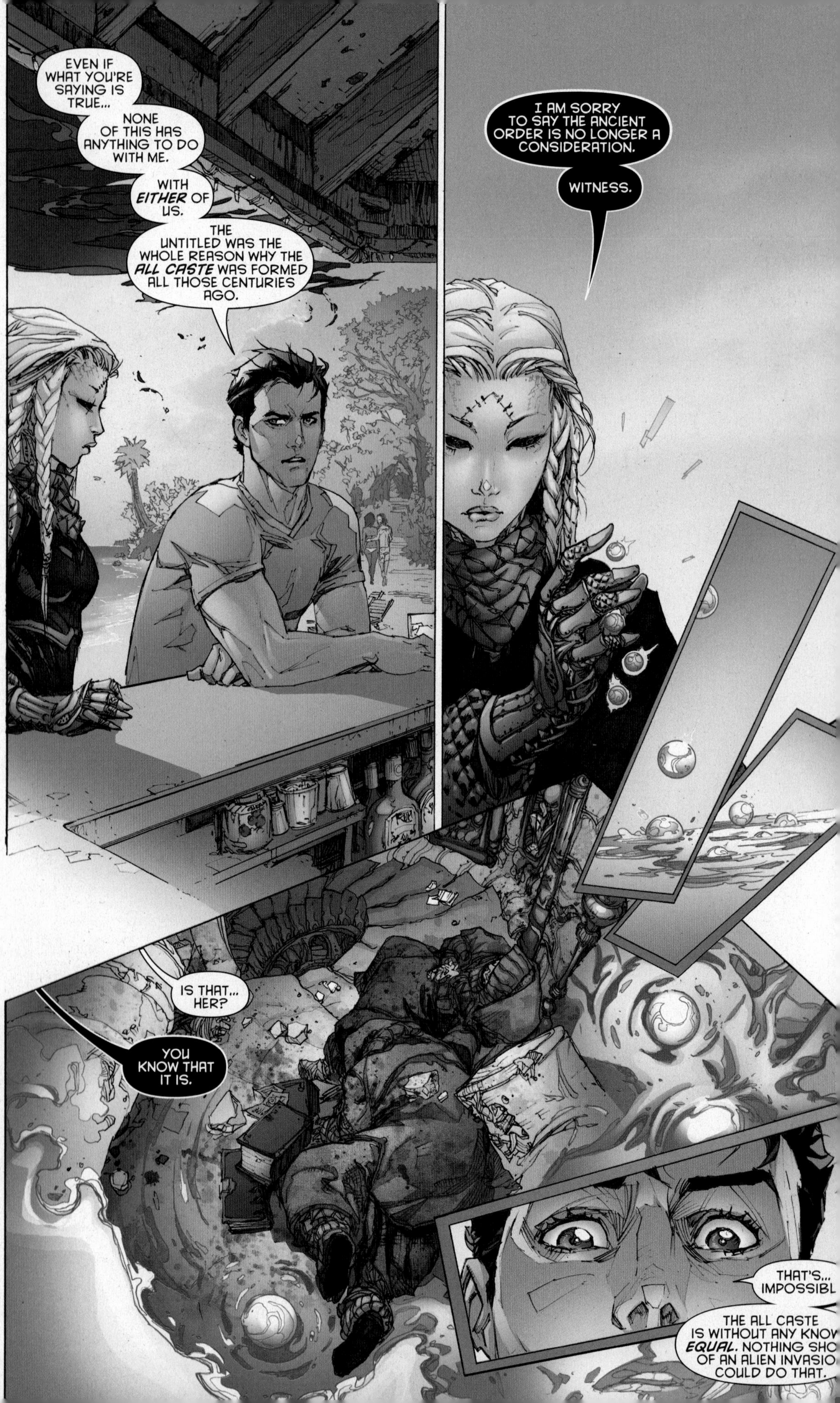
EVEN IF WHAT YOU'RE SAYING IS TRUE...
NONE OF THIS HAS ANYTHING TO DO WITH ME.
WITH EITHER OF US.
THE UNTITLED WAS THE WHOLE REASON WHY THE ALL CASTE WAS FORMED ALL THOSE CENTURIES AGO.
I AM SORRY TO SAY THE ANCIENT ORDER IS NO LONGER A CONSIDERATION.
WITNESS.
IS THAT... HER?
YOU KNOW THAT IT IS.
THAT'S... IMPOSSIBL
THE ALL CASTE IS WITHOUT ANY KNOV EQUAL. NOTHING SHO OF AN ALIEN INVASIO COULD DO THAT.

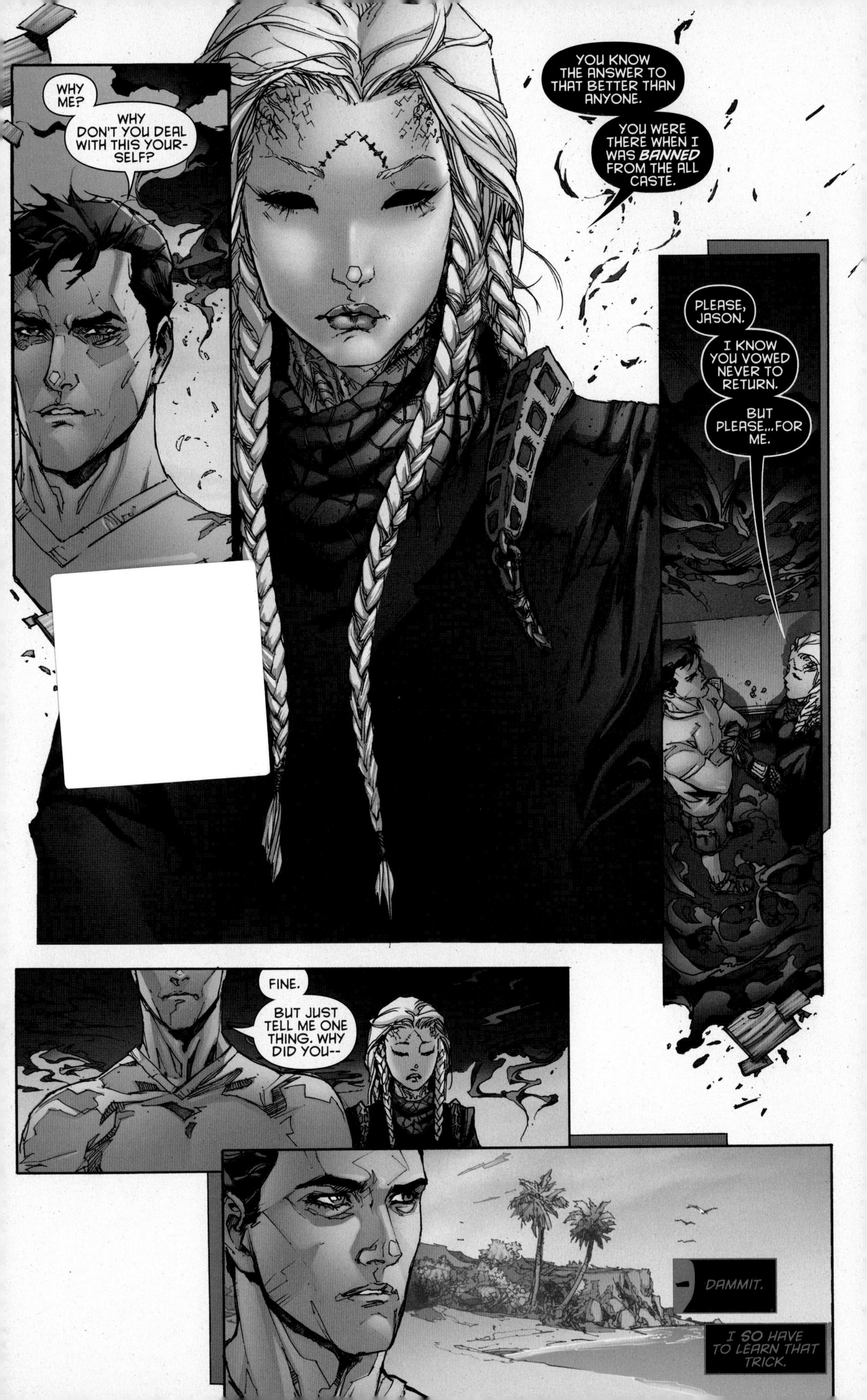
WHY ME?
WHY DON'T YOU DEAL WITH THIS YOUR-SELF?
YOU KNOW THE ANSWER TO THAT BETTER THAN ANYONE.
YOU WERE THERE WHEN I WAS *BANNED* FROM THE ALL CASTE.
PLEASE, JASON.
I KNOW YOU VOWED NEVER TO RETURN.
BUT PLEASE...FOR ME.
FINE.
BUT JUST TELL ME ONE THING. WHY DID YOU--
DAMMIT.
I *SO* HAVE TO LEARN THAT TRICK.

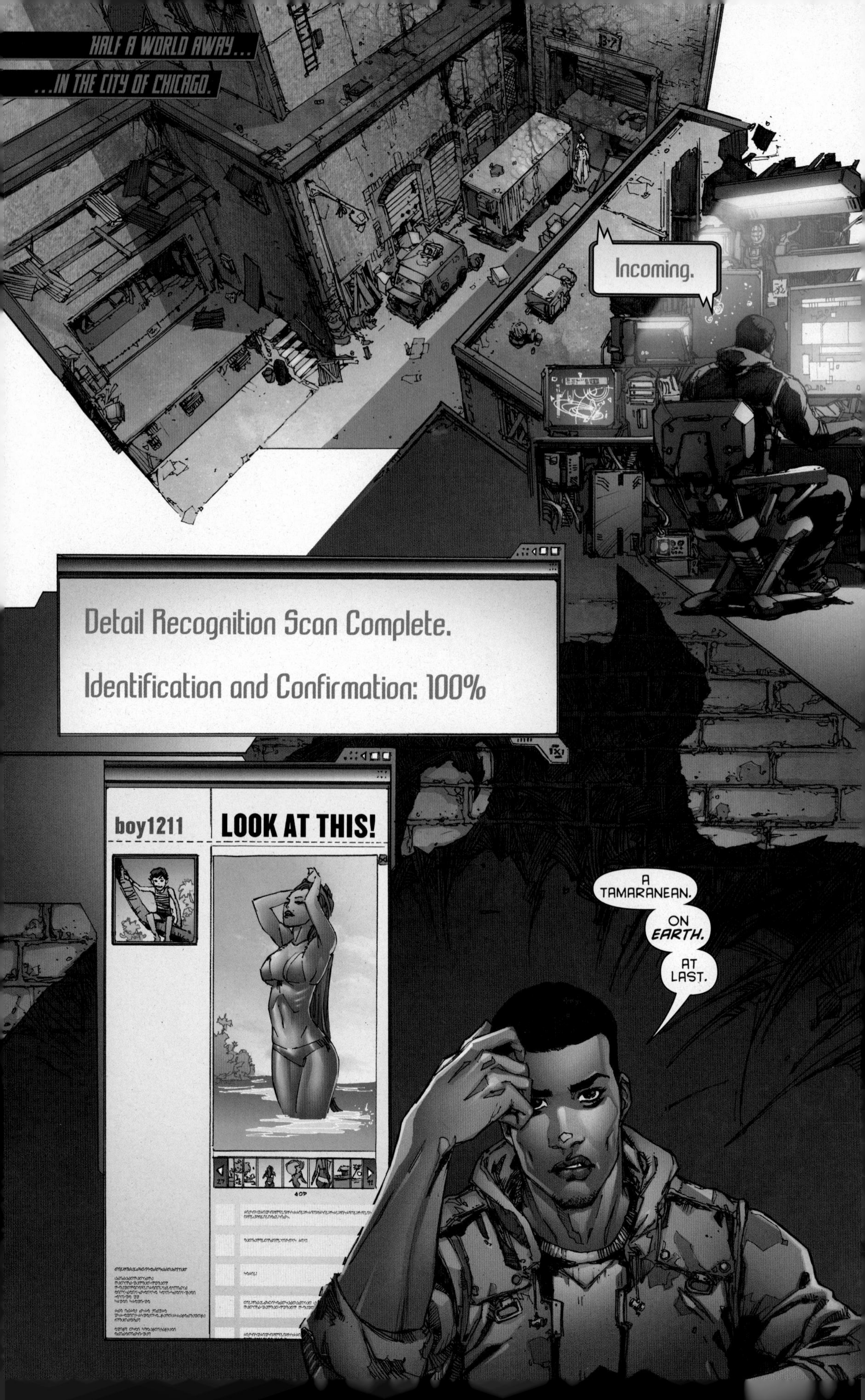
HALF A WORLD AWAY...
...IN THE CITY OF CHICAGO.
Incoming.
Detail Recognition Scan Complete.
Identification and Confirmation: 100%
boy1211
LOOK AT THIS!
A TAMARANEAN.
ON EARTH.
AT LAST.

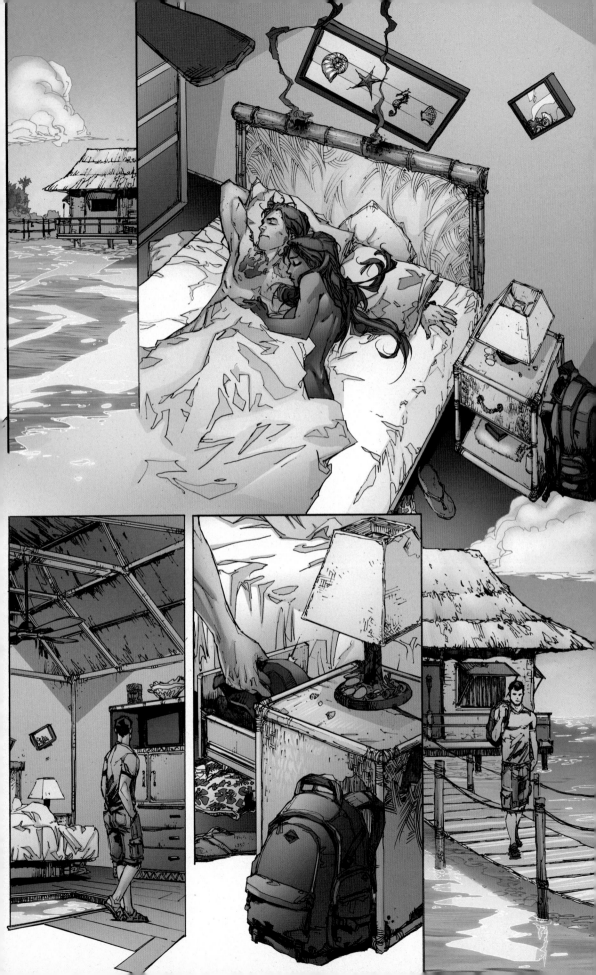

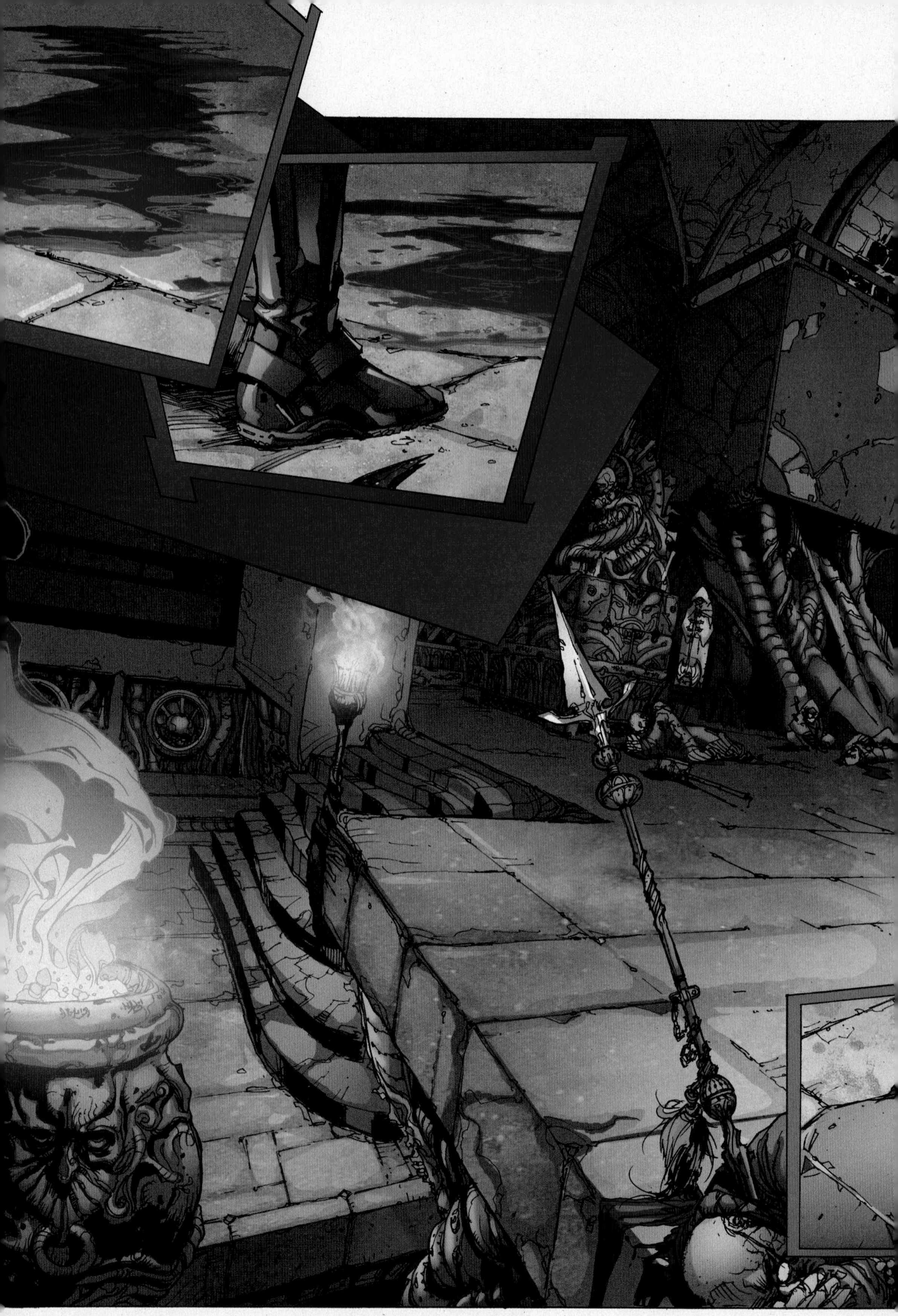

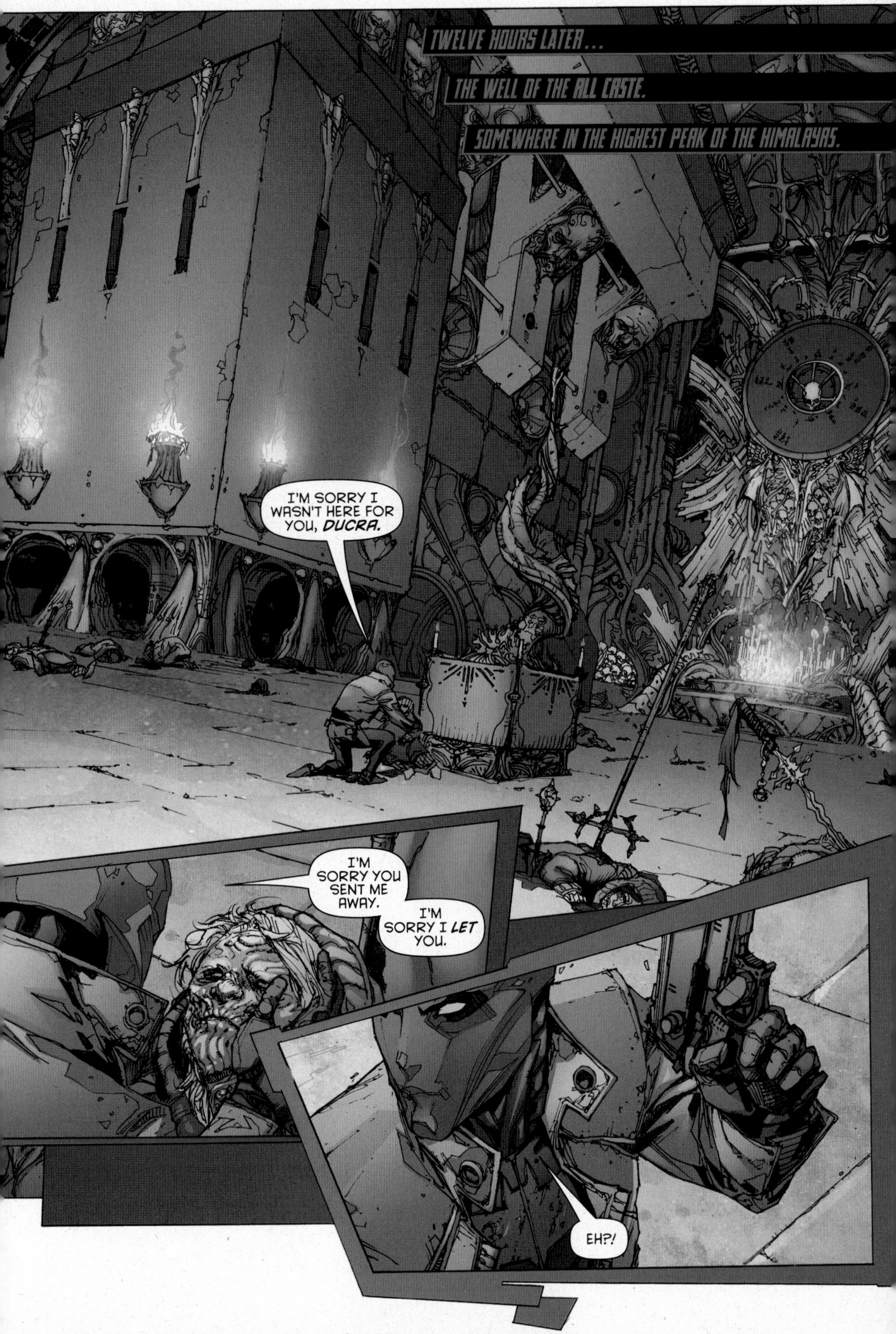
TWELVE HOURS LATER...
THE WELL OF THE ALL CASTE.
SOMEWHERE IN THE HIGHEST PEAK OF THE HIMALAYAS.
I'M SORRY I WASN'T HERE FOR YOU, DUCRA.
I'M SORRY YOU SENT ME AWAY.
I'M SORRY I LET YOU.
EH?!

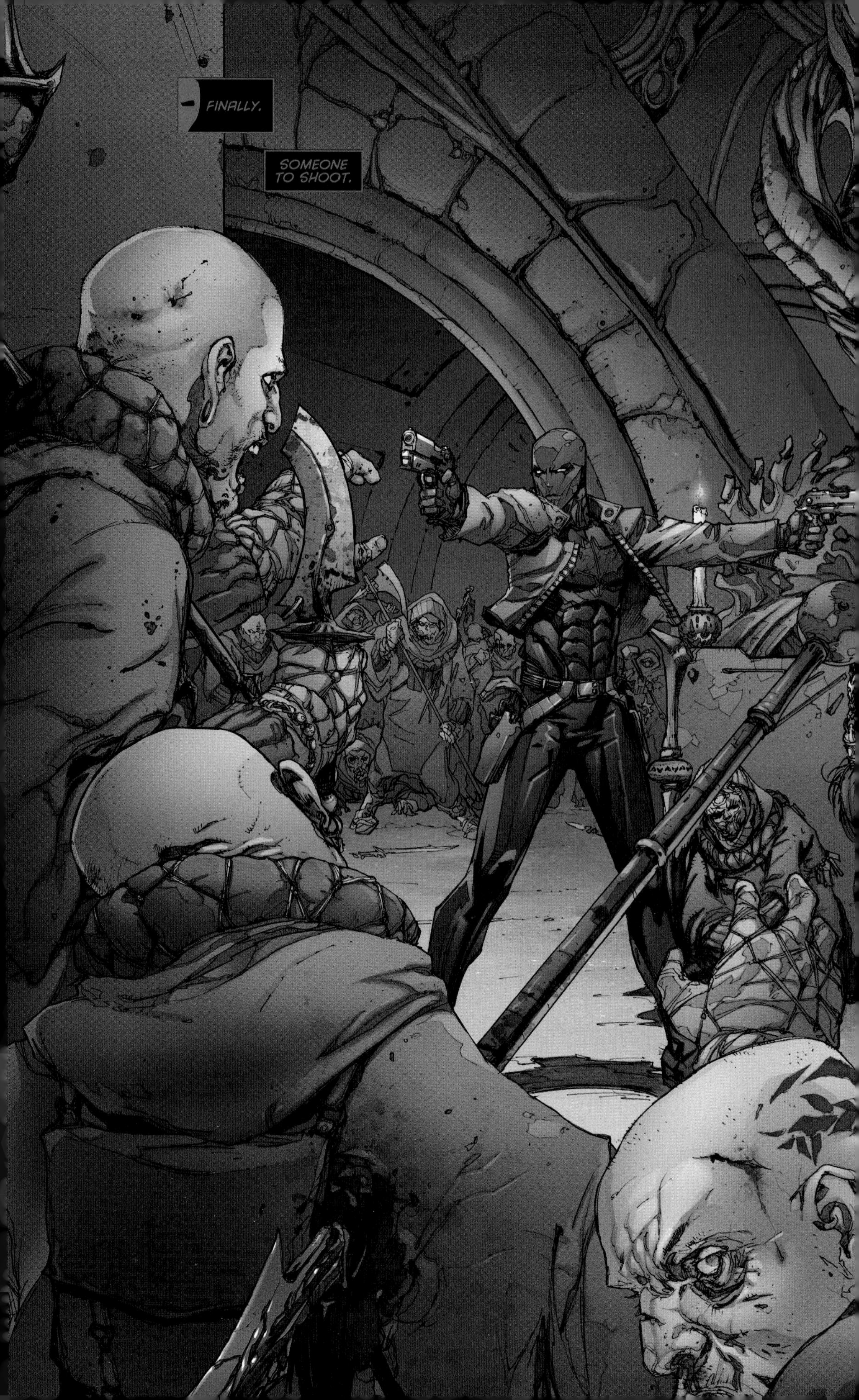
—FINALLY.
SOMEONE TO SHOOT.

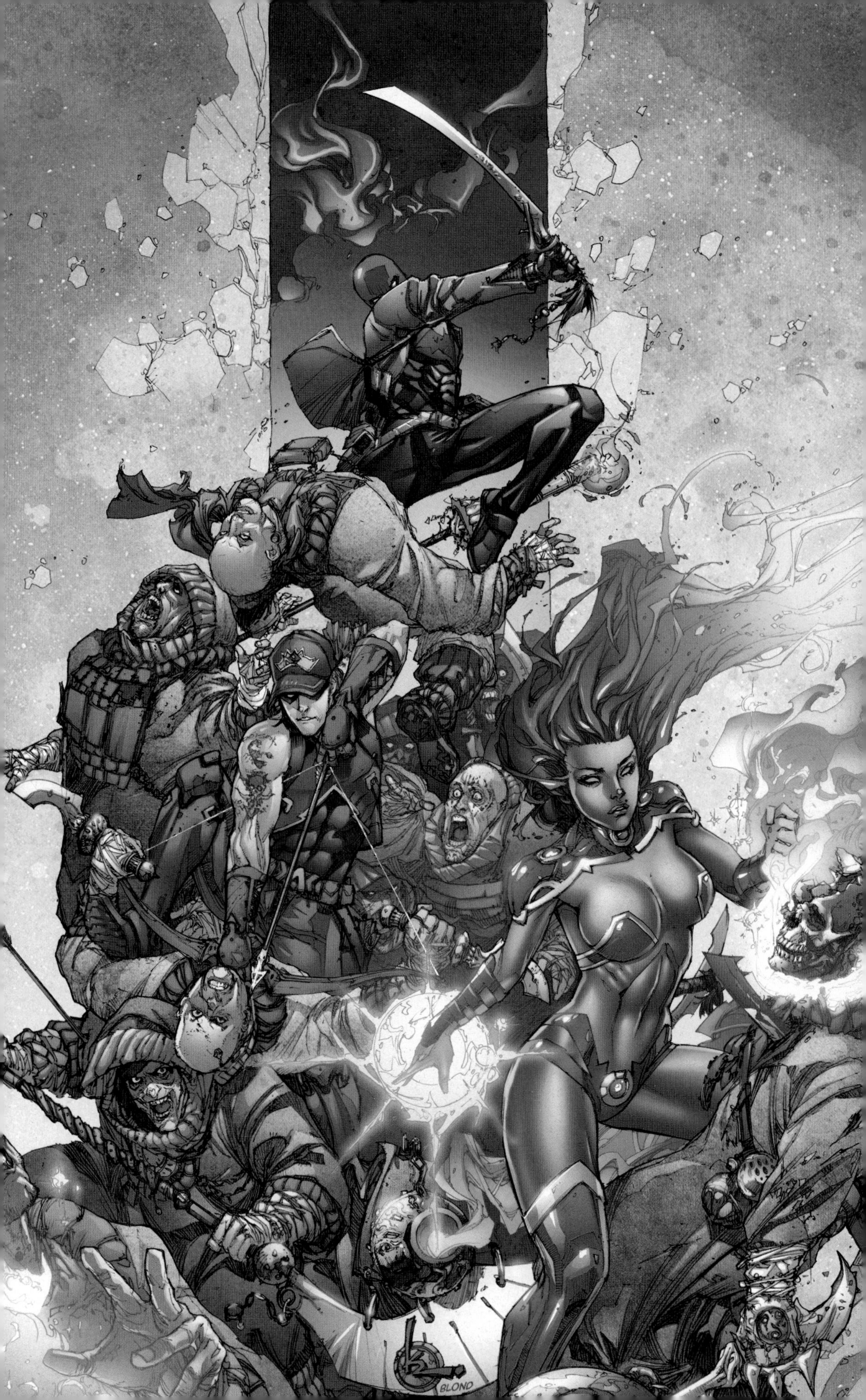
BLOND

VERTIGO WS TITLE THE RED HOOD ISSUE # 2 PAGE# MONTH **INTERIORS**

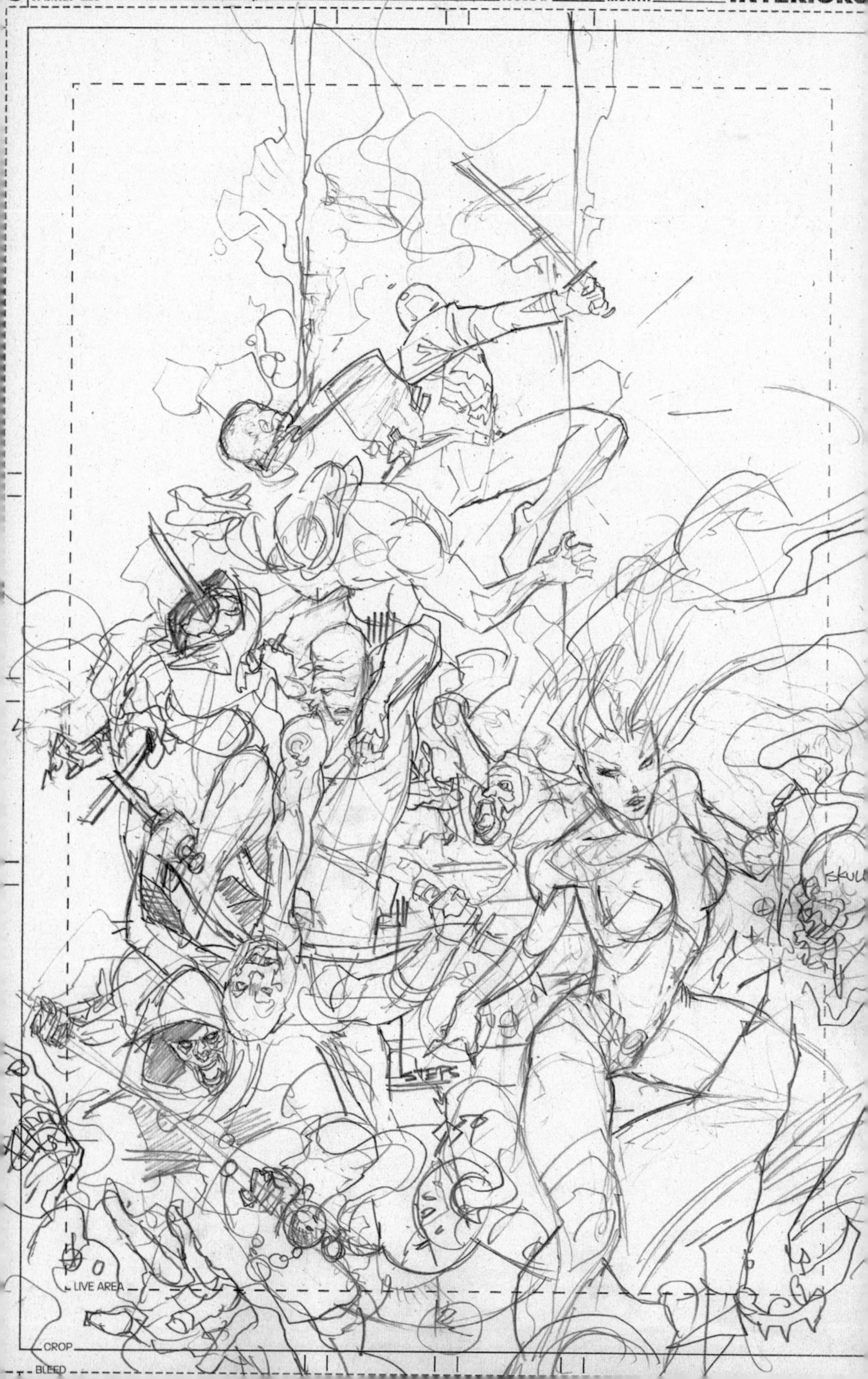
LIVE AREA
CROP
BLEED

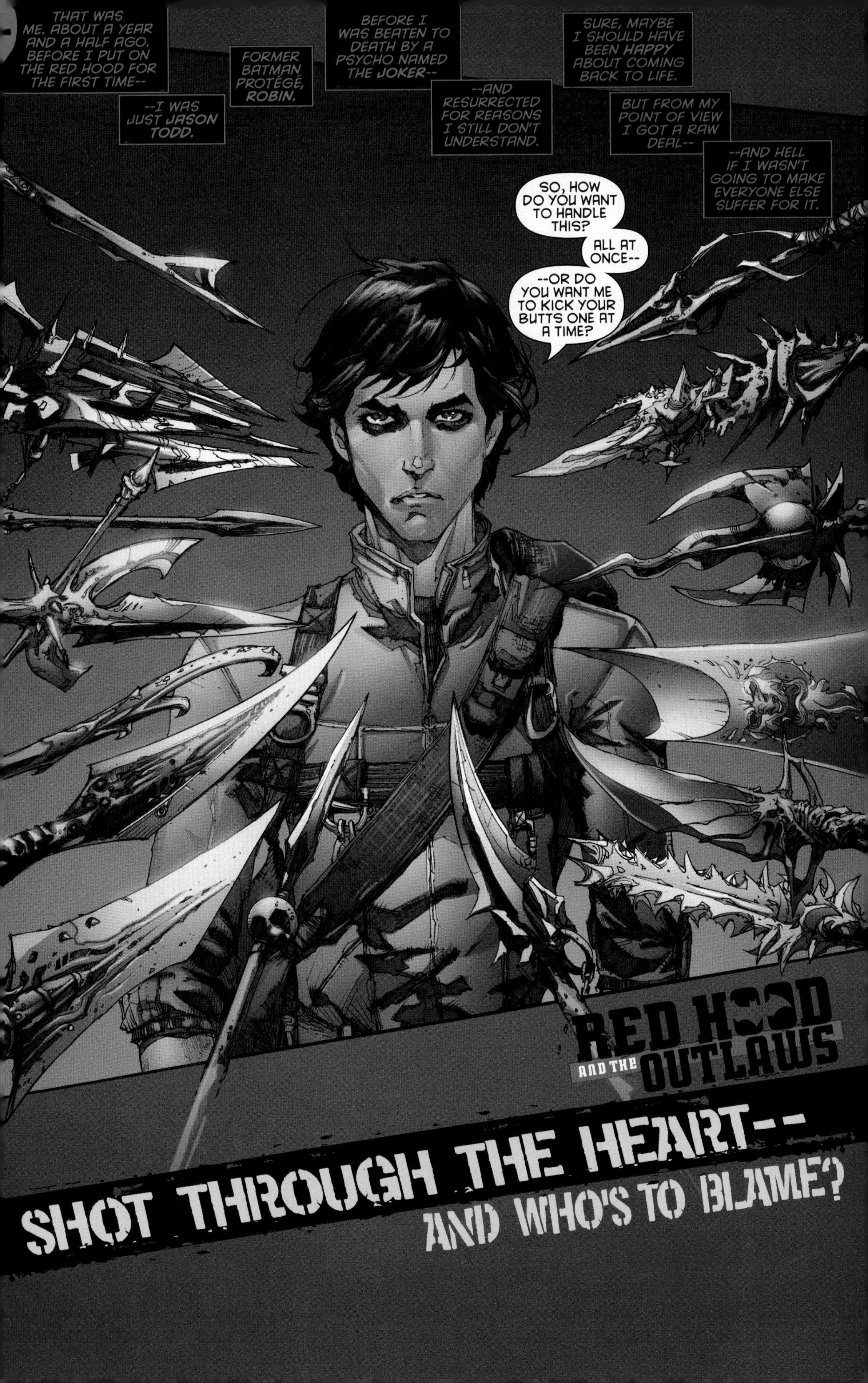
THAT WAS ME. ABOUT A YEAR AND A HALF AGO. BEFORE I PUT ON THE RED HOOD FOR THE FIRST TIME--
--I WAS JUST JASON TODD.
FORMER BATMAN PROTÉGÉ, ROBIN.
BEFORE I WAS BEATEN TO DEATH BY A PSYCHO NAMED THE JOKER--
--AND RESURRECTED FOR REASONS I STILL DON'T UNDERSTAND.
SURE, MAYBE I SHOULD HAVE BEEN HAPPY ABOUT COMING BACK TO LIFE.
BUT FROM MY POINT OF VIEW I GOT A RAW DEAL--
--AND HELL IF I WASN'T GOING TO MAKE EVERYONE ELSE SUFFER FOR IT.
SO, HOW DO YOU WANT TO HANDLE THIS?
ALL AT ONCE--
--OR DO YOU WANT ME TO KICK YOUR BUTTS ONE AT A TIME?
RED HOOD AND THE OUTLAWS
SHOT THROUGH THE HEART--
AND WHO'S TO BLAME?

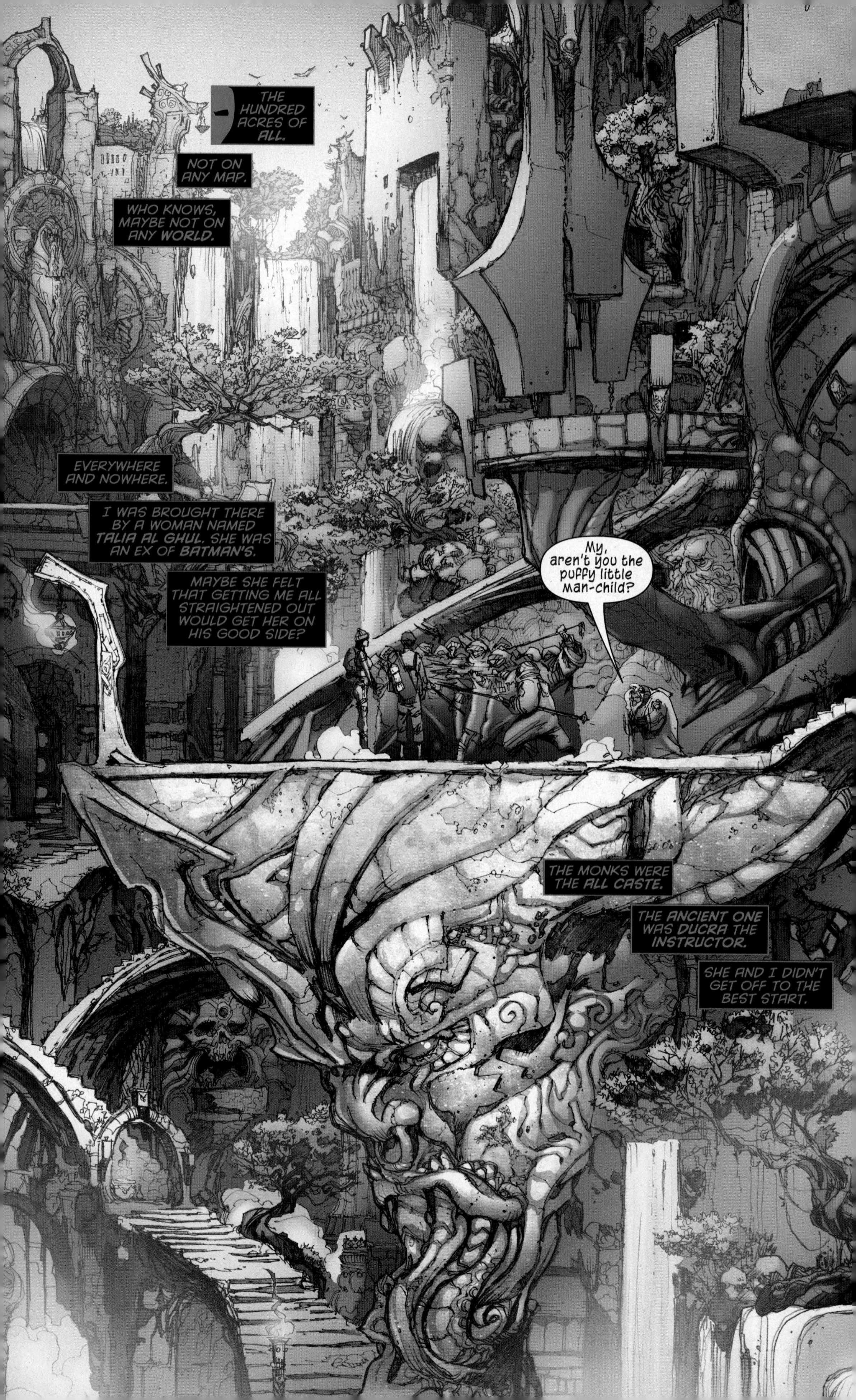

THE HUNDRED ACRES OF ALL.
NOT ON ANY MAP.
WHO KNOWS, MAYBE NOT ON ANY WORLD.
EVERYWHERE AND NOWHERE.
I WAS BROUGHT THERE BY A WOMAN NAMED TALIA AL GHUL. SHE WAS AN EX OF BATMAN'S.
MAYBE SHE FELT THAT GETTING ME ALL STRAIGHTENED OUT WOULD GET HER ON HIS GOOD SIDE?
My, aren't you the puffy little Man-child?
THE MONKS WERE THE ALL CASTE.
THE ANCIENT ONE WAS DUCRA THE INSTRUCTOR.
SHE AND I DIDN'T GET OFF TO THE BEST START.

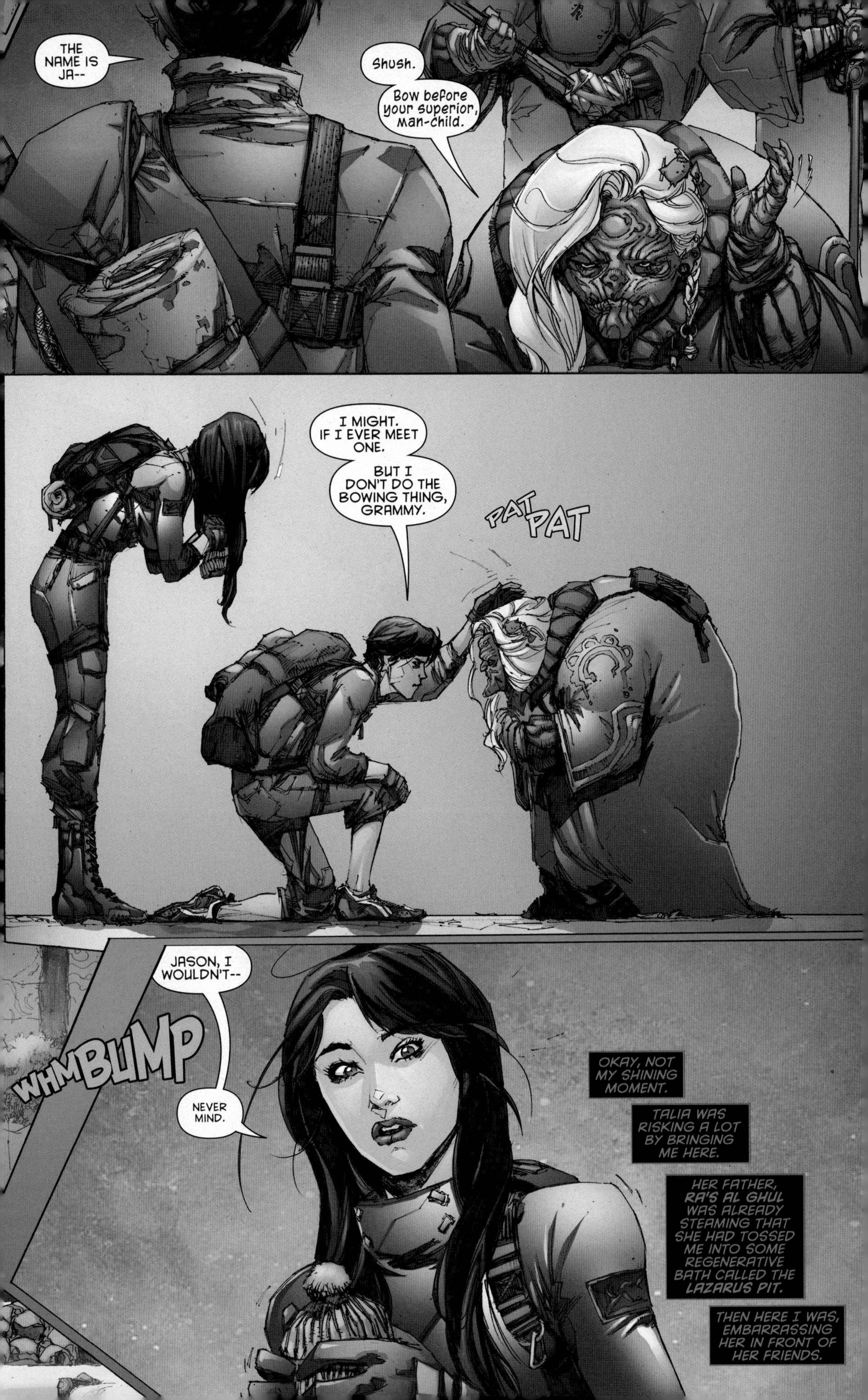
THE NAME IS JA--
Shush.
Bow before your superior, man-child.
I MIGHT. IF I EVER MEET ONE.
BUT I DON'T DO THE BOWING THING, GRAMMY.
PAT PAT
JASON, I WOULDN'T--
WHMBUMP
NEVER MIND.
OKAY, NOT MY SHINING MOMENT.
TALIA WAS RISKING A LOT BY BRINGING ME HERE.
HER FATHER, RA'S AL GHUL WAS ALREADY STEAMING THAT SHE HAD TOSSED ME INTO SOME REGENERATIVE BATH CALLED THE LAZARUS PIT.
THEN HERE I WAS, EMBARRASSING HER IN FRONT OF HER FRIENDS.

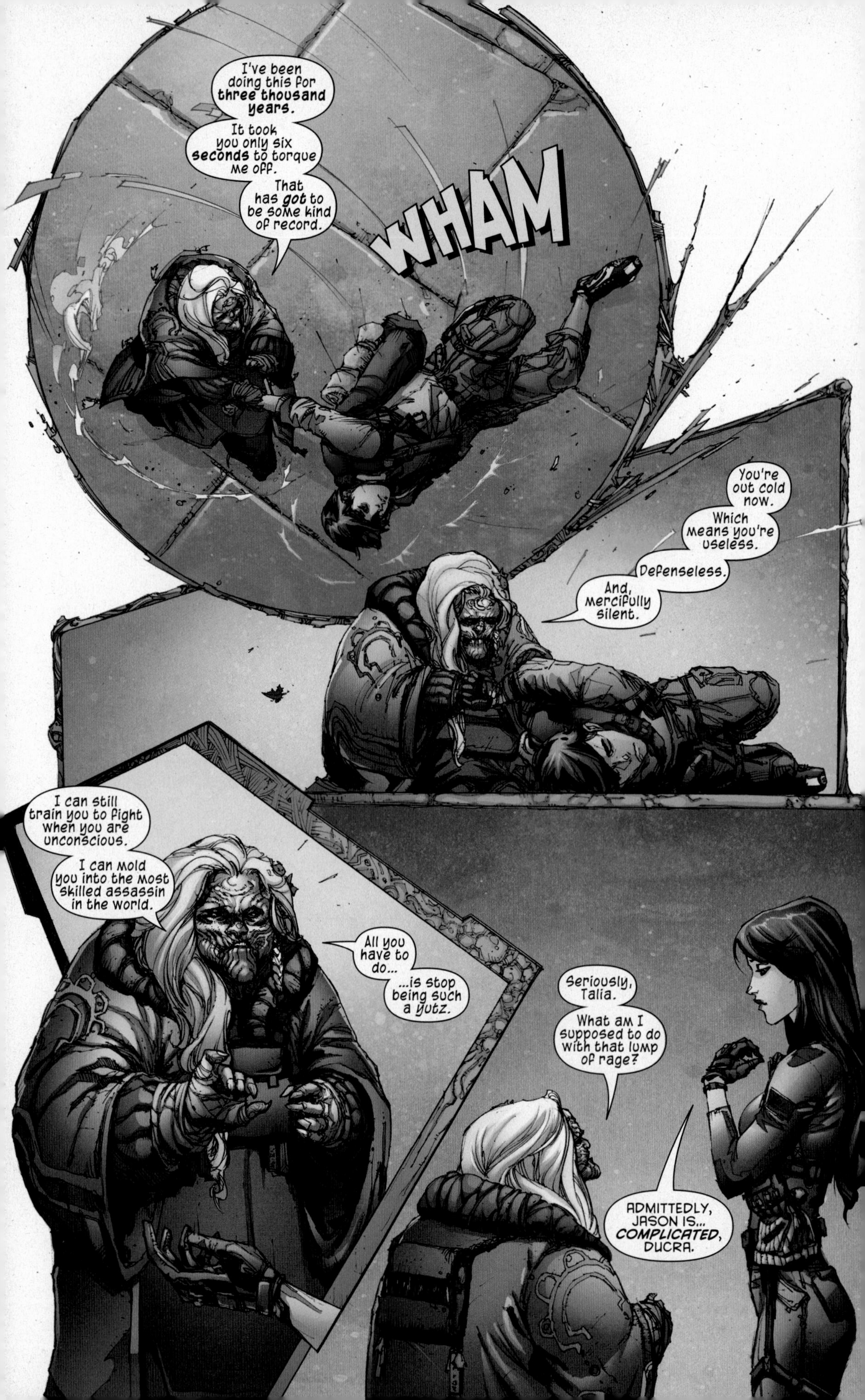

I've been doing this for **three thousand years.**
It took you only six **seconds** to torque me off.
That has **got** to be some kind of record.
WHAM
You're out cold now.
Which means you're useless.
Defenseless.
And, mercifully silent.
I can still train you to fight when you are unconscious.
I can mold you into the most skilled assassin in the world.
All you have to do...
...is stop being such a yutz.
Seriously, Talia.
What am I supposed to do with that lump of rage?
ADMITTEDLY, JASON IS... *COMPLICATED*, DUCRA.

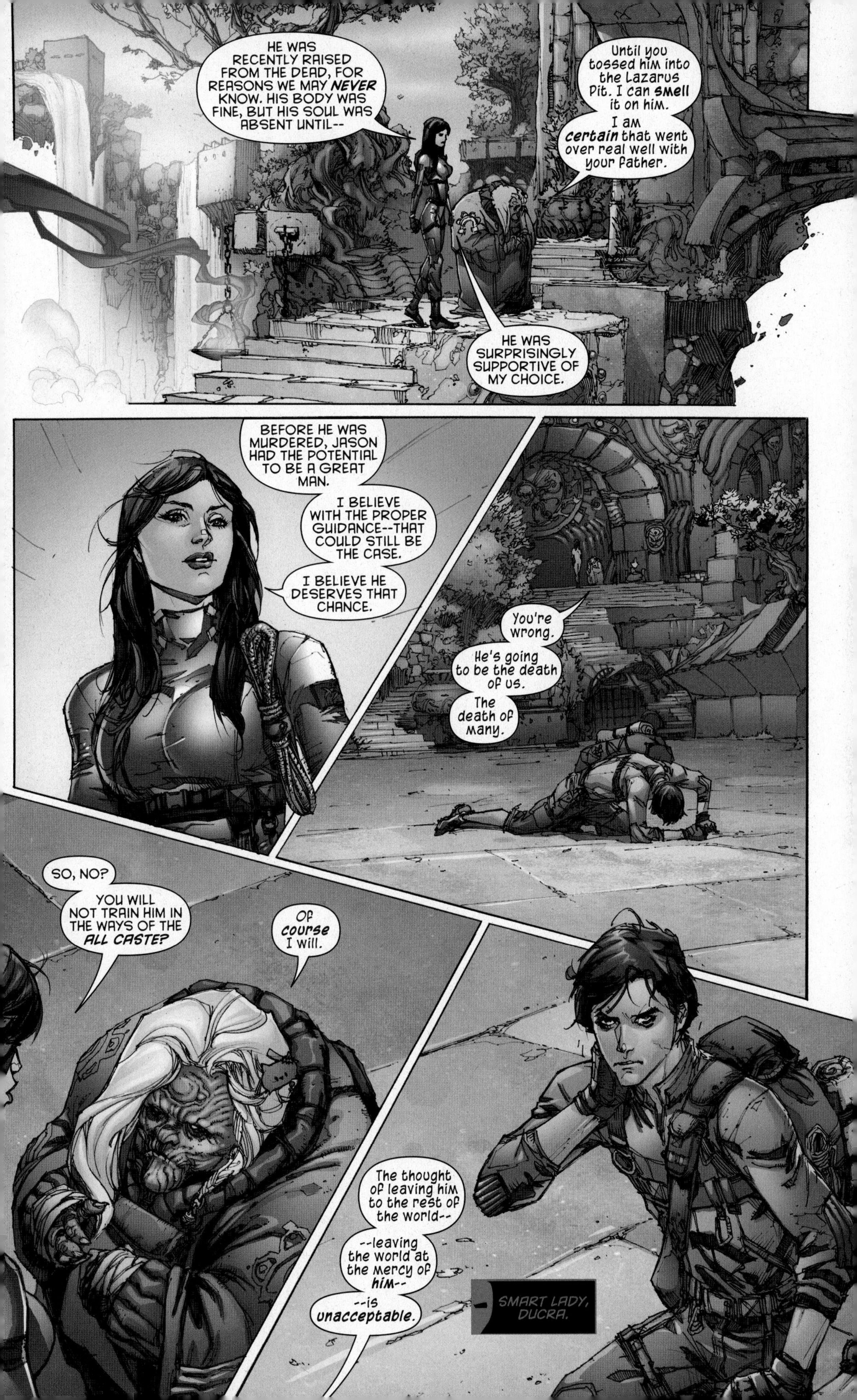

HE WAS RECENTLY RAISED FROM THE DEAD, FOR REASONS WE MAY NEVER KNOW. HIS BODY WAS FINE, BUT HIS SOUL WAS ABSENT UNTIL--
Until you tossed him into the Lazarus Pit. I can smell it on him.
I am certain that went over real well with your father.
HE WAS SURPRISINGLY SUPPORTIVE OF MY CHOICE.
BEFORE HE WAS MURDERED, JASON HAD THE POTENTIAL TO BE A GREAT MAN.
I BELIEVE WITH THE PROPER GUIDANCE--THAT COULD STILL BE THE CASE.
I BELIEVE HE DESERVES THAT CHANCE.
You're wrong.
He's going to be the death of us.
The death of many.
SO, NO?
YOU WILL NOT TRAIN HIM IN THE WAYS OF THE ALL CASTE?
Of course I will.
The thought of leaving him to the rest of the world--
--leaving the world at the mercy of him--
--is unacceptable.
SMART LADY, DUCRA.

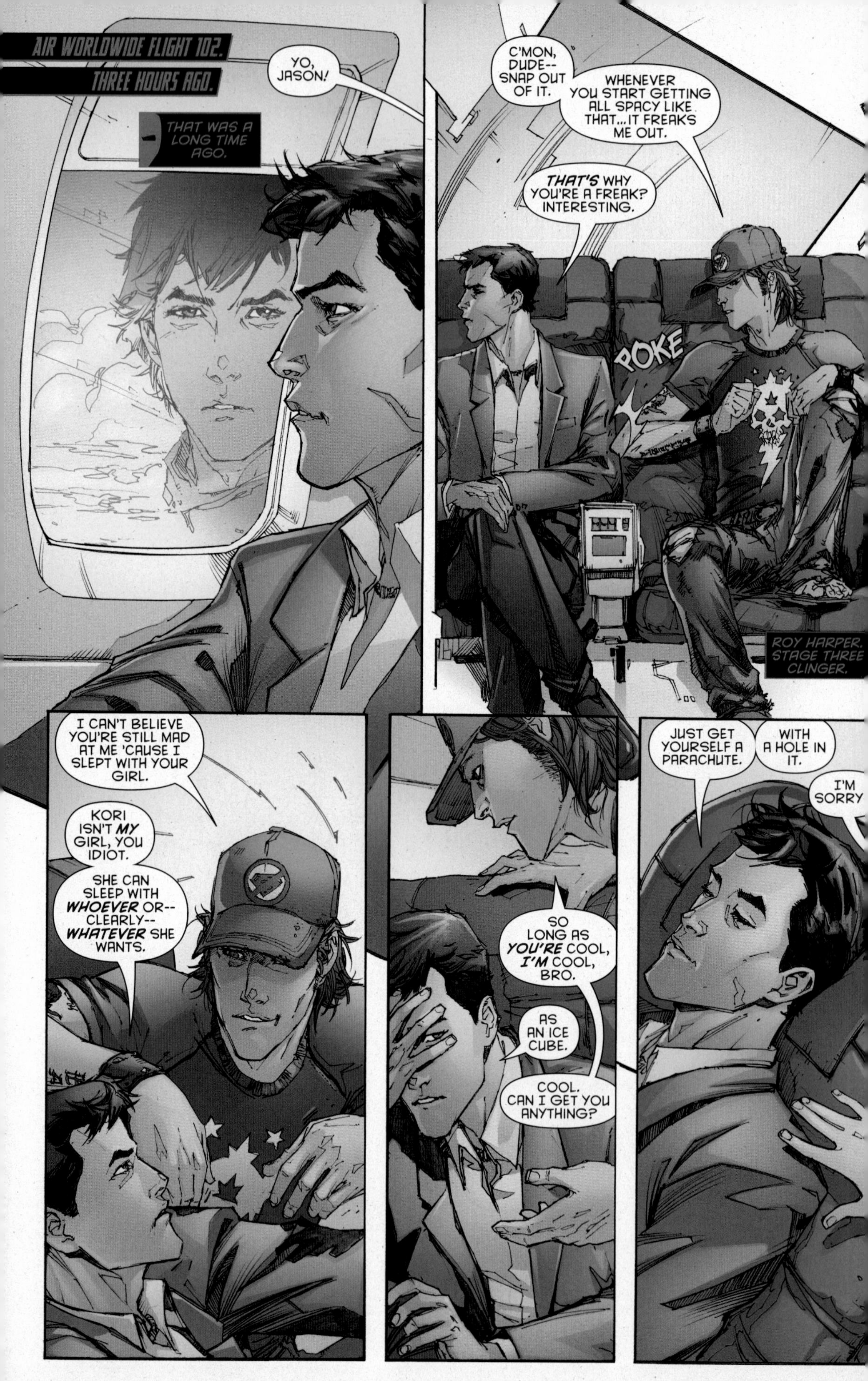

AIR WORLDWIDE FLIGHT 102.
THREE HOURS AGO.
YO, JASON!
THAT WAS A LONG TIME AGO.
C'MON, DUDE-- SNAP OUT OF IT.
WHENEVER YOU START GETTING ALL SPACY LIKE THAT... IT FREAKS ME OUT.
THAT'S WHY YOU'RE A FREAK? INTERESTING.
POKE
ROY HARPER. STAGE THREE CLINGER.
I CAN'T BELIEVE YOU'RE STILL MAD AT ME 'CAUSE I SLEPT WITH YOUR GIRL.
KORI ISN'T MY GIRL, YOU IDIOT.
SHE CAN SLEEP WITH WHOEVER OR-- CLEARLY-- WHATEVER SHE WANTS.
SO LONG AS YOU'RE COOL, I'M COOL, BRO.
AS AN ICE CUBE.
COOL. CAN I GET YOU ANYTHING?
JUST GET YOURSELF A PARACHUTE.
WITH A HOLE IN IT.
I'M SORRY

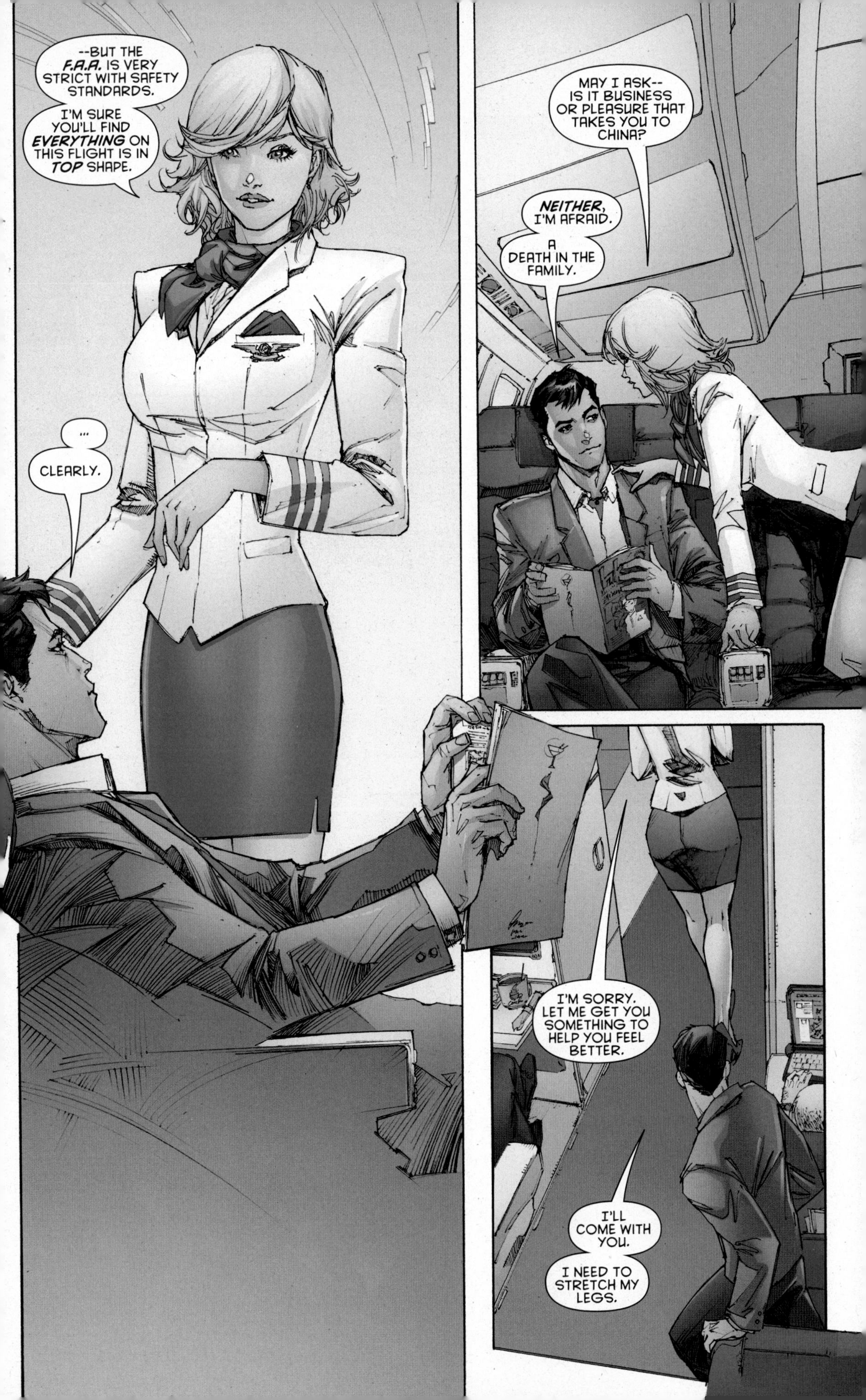
--BUT THE F.A.A. IS VERY STRICT WITH SAFETY STANDARDS.
I'M SURE YOU'LL FIND EVERYTHING ON THIS FLIGHT IS IN TOP SHAPE.
...
CLEARLY.
MAY I ASK-- IS IT BUSINESS OR PLEASURE THAT TAKES YOU TO CHINA?
NEITHER, I'M AFRAID.
A DEATH IN THE FAMILY.
I'M SORRY. LET ME GET YOU SOMETHING TO HELP YOU FEEL BETTER.
I'LL COME WITH YOU.
I NEED TO STRETCH MY LEGS.

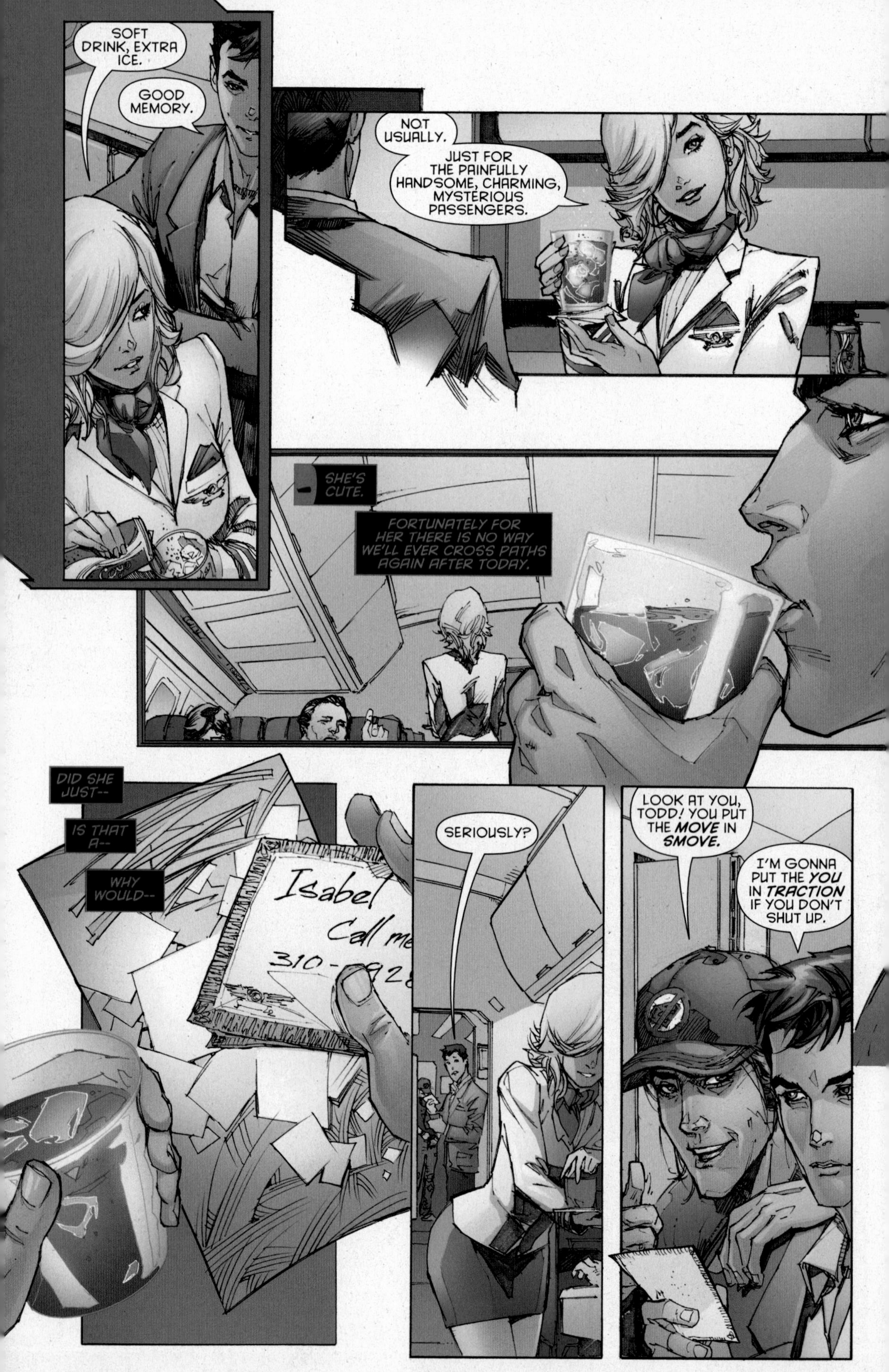
SOFT DRINK, EXTRA ICE.
GOOD MEMORY.
NOT USUALLY.
JUST FOR THE PAINFULLY HANDSOME, CHARMING, MYSTERIOUS PASSENGERS.
SHE'S CUTE.
FORTUNATELY FOR HER THERE IS NO WAY WE'LL EVER CROSS PATHS AGAIN AFTER TODAY.
DID SHE JUST--
IS THAT A--
WHY WOULD--
Isabel
Call me
SERIOUSLY?
LOOK AT YOU, TODD! YOU PUT THE MOVE IN SMOVE.
I'M GONNA PUT THE YOU IN TRACTION IF YOU DON'T SHUT UP.

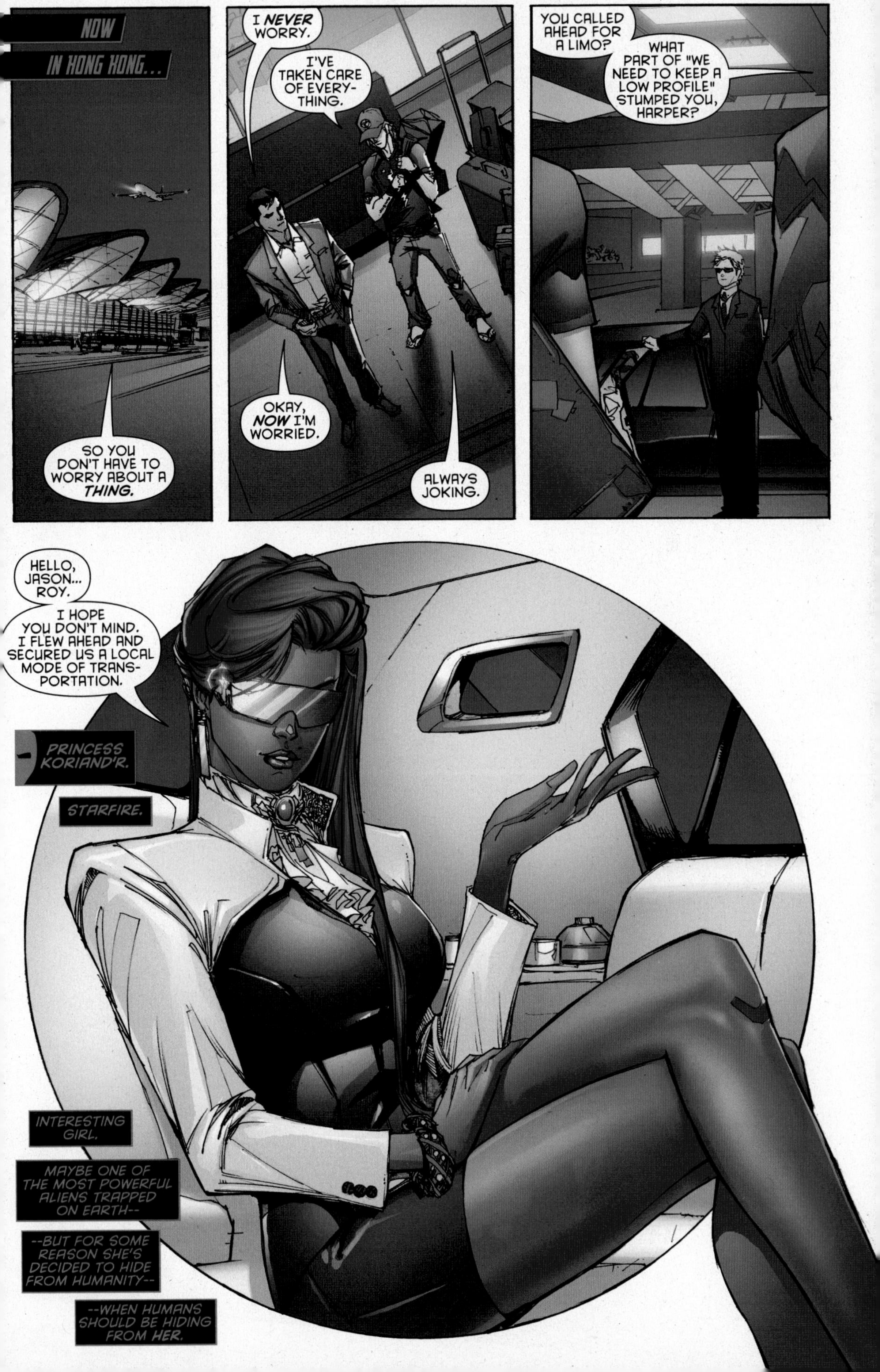
NOW
IN HONG KONG...
SO YOU DON'T HAVE TO WORRY ABOUT A THING.
I NEVER WORRY.
I'VE TAKEN CARE OF EVERY-THING.
OKAY, NOW I'M WORRIED.
ALWAYS JOKING.
YOU CALLED AHEAD FOR A LIMO?
WHAT PART OF "WE NEED TO KEEP A LOW PROFILE" STUMPED YOU, HARPER?
HELLO, JASON... ROY.
I HOPE YOU DON'T MIND. I FLEW AHEAD AND SECURED US A LOCAL MODE OF TRANS-PORTATION.
PRINCESS KORIAND'R.
STARFIRE.
INTERESTING GIRL.
MAYBE ONE OF THE MOST POWERFUL ALIENS TRAPPED ON EARTH--
--BUT FOR SOME REASON SHE'S DECIDED TO HIDE FROM HUMANITY--
--WHEN HUMANS SHOULD BE HIDING FROM HER.

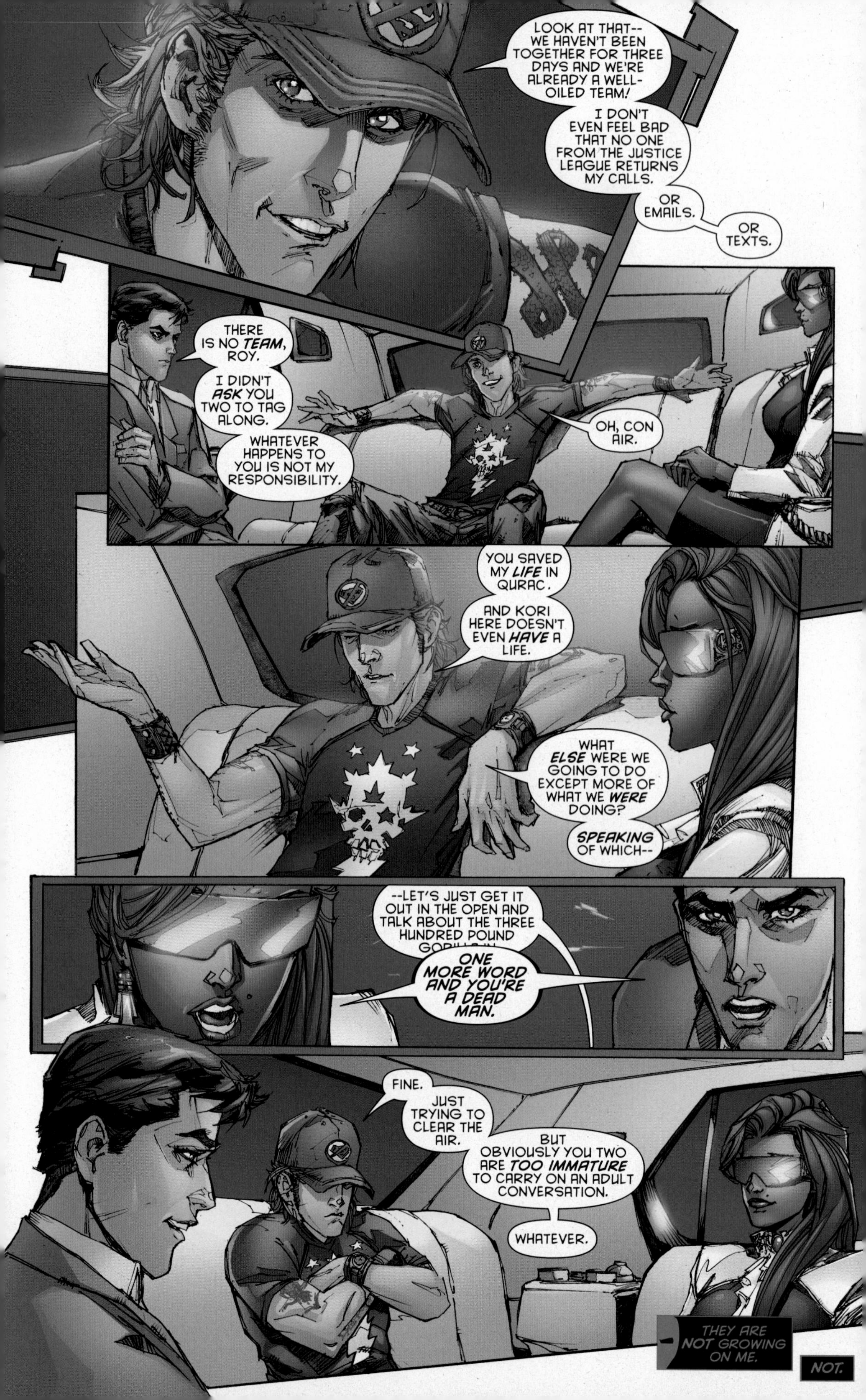
LOOK AT THAT-- WE HAVEN'T BEEN TOGETHER FOR THREE DAYS AND WE'RE ALREADY A WELL-OILED TEAM!
I DON'T EVEN FEEL BAD THAT NO ONE FROM THE JUSTICE LEAGUE RETURNS MY CALLS.
OR EMAILS.
OR TEXTS.
THERE IS NO TEAM, ROY.
I DIDN'T ASK YOU TWO TO TAG ALONG.
WHATEVER HAPPENS TO YOU IS NOT MY RESPONSIBILITY.
OH, CON AIR.
YOU SAVED MY LIFE IN QURAC.
AND KORI HERE DOESN'T EVEN HAVE A LIFE.
WHAT ELSE WERE WE GOING TO DO EXCEPT MORE OF WHAT WE WERE DOING?
SPEAKING OF WHICH--
--LET'S JUST GET IT OUT IN THE OPEN AND TALK ABOUT THE THREE HUNDRED POUND
ONE MORE WORD AND YOU'RE A DEAD MAN.
FINE.
JUST TRYING TO CLEAR THE AIR.
BUT OBVIOUSLY YOU TWO ARE TOO IMMATURE TO CARRY ON AN ADULT CONVERSATION.
WHATEVER.
THEY ARE NOT GROWING ON ME.
NOT.

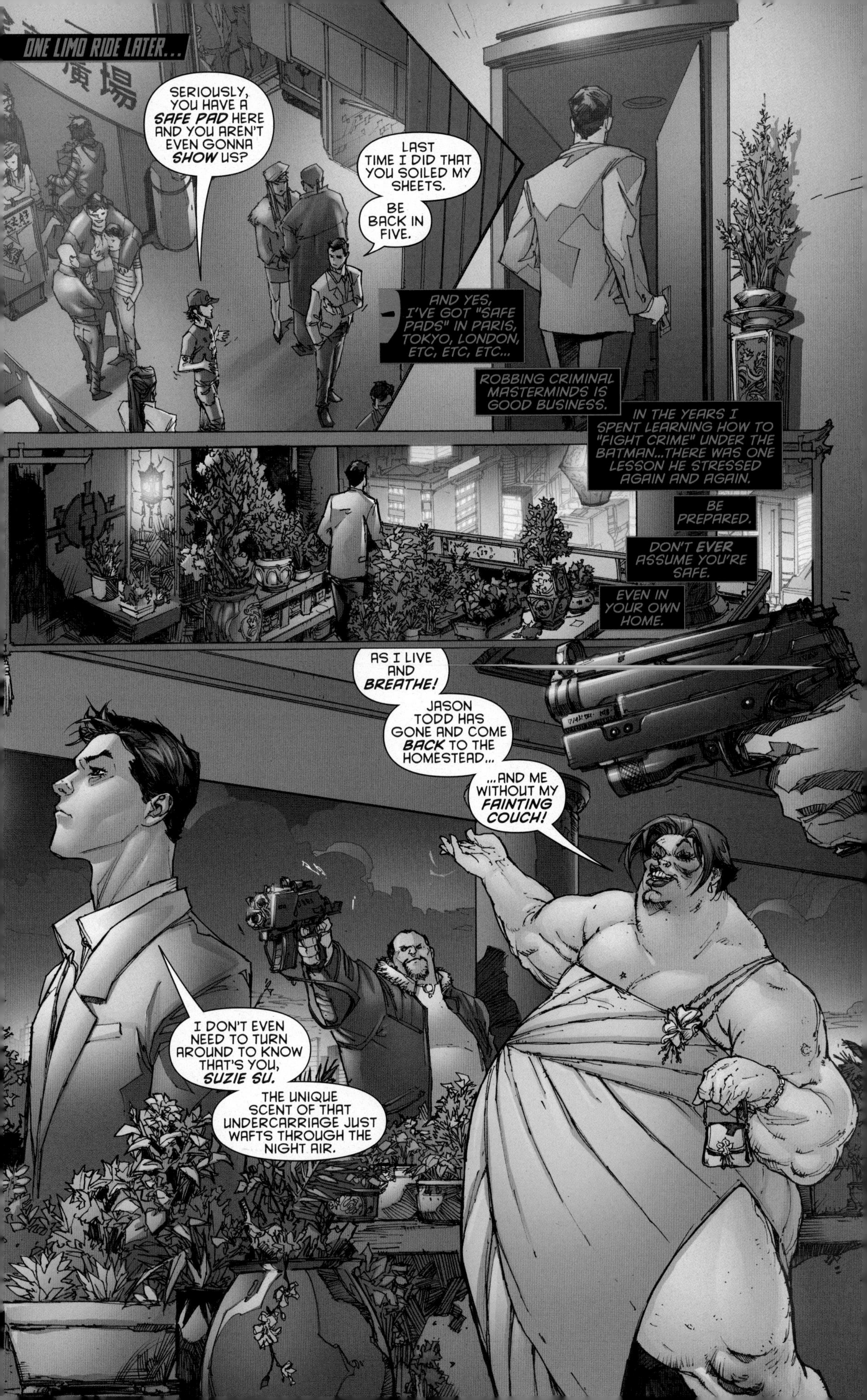
ONE LIMO RIDE LATER...
SERIOUSLY, YOU HAVE A SAFE PAD HERE AND YOU AREN'T EVEN GONNA SHOW US?
LAST TIME I DID THAT YOU SOILED MY SHEETS.
BE BACK IN FIVE.
AND YES, I'VE GOT "SAFE PADS" IN PARIS, TOKYO, LONDON, ETC, ETC, ETC...
ROBBING CRIMINAL MASTERMINDS IS GOOD BUSINESS.
IN THE YEARS I SPENT LEARNING HOW TO "FIGHT CRIME" UNDER THE BATMAN...THERE WAS ONE LESSON HE STRESSED AGAIN AND AGAIN.
BE PREPARED.
DON'T EVER ASSUME YOU'RE SAFE.
EVEN IN YOUR OWN HOME.
AS I LIVE AND BREATHE!
JASON TODD HAS GONE AND COME BACK TO THE HOMESTEAD...
...AND ME WITHOUT MY FAINTING COUCH!
I DON'T EVEN NEED TO TURN AROUND TO KNOW THAT'S YOU, SUZIE SU.
THE UNIQUE SCENT OF THAT UNDERCARRIAGE JUST WAFTS THROUGH THE NIGHT AIR.

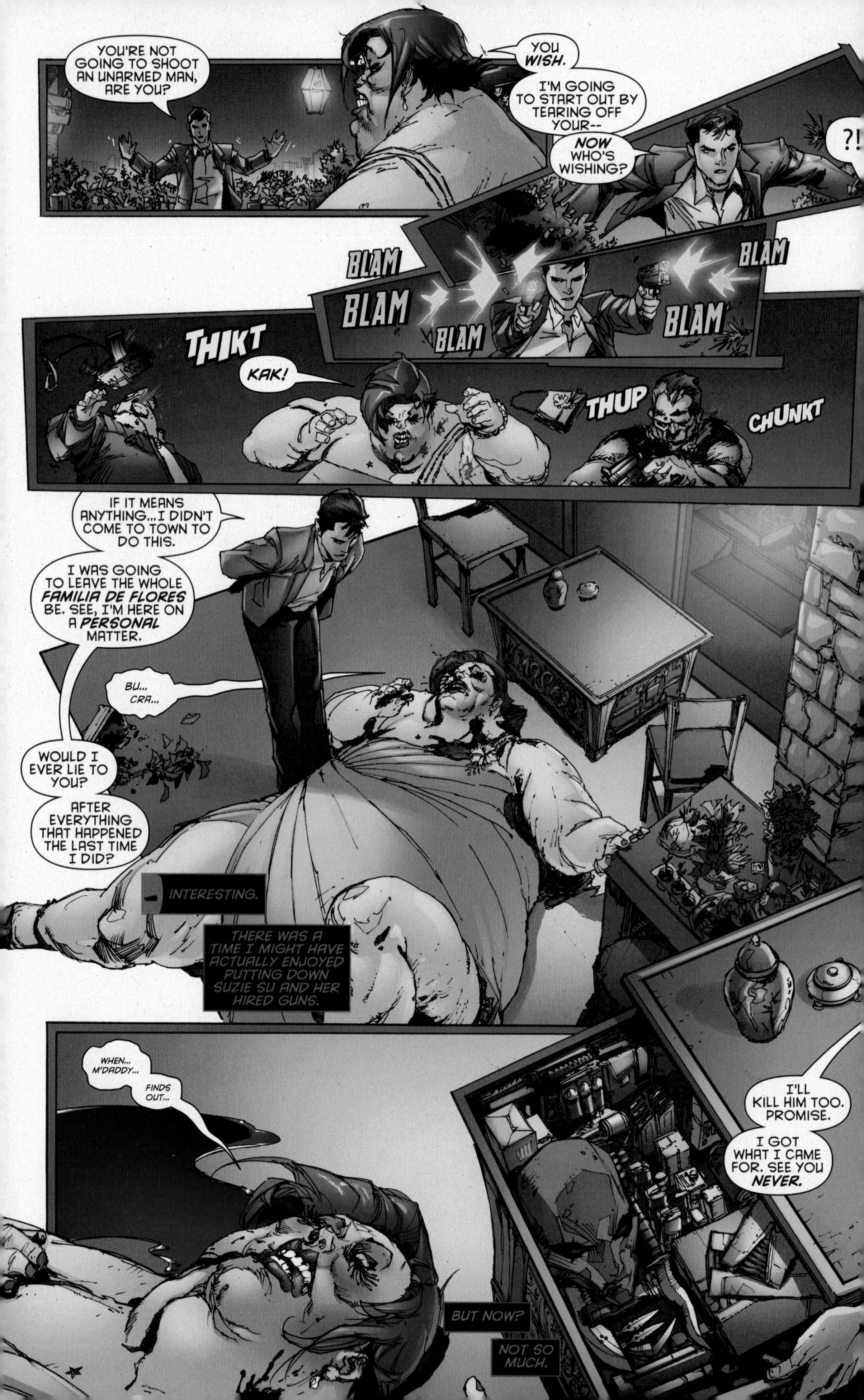

YOU'RE NOT GOING TO SHOOT AN UNARMED MAN, ARE YOU?
YOU WISH.
I'M GOING TO START OUT BY TEARING OFF YOUR--
NOW WHO'S WISHING?
?!
BLAM
BLAM
BLAM
BLAM
BLAM
THIKT
KAK!
THUP
CHUNKT
IF IT MEANS ANYTHING...I DIDN'T COME TO TOWN TO DO THIS.
I WAS GOING TO LEAVE THE WHOLE FAMILIA DE FLORES BE. SEE, I'M HERE ON A PERSONAL MATTER.
BU... CRA...
WOULD I EVER LIE TO YOU?
AFTER EVERYTHING THAT HAPPENED THE LAST TIME I DID?
INTERESTING.
THERE WAS A TIME I MIGHT HAVE ACTUALLY ENJOYED PUTTING DOWN SUZIE SU AND HER HIRED GUNS.
WHEN... M'DADDY... FINDS OUT...
I'LL KILL HIM TOO. PROMISE.
I GOT WHAT I CAME FOR. SEE YOU NEVER.
BUT NOW?
NOT SO MUCH.

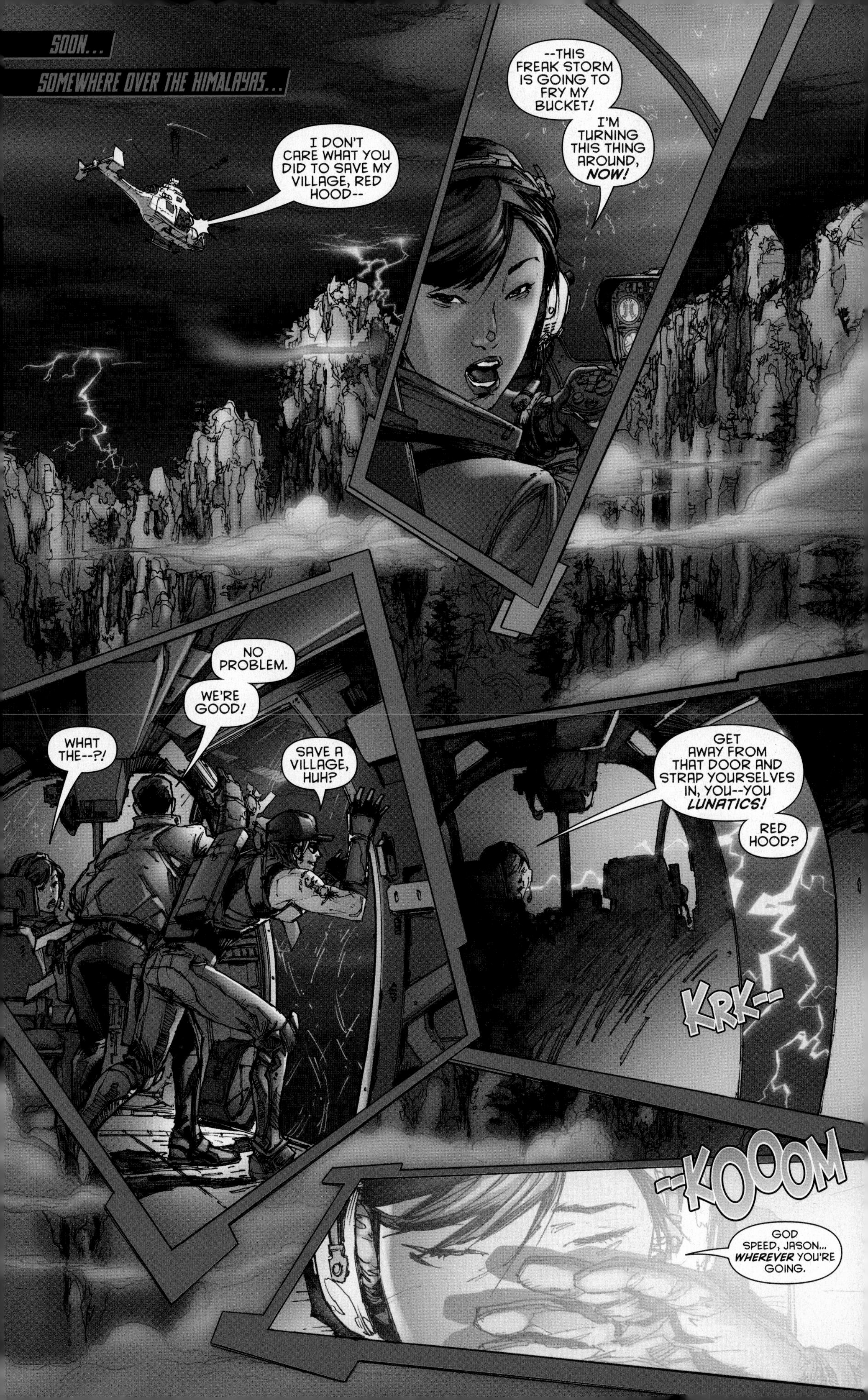
SOON...
SOMEWHERE OVER THE HIMALAYAS...
I DON'T CARE WHAT YOU DID TO SAVE MY VILLAGE, RED HOOD--
--THIS FREAK STORM IS GOING TO FRY MY BUCKET!
I'M TURNING THIS THING AROUND, NOW!
WHAT THE--?!
NO PROBLEM.
WE'RE GOOD!
SAVE A VILLAGE, HUH?
GET AWAY FROM THAT DOOR AND STRAP YOURSELVES IN, YOU--YOU LUNATICS!
RED HOOD?
KRK--
--KOOOM
GOD SPEED, JASON... WHEREVER YOU'RE GOING.

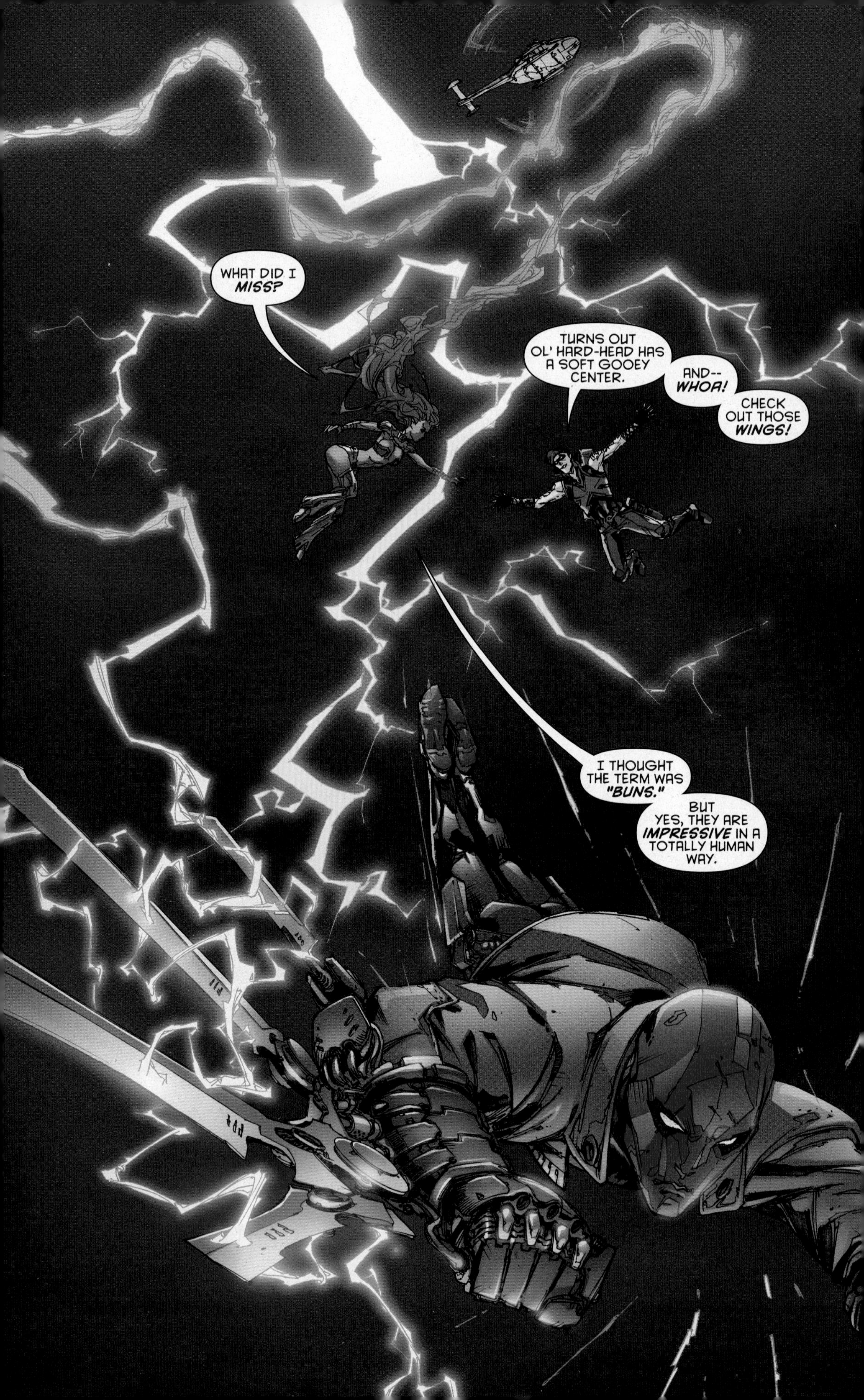
WHAT DID I *MISS?*
TURNS OUT OL' HARD-HEAD HAS A SOFT GOOEY CENTER.
AND-- *WHOA!*
CHECK OUT THOSE *WINGS!*
I THOUGHT THE TERM WAS *"BUNS."*
BUT YES, THEY ARE *IMPRESSIVE* IN A TOTALLY HUMAN WAY.

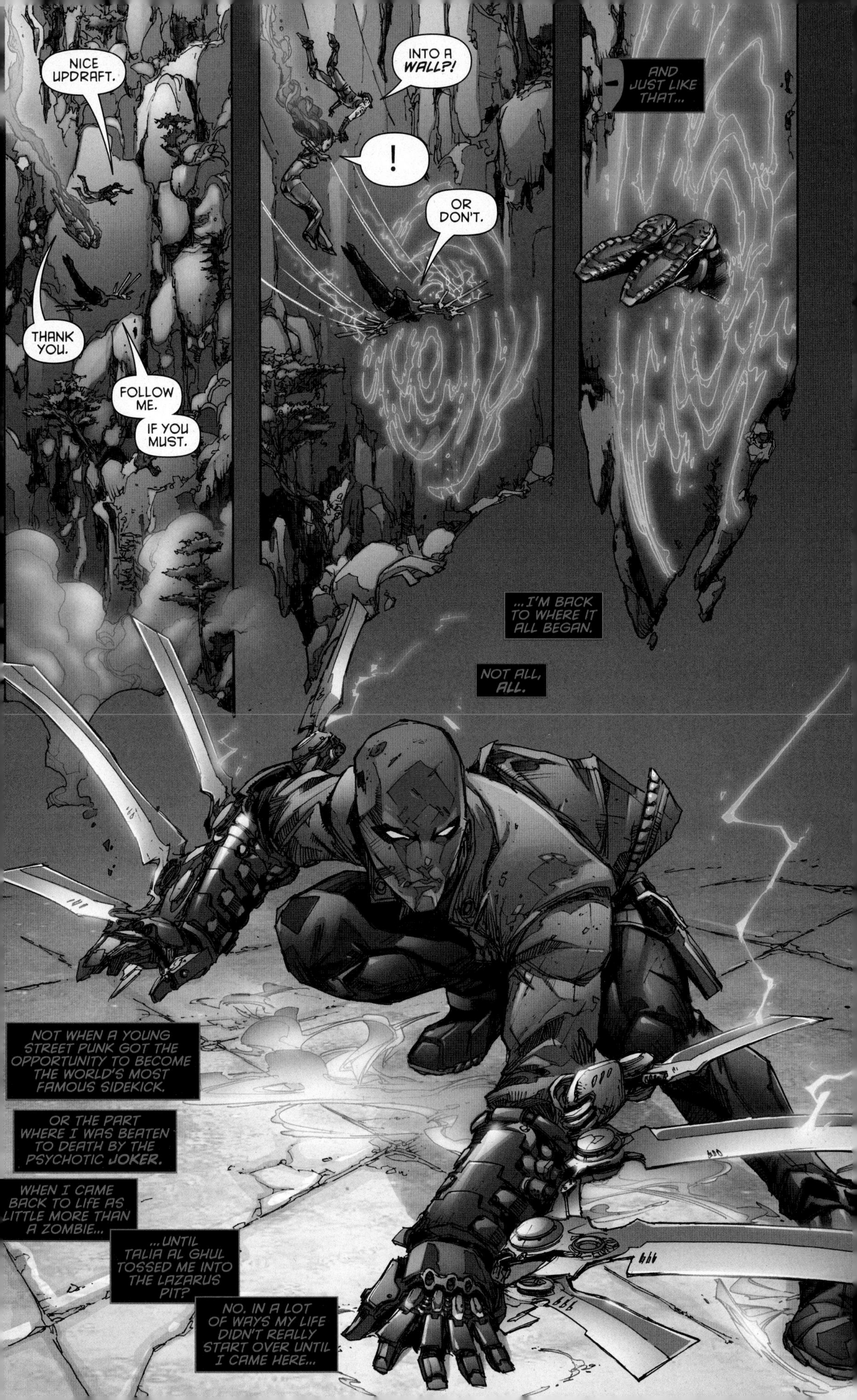
NICE UPDRAFT.
THANK YOU.
FOLLOW ME.
IF YOU MUST.
INTO A WALL?!
!
OR DON'T.
AND JUST LIKE THAT...
...I'M BACK TO WHERE IT ALL BEGAN.
NOT ALL, ALL.
NOT WHEN A YOUNG STREET PUNK GOT THE OPPORTUNITY TO BECOME THE WORLD'S MOST FAMOUS SIDEKICK.
OR THE PART WHERE I WAS BEATEN TO DEATH BY THE PSYCHOTIC JOKER.
WHEN I CAME BACK TO LIFE AS LITTLE MORE THAN A ZOMBIE...
...UNTIL TALIA AL GHUL TOSSED ME INTO THE LAZARUS PIT?
NO. IN A LOT OF WAYS MY LIFE DIDN'T REALLY START OVER UNTIL I CAME HERE...

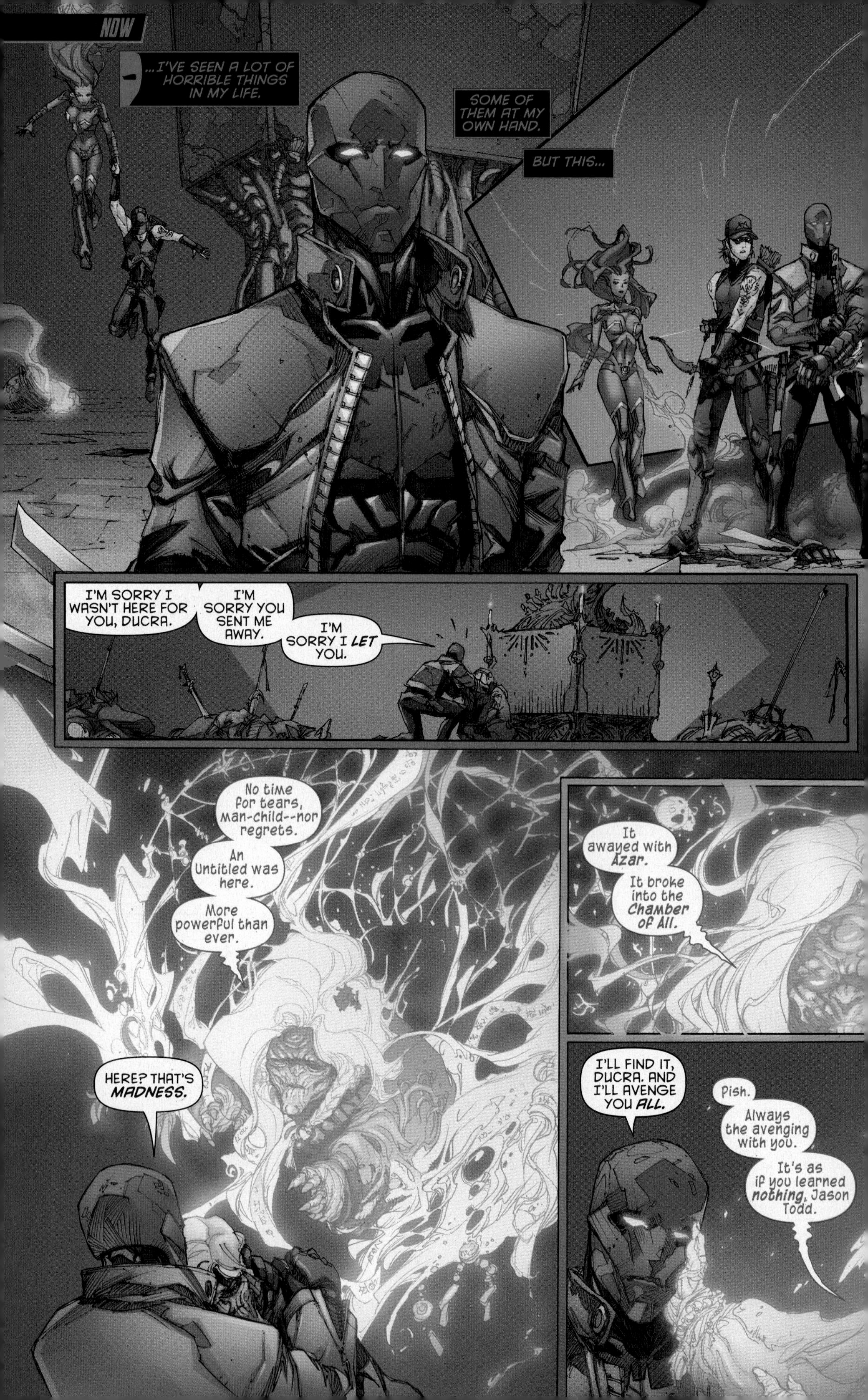
NOW
...I'VE SEEN A LOT OF HORRIBLE THINGS IN MY LIFE.
SOME OF THEM AT MY OWN HAND.
BUT THIS...
I'M SORRY I WASN'T HERE FOR YOU, DUCRA.
I'M SORRY YOU SENT ME AWAY.
I'M SORRY I LET YOU.
No time for tears, Man-child--nor regrets.
An Untitled was here.
More powerful than ever.
HERE? THAT'S MADNESS.
It awayed with Azar.
It broke into the Chamber of All.
I'LL FIND IT, DUCRA. AND I'LL AVENGE YOU ALL.
Pish.
Always the avenging with you.
It's as if you learned nothing, Jason Todd.

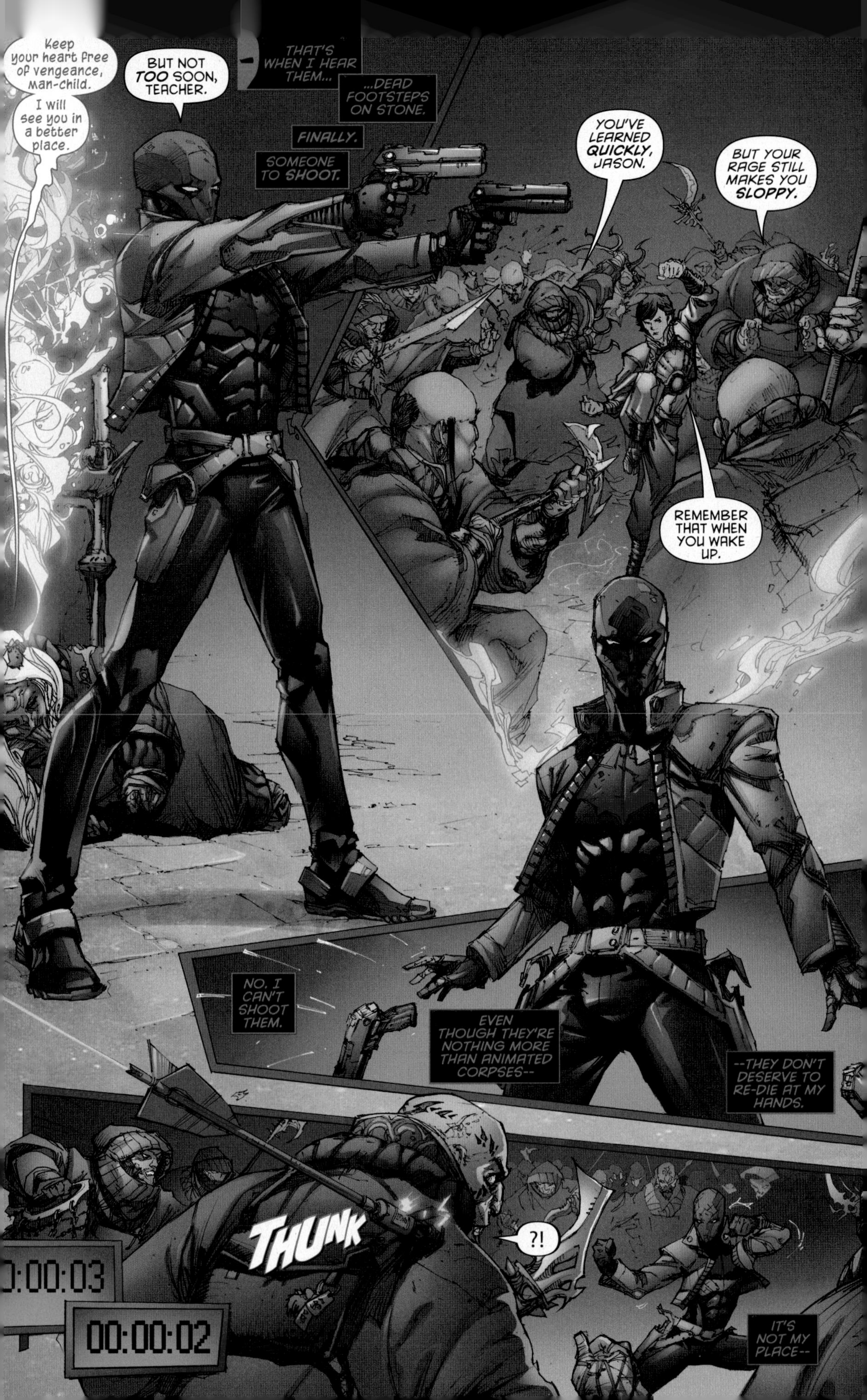
Keep your heart free of vengeance, man-child.
I will see you in a better place.
BUT NOT TOO SOON, TEACHER.
THAT'S WHEN I HEAR THEM...
...DEAD FOOTSTEPS ON STONE.
FINALLY.
SOMEONE TO SHOOT.
YOU'VE LEARNED QUICKLY, JASON.
BUT YOUR RAGE STILL MAKES YOU SLOPPY.
REMEMBER THAT WHEN YOU WAKE UP.
NO. I CAN'T SHOOT THEM.
EVEN THOUGH THEY'RE NOTHING MORE THAN ANIMATED CORPSES--
--THEY DON'T DESERVE TO RE-DIE AT MY HANDS.
THUNK
?!
0:00:03
00:00:02
IT'S NOT MY PLACE--

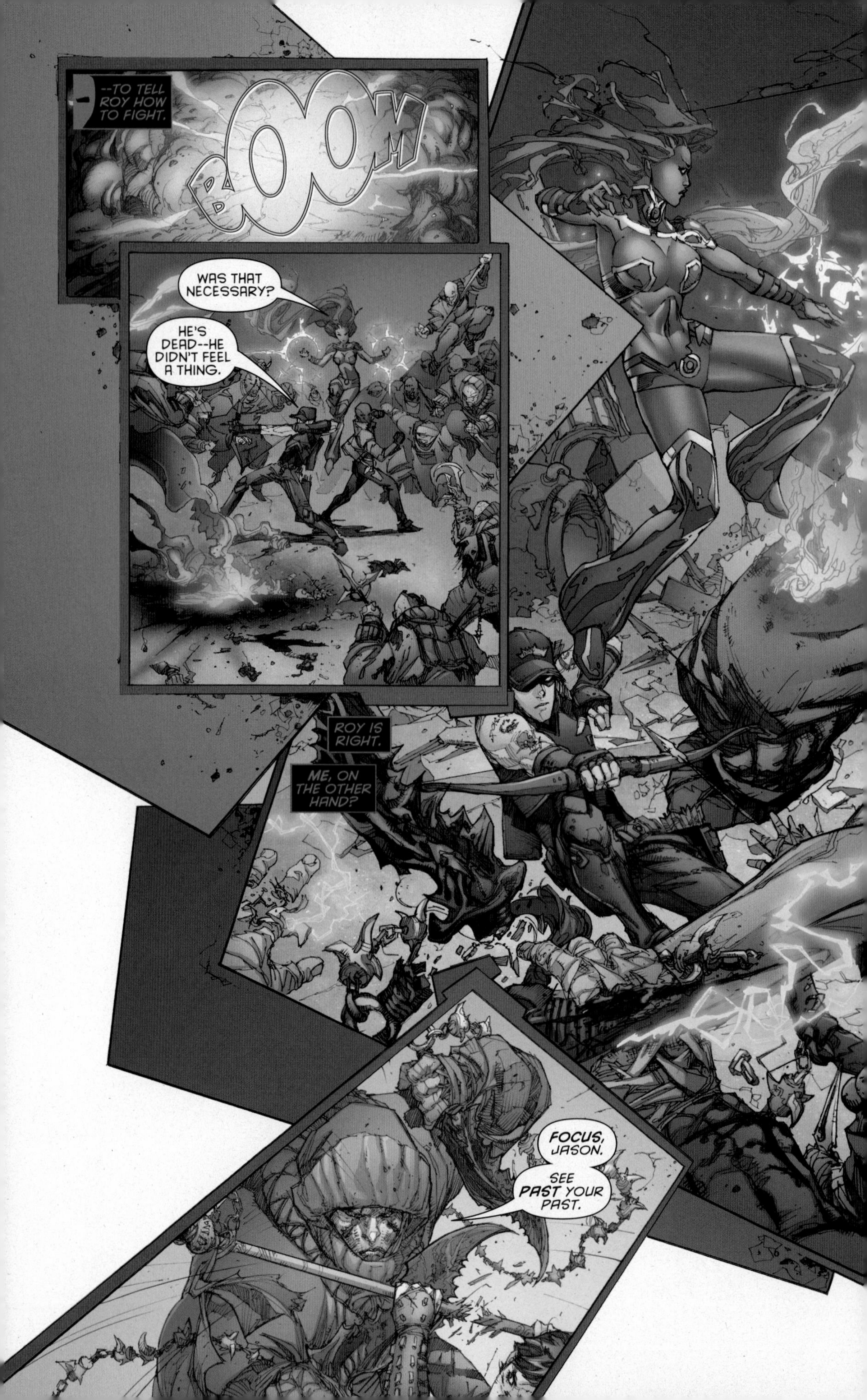
--TO TELL ROY HOW TO FIGHT.
BOOM
WAS THAT NECESSARY?
HE'S DEAD--HE DIDN'T FEEL A THING.
ROY IS RIGHT.
ME, ON THE OTHER HAND?
FOCUS, JASON.
SEE PAST YOUR PAST.

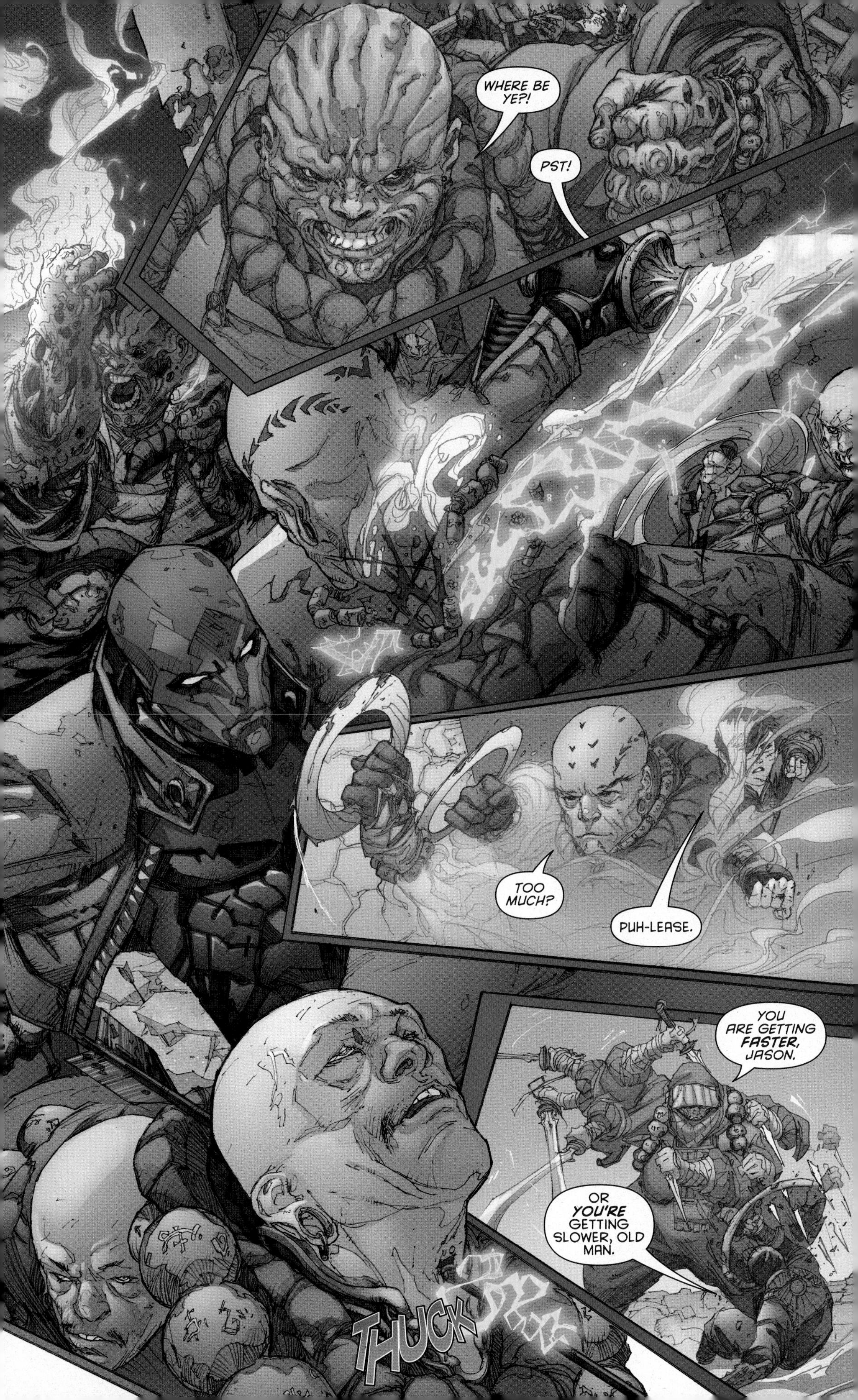
WHERE BE YE?!
PST!
TOO MUCH?
PUH-LEASE.
YOU ARE GETTING FASTER, JASON.
OR YOU'RE GETTING SLOWER, OLD MAN.
THUCK

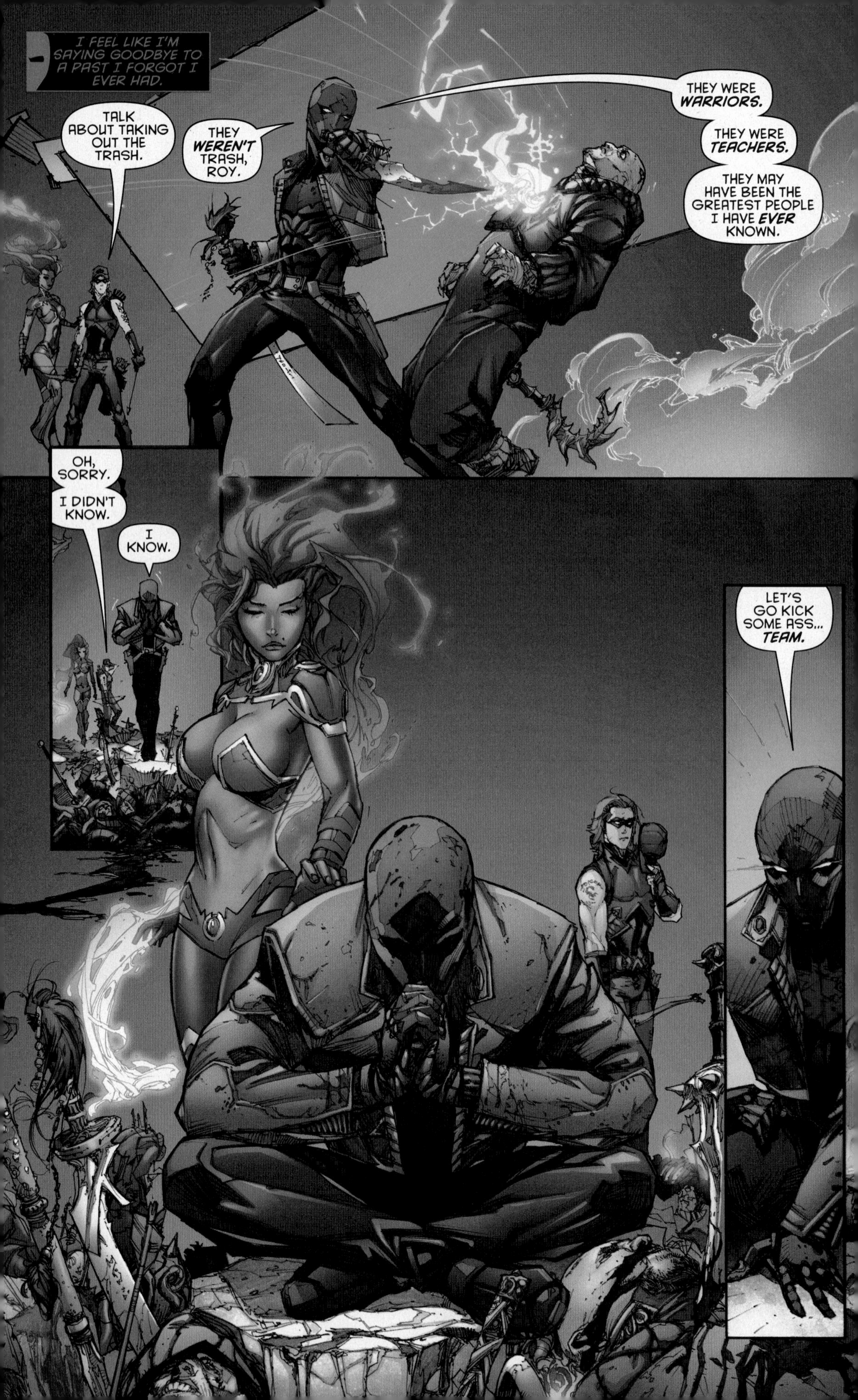
I FEEL LIKE I'M SAYING GOODBYE TO A PAST I FORGOT I EVER HAD.
TALK ABOUT TAKING OUT THE TRASH.
THEY *WEREN'T* TRASH, ROY.
THEY WERE *WARRIORS.*
THEY WERE *TEACHERS.*
THEY MAY HAVE BEEN THE GREATEST PEOPLE I HAVE *EVER* KNOWN.
OH, SORRY.
I DIDN'T KNOW.
I KNOW.
LET'S GO KICK SOME ASS... *TEAM.*

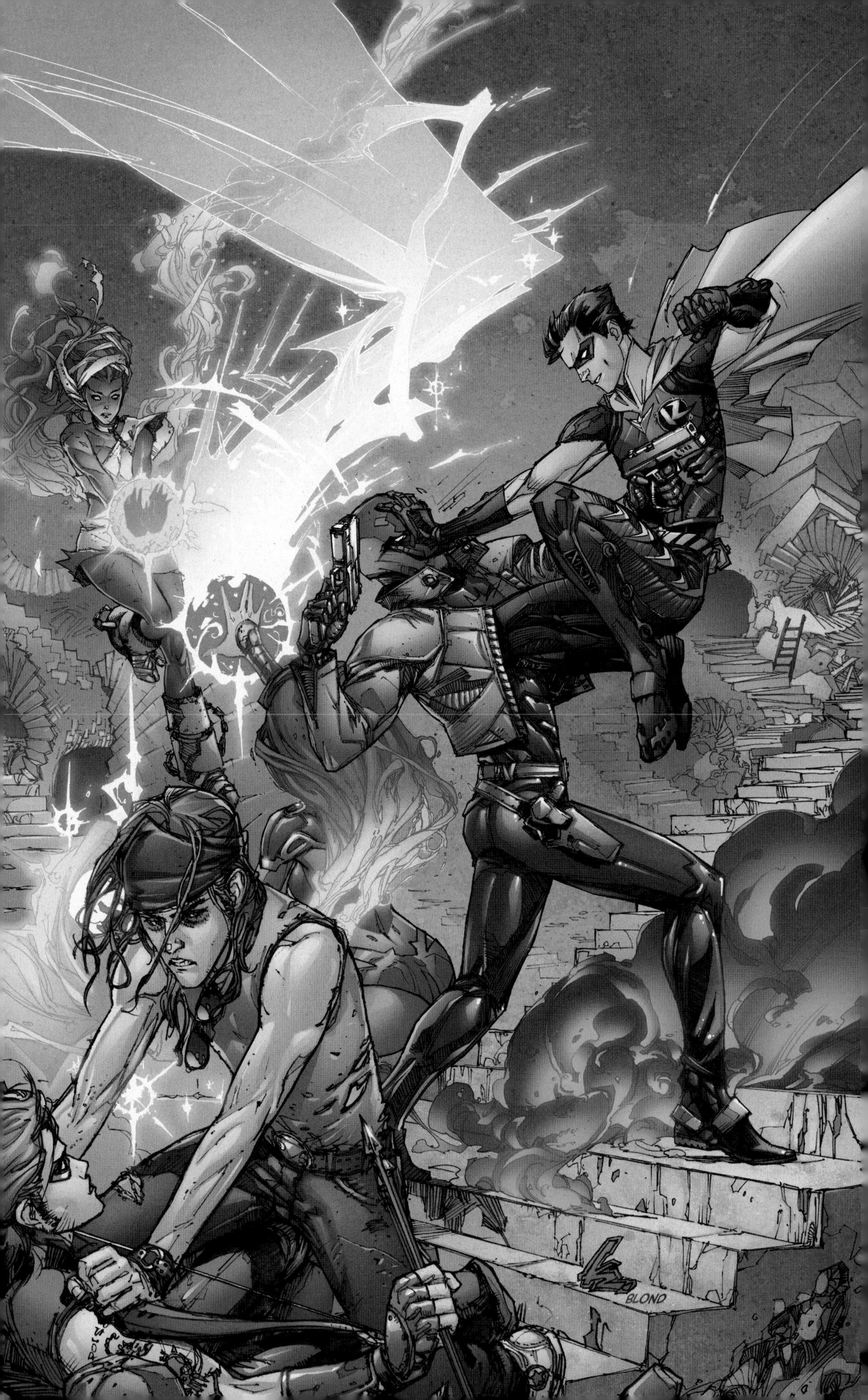
BLOND

PENCILLER KENNETH ROCAFORT INKER PAGE# COVER

TITLE RED HOOD AND THE OUTLAWS ISSUE # 3 MONTH

INTERIORS

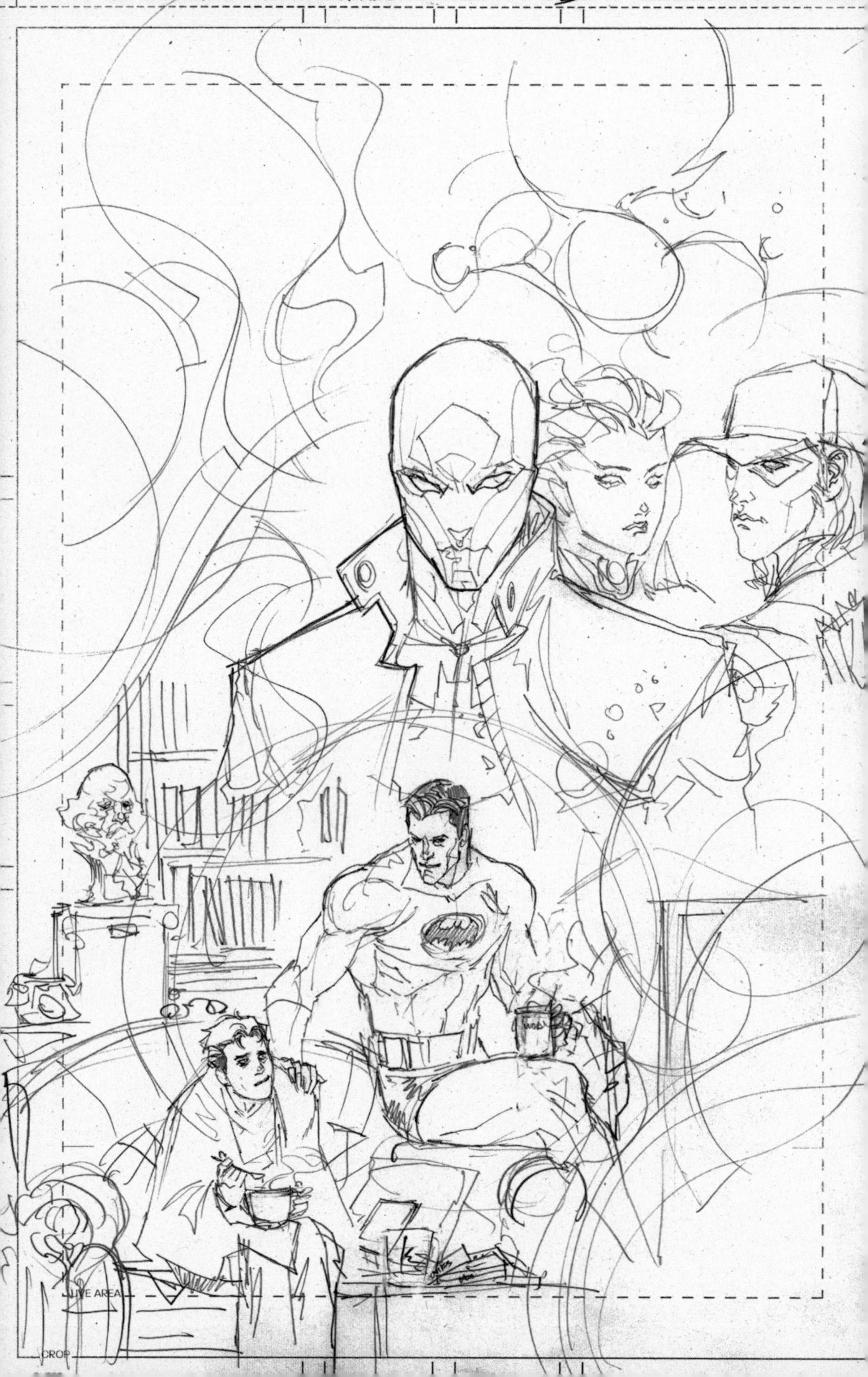
LIVE AREA
CROP

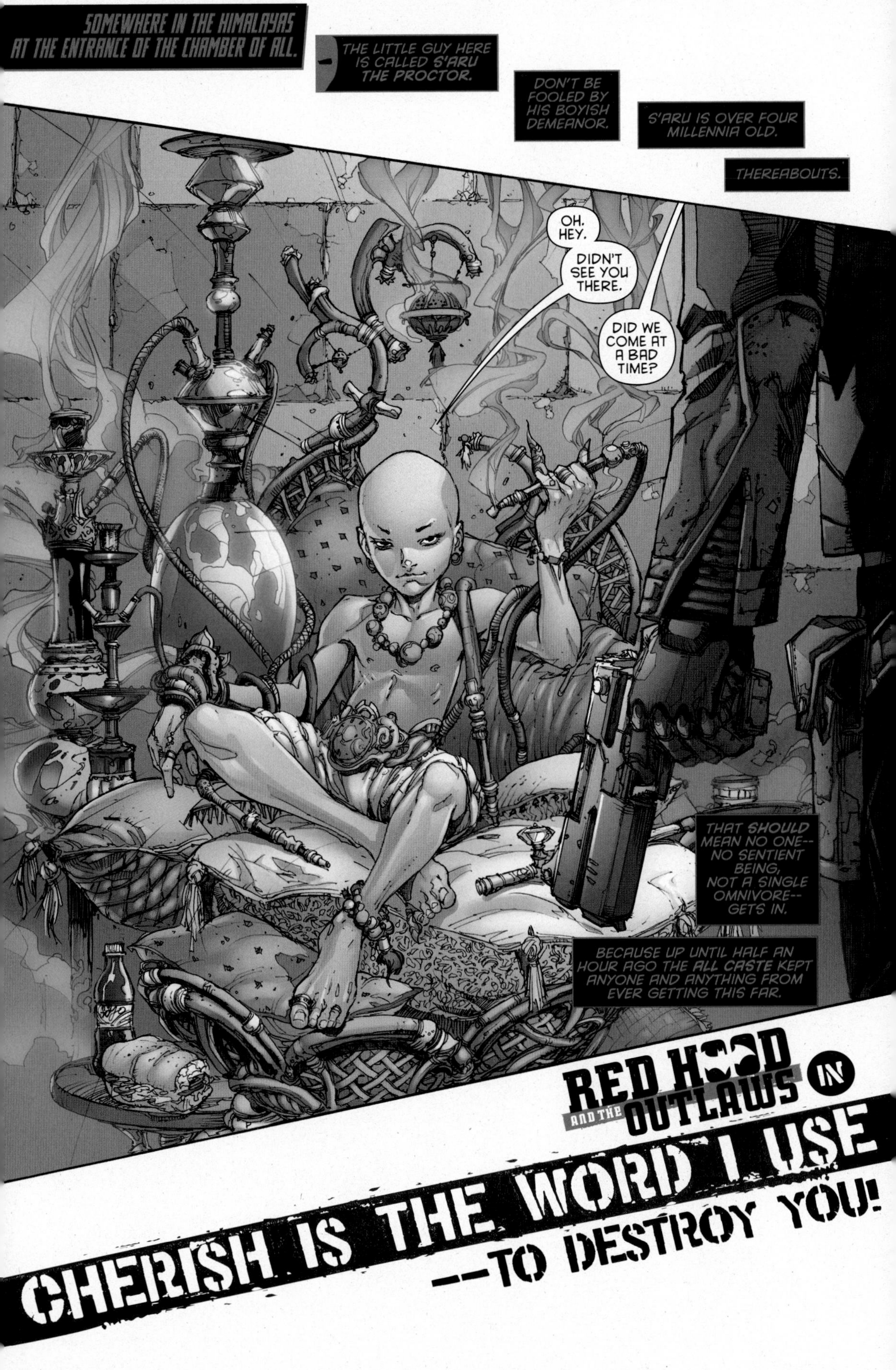
SOMEWHERE IN THE HIMALAYAS AT THE ENTRANCE OF THE CHAMBER OF ALL.
THE LITTLE GUY HERE IS CALLED S'ARU THE PROCTOR.
DON'T BE FOOLED BY HIS BOYISH DEMEANOR.
S'ARU IS OVER FOUR MILLENNIA OLD.
THEREABOUTS.
OH. HEY.
DIDN'T SEE YOU THERE.
DID WE COME AT A BAD TIME?
THAT SHOULD MEAN NO ONE-- NO SENTIENT BEING, NOT A SINGLE OMNIVORE-- GETS IN.
BECAUSE UP UNTIL HALF AN HOUR AGO THE ALL CASTE KEPT ANYONE AND ANYTHING FROM EVER GETTING THIS FAR.
RED HOOD AND THE OUTLAWS IN
CHERISH IS THE WORD I USE
--TO DESTROY YOU!

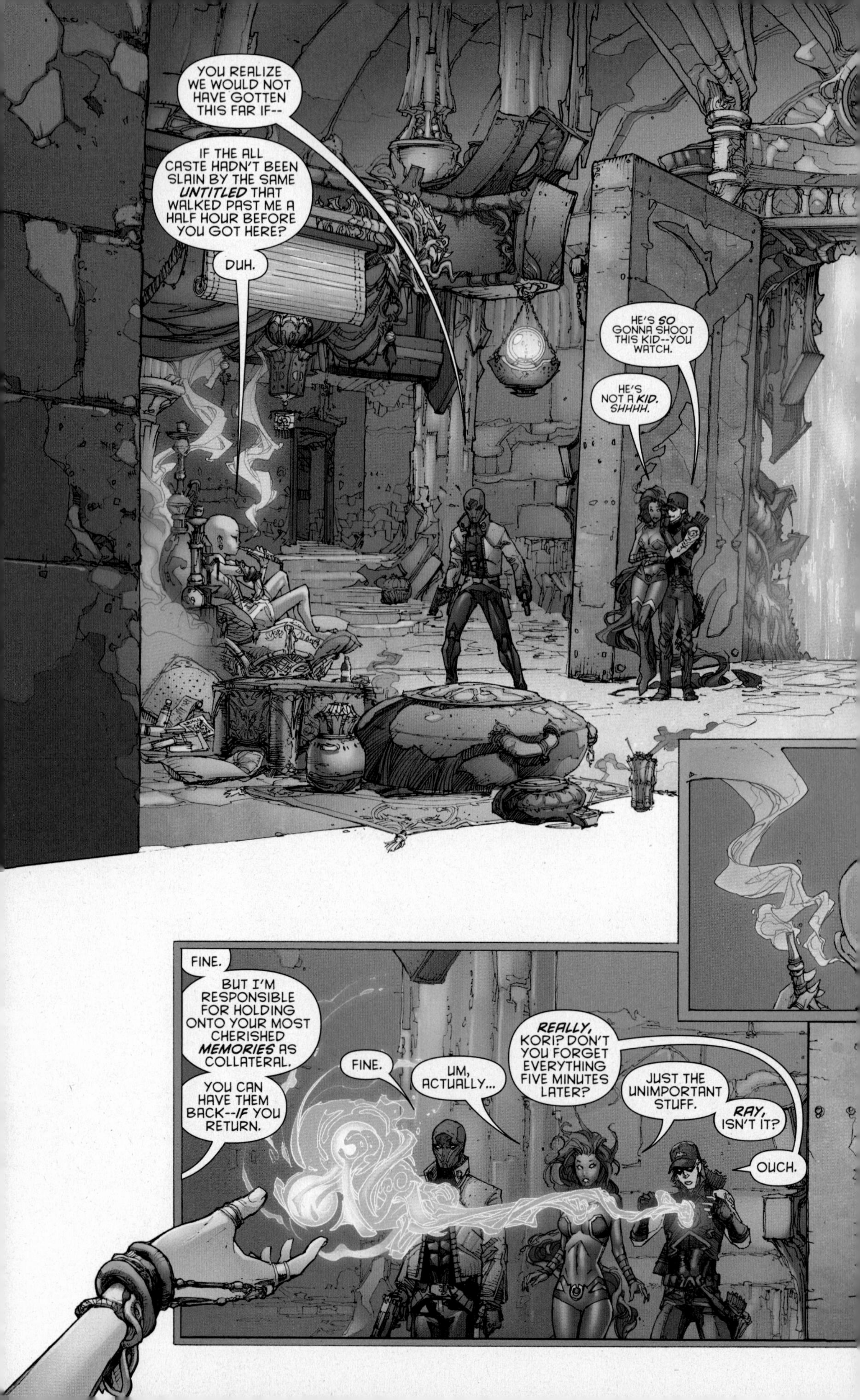
YOU REALIZE WE WOULD NOT HAVE GOTTEN THIS FAR IF--
IF THE ALL CASTE HADN'T BEEN SLAIN BY THE SAME *UNTITLED* THAT WALKED PAST ME A HALF HOUR BEFORE YOU GOT HERE?
DUH.
HE'S *SO* GONNA SHOOT THIS KID--YOU WATCH.
HE'S NOT A *KID*. *SHHHH.*
FINE.
BUT I'M RESPONSIBLE FOR HOLDING ONTO YOUR MOST CHERISHED *MEMORIES* AS COLLATERAL.
YOU CAN HAVE THEM BACK--*IF* YOU RETURN.
FINE.
UM, ACTUALLY...
REALLY, KORI? DON'T YOU FORGET EVERYTHING FIVE MINUTES LATER?
JUST THE UNIMPORTANT STUFF.
RAY, ISN'T IT?
OUCH.

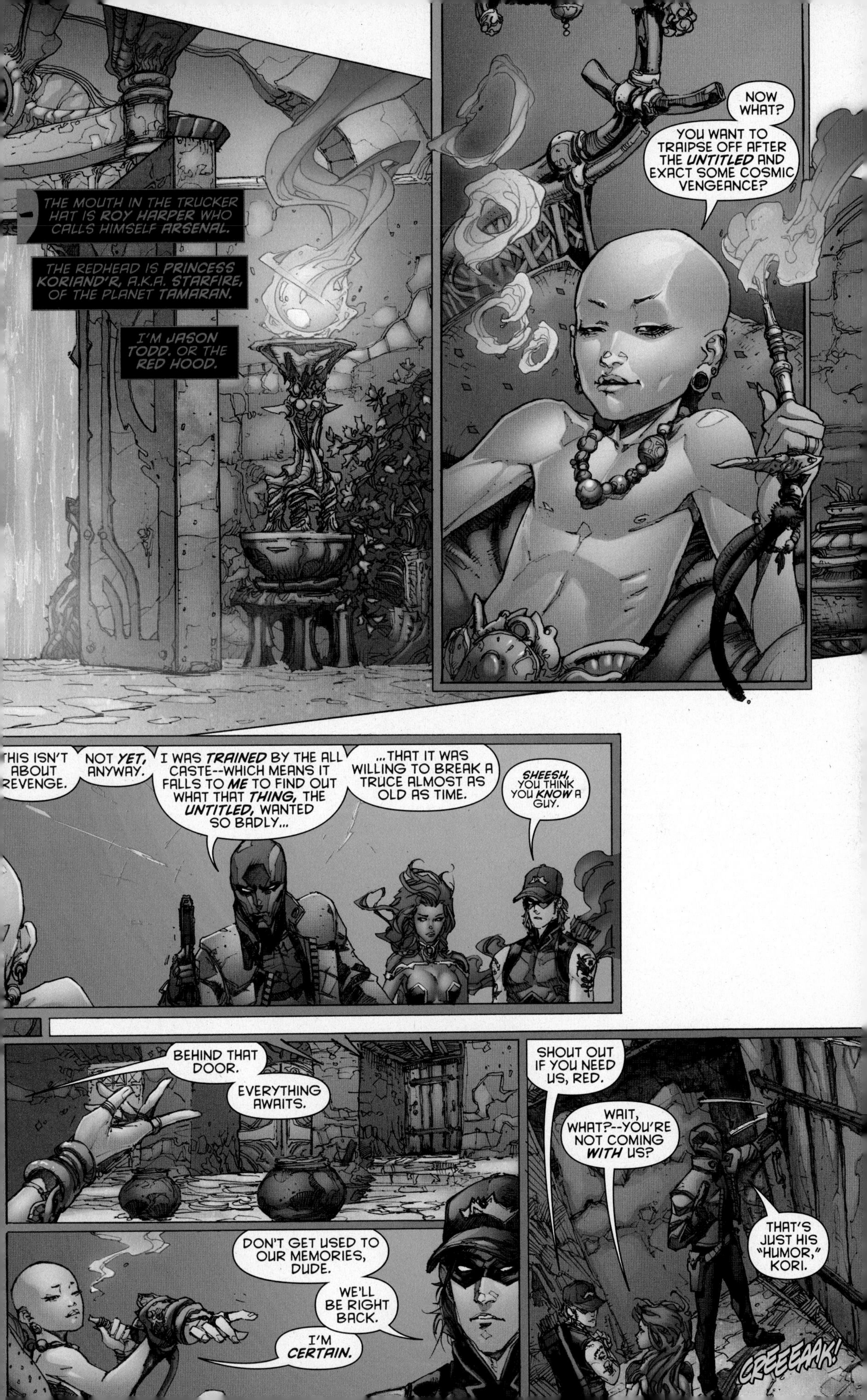
THE MOUTH IN THE TRUCKER HAT IS ROY HARPER WHO CALLS HIMSELF ARSENAL.
THE REDHEAD IS PRINCESS KORIAND'R, A.K.A. STARFIRE, OF THE PLANET TAMARAN.
I'M JASON TODD. OR THE RED HOOD.
NOW WHAT?
YOU WANT TO TRAIPSE OFF AFTER THE UNTITLED AND EXACT SOME COSMIC VENGEANCE?
THIS ISN'T ABOUT REVENGE.
NOT YET, ANYWAY.
I WAS TRAINED BY THE ALL CASTE--WHICH MEANS IT FALLS TO ME TO FIND OUT WHAT THAT THING, THE UNTITLED, WANTED SO BADLY...
...THAT IT WAS WILLING TO BREAK A TRUCE ALMOST AS OLD AS TIME.
SHEESH, YOU THINK YOU KNOW A GUY.
BEHIND THAT DOOR.
EVERYTHING AWAITS.
DON'T GET USED TO OUR MEMORIES, DUDE.
WE'LL BE RIGHT BACK.
I'M CERTAIN.
SHOUT OUT IF YOU NEED US, RED.
WAIT, WHAT?--YOU'RE NOT COMING WITH US?
THAT'S JUST HIS "HUMOR," KORI.
CREEEAAK!

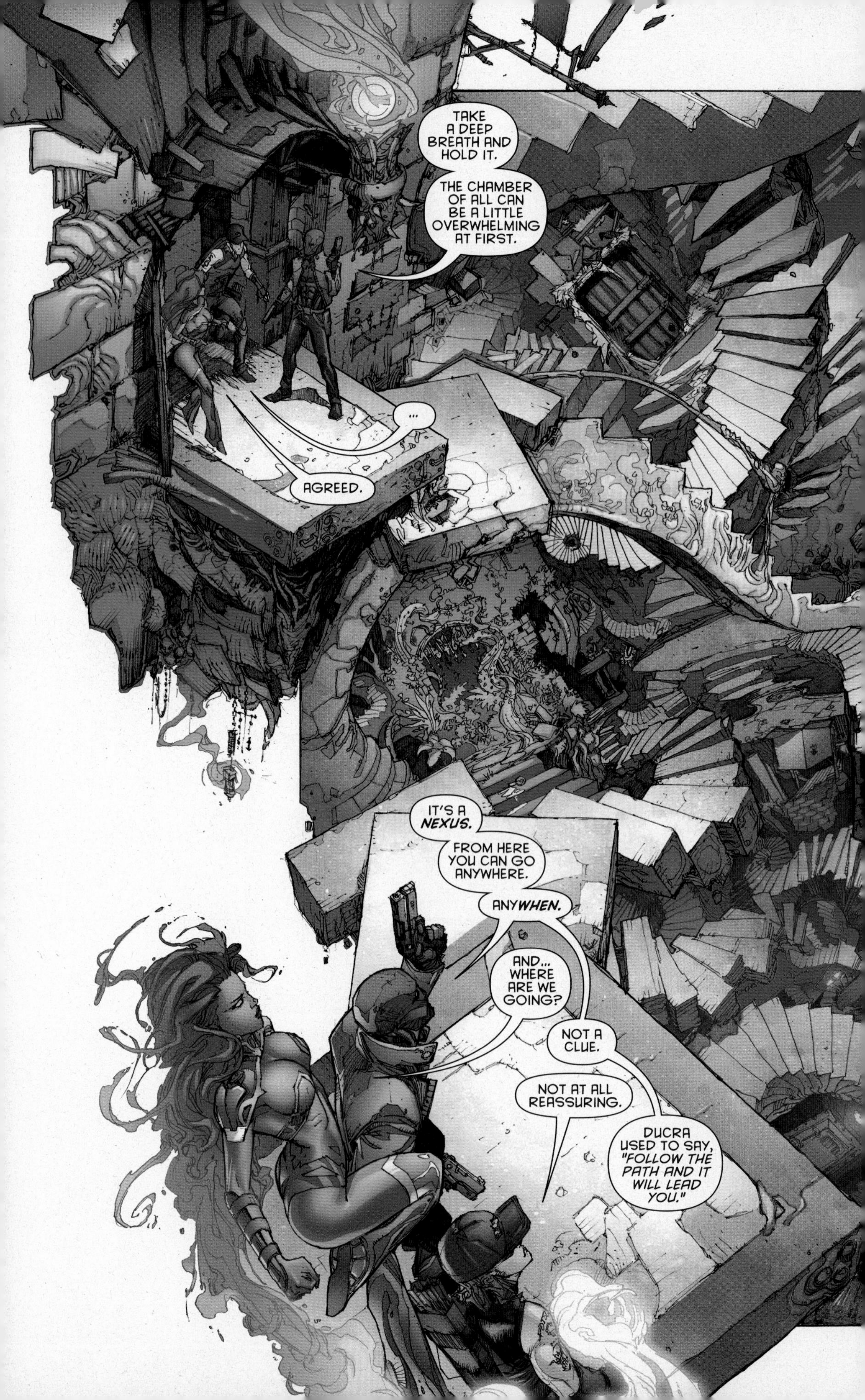

TAKE A DEEP BREATH AND HOLD IT.
THE CHAMBER OF ALL CAN BE A LITTLE OVERWHELMING AT FIRST.
...
AGREED.
IT'S A NEXUS.
FROM HERE YOU CAN GO ANYWHERE.
ANYWHEN.
AND... WHERE ARE WE GOING?
NOT A CLUE.
NOT AT ALL REASSURING.
DUCRA USED TO SAY, "FOLLOW THE PATH AND IT WILL LEAD YOU."

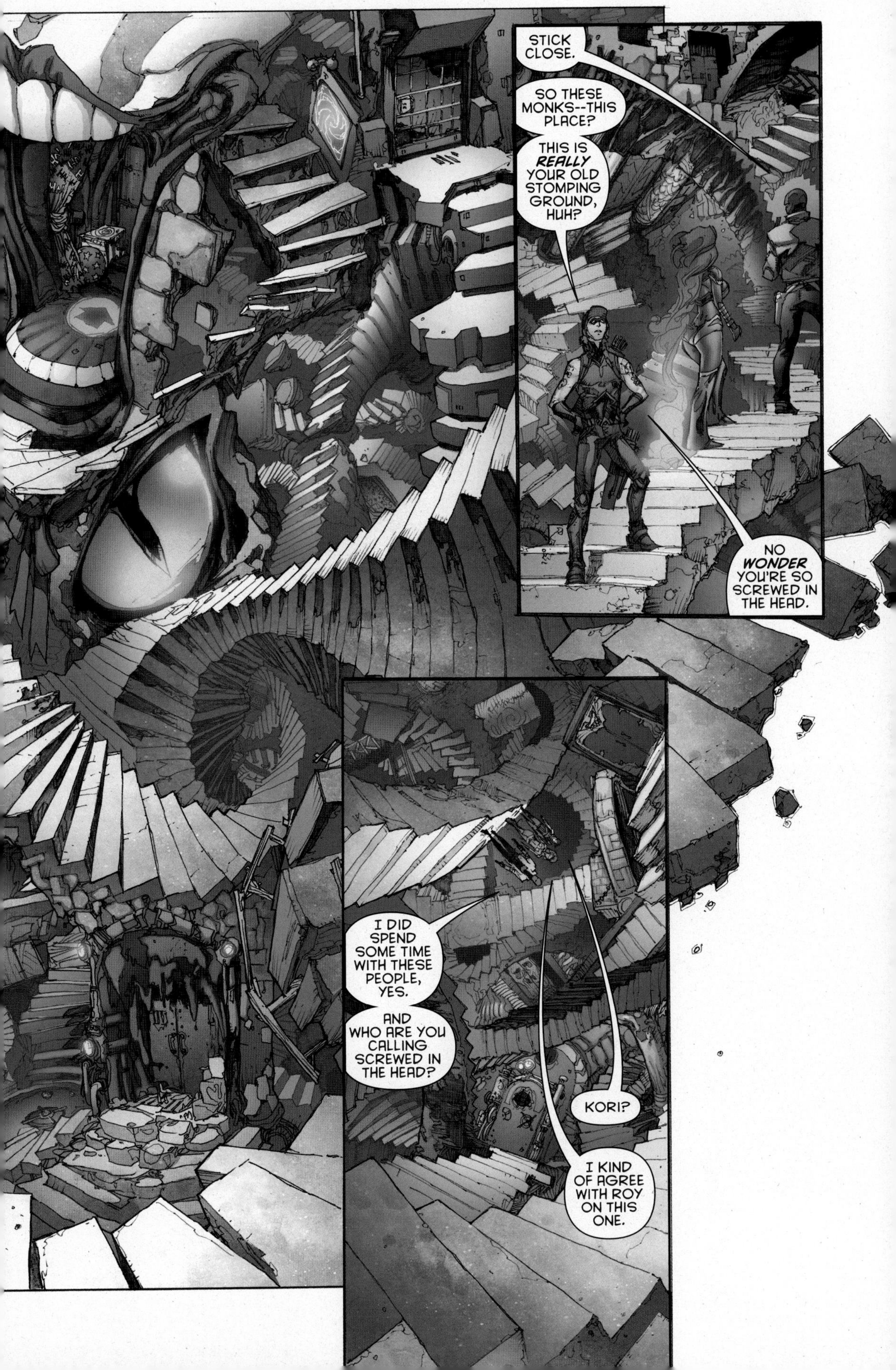
STICK CLOSE.
SO THESE MONKS--THIS PLACE?
THIS IS REALLY YOUR OLD STOMPING GROUND, HUH?
NO WONDER YOU'RE SO SCREWED IN THE HEAD.
I DID SPEND SOME TIME WITH THESE PEOPLE, YES.
AND WHO ARE YOU CALLING SCREWED IN THE HEAD?
KORI?
I KIND OF AGREE WITH ROY ON THIS ONE.

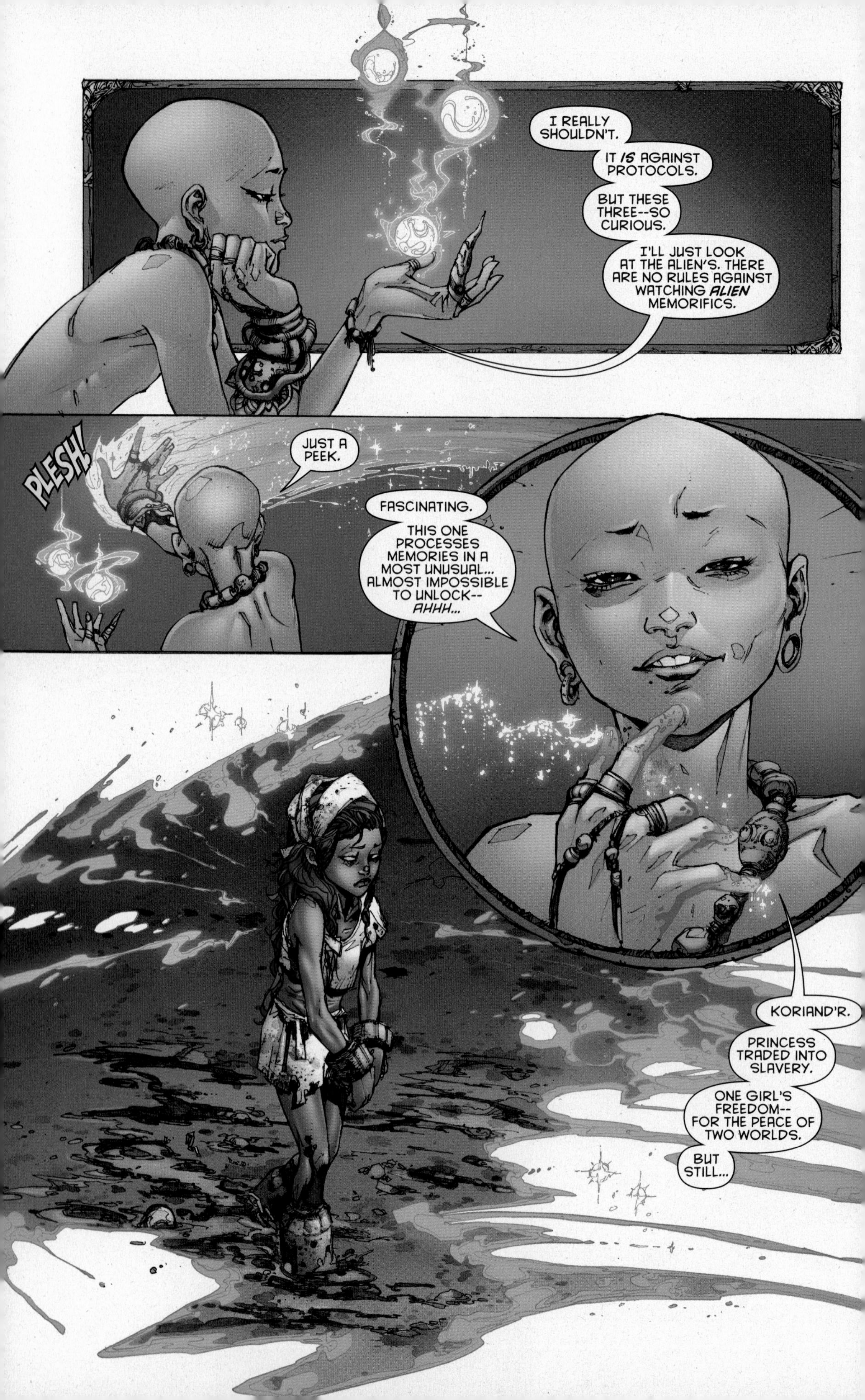

I REALLY SHOULDN'T.
IT *IS* AGAINST PROTOCOLS.
BUT THESE THREE--SO CURIOUS.
I'LL JUST LOOK AT THE ALIEN'S. THERE ARE NO RULES AGAINST WATCHING *ALIEN* MEMORIFICS.
PLESH!
JUST A PEEK.
FASCINATING.
THIS ONE PROCESSES MEMORIES IN A MOST UNUSUAL... ALMOST IMPOSSIBLE TO UNLOCK-- *AHHH...*
KORIAND'R.
PRINCESS TRADED INTO SLAVERY.
ONE GIRL'S FREEDOM-- FOR THE PEACE OF TWO WORLDS.
BUT STILL...

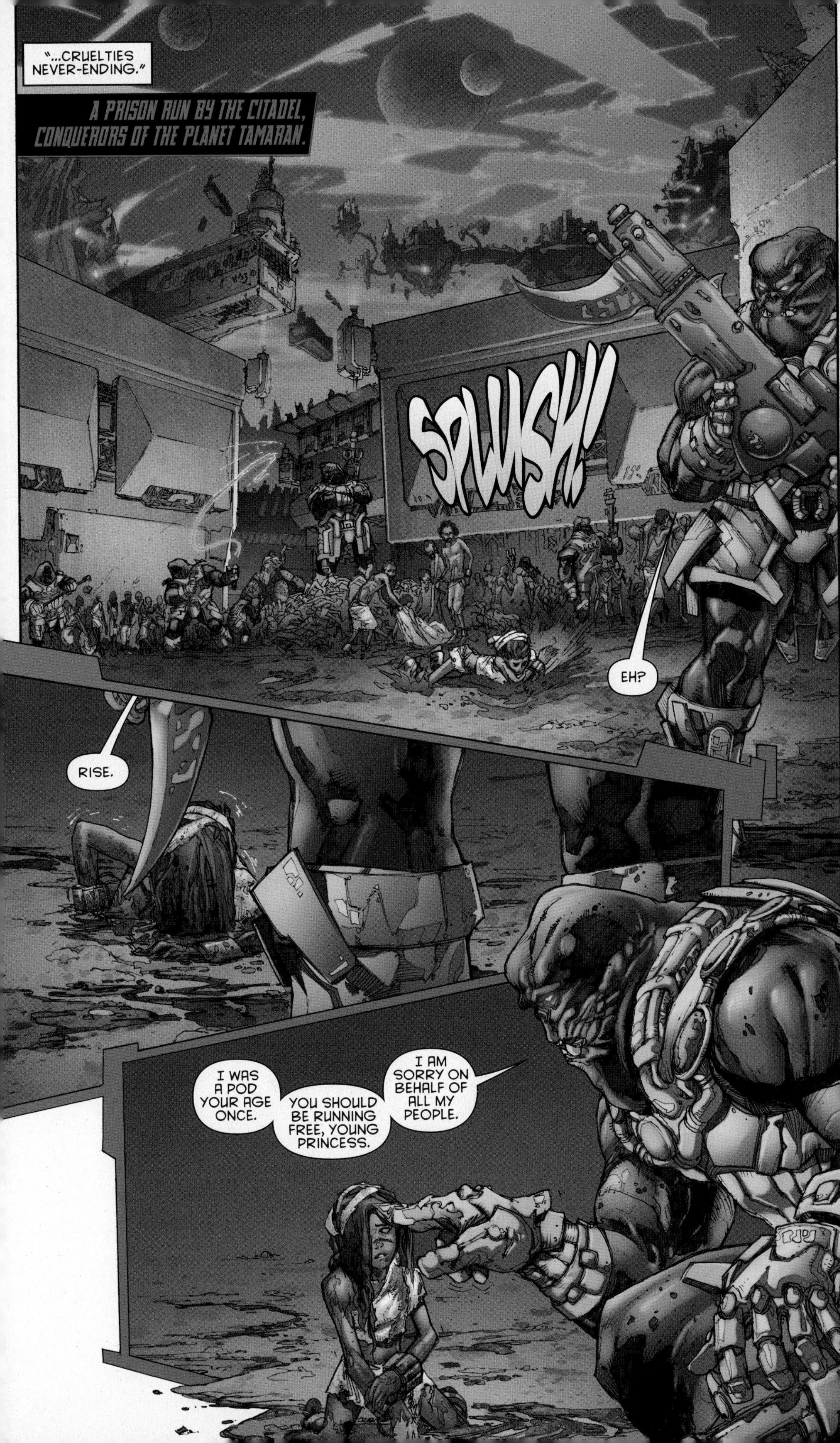
"...CRUELTIES NEVER-ENDING."
A PRISON RUN BY THE CITADEL, CONQUERORS OF THE PLANET TAMARAN.
SPLUSH!
EH?
RISE.
I WAS A POD YOUR AGE ONCE.
YOU SHOULD BE RUNNING FREE, YOUNG PRINCESS.
I AM SORRY ON BEHALF OF ALL MY PEOPLE.

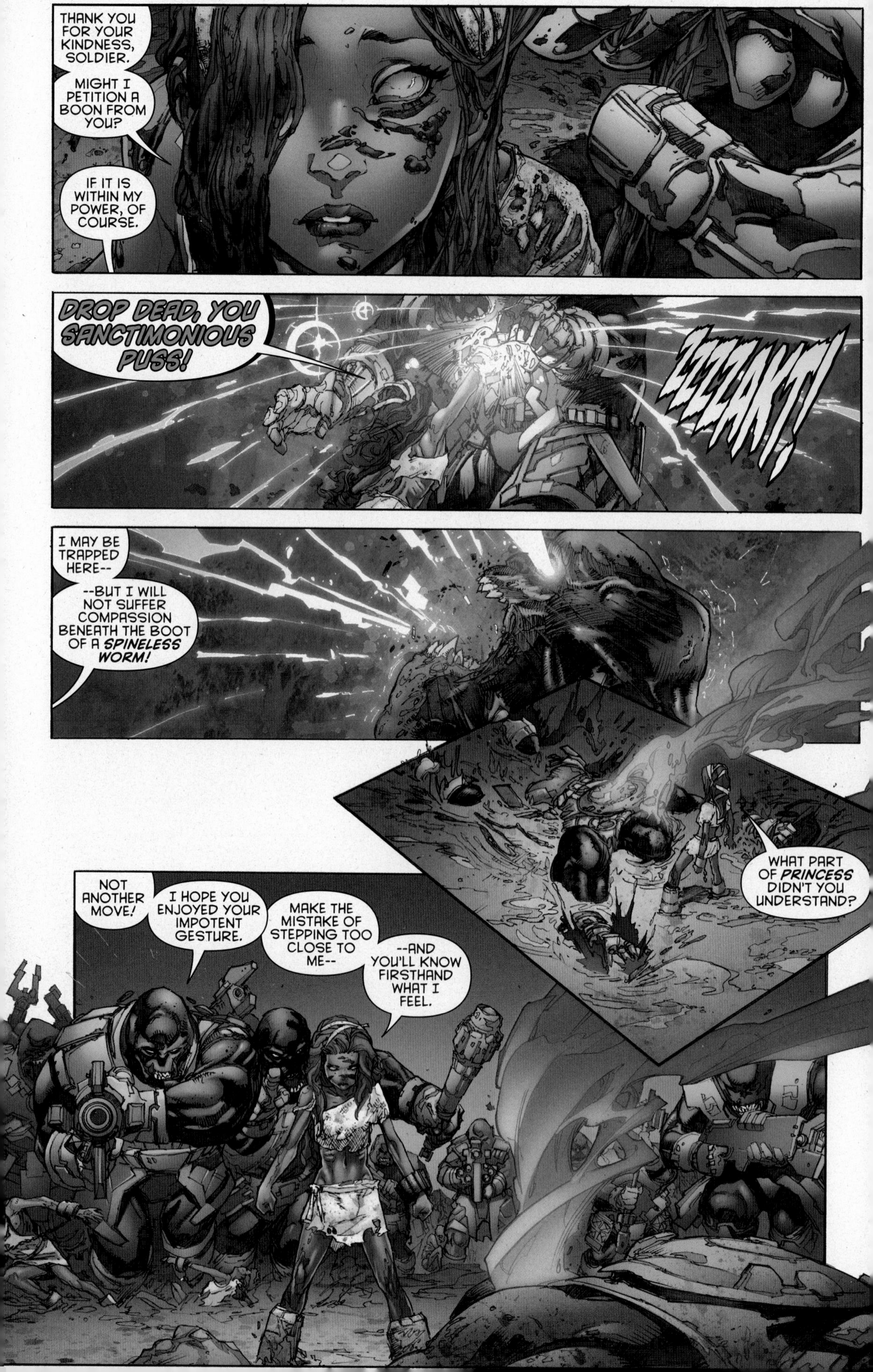
THANK YOU FOR YOUR KINDNESS, SOLDIER.
MIGHT I PETITION A BOON FROM YOU?
IF IT IS WITHIN MY POWER, OF COURSE.
DROP DEAD, YOU SANCTIMONIOUS PUSS!
ZZZZAKT!
I MAY BE TRAPPED HERE--
--BUT I WILL NOT SUFFER COMPASSION BENEATH THE BOOT OF A SPINELESS WORM!
WHAT PART OF PRINCESS DIDN'T YOU UNDERSTAND?
NOT ANOTHER MOVE!
I HOPE YOU ENJOYED YOUR IMPOTENT GESTURE.
MAKE THE MISTAKE OF STEPPING TOO CLOSE TO ME--
--AND YOU'LL KNOW FIRSTHAND WHAT I FEEL.

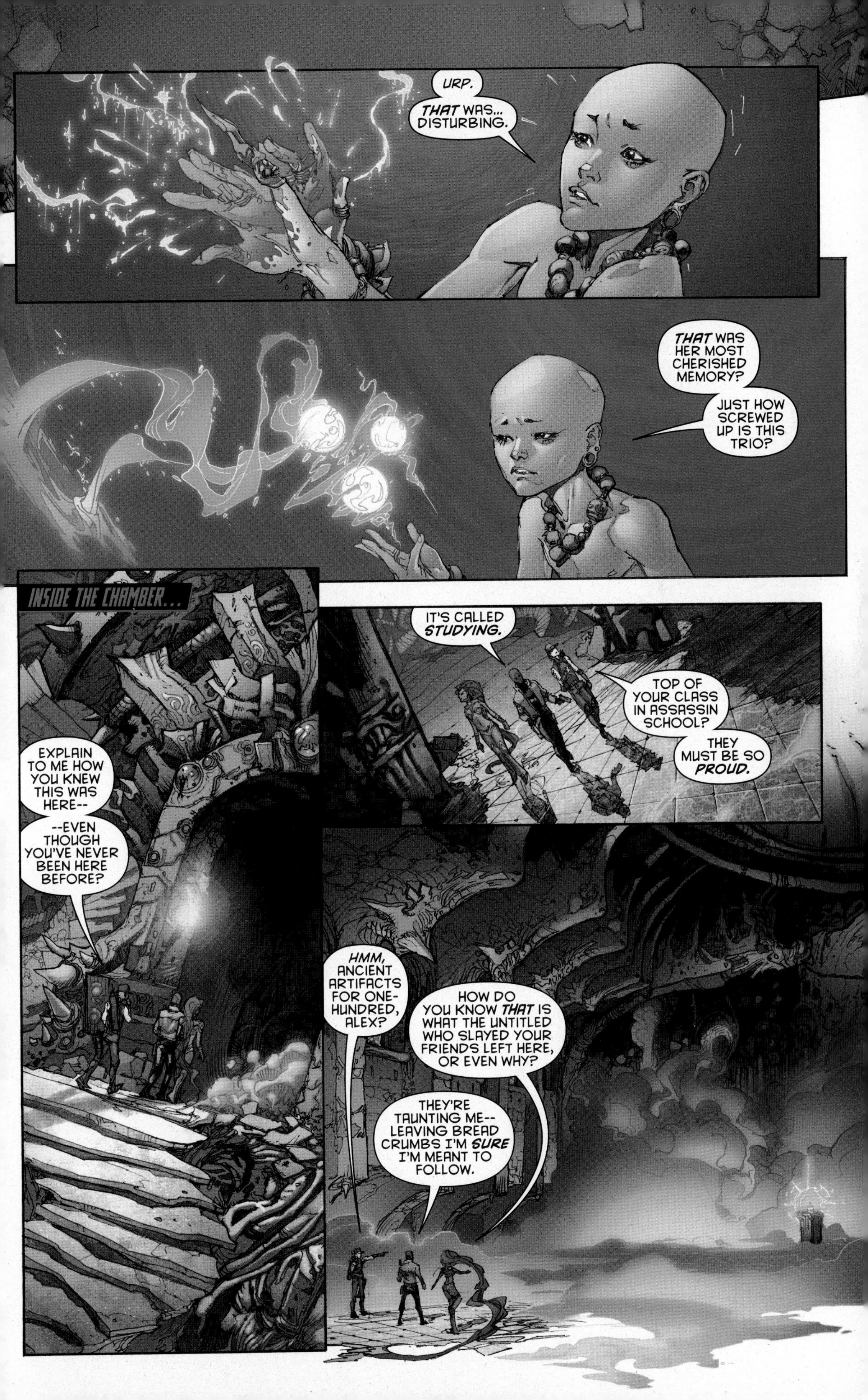
URP.
THAT WAS... DISTURBING.
THAT WAS HER MOST CHERISHED MEMORY?
JUST HOW SCREWED UP IS THIS TRIO?
INSIDE THE CHAMBER...
EXPLAIN TO ME HOW YOU KNEW THIS WAS HERE--
--EVEN THOUGH YOU'VE NEVER BEEN HERE BEFORE?
IT'S CALLED STUDYING.
TOP OF YOUR CLASS IN ASSASSIN SCHOOL?
THEY MUST BE SO PROUD.
HMM, ANCIENT ARTIFACTS FOR ONE-HUNDRED, ALEX?
HOW DO YOU KNOW THAT IS WHAT THE UNTITLED WHO SLAYED YOUR FRIENDS LEFT HERE, OR EVEN WHY?
THEY'RE TAUNTING ME-- LEAVING BREAD CRUMBS I'M SURE I'M MEANT TO FOLLOW.

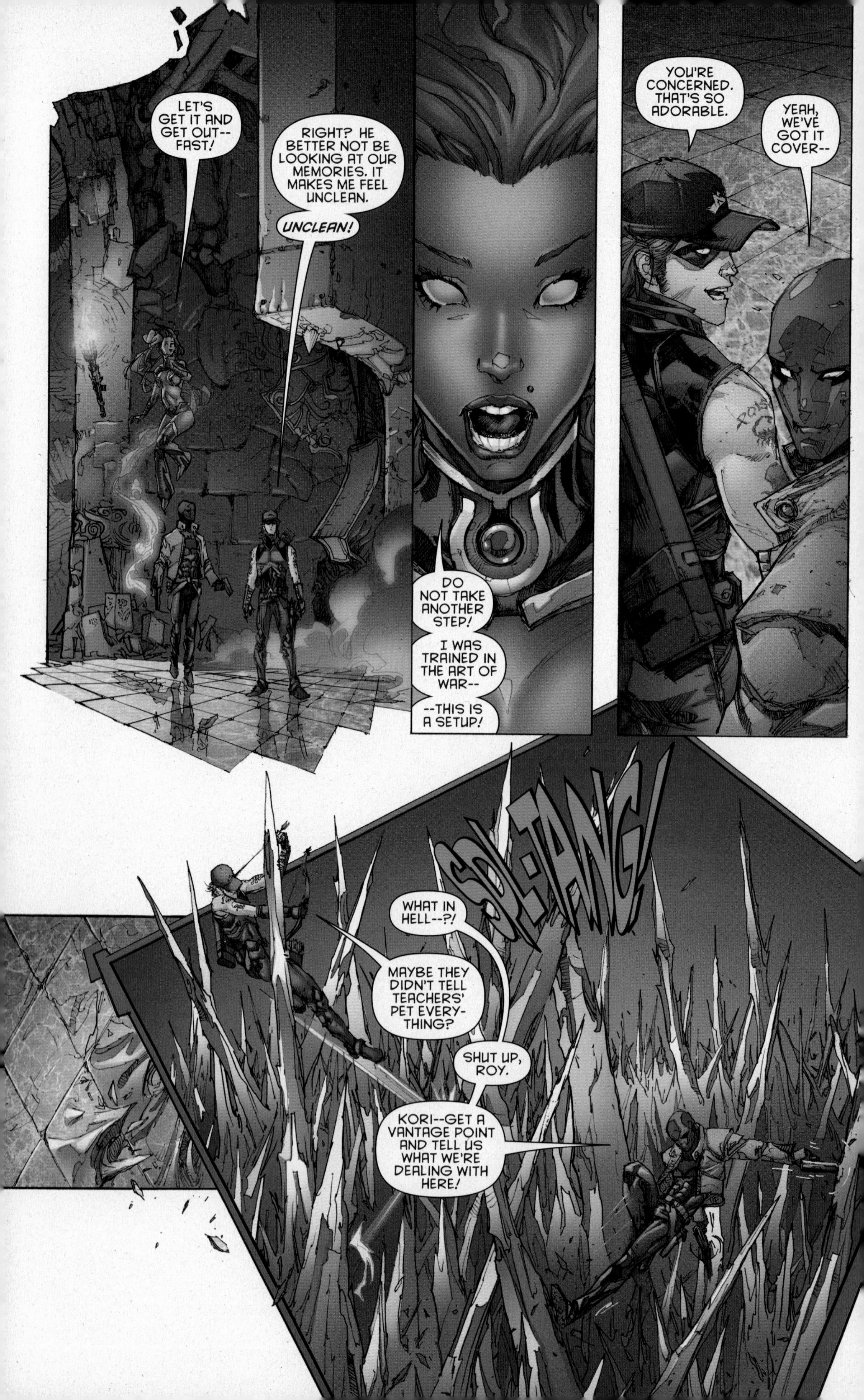
LET'S GET IT AND GET OUT-- FAST!
RIGHT? HE BETTER NOT BE LOOKING AT OUR MEMORIES. IT MAKES ME FEEL UNCLEAN.
UNCLEAN!
DO NOT TAKE ANOTHER STEP!
I WAS TRAINED IN THE ART OF WAR--
--THIS IS A SETUP!
YOU'RE CONCERNED. THAT'S SO ADORABLE.
YEAH, WE'VE GOT IT COVER--
SPL-TANG!
WHAT IN HELL--?!
MAYBE THEY DIDN'T TELL TEACHERS' PET EVERY-THING?
SHUT UP, ROY.
KORI--GET A VANTAGE POINT AND TELL US WHAT WE'RE DEALING WITH HERE!

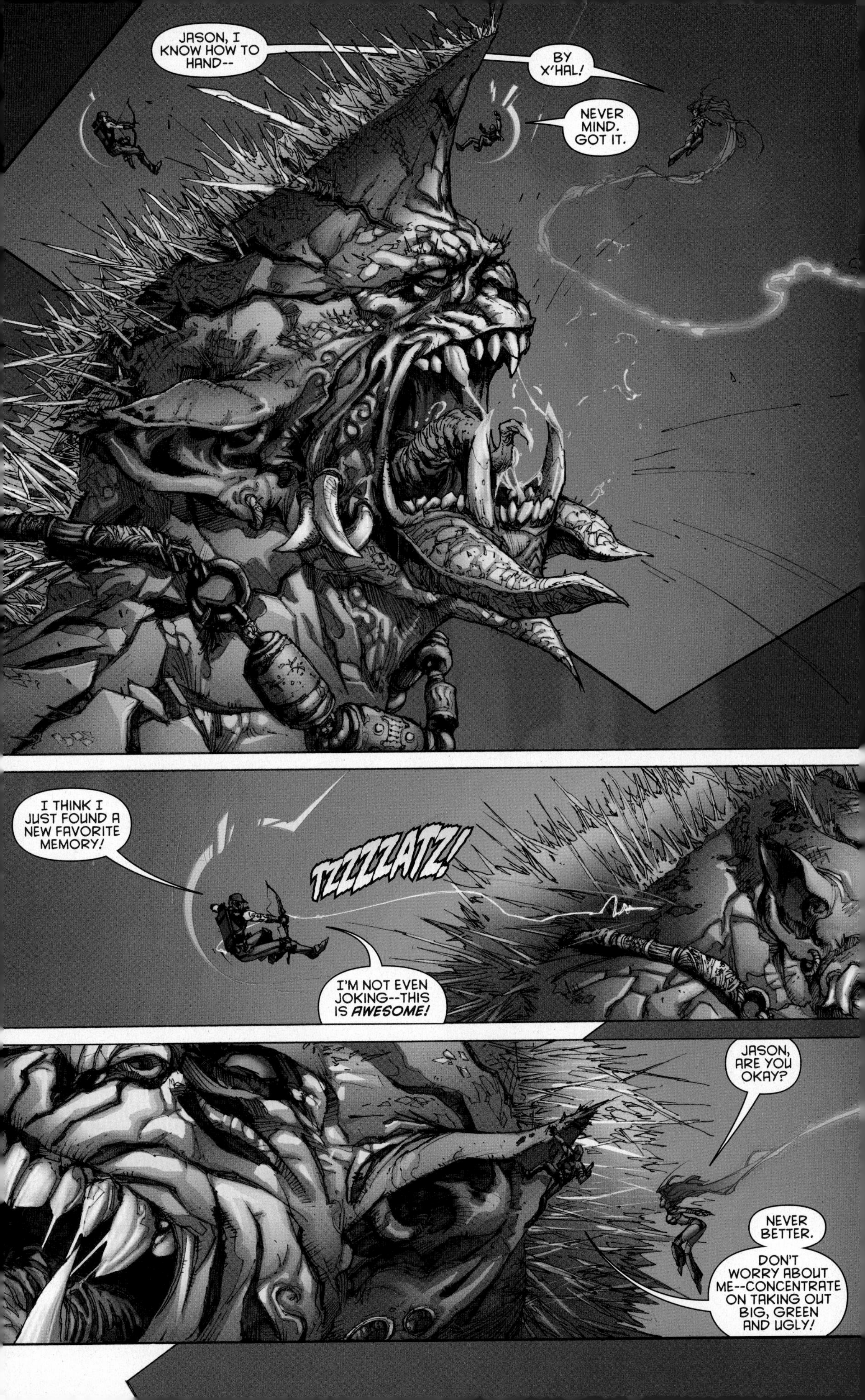
JASON, I KNOW HOW TO HAND--
BY X'HAL!
NEVER MIND. GOT IT.
I THINK I JUST FOUND A NEW FAVORITE MEMORY!
TZZZZZATZ!
I'M NOT EVEN JOKING--THIS IS AWESOME!
JASON, ARE YOU OKAY?
NEVER BETTER.
DON'T WORRY ABOUT ME--CONCENTRATE ON TAKING OUT BIG, GREEN AND UGLY!

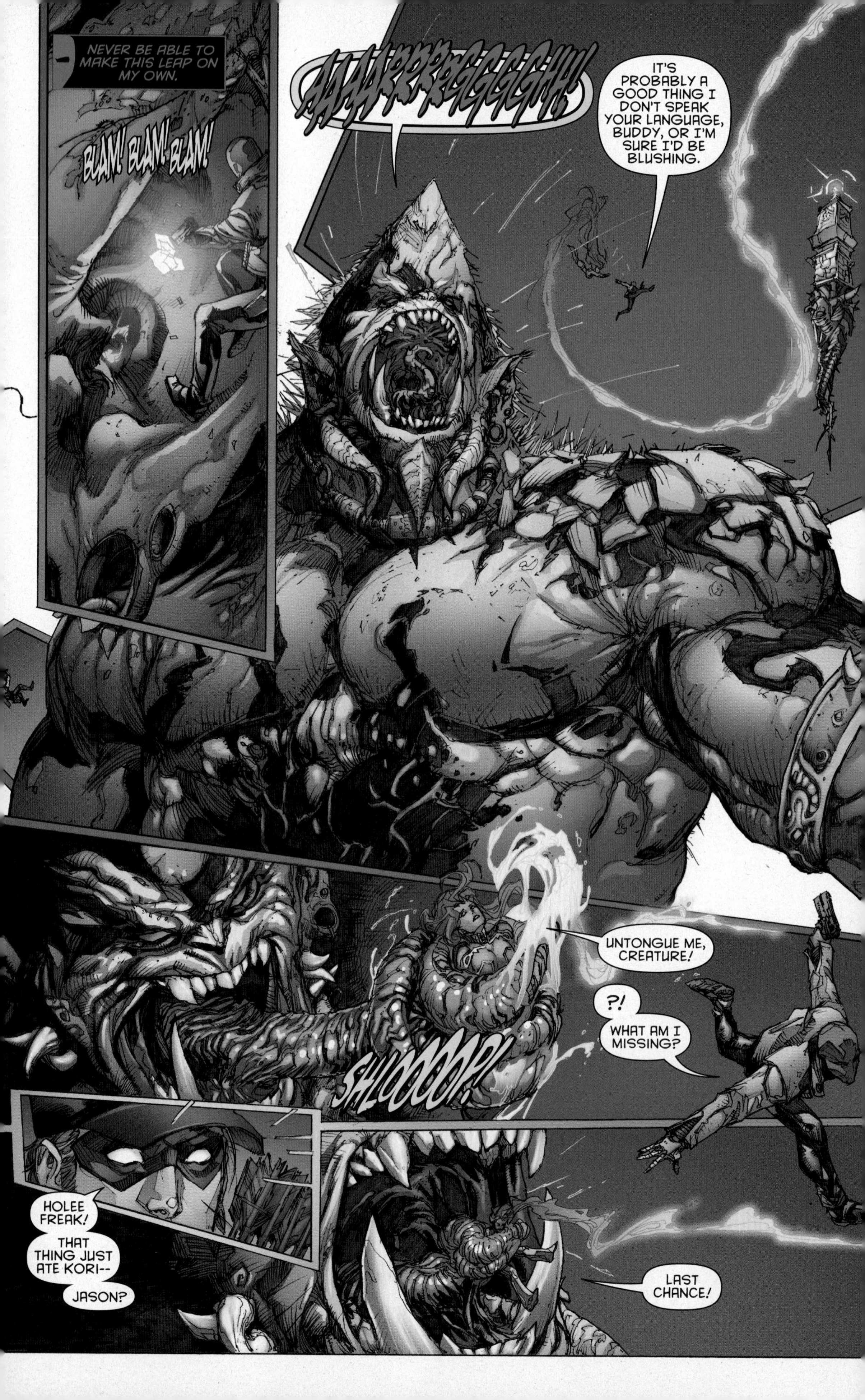
NEVER BE ABLE TO MAKE THIS LEAP ON MY OWN.
BLAM! BLAM! BLAM!
AAAARRRRGGGGGH!!
IT'S PROBABLY A GOOD THING I DON'T SPEAK YOUR LANGUAGE, BUDDY, OR I'M SURE I'D BE BLUSHING.
UNTONGUE ME, CREATURE!
?!
WHAT AM I MISSING?
SHLOOOOP!
HOLEE FREAK!
THAT THING JUST ATE KORI--
JASON?
LAST CHANCE!

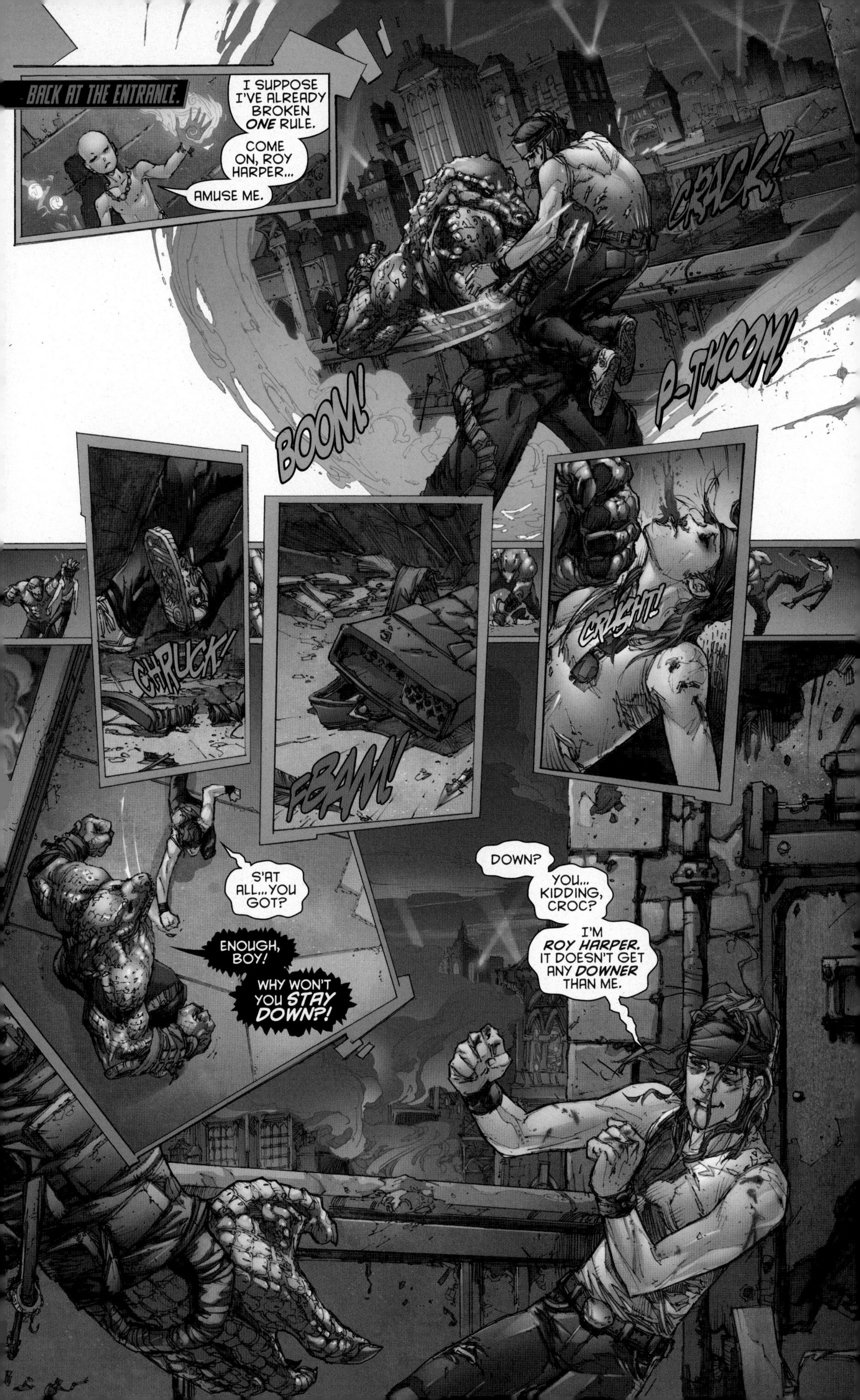

BACK AT THE ENTRANCE.
I SUPPOSE I'VE ALREADY BROKEN ONE RULE.
COME ON, ROY HARPER...
AMUSE ME.
CRACK!
P-THOOM!
BOOM!
CHRUCK!
FBAM!
CRUSHT!
S'AT ALL...YOU GOT?
ENOUGH, BOY!
WHY WON'T YOU STAY DOWN?!
DOWN?
YOU... KIDDING, CROC?
I'M ROY HARPER. IT DOESN'T GET ANY DOWNER THAN ME.

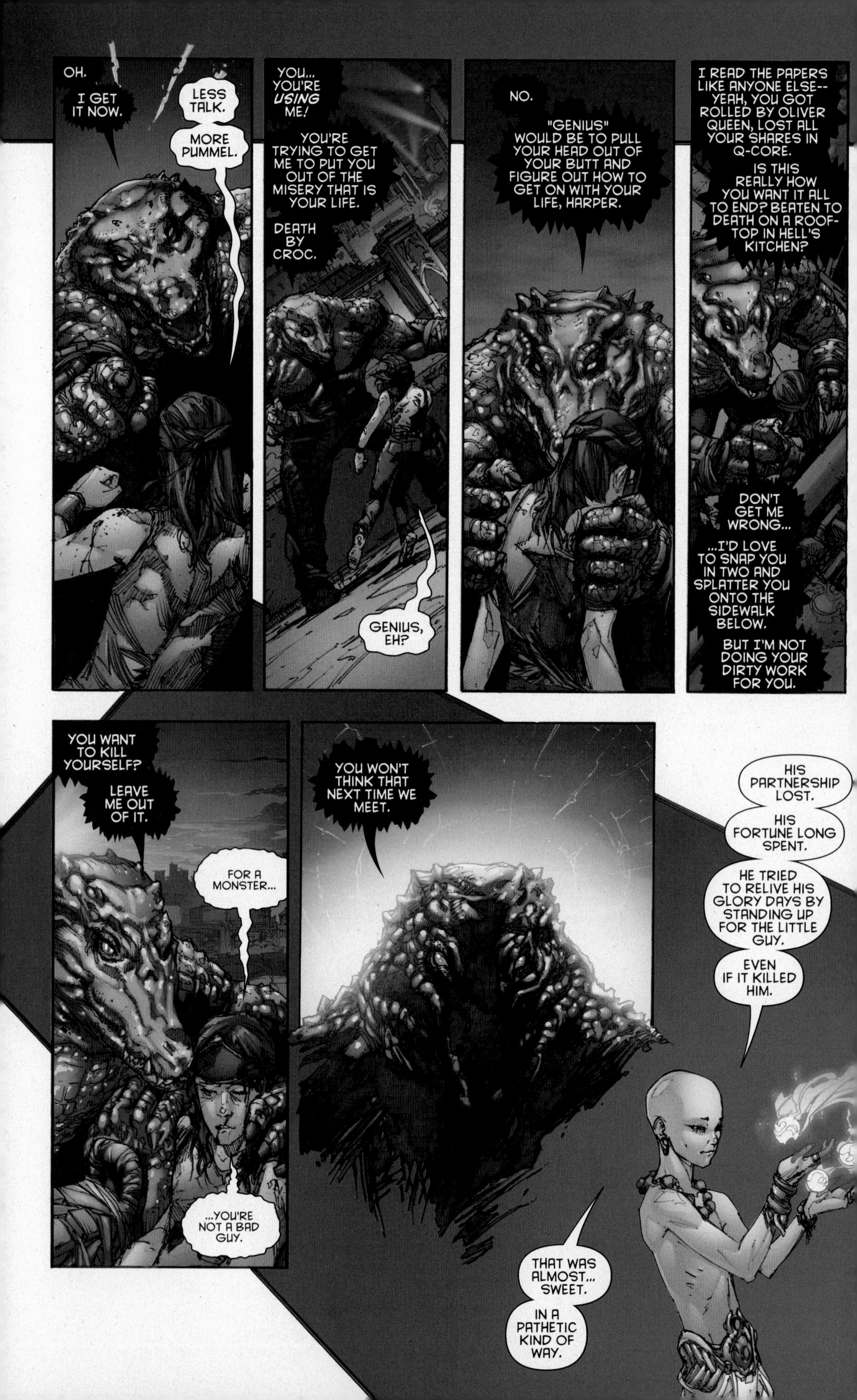

OH.
I GET IT NOW.
LESS TALK.
MORE PUMMEL.
YOU... YOU'RE USING ME!
YOU'RE TRYING TO GET ME TO PUT YOU OUT OF THE MISERY THAT IS YOUR LIFE.
DEATH BY CROC.
GENIUS, EH?
NO.
"GENIUS" WOULD BE TO PULL YOUR HEAD OUT OF YOUR BUTT AND FIGURE OUT HOW TO GET ON WITH YOUR LIFE, HARPER.
I READ THE PAPERS LIKE ANYONE ELSE-- YEAH, YOU GOT ROLLED BY OLIVER QUEEN, LOST ALL YOUR SHARES IN Q-CORE.
IS THIS REALLY HOW YOU WANT IT ALL TO END? BEATEN TO DEATH ON A ROOF-TOP IN HELL'S KITCHEN?
DON'T GET ME WRONG...
...I'D LOVE TO SNAP YOU IN TWO AND SPLATTER YOU ONTO THE SIDEWALK BELOW.
BUT I'M NOT DOING YOUR DIRTY WORK FOR YOU.
YOU WANT TO KILL YOURSELF?
LEAVE ME OUT OF IT.
FOR A MONSTER...
...YOU'RE NOT A BAD GUY.
YOU WON'T THINK THAT NEXT TIME WE MEET.
HIS PARTNERSHIP LOST.
HIS FORTUNE LONG SPENT.
HE TRIED TO RELIVE HIS GLORY DAYS BY STANDING UP FOR THE LITTLE GUY.
EVEN IF IT KILLED HIM.
THAT WAS ALMOST... SWEET.
IN A PATHETIC KIND OF WAY.

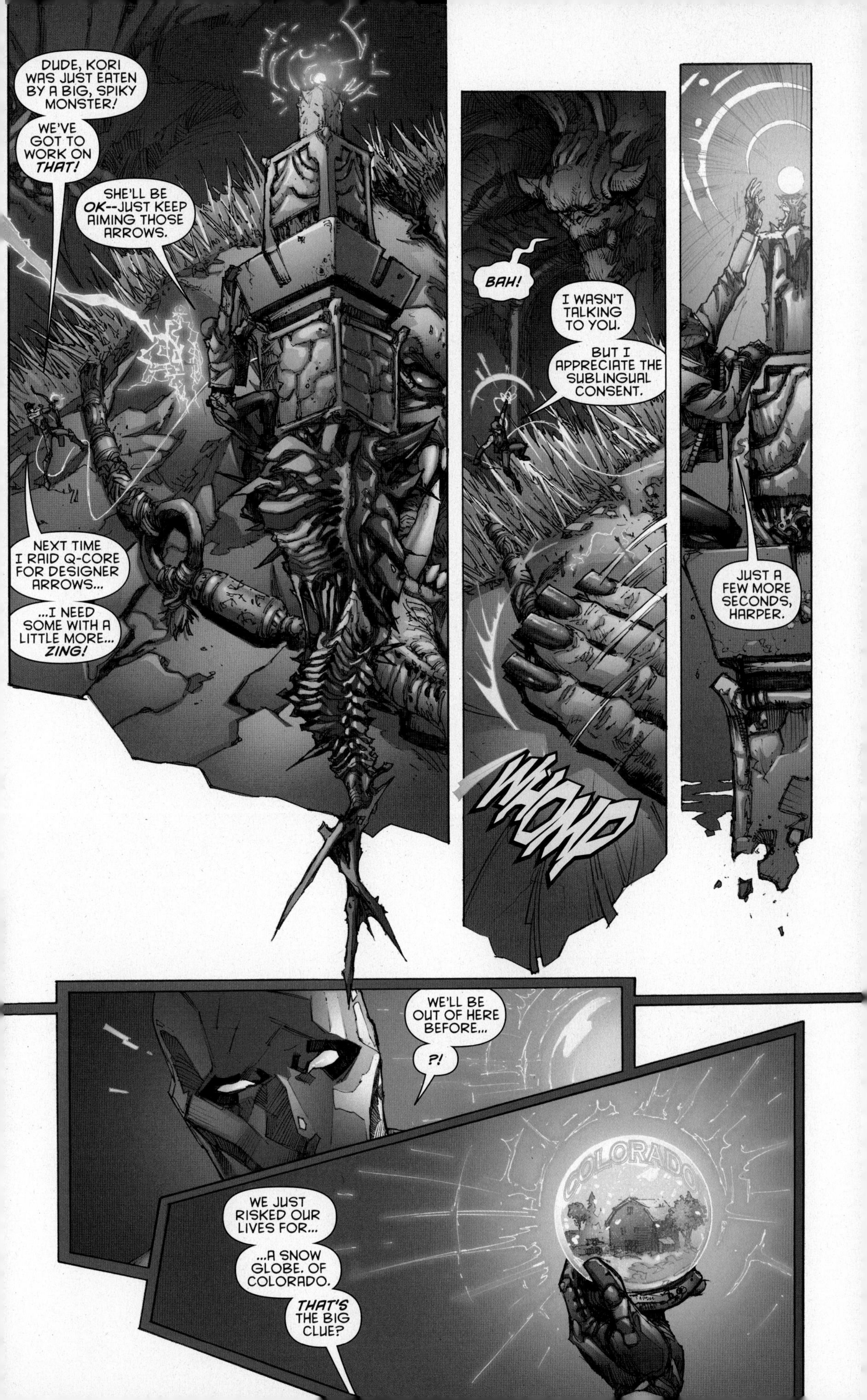
DUDE, KORI WAS JUST EATEN BY A BIG, SPIKY MONSTER!
WE'VE GOT TO WORK ON THAT!
SHE'LL BE OK--JUST KEEP AIMING THOSE ARROWS.
NEXT TIME I RAID Q-CORE FOR DESIGNER ARROWS...
...I NEED SOME WITH A LITTLE MORE... ZING!
BAH!
I WASN'T TALKING TO YOU.
BUT I APPRECIATE THE SUBLINGUAL CONSENT.
WHOMP
JUST A FEW MORE SECONDS, HARPER.
WE'LL BE OUT OF HERE BEFORE...
?!
COLORADO
WE JUST RISKED OUR LIVES FOR...
...A SNOW GLOBE. OF COLORADO.
THAT'S THE BIG CLUE?

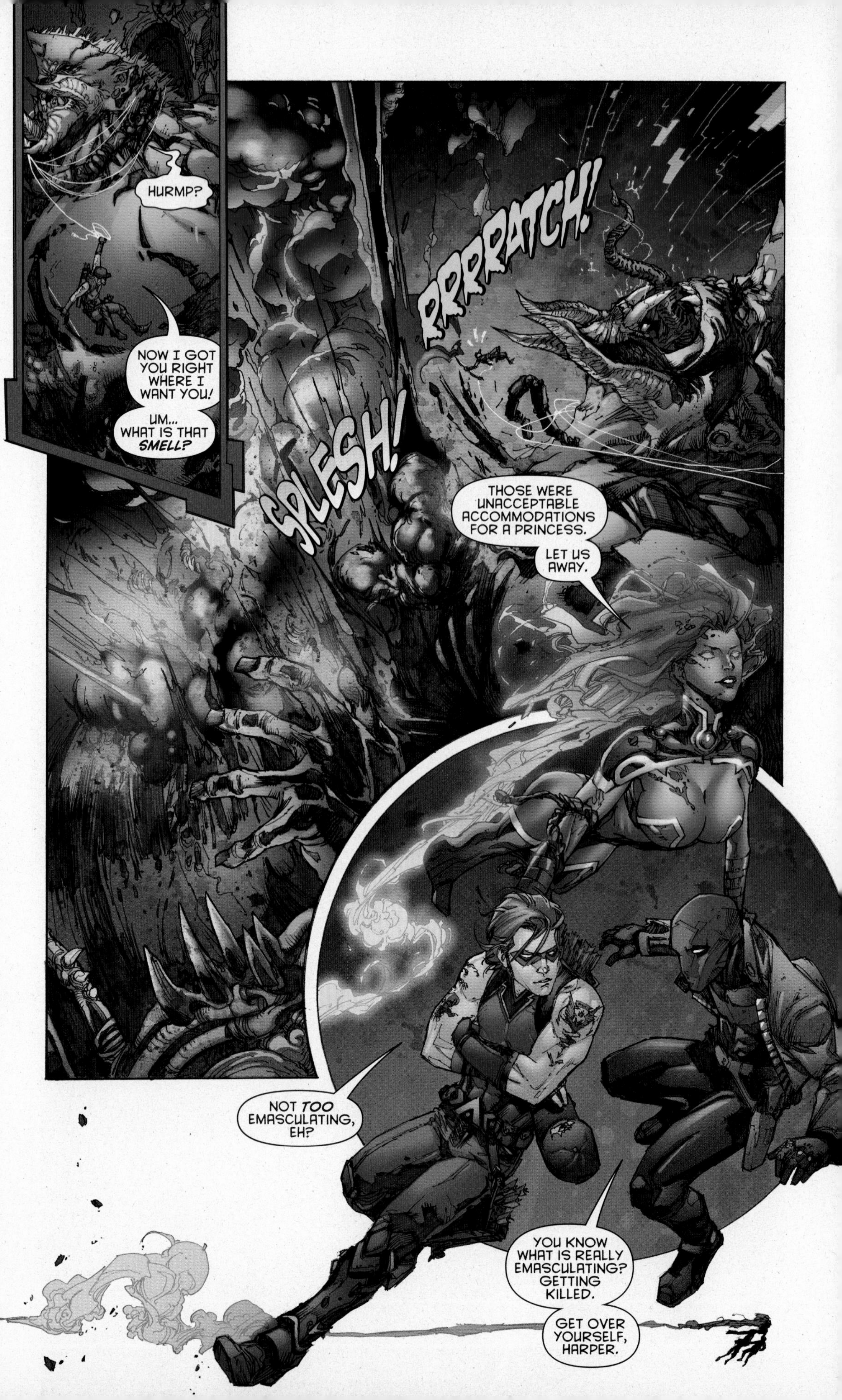
HURMP?
NOW I GOT YOU RIGHT WHERE I WANT YOU!
UM... WHAT IS THAT SMELL?
RRRRATCH!
SPLESH!
THOSE WERE UNACCEPTABLE ACCOMMODATIONS FOR A PRINCESS.
LET US AWAY.
NOT TOO EMASCULATING, EH?
YOU KNOW WHAT IS REALLY EMASCULATING? GETTING KILLED.
GET OVER YOURSELF, HARPER.

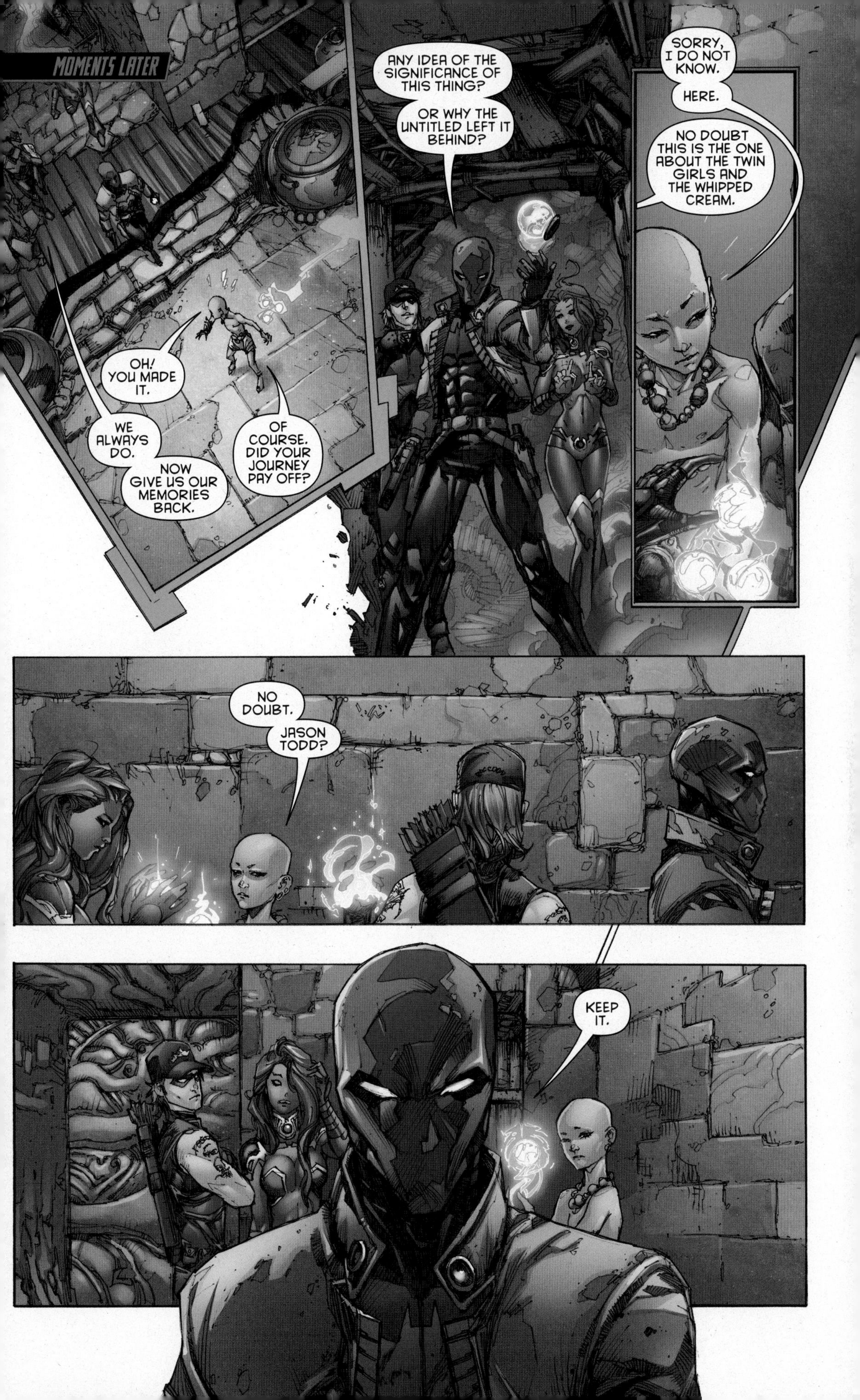
MOMENTS LATER
OH! YOU MADE IT.
WE ALWAYS DO.
NOW GIVE US OUR MEMORIES BACK.
OF COURSE. DID YOUR JOURNEY PAY OFF?
ANY IDEA OF THE SIGNIFICANCE OF THIS THING?
OR WHY THE UNTITLED LEFT IT BEHIND?
SORRY, I DO NOT KNOW.
HERE.
NO DOUBT THIS IS THE ONE ABOUT THE TWIN GIRLS AND THE WHIPPED CREAM.
NO DOUBT.
JASON TODD?
KEEP IT.

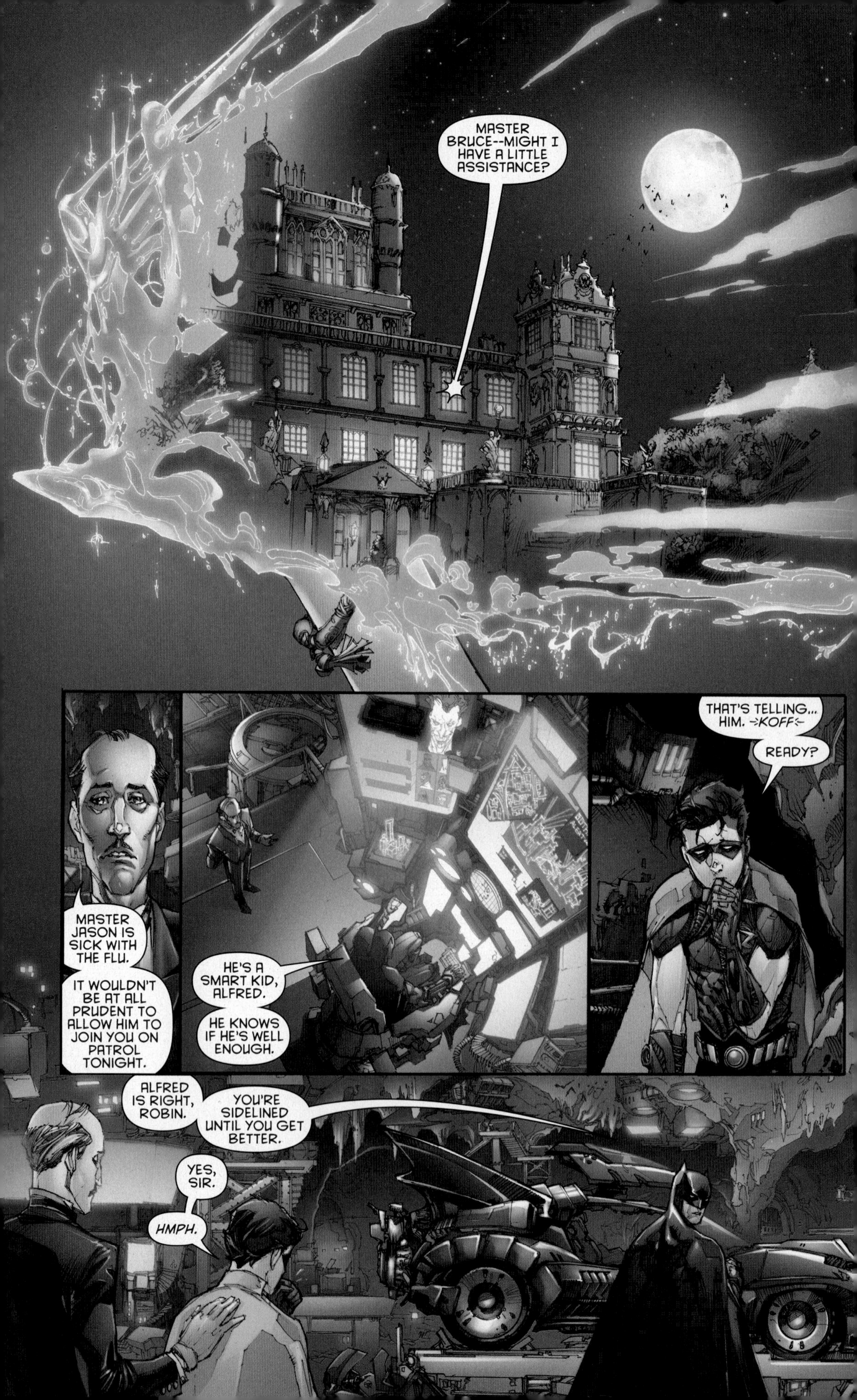
MASTER BRUCE--MIGHT I HAVE A LITTLE ASSISTANCE?
MASTER JASON IS SICK WITH THE FLU.
IT WOULDN'T BE AT ALL PRUDENT TO ALLOW HIM TO JOIN YOU ON PATROL TONIGHT.
HE'S A SMART KID, ALFRED.
HE KNOWS IF HE'S WELL ENOUGH.
THAT'S TELLING... HIM. -KOFF-
READY?
ALFRED IS RIGHT, ROBIN.
YOU'RE SIDELINED UNTIL YOU GET BETTER.
YES, SIR.
HMPH.

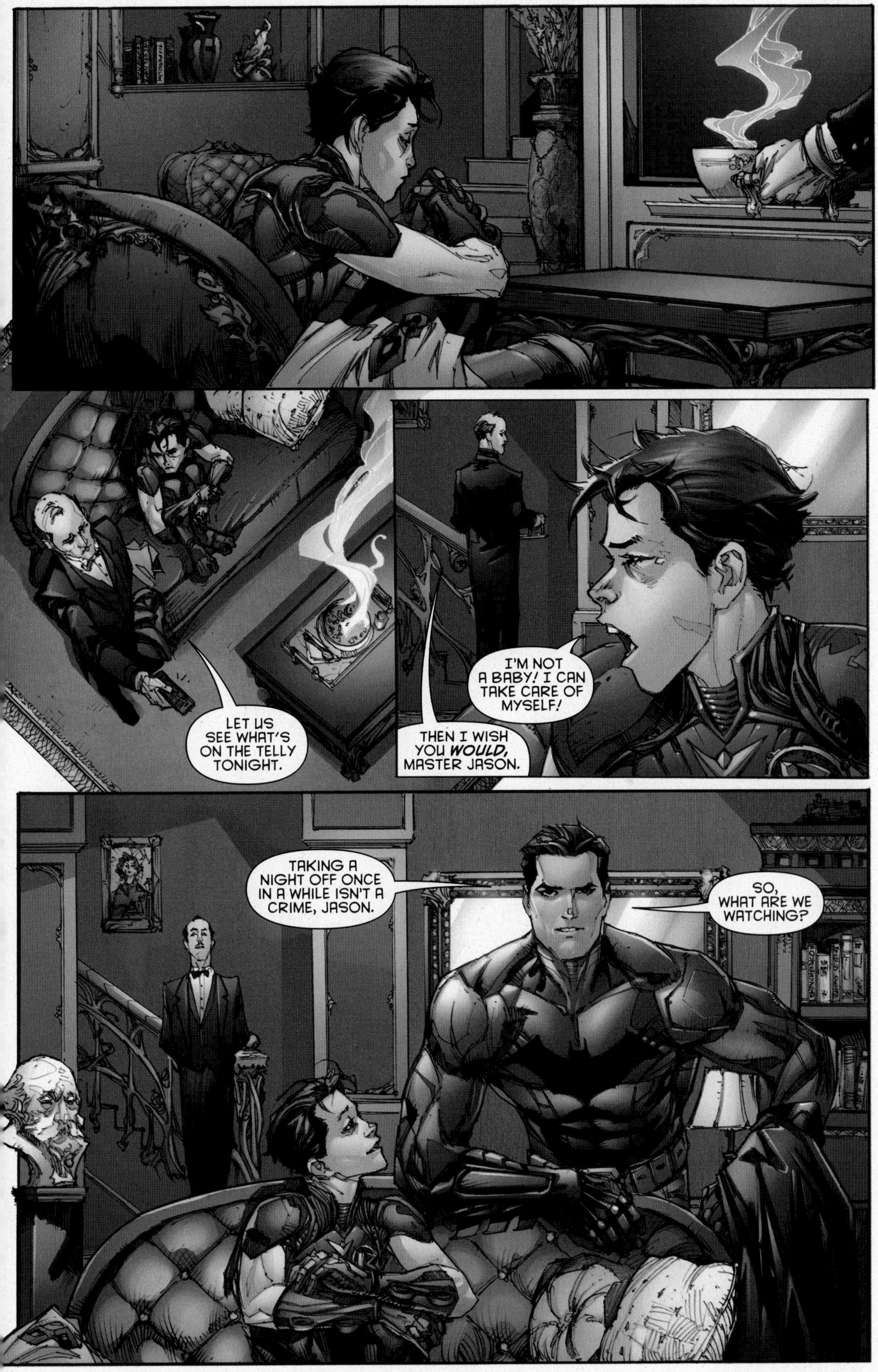
LET US SEE WHAT'S ON THE TELLY TONIGHT.
I'M NOT A BABY! I CAN TAKE CARE OF MYSELF!
THEN I WISH YOU *WOULD,* MASTER JASON.
TAKING A NIGHT OFF ONCE IN A WHILE ISN'T A CRIME, JASON.
SO, WHAT ARE WE WATCHING?

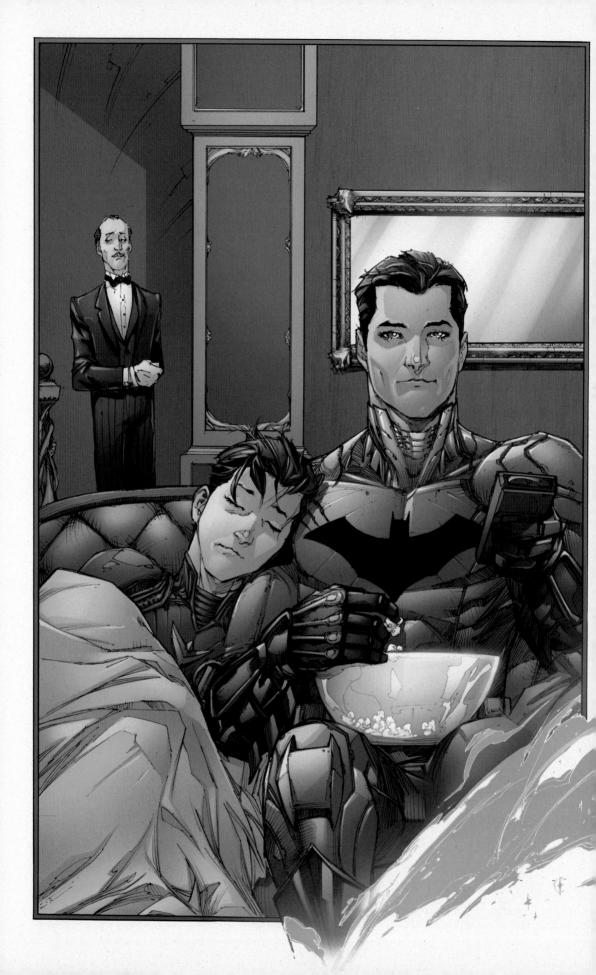

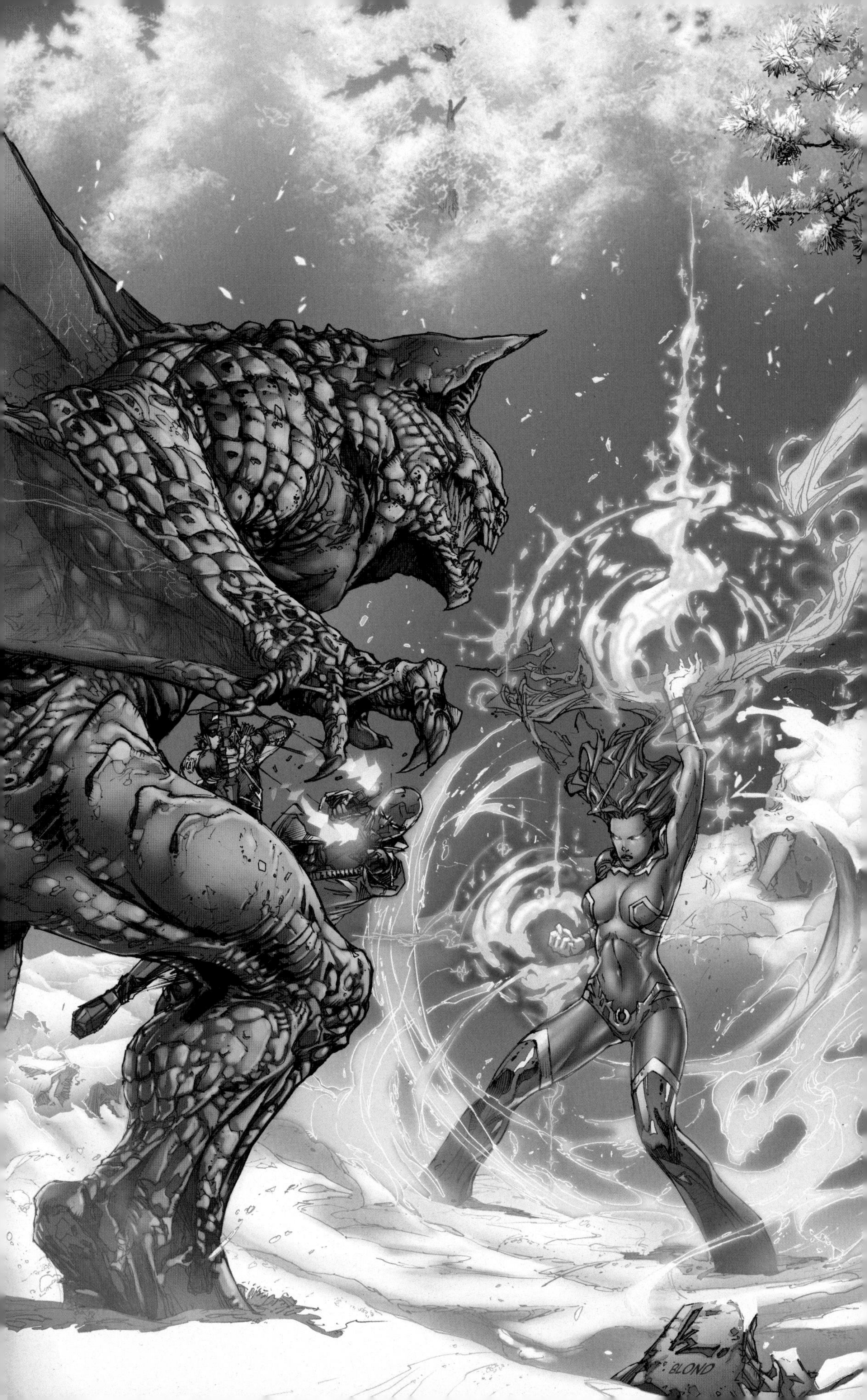
BLOND

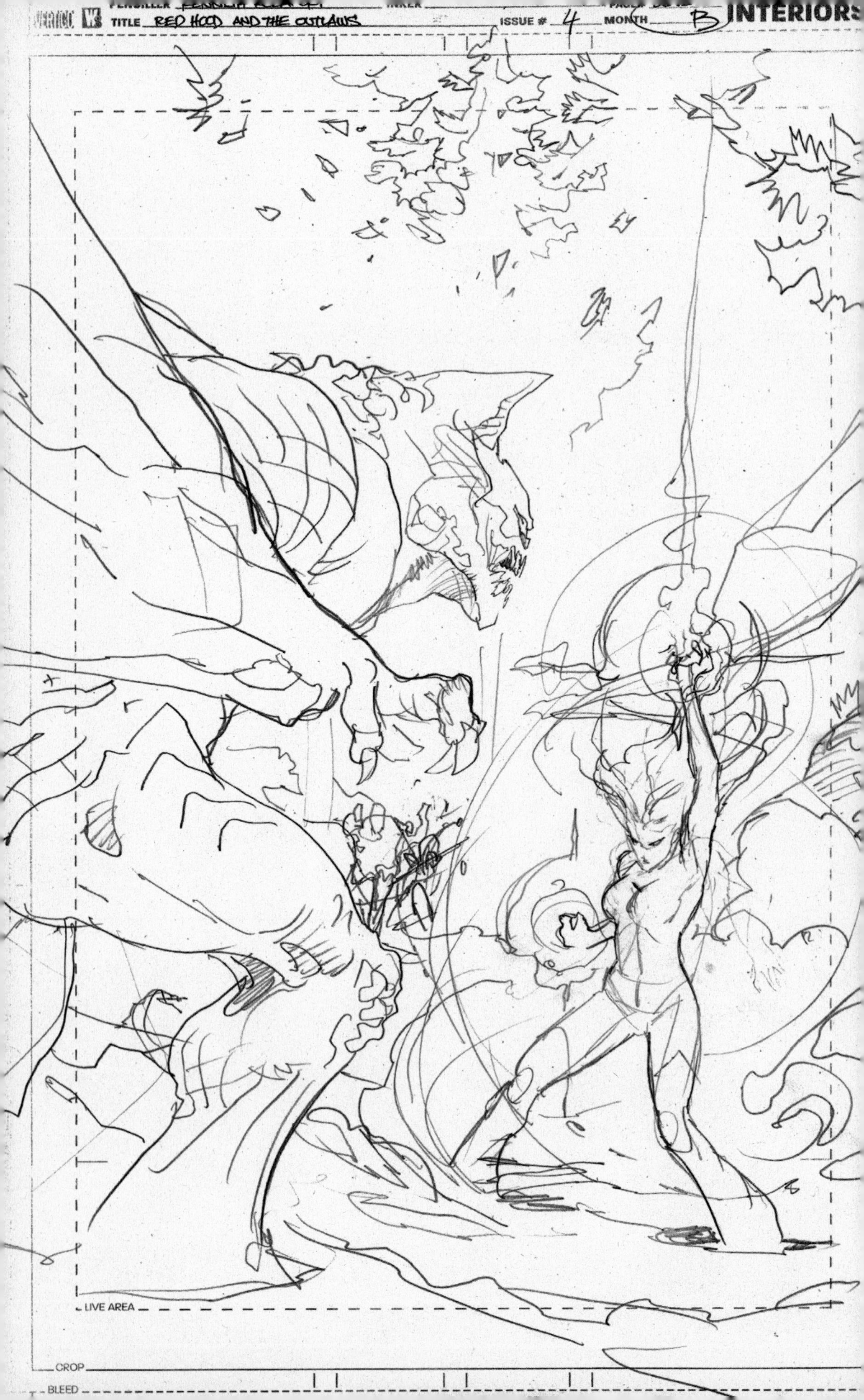
TITLE RED HOOD AND THE OUTLAWS
ISSUE # 4
MONTH
INTERIORS
LIVE AREA
CROP
BLEED

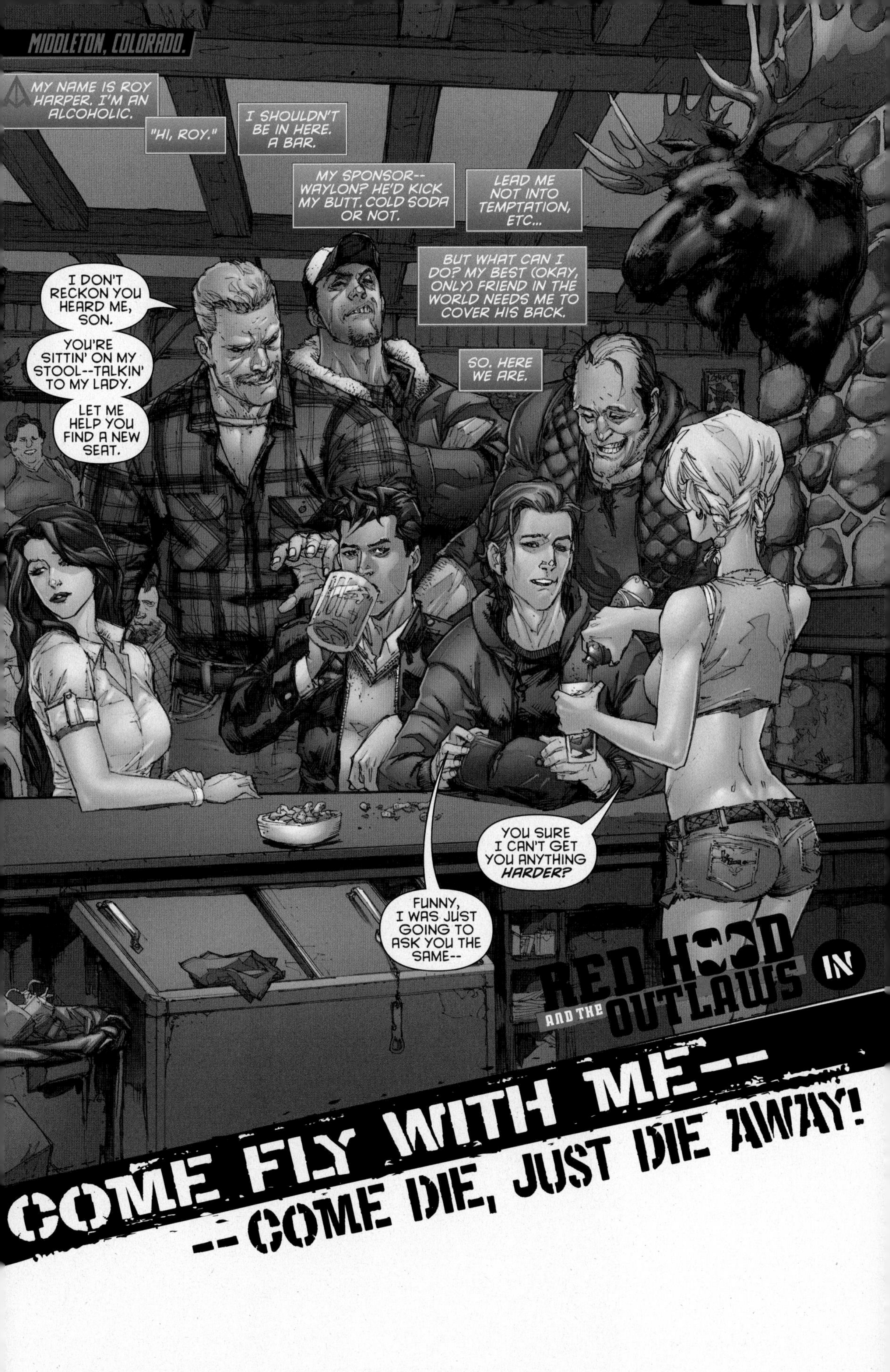
MIDDLETON, COLORADO.
MY NAME IS ROY HARPER. I'M AN ALCOHOLIC.
"HI, ROY."
I SHOULDN'T BE IN HERE. A BAR.
MY SPONSOR-- WAYLON? HE'D KICK MY BUTT. COLD SODA OR NOT.
LEAD ME NOT INTO TEMPTATION, ETC...
BUT WHAT CAN I DO? MY BEST (OKAY, ONLY) FRIEND IN THE WORLD NEEDS ME TO COVER HIS BACK.
SO. HERE WE ARE.
I DON'T RECKON YOU HEARD ME, SON.
YOU'RE SITTIN' ON MY STOOL--TALKIN' TO MY LADY.
LET ME HELP YOU FIND A NEW SEAT.
YOU SURE I CAN'T GET YOU ANYTHING *HARDER?*
FUNNY, I WAS JUST GOING TO ASK YOU THE SAME--
RED HOOD AND THE OUTLAWS IN
COME FLY WITH ME--
--COME DIE, JUST DIE AWAY!

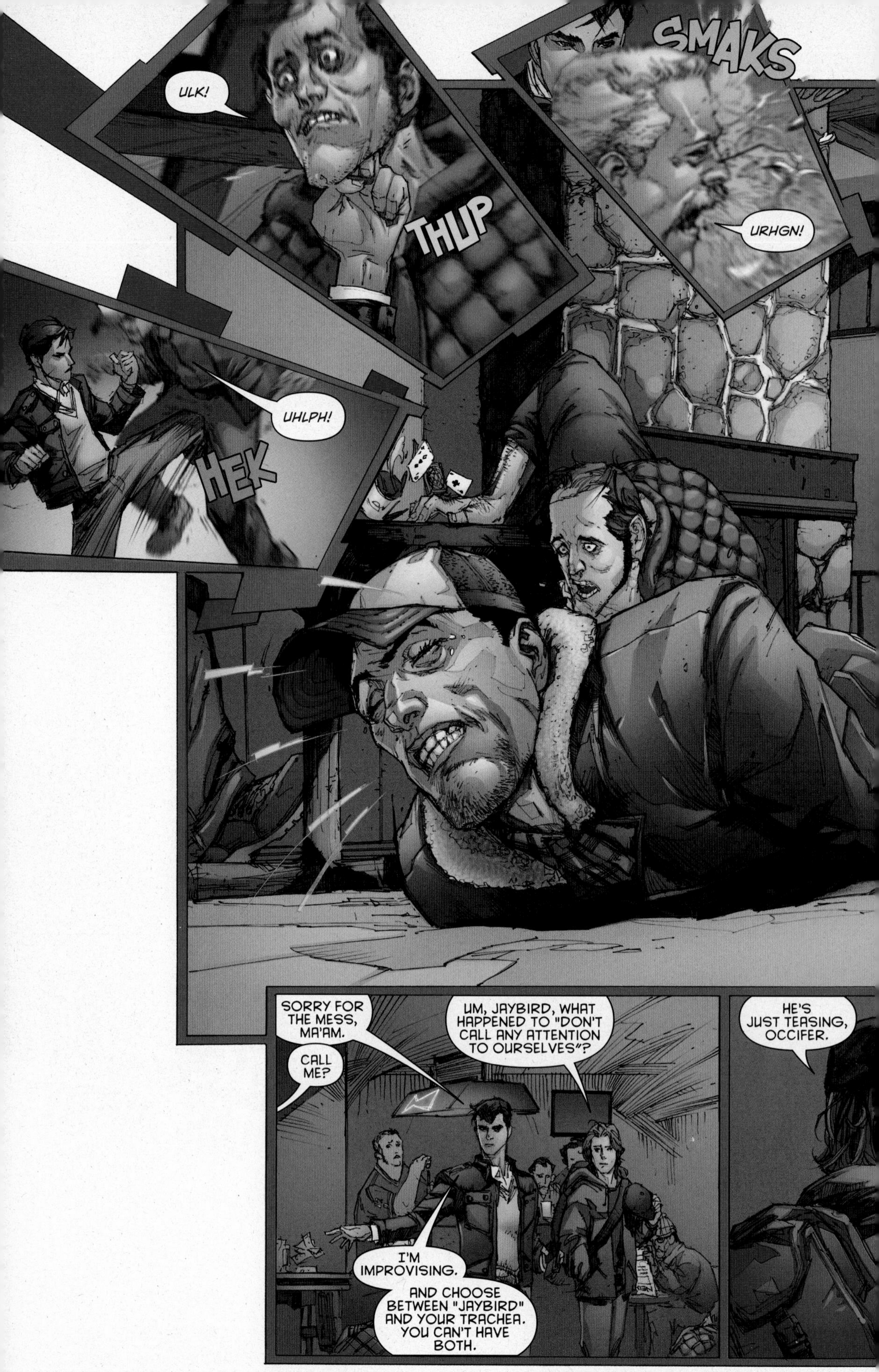
ULK!
THUP
SMAKS
URHGN!
UHLPH!
HEK
SORRY FOR THE MESS, MA'AM.
CALL ME?
UM, JAYBIRD, WHAT HAPPENED TO "DON'T CALL ANY ATTENTION TO OURSELVES"?
I'M IMPROVISING.
AND CHOOSE BETWEEN "JAYBIRD" AND YOUR TRACHEA. YOU CAN'T HAVE BOTH.
HE'S JUST TEASING, OCCIFER.

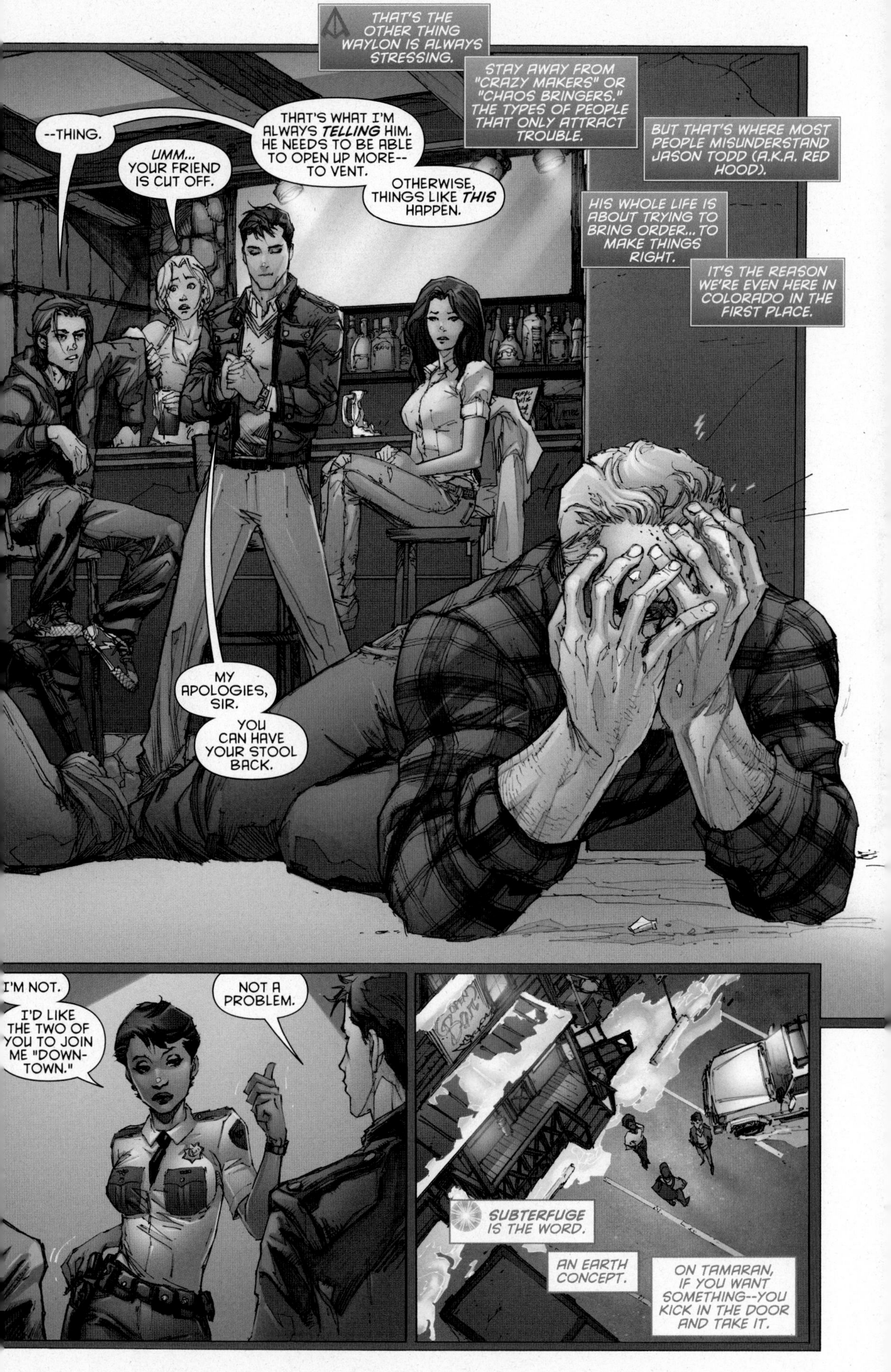
THAT'S THE OTHER THING WAYLON IS ALWAYS STRESSING.
STAY AWAY FROM "CRAZY MAKERS" OR "CHAOS BRINGERS." THE TYPES OF PEOPLE THAT ONLY ATTRACT TROUBLE.
BUT THAT'S WHERE MOST PEOPLE MISUNDERSTAND JASON TODD (A.K.A. RED HOOD).
HIS WHOLE LIFE IS ABOUT TRYING TO BRING ORDER...TO MAKE THINGS RIGHT.
IT'S THE REASON WE'RE EVEN HERE IN COLORADO IN THE FIRST PLACE.
--THING.
UMM... YOUR FRIEND IS CUT OFF.
THAT'S WHAT I'M ALWAYS TELLING HIM. HE NEEDS TO BE ABLE TO OPEN UP MORE--TO VENT.
OTHERWISE, THINGS LIKE THIS HAPPEN.
MY APOLOGIES, SIR.
YOU CAN HAVE YOUR STOOL BACK.
I'M NOT.
I'D LIKE THE TWO OF YOU TO JOIN ME "DOWN-TOWN."
NOT A PROBLEM.
SUBTERFUGE IS THE WORD.
AN EARTH CONCEPT.
ON TAMARAN, IF YOU WANT SOMETHING--YOU KICK IN THE DOOR AND TAKE IT.

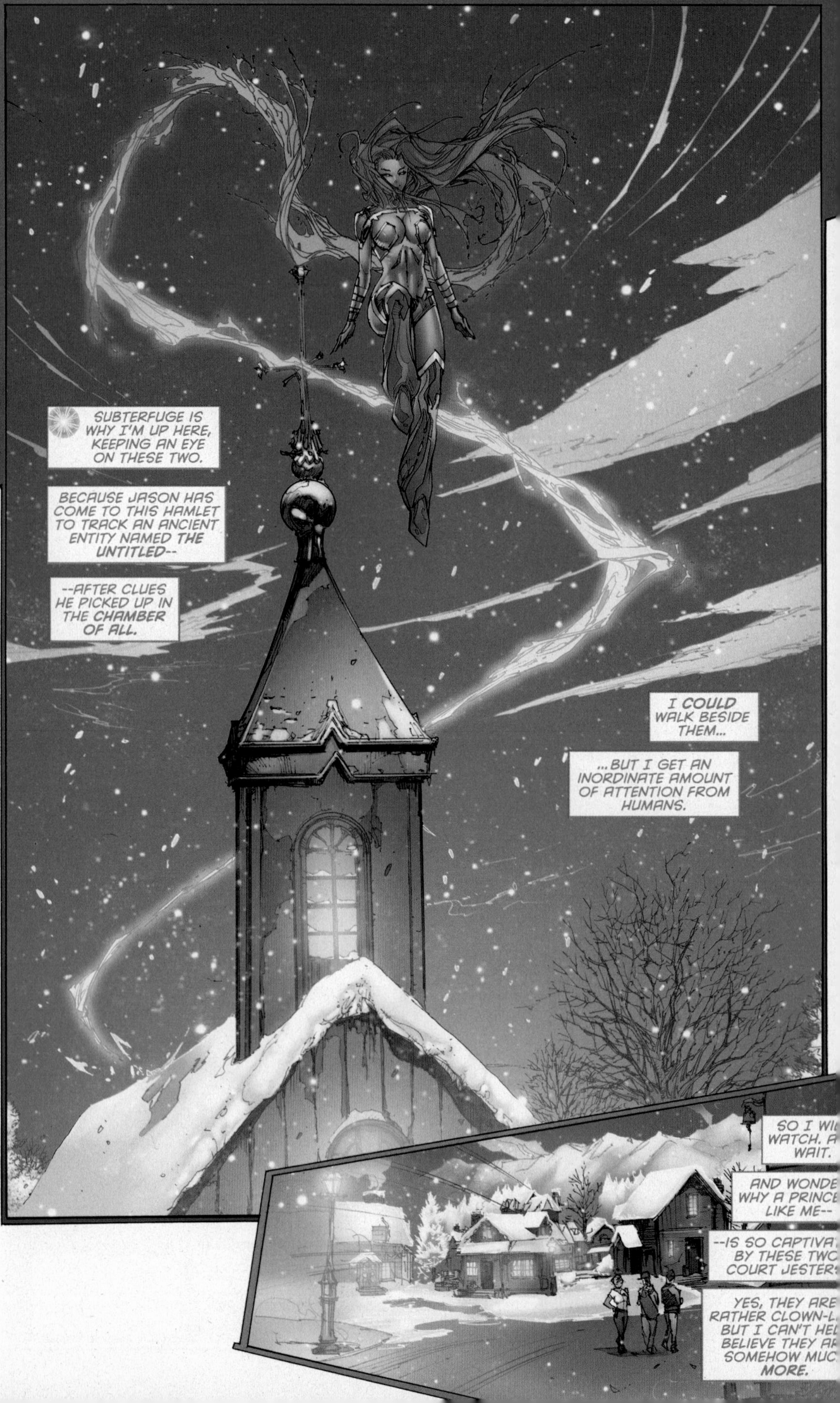

SUBTERFUGE IS WHY I'M UP HERE, KEEPING AN EYE ON THESE TWO.
BECAUSE JASON HAS COME TO THIS HAMLET TO TRACK AN ANCIENT ENTITY NAMED THE UNTITLED--
--AFTER CLUES HE PICKED UP IN THE CHAMBER OF ALL.
I COULD WALK BESIDE THEM...
...BUT I GET AN INORDINATE AMOUNT OF ATTENTION FROM HUMANS.
SO I WI WATCH. A WAIT.
AND WONDE WHY A PRINCE LIKE ME--
--IS SO CAPTIVA BY THESE TWO COURT JESTER
YES, THEY ARE RATHER CLOWN-L BUT I CAN'T HE BELIEVE THEY A SOMEHOW MUC MORE.

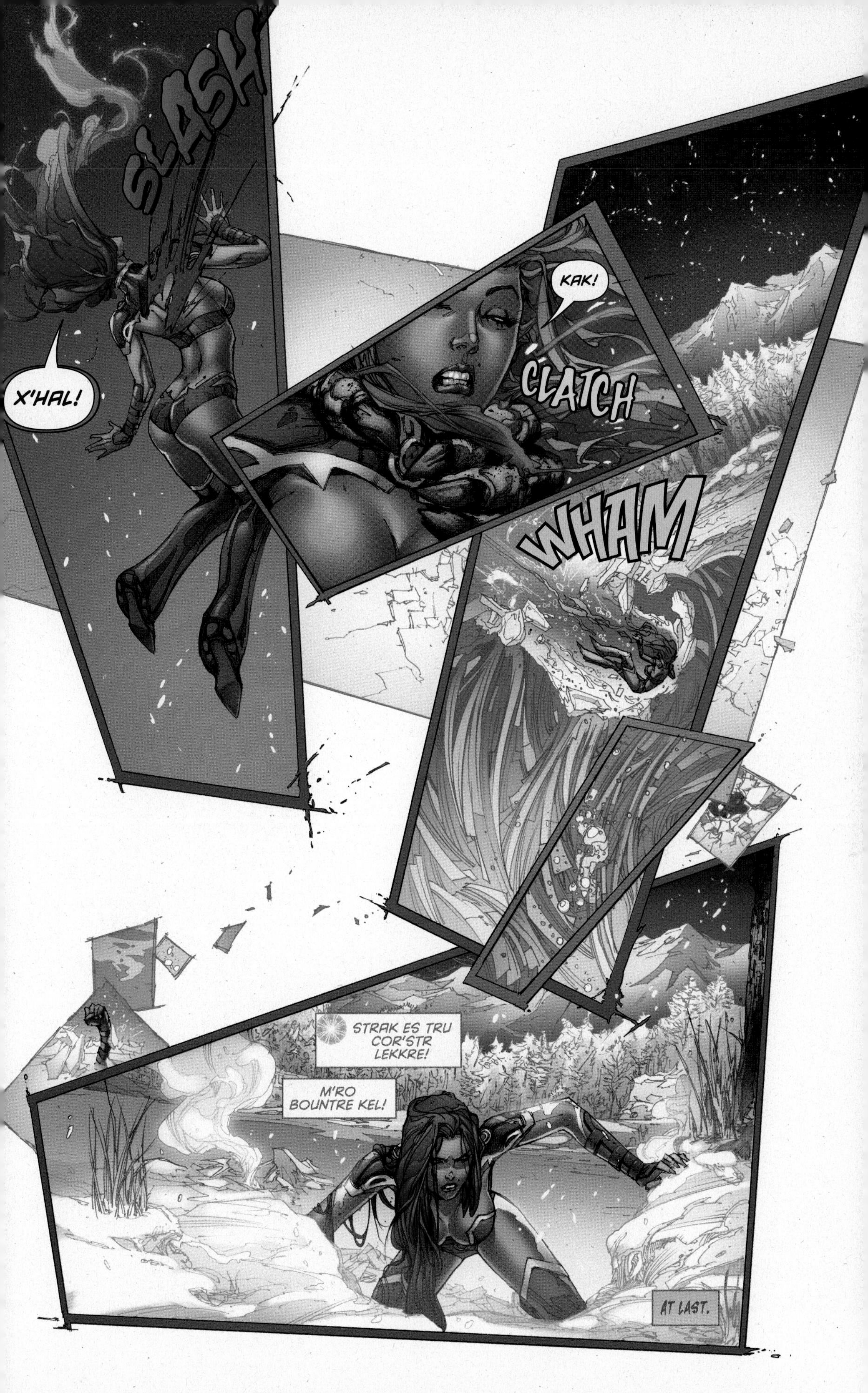
SLASH
X'HAL!
KAK!
CLATCH
WHAM
STRAK ES TRU COR'STR LEKKRE!
M'RO BOUNTRE KEL!
AT LAST.

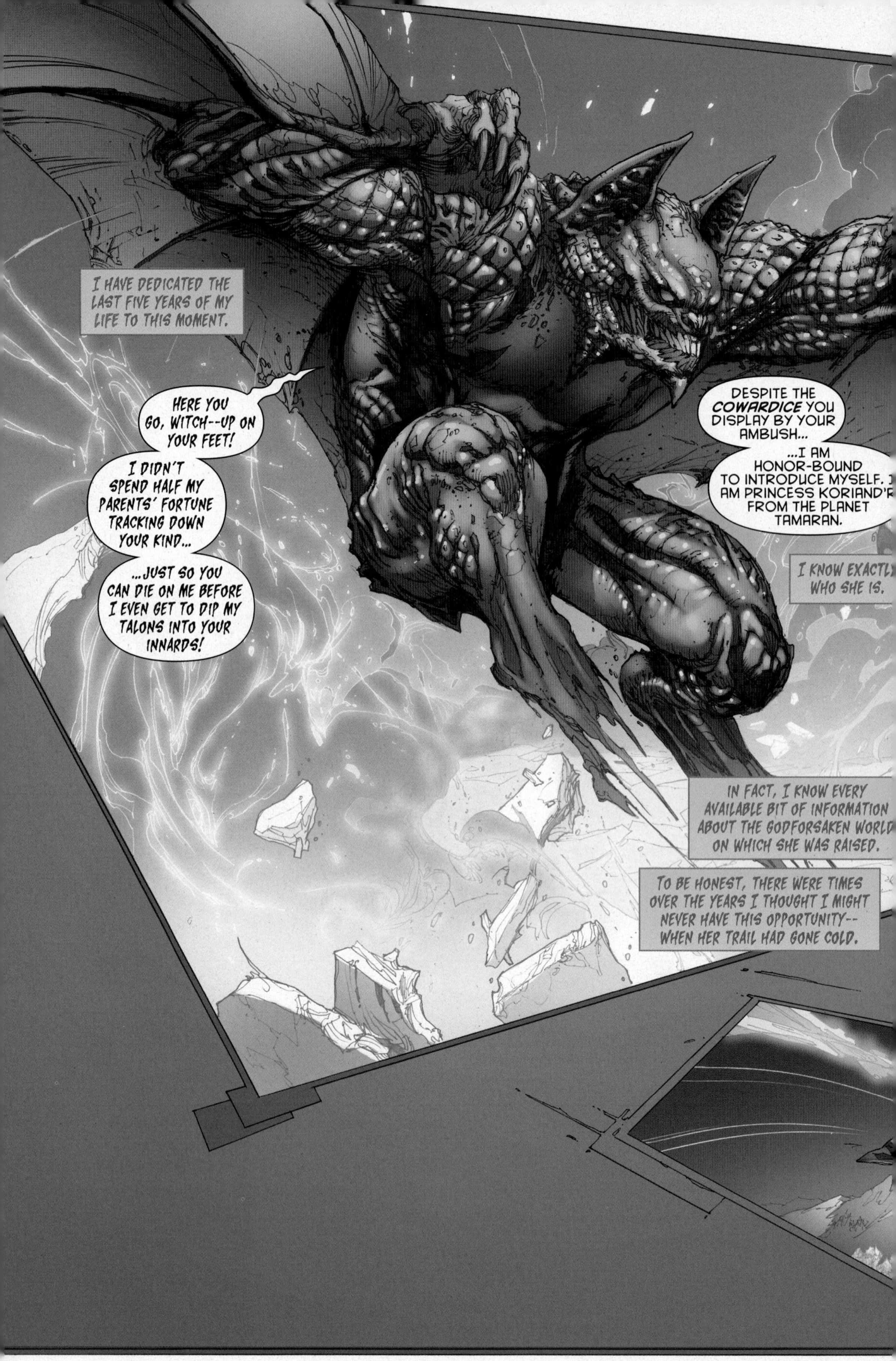
I HAVE DEDICATED THE LAST FIVE YEARS OF MY LIFE TO THIS MOMENT.
HERE YOU GO, WITCH--UP ON YOUR FEET!
I DIDN'T SPEND HALF MY PARENTS' FORTUNE TRACKING DOWN YOUR KIND...
...JUST SO YOU CAN DIE ON ME BEFORE I EVEN GET TO DIP MY TALONS INTO YOUR INNARDS!
DESPITE THE COWARDICE YOU DISPLAY BY YOUR AMBUSH...
...I AM HONOR-BOUND TO INTRODUCE MYSELF. I AM PRINCESS KORIAND'R FROM THE PLANET TAMARAN.
I KNOW EXACTLY WHO SHE IS.
IN FACT, I KNOW EVERY AVAILABLE BIT OF INFORMATION ABOUT THE GODFORSAKEN WORLD ON WHICH SHE WAS RAISED.
TO BE HONEST, THERE WERE TIMES OVER THE YEARS I THOUGHT I MIGHT NEVER HAVE THIS OPPORTUNITY-- WHEN HER TRAIL HAD GONE COLD.

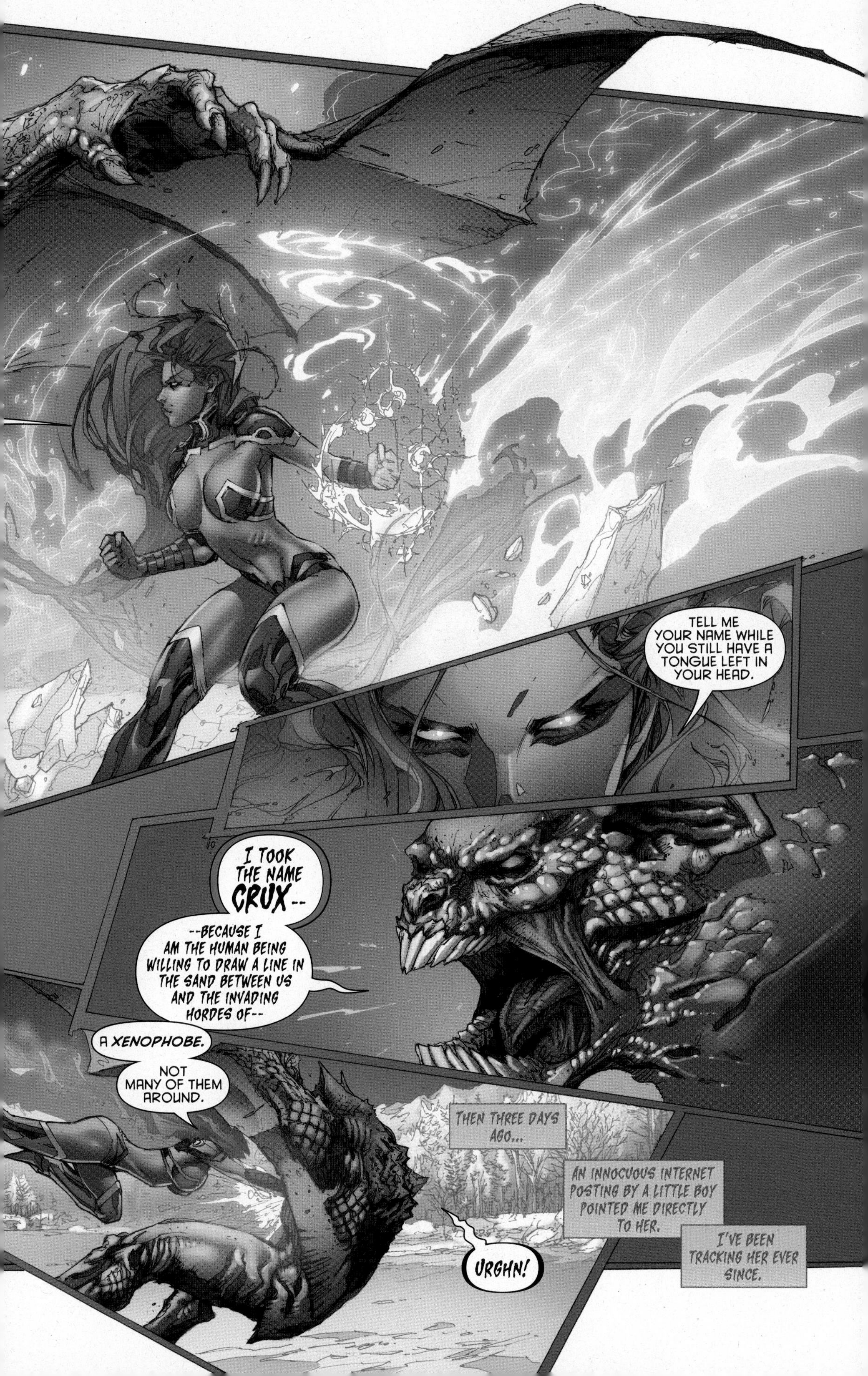
TELL ME YOUR NAME WHILE YOU STILL HAVE A TONGUE LEFT IN YOUR HEAD.
I TOOK THE NAME CRUX--
--BECAUSE I AM THE HUMAN BEING WILLING TO DRAW A LINE IN THE SAND BETWEEN US AND THE INVADING HORDES OF--
A XENOPHOBE.
NOT MANY OF THEM AROUND.
THEN THREE DAYS AGO...
AN INNOCUOUS INTERNET POSTING BY A LITTLE BOY POINTED ME DIRECTLY TO HER.
I'VE BEEN TRACKING HER EVER SINCE.
URGHN!

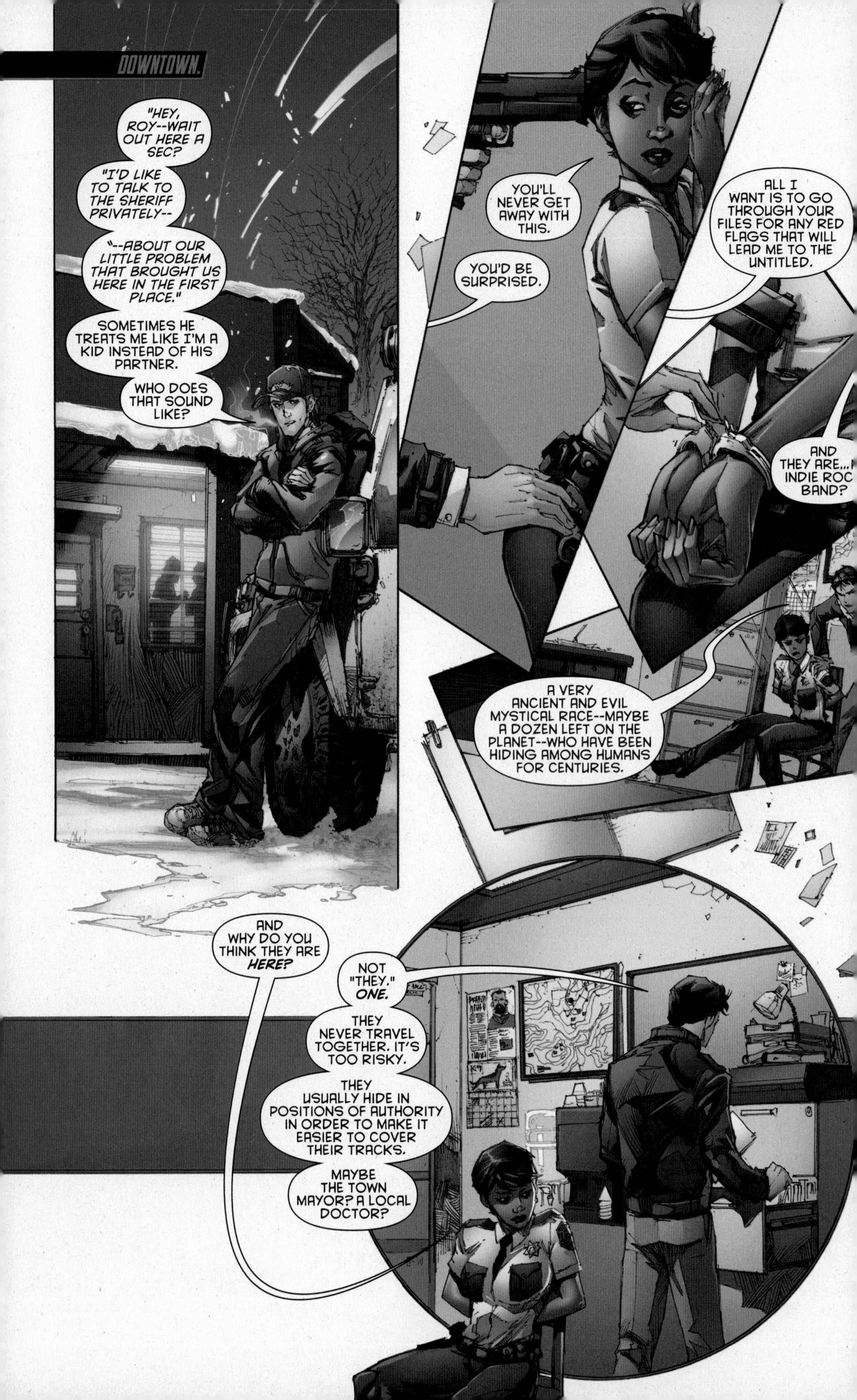
DOWNTOWN.
"HEY, ROY--WAIT OUT HERE A SEC?
"I'D LIKE TO TALK TO THE SHERIFF PRIVATELY--
"--ABOUT OUR LITTLE PROBLEM THAT BROUGHT US HERE IN THE FIRST PLACE."
SOMETIMES HE TREATS ME LIKE I'M A KID INSTEAD OF HIS PARTNER.
WHO DOES THAT SOUND LIKE?
YOU'LL NEVER GET AWAY WITH THIS.
YOU'D BE SURPRISED.
ALL I WANT IS TO GO THROUGH YOUR FILES FOR ANY RED FLAGS THAT WILL LEAD ME TO THE UNTITLED.
AND THEY ARE...
A VERY ANCIENT AND EVIL MYSTICAL RACE--MAYBE A DOZEN LEFT ON THE PLANET--WHO HAVE BEEN HIDING AMONG HUMANS FOR CENTURIES.
AND WHY DO YOU THINK THEY ARE HERE?
NOT "THEY." ONE.
THEY NEVER TRAVEL TOGETHER. IT'S TOO RISKY.
THEY USUALLY HIDE IN POSITIONS OF AUTHORITY IN ORDER TO MAKE IT EASIER TO COVER THEIR TRACKS.
MAYBE THE TOWN MAYOR? A LOCAL DOCTOR?

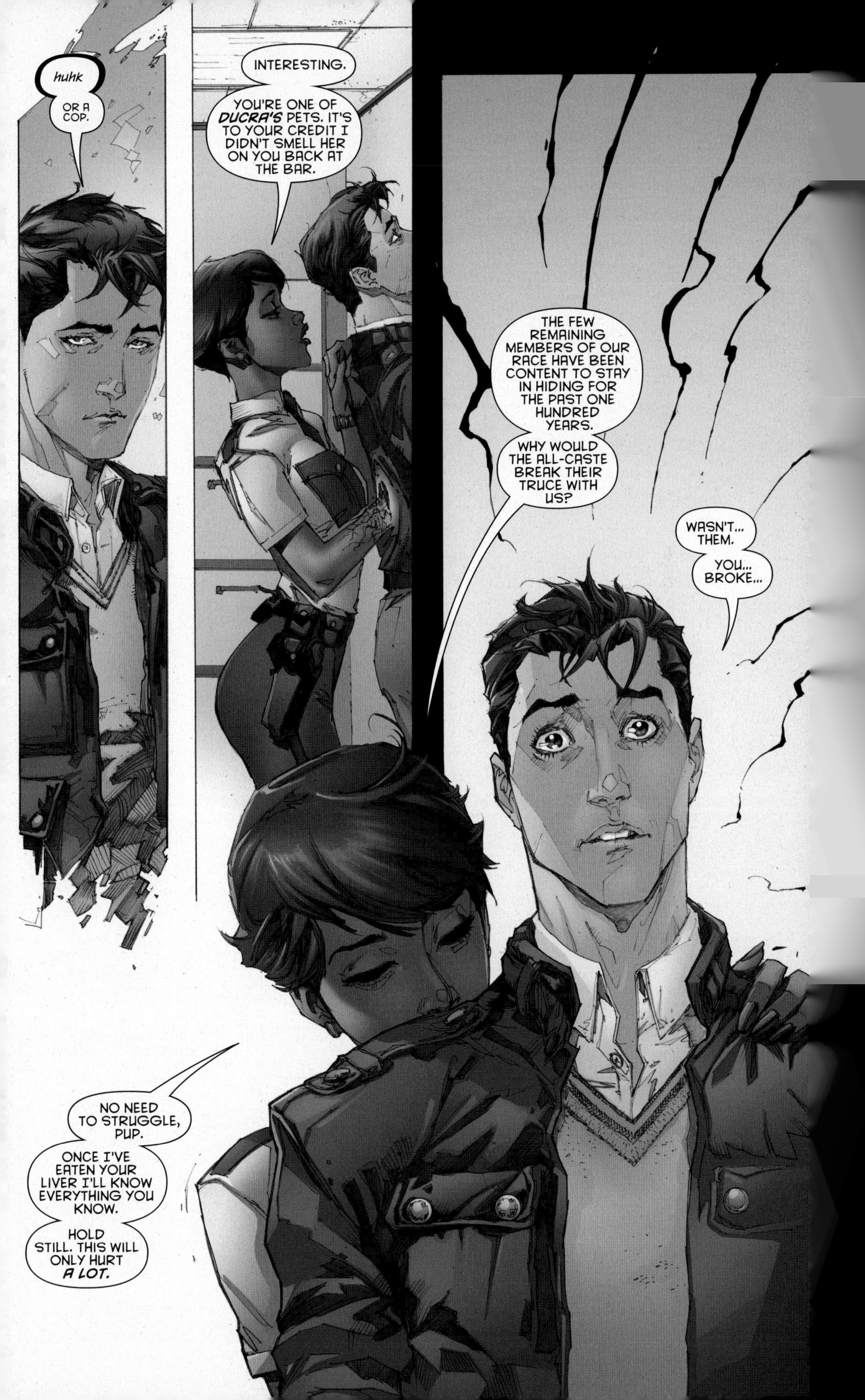
huhk
OR A COP.
INTERESTING.
YOU'RE ONE OF DUCRA'S PETS. IT'S TO YOUR CREDIT I DIDN'T SMELL HER ON YOU BACK AT THE BAR.
THE FEW REMAINING MEMBERS OF OUR RACE HAVE BEEN CONTENT TO STAY IN HIDING FOR THE PAST ONE HUNDRED YEARS.
WHY WOULD THE ALL-CASTE BREAK THEIR TRUCE WITH US?
WASN'T... THEM.
YOU... BROKE...
NO NEED TO STRUGGLE, PUP.
ONCE I'VE EATEN YOUR LIVER I'LL KNOW EVERYTHING YOU KNOW.
HOLD STILL. THIS WILL ONLY HURT A LOT.

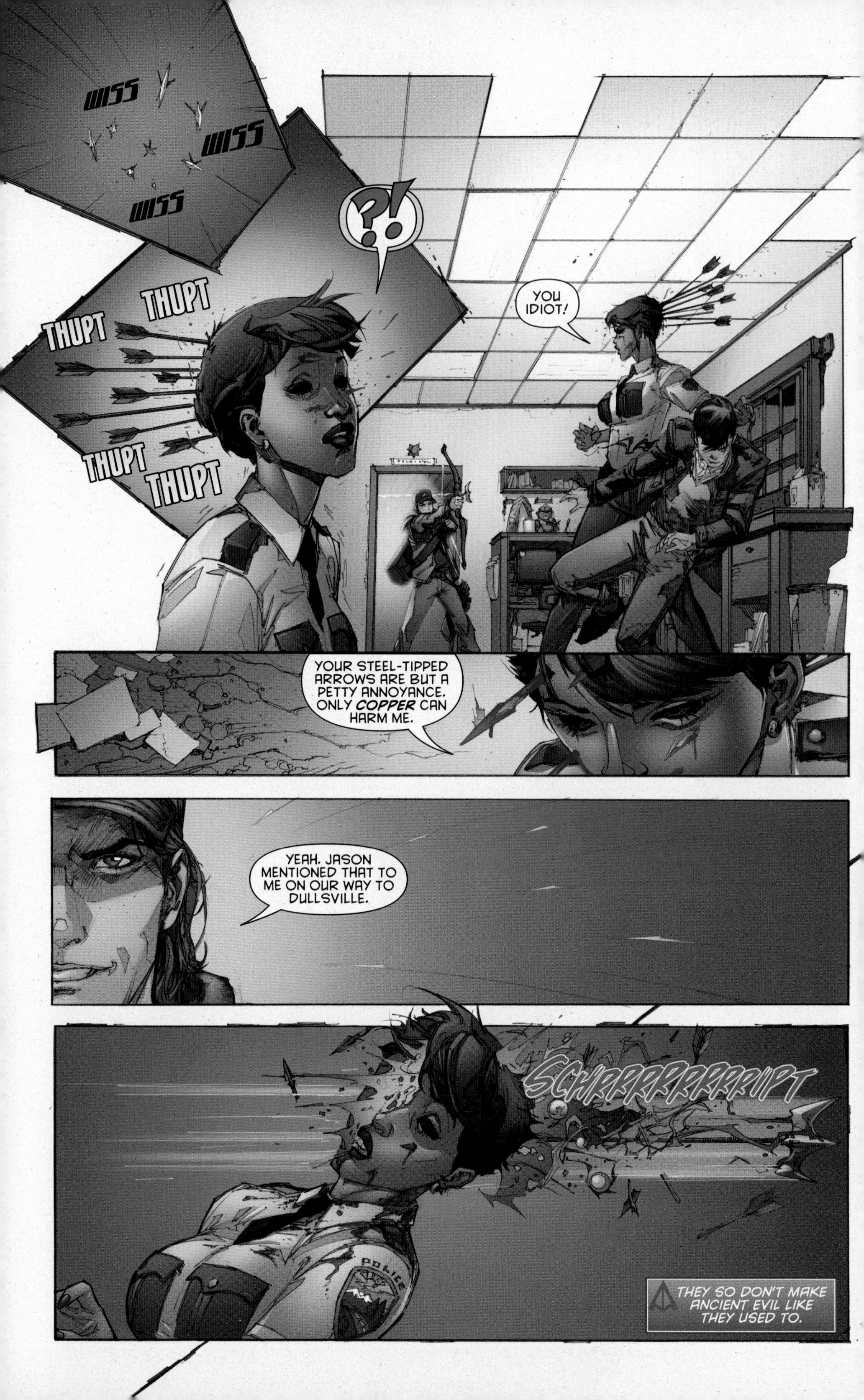
WISS
WISS
WISS
?!
THUPT
THUPT
THUPT
THUPT
YOU IDIOT!
YOUR STEEL-TIPPED ARROWS ARE BUT A PETTY ANNOYANCE. ONLY COPPER CAN HARM ME.
YEAH. JASON MENTIONED THAT TO ME ON OUR WAY TO DULLSVILLE.
SCHRRRRRRRRRIPT
POLICE
THEY SO DON'T MAKE ANCIENT EVIL LIKE THEY USED TO.

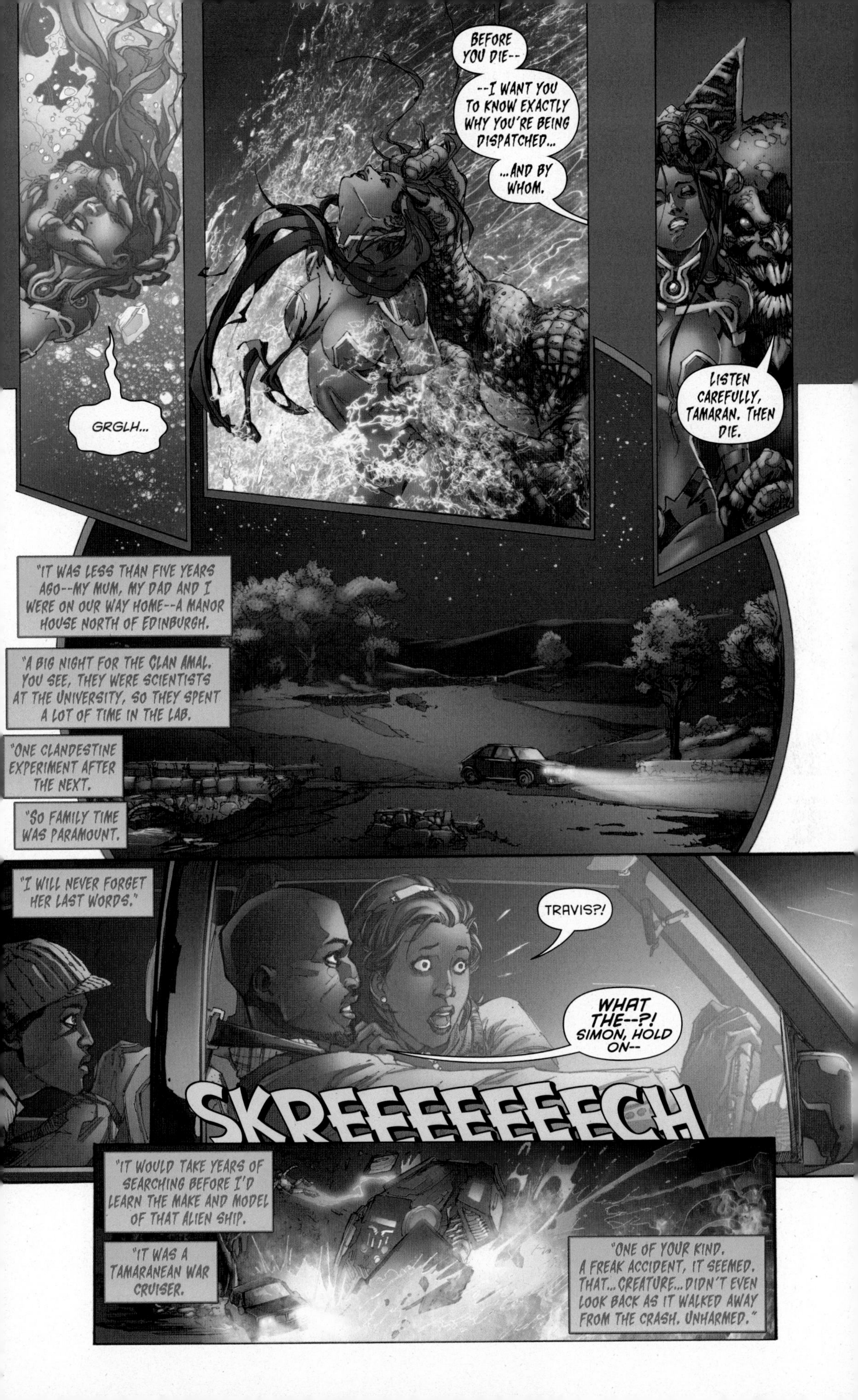
GRGLH...
BEFORE YOU DIE--
--I WANT YOU TO KNOW EXACTLY WHY YOU'RE BEING DISPATCHED...
...AND BY WHOM.
LISTEN CAREFULLY, TAMARAN. THEN DIE.
"IT WAS LESS THAN FIVE YEARS AGO--MY MUM, MY DAD AND I WERE ON OUR WAY HOME--A MANOR HOUSE NORTH OF EDINBURGH.
"A BIG NIGHT FOR THE CLAN AMAL. YOU SEE, THEY WERE SCIENTISTS AT THE UNIVERSITY, SO THEY SPENT A LOT OF TIME IN THE LAB.
"ONE CLANDESTINE EXPERIMENT AFTER THE NEXT.
"SO FAMILY TIME WAS PARAMOUNT.
"I WILL NEVER FORGET HER LAST WORDS."
TRAVIS?!
WHAT THE--?! SIMON, HOLD ON--
SKREEEEEEEECH
"IT WOULD TAKE YEARS OF SEARCHING BEFORE I'D LEARN THE MAKE AND MODEL OF THAT ALIEN SHIP.
"IT WAS A TAMARANEAN WAR CRUISER.
"ONE OF YOUR KIND. A FREAK ACCIDENT, IT SEEMED. THAT...CREATURE...DIDN'T EVEN LOOK BACK AS IT WALKED AWAY FROM THE CRASH. UNHARMED."

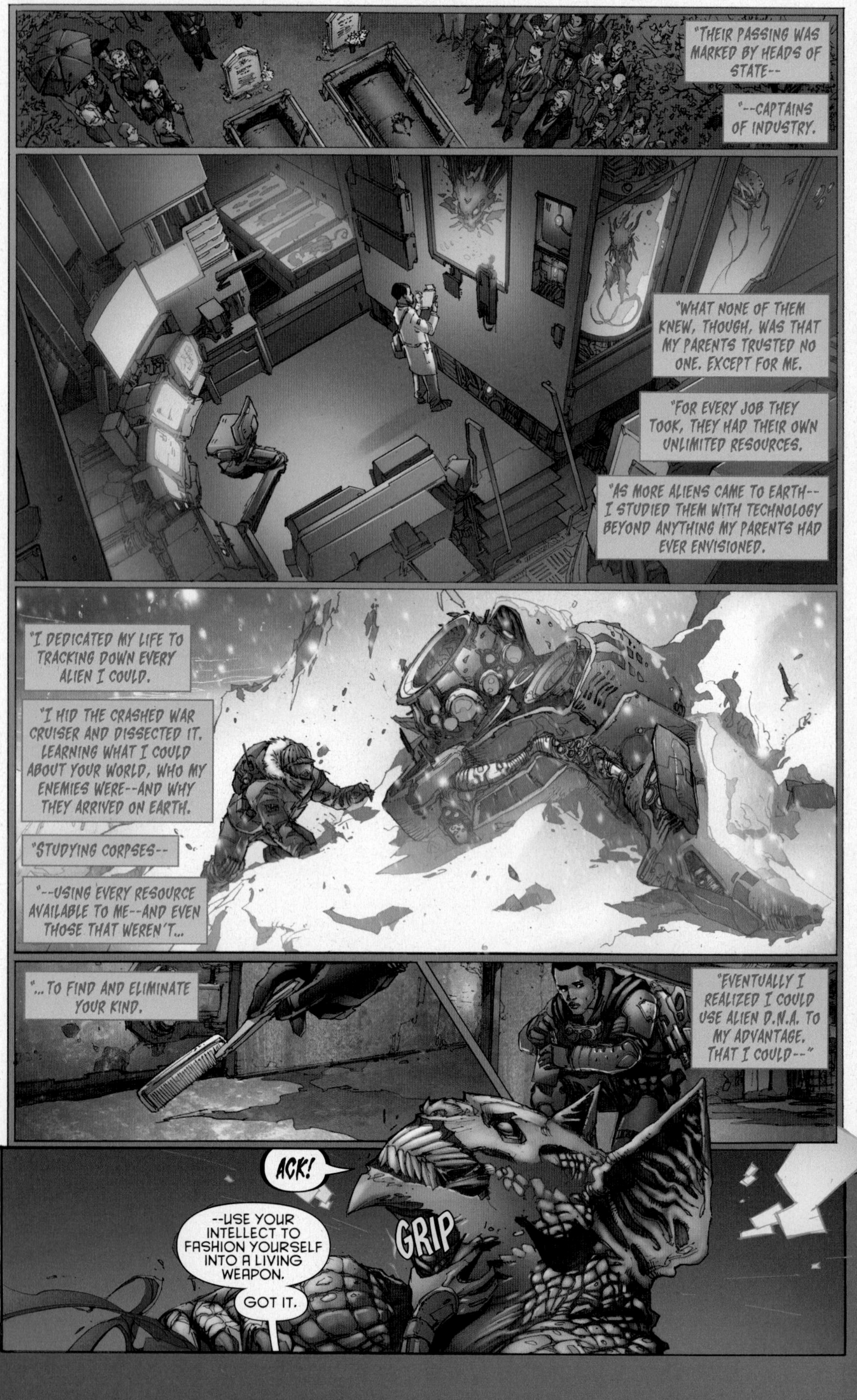
"THEIR PASSING WAS MARKED BY HEADS OF STATE--
"--CAPTAINS OF INDUSTRY.
"WHAT NONE OF THEM KNEW, THOUGH, WAS THAT MY PARENTS TRUSTED NO ONE. EXCEPT FOR ME.
"FOR EVERY JOB THEY TOOK, THEY HAD THEIR OWN UNLIMITED RESOURCES.
"AS MORE ALIENS CAME TO EARTH-- I STUDIED THEM WITH TECHNOLOGY BEYOND ANYTHING MY PARENTS HAD EVER ENVISIONED.
"I DEDICATED MY LIFE TO TRACKING DOWN EVERY ALIEN I COULD.
"I HID THE CRASHED WAR CRUISER AND DISSECTED IT. LEARNING WHAT I COULD ABOUT YOUR WORLD, WHO MY ENEMIES WERE--AND WHY THEY ARRIVED ON EARTH.
"STUDYING CORPSES--
"--USING EVERY RESOURCE AVAILABLE TO ME--AND EVEN THOSE THAT WEREN'T...
"...TO FIND AND ELIMINATE YOUR KIND.
"EVENTUALLY I REALIZED I COULD USE ALIEN D.N.A. TO MY ADVANTAGE. THAT I COULD--"
ACK!
--USE YOUR INTELLECT TO FASHION YOURSELF INTO A LIVING WEAPON.
GOT IT.
GRIP

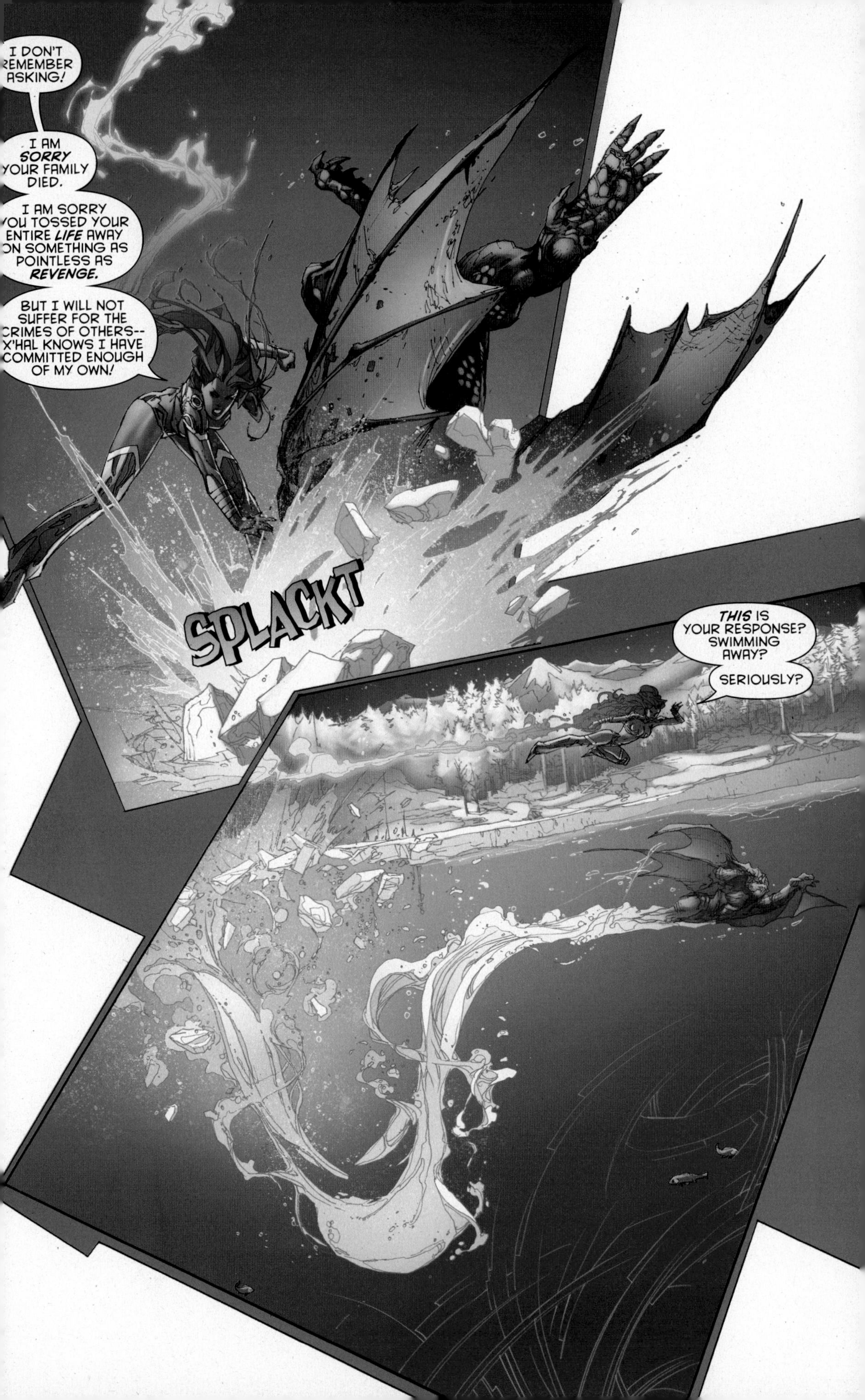

I DON'T REMEMBER ASKING!
I AM SORRY YOUR FAMILY DIED.
I AM SORRY YOU TOSSED YOUR ENTIRE LIFE AWAY ON SOMETHING AS POINTLESS AS REVENGE.
BUT I WILL NOT SUFFER FOR THE CRIMES OF OTHERS-- X'HAL KNOWS I HAVE COMMITTED ENOUGH OF MY OWN!
SPLACKT
THIS IS YOUR RESPONSE? SWIMMING AWAY?
SERIOUSLY?

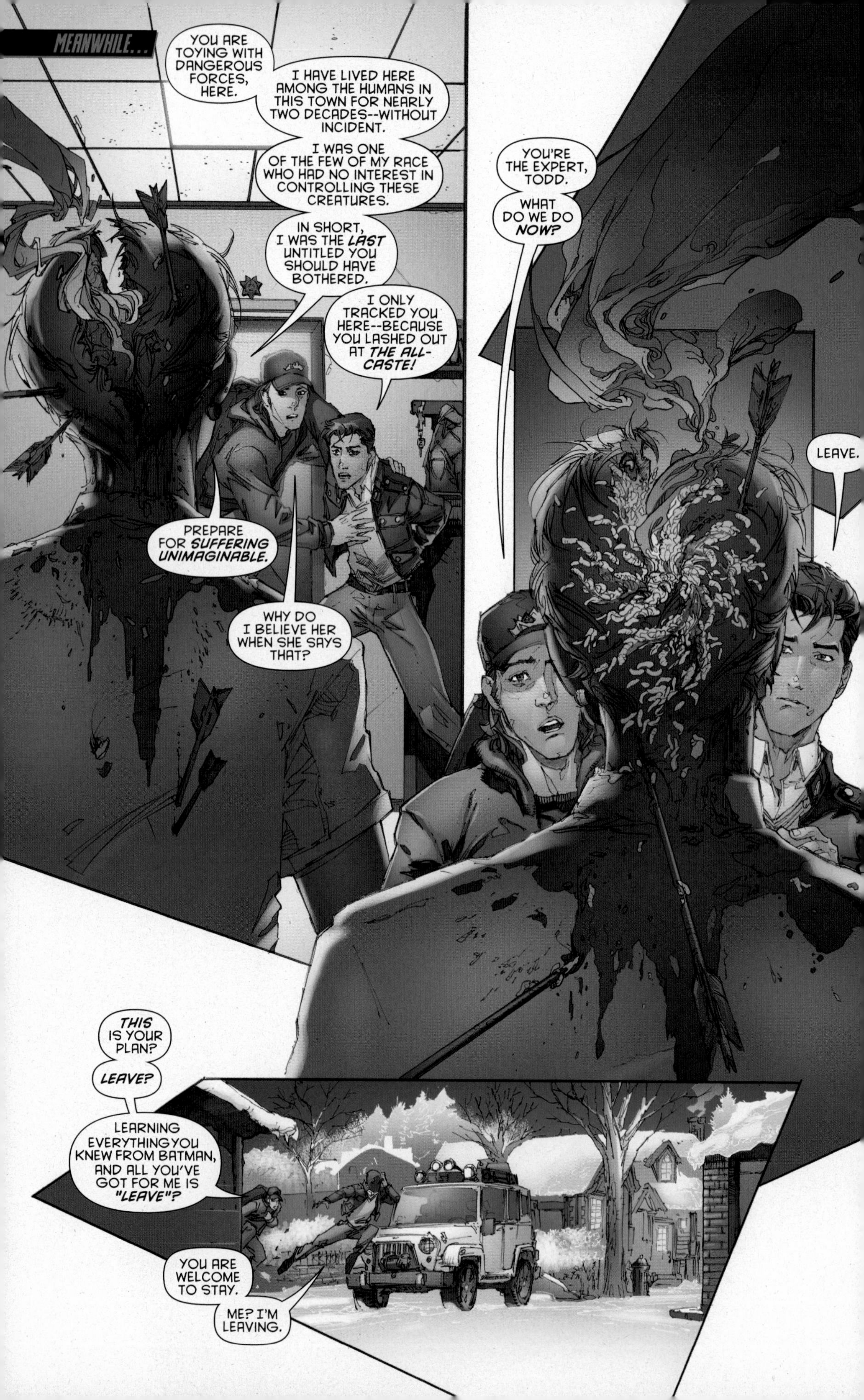
MEANWHILE...
YOU ARE TOYING WITH DANGEROUS FORCES, HERE.
I HAVE LIVED HERE AMONG THE HUMANS IN THIS TOWN FOR NEARLY TWO DECADES--WITHOUT INCIDENT.
I WAS ONE OF THE FEW OF MY RACE WHO HAD NO INTEREST IN CONTROLLING THESE CREATURES.
IN SHORT, I WAS THE LAST UNTITLED YOU SHOULD HAVE BOTHERED.
I ONLY TRACKED YOU HERE--BECAUSE YOU LASHED OUT AT THE ALL-CASTE!
PREPARE FOR SUFFERING UNIMAGINABLE.
WHY DO I BELIEVE HER WHEN SHE SAYS THAT?
YOU'RE THE EXPERT, TODD.
WHAT DO WE DO NOW?
LEAVE.
THIS IS YOUR PLAN?
LEAVE?
LEARNING EVERYTHING YOU KNEW FROM BATMAN, AND ALL YOU'VE GOT FOR ME IS "LEAVE"?
YOU ARE WELCOME TO STAY.
ME? I'M LEAVING.

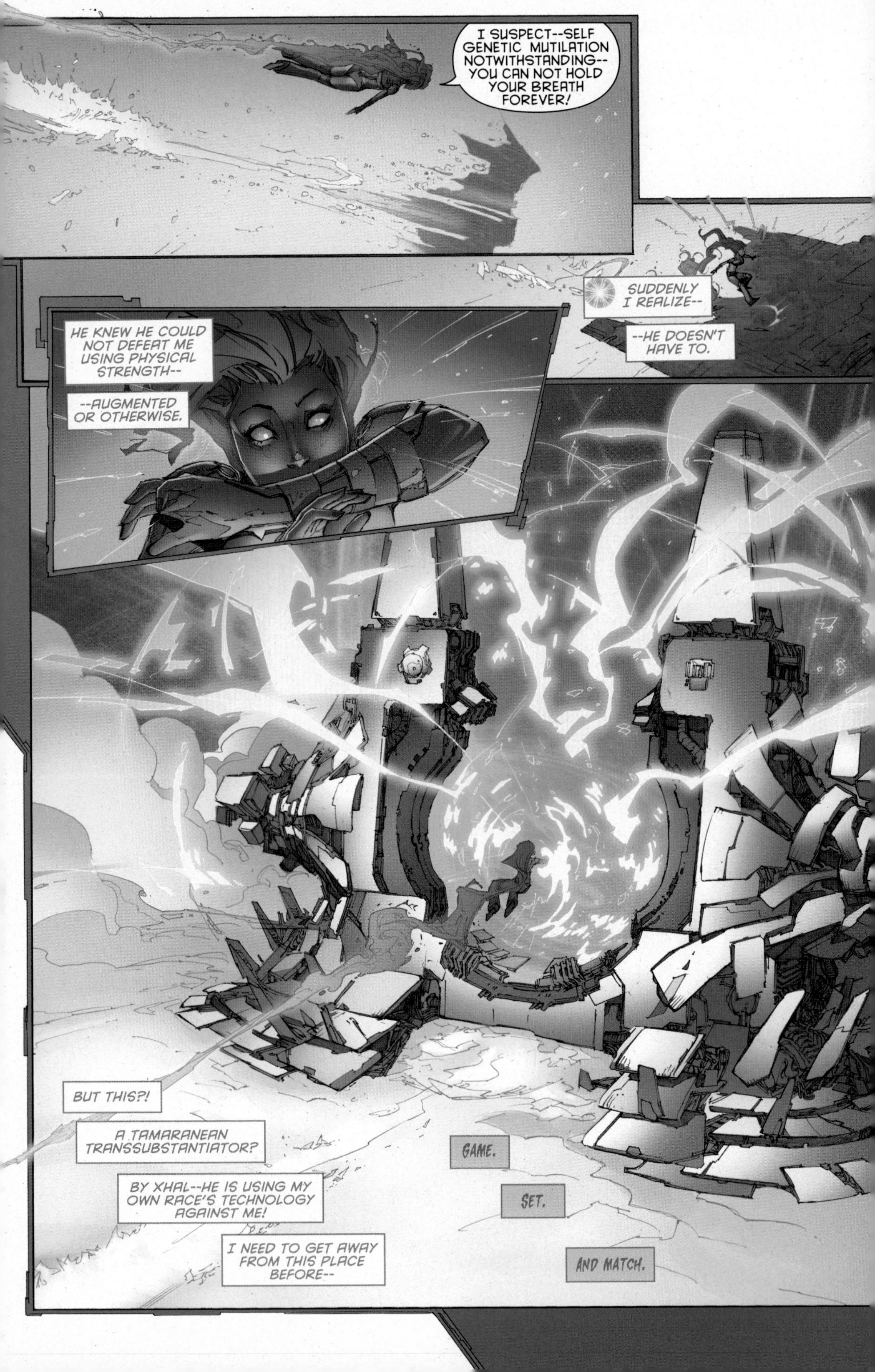
I SUSPECT--SELF GENETIC MUTILATION NOTWITHSTANDING--YOU CAN NOT HOLD YOUR BREATH FOREVER!
SUDDENLY I REALIZE--
--HE DOESN'T HAVE TO.
HE KNEW HE COULD NOT DEFEAT ME USING PHYSICAL STRENGTH--
--AUGMENTED OR OTHERWISE.
BUT THIS?!
A TAMARANEAN TRANSSUBSTANTIATOR?
BY XHAL--HE IS USING MY OWN RACE'S TECHNOLOGY AGAINST ME!
I NEED TO GET AWAY FROM THIS PLACE BEFORE--
GAME.
SET.
AND MATCH.

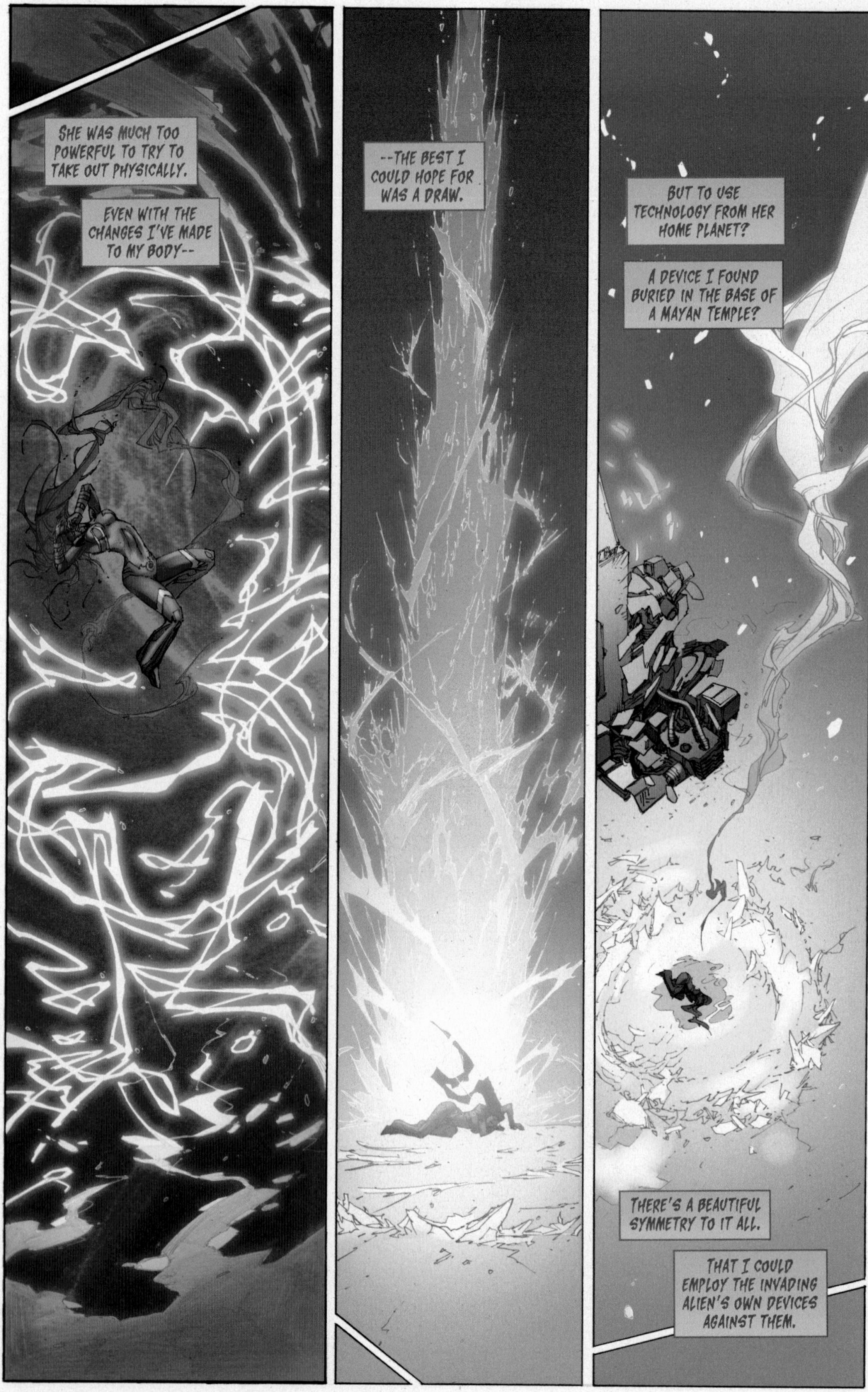
SHE WAS MUCH TOO POWERFUL TO TRY TO TAKE OUT PHYSICALLY.
EVEN WITH THE CHANGES I'VE MADE TO MY BODY--
--THE BEST I COULD HOPE FOR WAS A DRAW.
BUT TO USE TECHNOLOGY FROM HER HOME PLANET?
A DEVICE I FOUND BURIED IN THE BASE OF A MAYAN TEMPLE?
THERE'S A BEAUTIFUL SYMMETRY TO IT ALL.
THAT I COULD EMPLOY THE INVADING ALIEN'S OWN DEVICES AGAINST THEM.

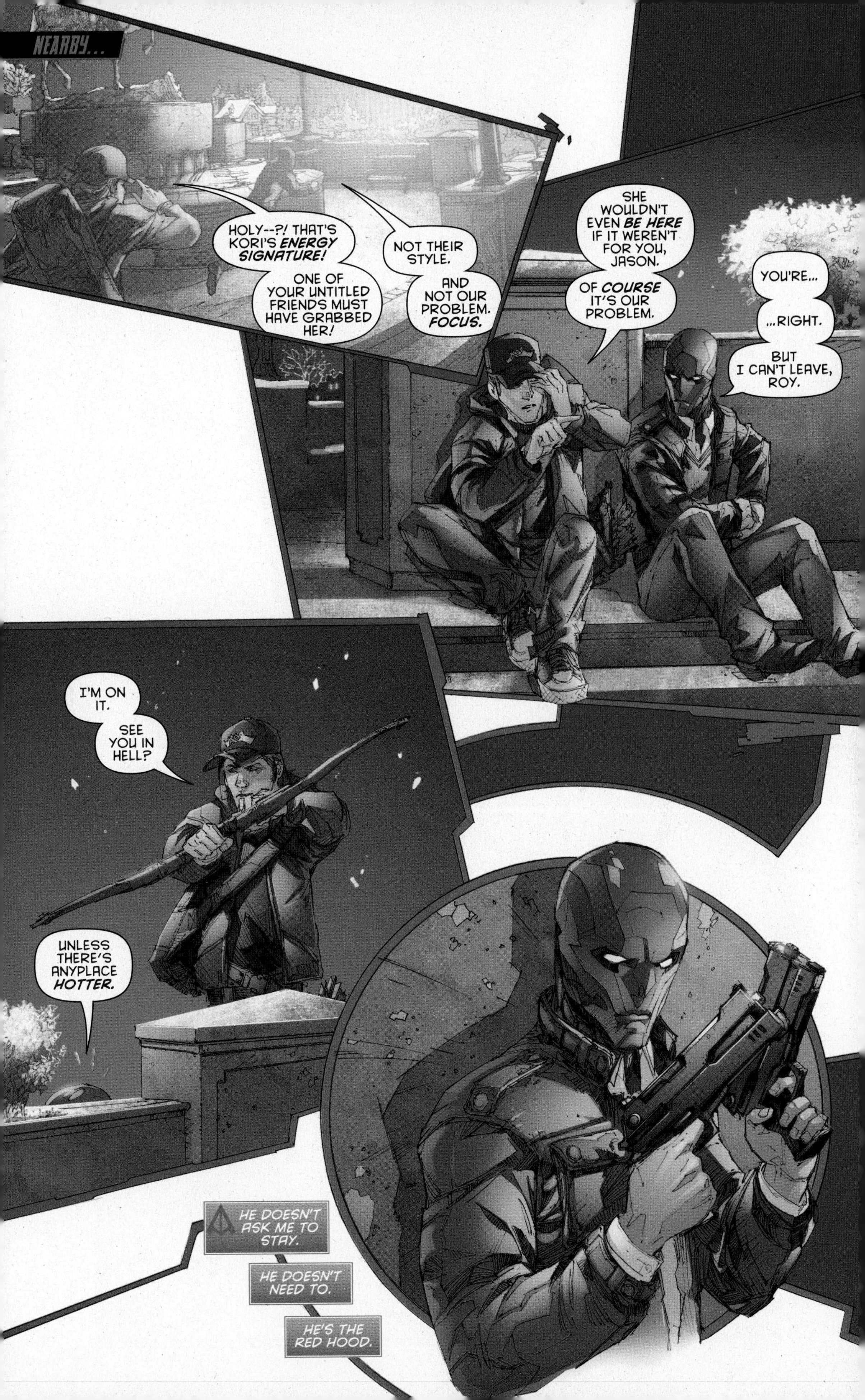
NEARBY...
HOLY--?! THAT'S KORI'S ENERGY SIGNATURE!
ONE OF YOUR UNTITLED FRIENDS MUST HAVE GRABBED HER!
NOT THEIR STYLE.
AND NOT OUR PROBLEM. FOCUS.
SHE WOULDN'T EVEN BE HERE IF IT WEREN'T FOR YOU, JASON.
OF COURSE IT'S OUR PROBLEM.
YOU'RE...
...RIGHT.
BUT I CAN'T LEAVE, ROY.
I'M ON IT.
SEE YOU IN HELL?
UNLESS THERE'S ANYPLACE HOTTER.
HE DOESN'T ASK ME TO STAY.
HE DOESN'T NEED TO.
HE'S THE RED HOOD.

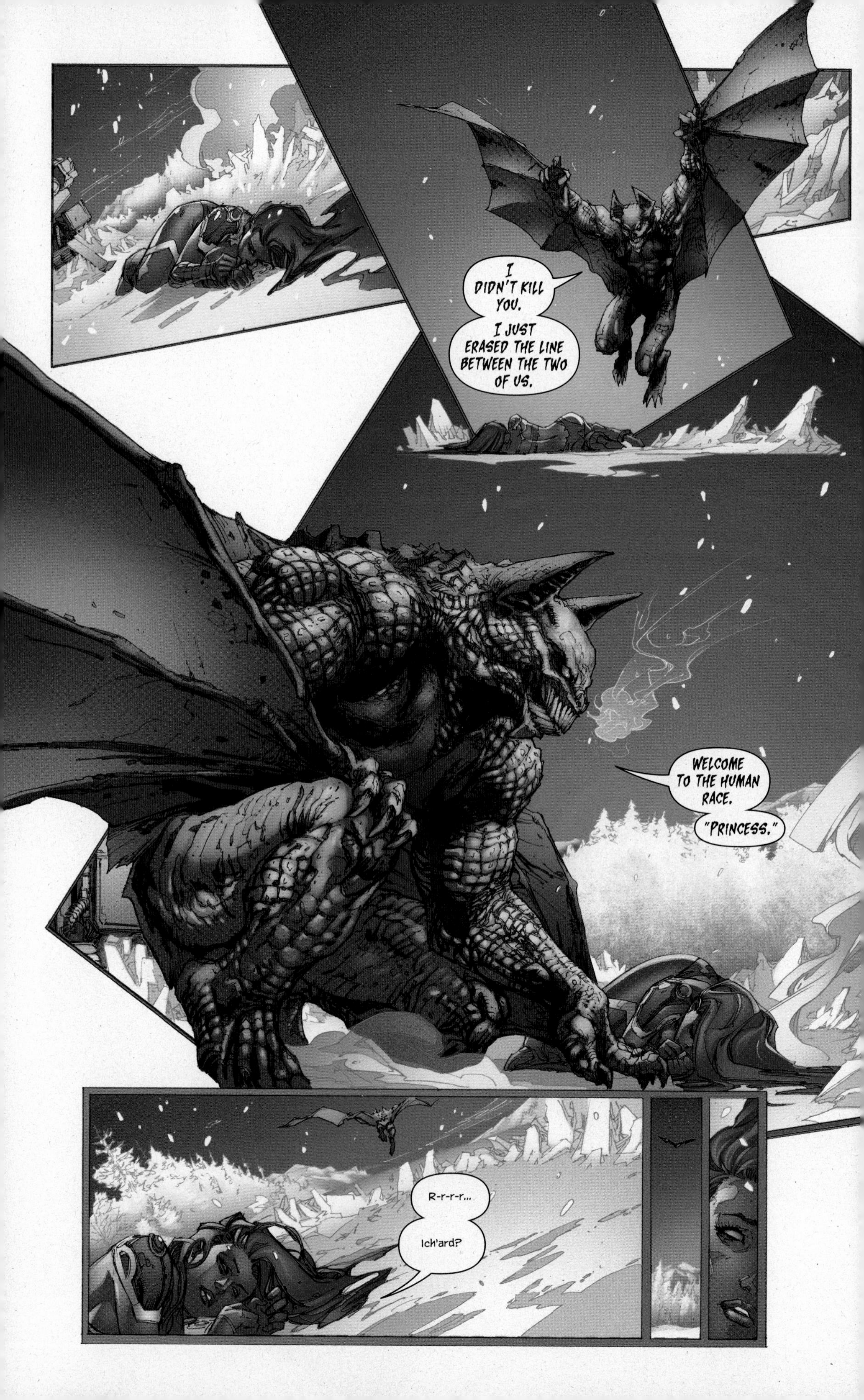
I DIDN'T KILL YOU.
I JUST ERASED THE LINE BETWEEN THE TWO OF US.
WELCOME TO THE HUMAN RACE.
"PRINCESS."
R-r-r-r...
Ich'ard?

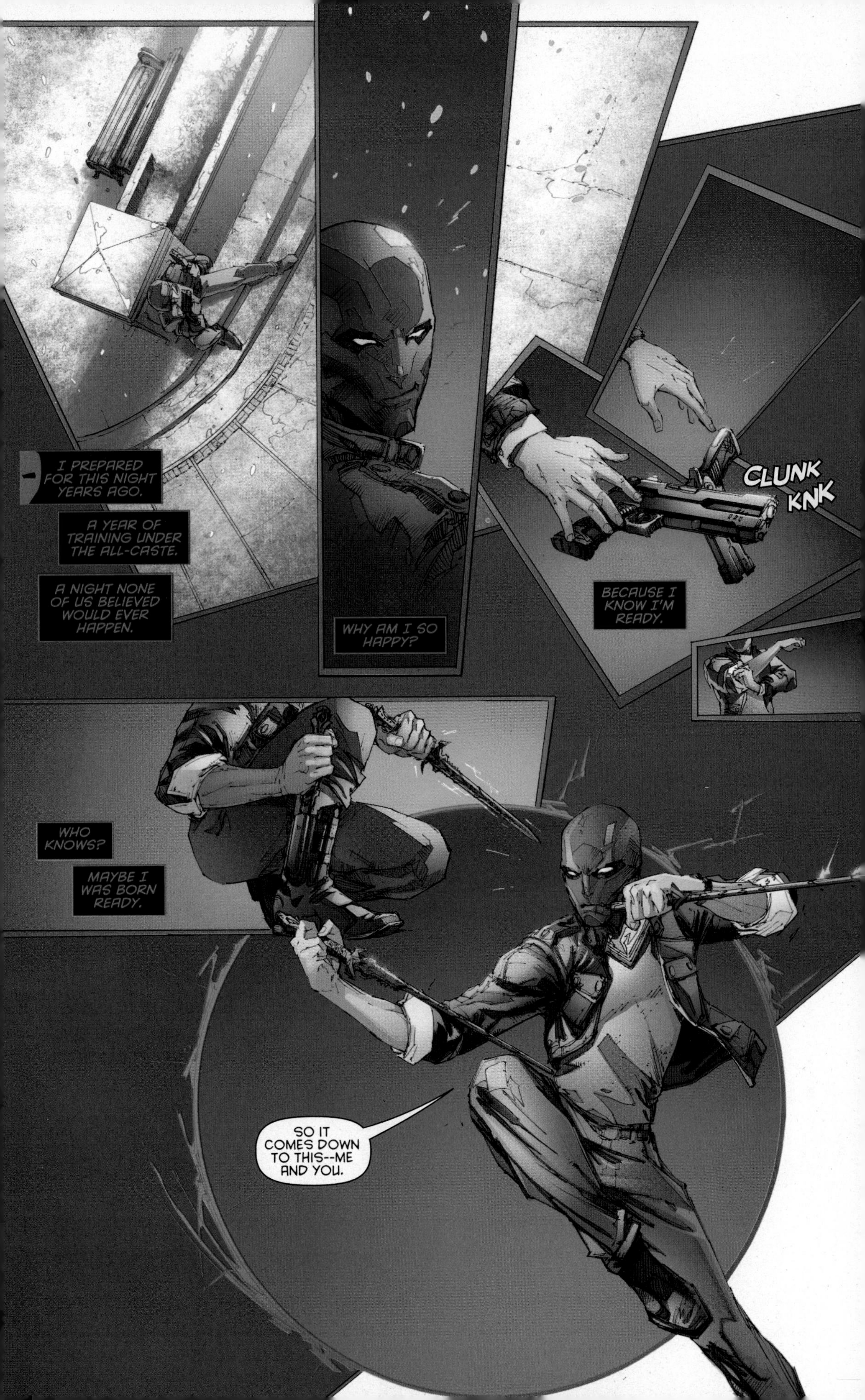
I PREPARED FOR THIS NIGHT YEARS AGO.
A YEAR OF TRAINING UNDER THE ALL-CASTE.
A NIGHT NONE OF US BELIEVED WOULD EVER HAPPEN.
WHY AM I SO HAPPY?
CLUNK
KNK
BECAUSE I KNOW I'M READY.
WHO KNOWS?
MAYBE I WAS BORN READY.
SO IT COMES DOWN TO THIS--ME AND YOU.

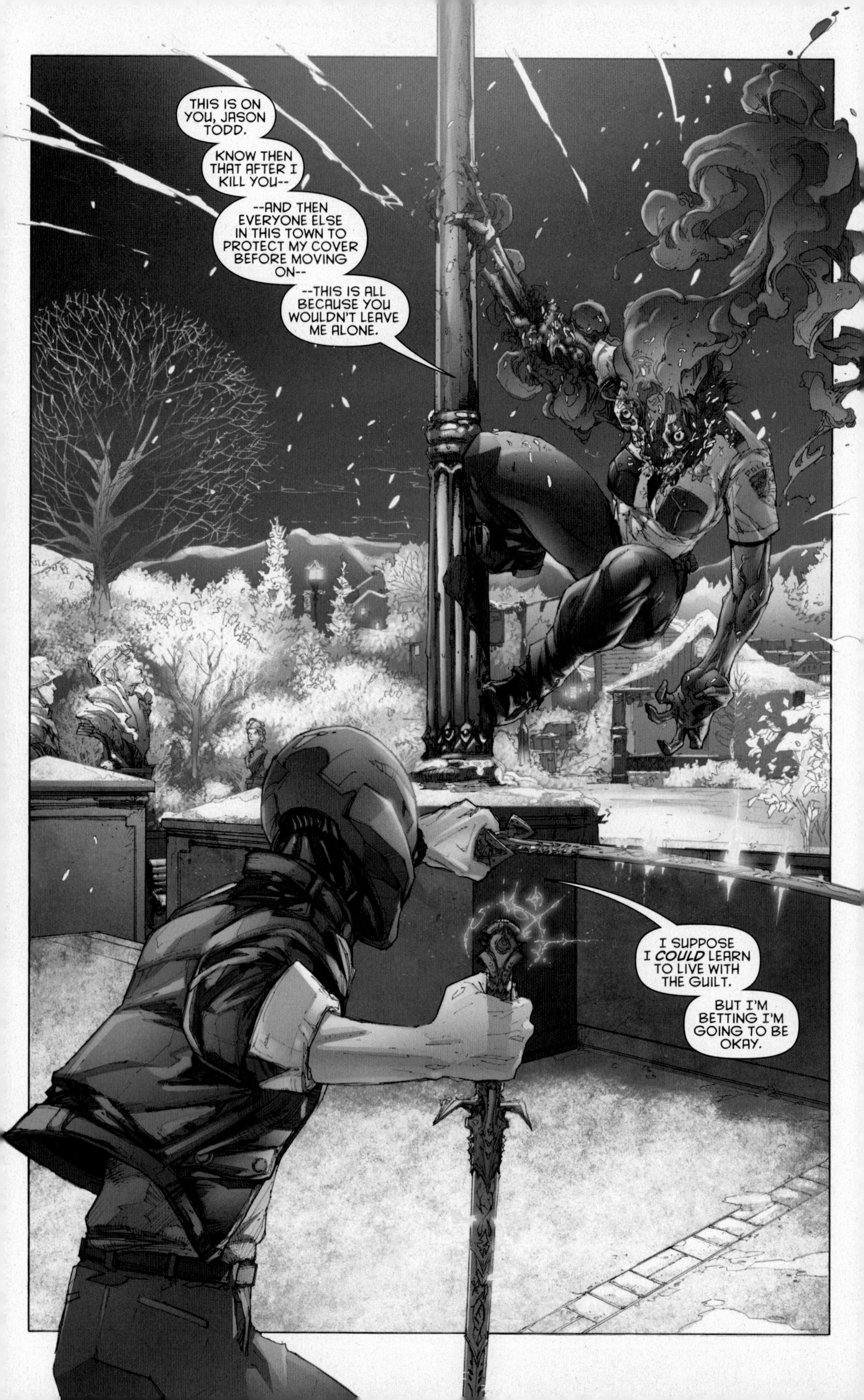
THIS IS ON YOU, JASON TODD.
KNOW THEN THAT AFTER I KILL YOU--
--AND THEN EVERYONE ELSE IN THIS TOWN TO PROTECT MY COVER BEFORE MOVING ON--
--THIS IS ALL BECAUSE YOU WOULDN'T LEAVE ME ALONE.
I SUPPOSE I ***COULD*** LEARN TO LIVE WITH THE GUILT.
BUT I'M BETTING I'M GOING TO BE OKAY.

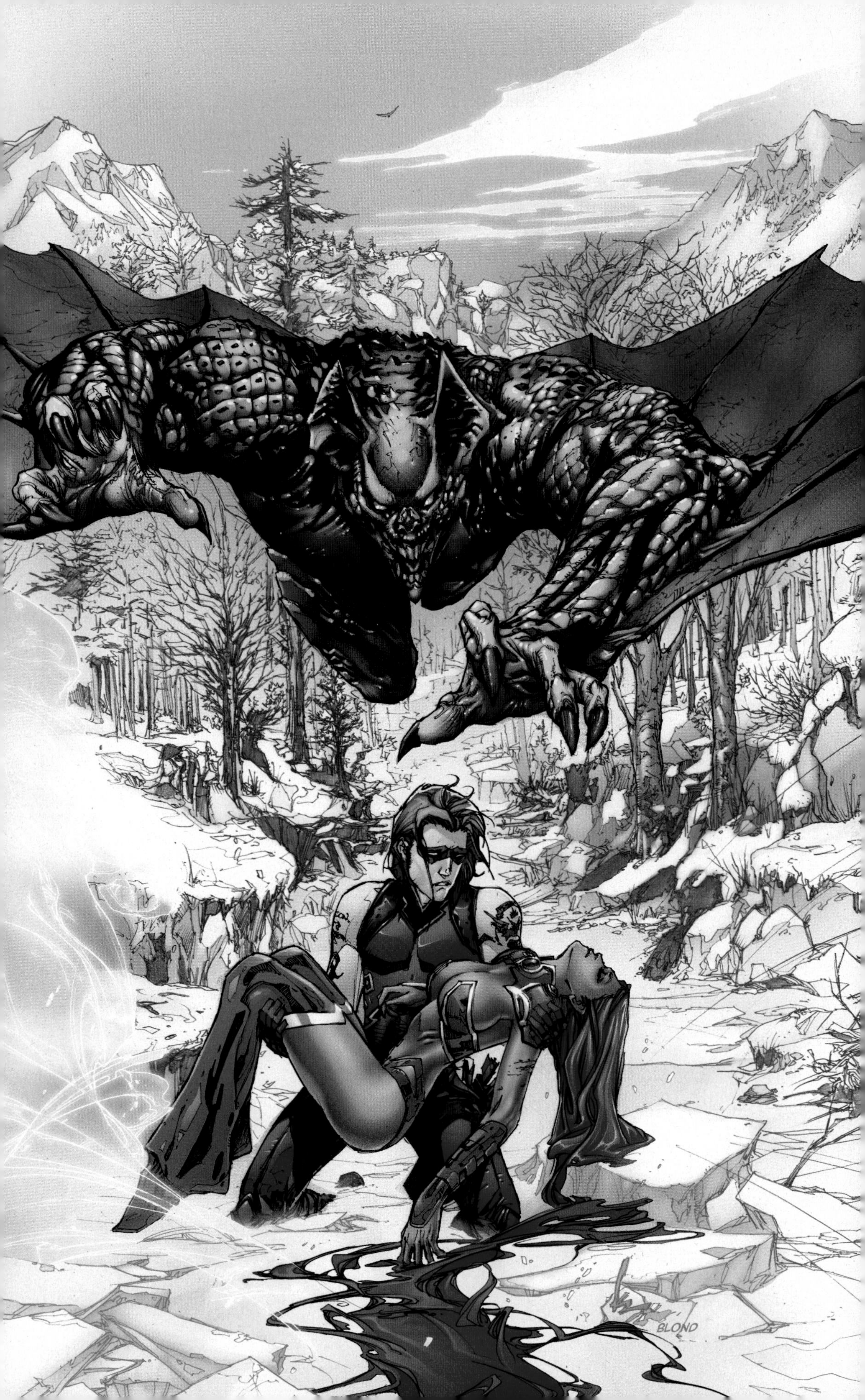
BLOND

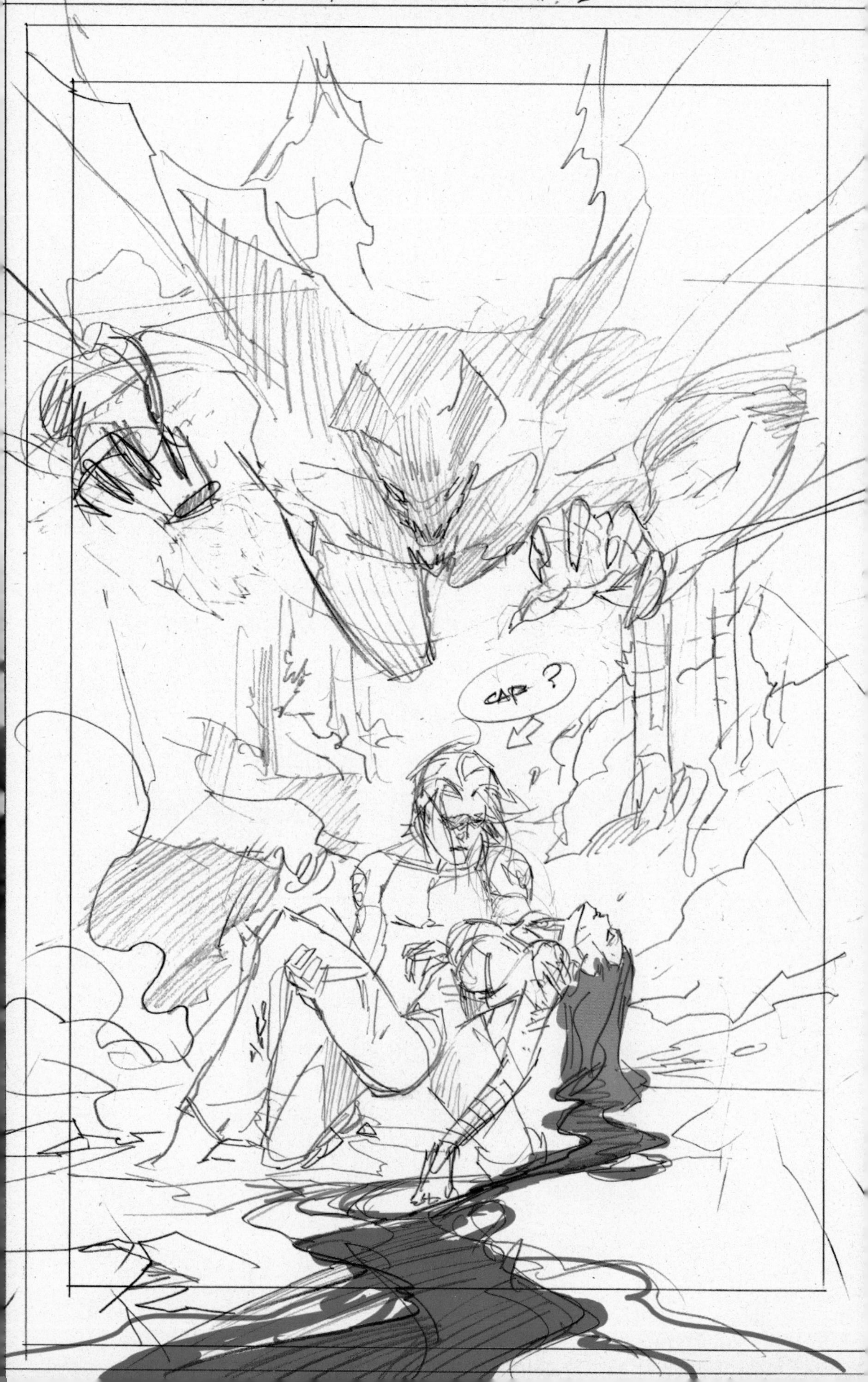
CAP ?

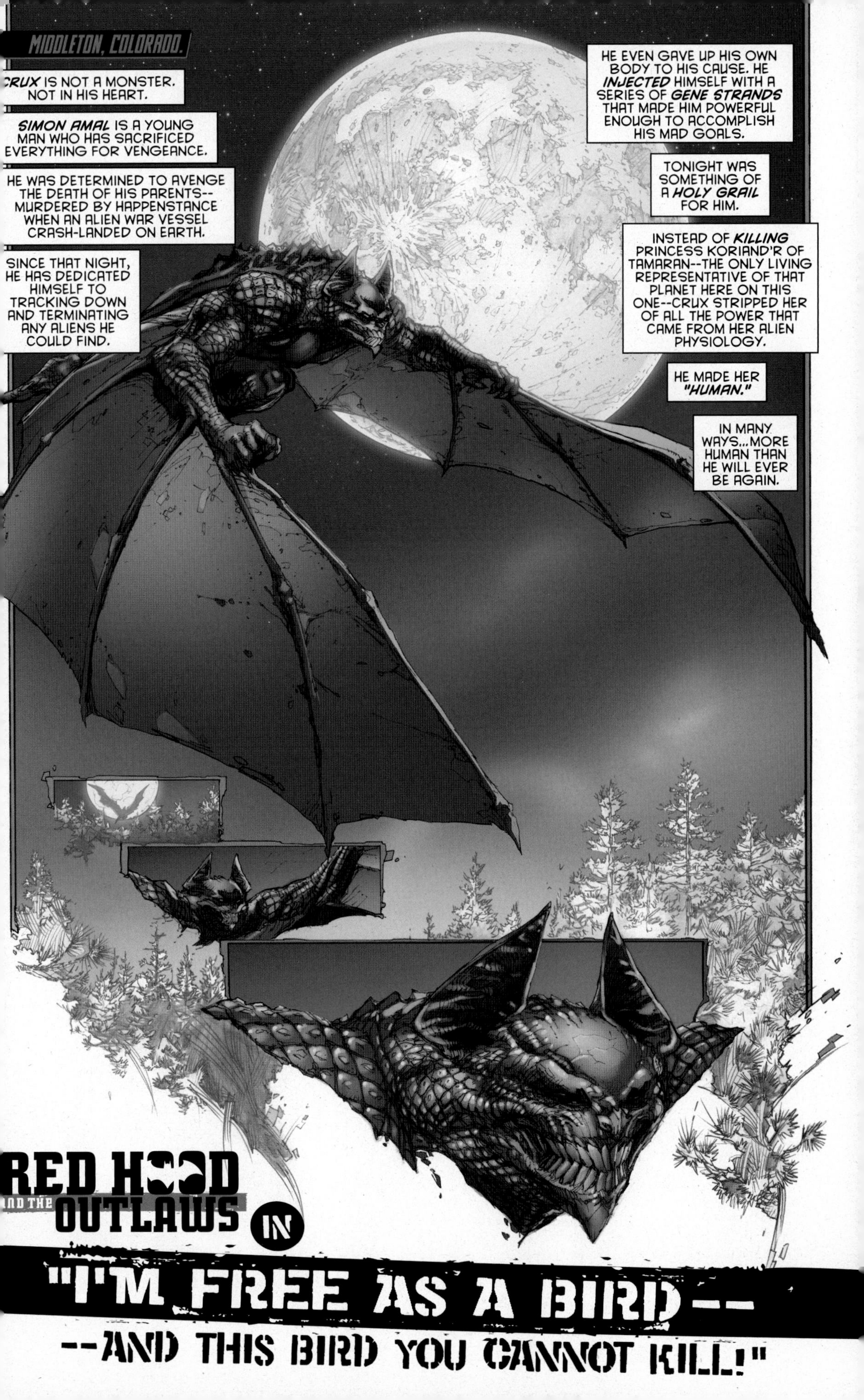
MIDDLETON, COLORADO.
CRUX IS NOT A MONSTER. NOT IN HIS HEART.
SIMON AMAL IS A YOUNG MAN WHO HAS SACRIFICED EVERYTHING FOR VENGEANCE.
HE WAS DETERMINED TO AVENGE THE DEATH OF HIS PARENTS-- MURDERED BY HAPPENSTANCE WHEN AN ALIEN WAR VESSEL CRASH-LANDED ON EARTH.
SINCE THAT NIGHT, HE HAS DEDICATED HIMSELF TO TRACKING DOWN AND TERMINATING ANY ALIENS HE COULD FIND.
HE EVEN GAVE UP HIS OWN BODY TO HIS CAUSE. HE INJECTED HIMSELF WITH A SERIES OF GENE STRANDS THAT MADE HIM POWERFUL ENOUGH TO ACCOMPLISH HIS MAD GOALS.
TONIGHT WAS SOMETHING OF A HOLY GRAIL FOR HIM.
INSTEAD OF KILLING PRINCESS KORIAND'R OF TAMARAN--THE ONLY LIVING REPRESENTATIVE OF THAT PLANET HERE ON THIS ONE--CRUX STRIPPED HER OF ALL THE POWER THAT CAME FROM HER ALIEN PHYSIOLOGY.
HE MADE HER "HUMAN."
IN MANY WAYS...MORE HUMAN THAN HE WILL EVER BE AGAIN.
RED HOOD AND THE OUTLAWS IN
"I'M FREE AS A BIRD--
--AND THIS BIRD YOU CANNOT KILL!"

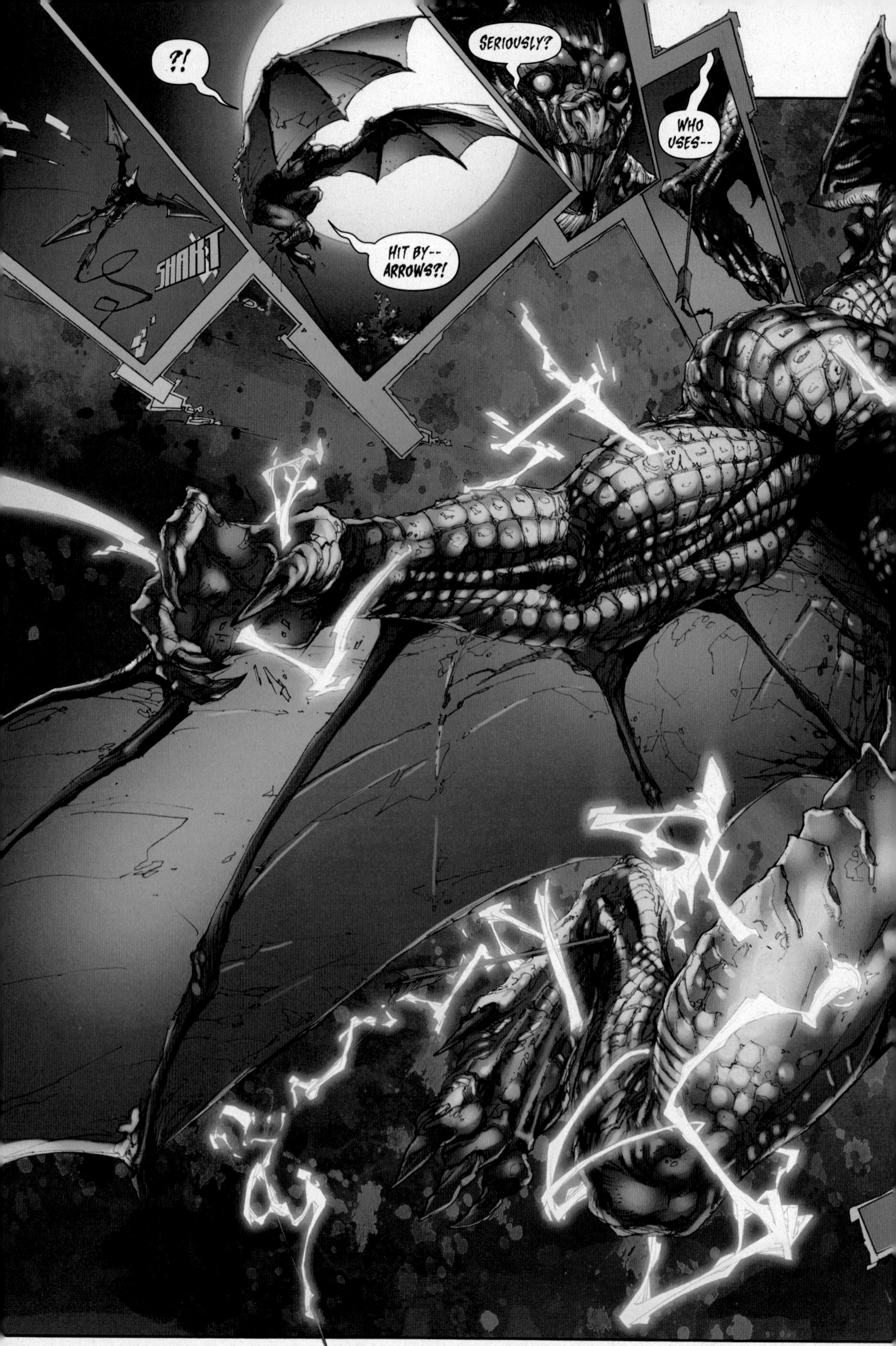
?!
SHAKT
HIT BY--
ARROWS?!
SERIOUSLY?
WHO
USES--

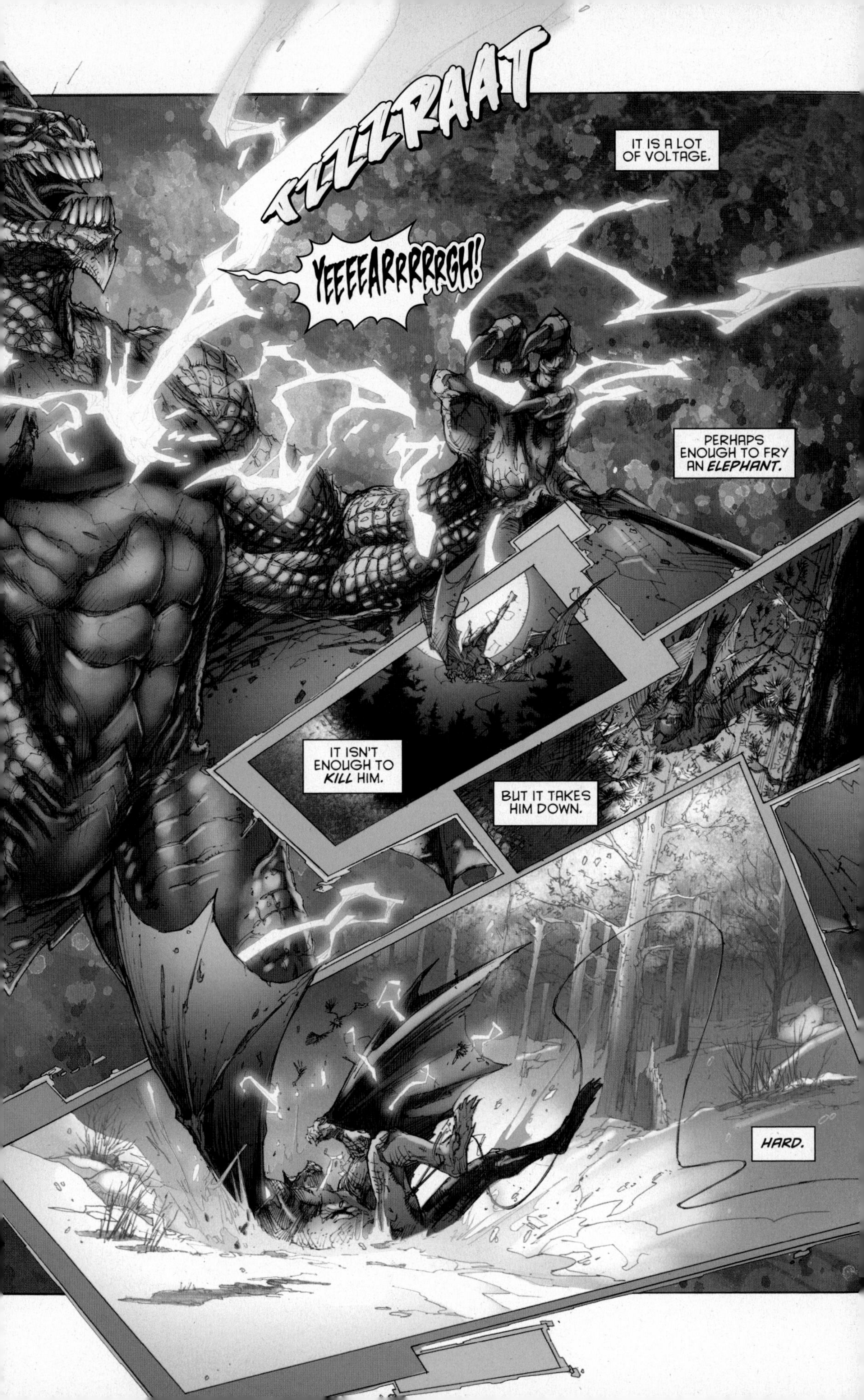
TZZZZRAAT
IT IS A LOT OF VOLTAGE.
YEEEEARRRRRGH!
PERHAPS ENOUGH TO FRY AN *ELEPHANT*.
IT ISN'T ENOUGH TO *KILL* HIM.
BUT IT TAKES HIM DOWN.
HARD.

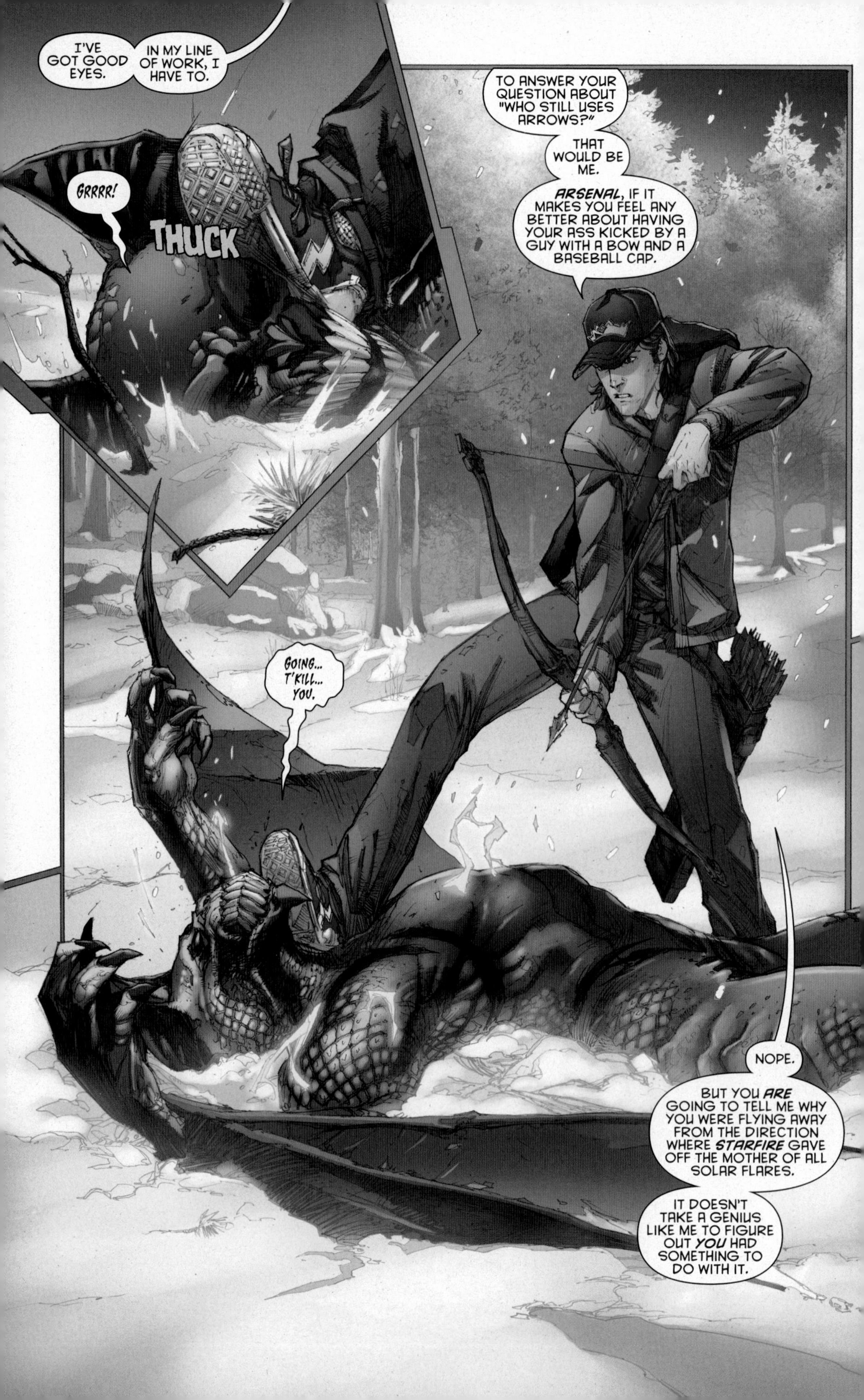
I'VE GOT GOOD EYES.
IN MY LINE OF WORK, I HAVE TO.
GRRRR!
THUCK
TO ANSWER YOUR QUESTION ABOUT "WHO STILL USES ARROWS?"
THAT WOULD BE ME.
ARSENAL, IF IT MAKES YOU FEEL ANY BETTER ABOUT HAVING YOUR ASS KICKED BY A GUY WITH A BOW AND A BASEBALL CAP.
GOING... T'KILL... YOU.
NOPE.
BUT YOU ARE GOING TO TELL ME WHY YOU WERE FLYING AWAY FROM THE DIRECTION WHERE STARFIRE GAVE OFF THE MOTHER OF ALL SOLAR FLARES.
IT DOESN'T TAKE A GENIUS LIKE ME TO FIGURE OUT YOU HAD SOMETHING TO DO WITH IT.

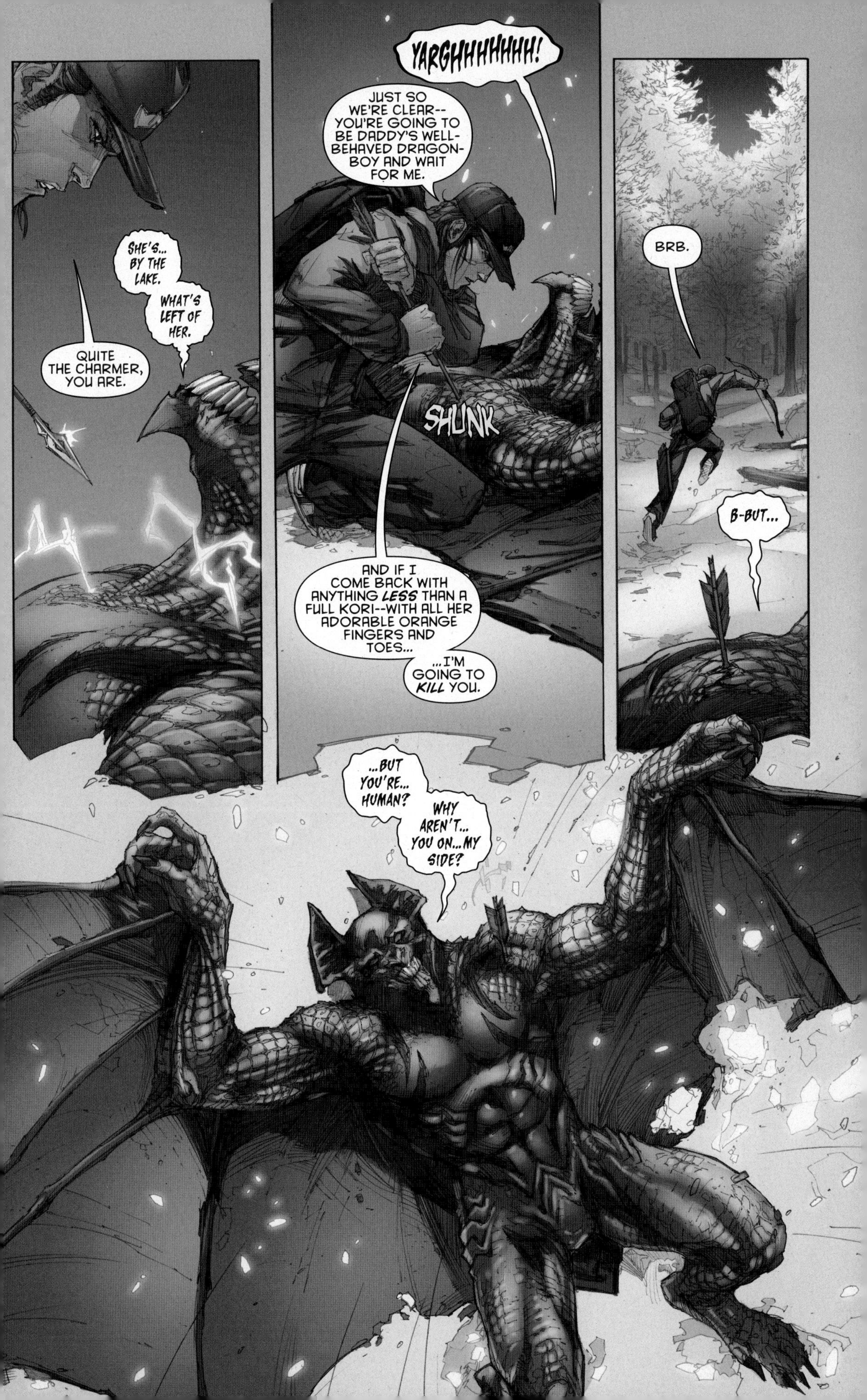
SHE'S... BY THE LAKE.
WHAT'S LEFT OF HER.
QUITE THE CHARMER, YOU ARE.
YARGHHHHHHH!
JUST SO WE'RE CLEAR-- YOU'RE GOING TO BE DADDY'S WELL-BEHAVED DRAGON-BOY AND WAIT FOR ME.
SHUNK
AND IF I COME BACK WITH ANYTHING *LESS* THAN A FULL KORI--WITH ALL HER ADORABLE ORANGE FINGERS AND TOES...
...I'M GOING TO *KILL* YOU.
BRB.
B-BUT...
...BUT YOU'RE... HUMAN?
WHY AREN'T... YOU ON...MY SIDE?

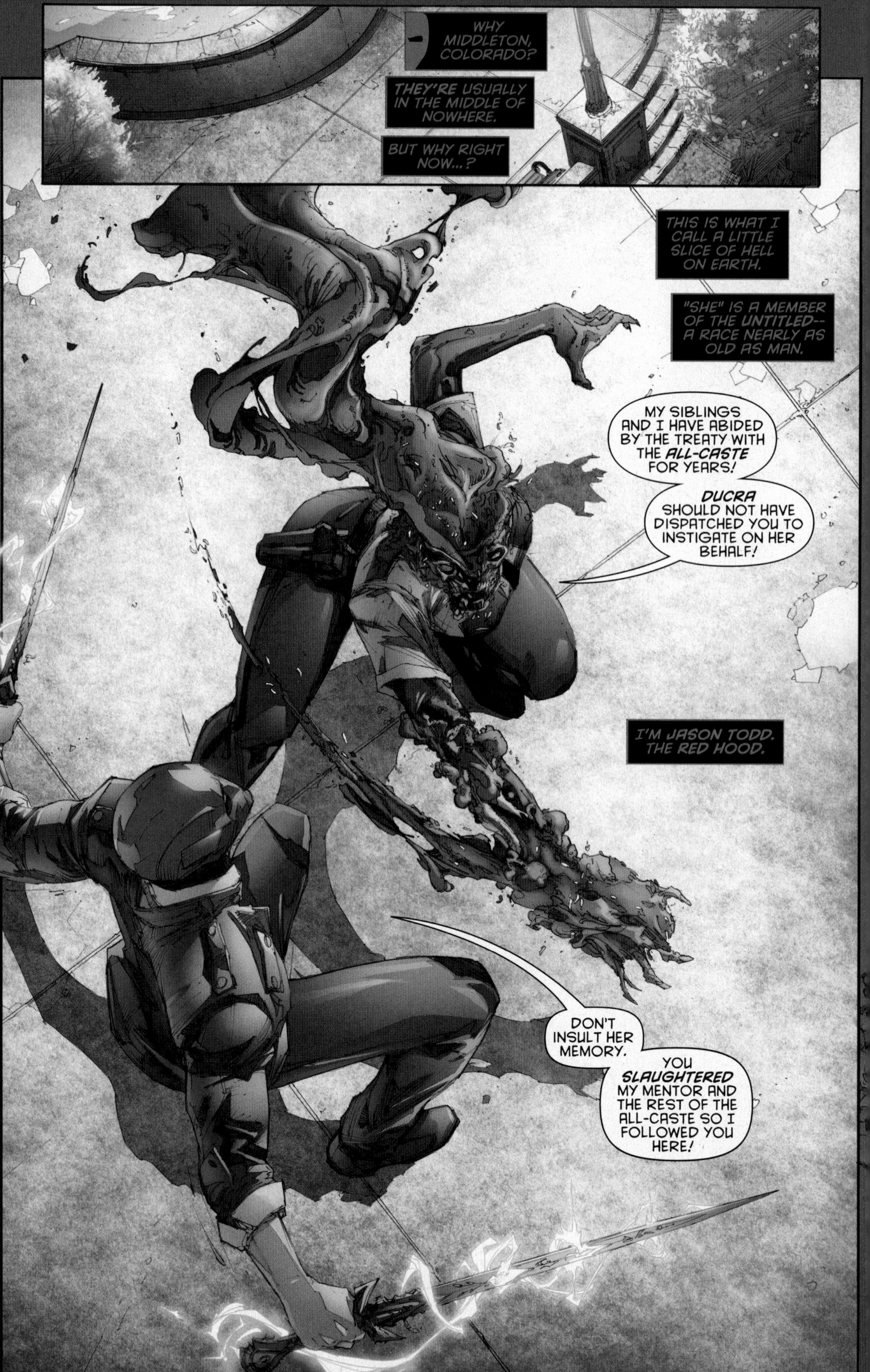
WHY MIDDLETON, COLORADO?
THEY'RE USUALLY IN THE MIDDLE OF NOWHERE.
BUT WHY RIGHT NOW...?
THIS IS WHAT I CALL A LITTLE SLICE OF HELL ON EARTH.
"SHE" IS A MEMBER OF THE UNTITLED-- A RACE NEARLY AS OLD AS MAN.
MY SIBLINGS AND I HAVE ABIDED BY THE TREATY WITH THE ALL-CASTE FOR YEARS!
DUCRA SHOULD NOT HAVE DISPATCHED YOU TO INSTIGATE ON HER BEHALF!
I'M JASON TODD. THE RED HOOD.
DON'T INSULT HER MEMORY.
YOU SLAUGHTERED MY MENTOR AND THE REST OF THE ALL-CASTE SO I FOLLOWED YOU HERE!

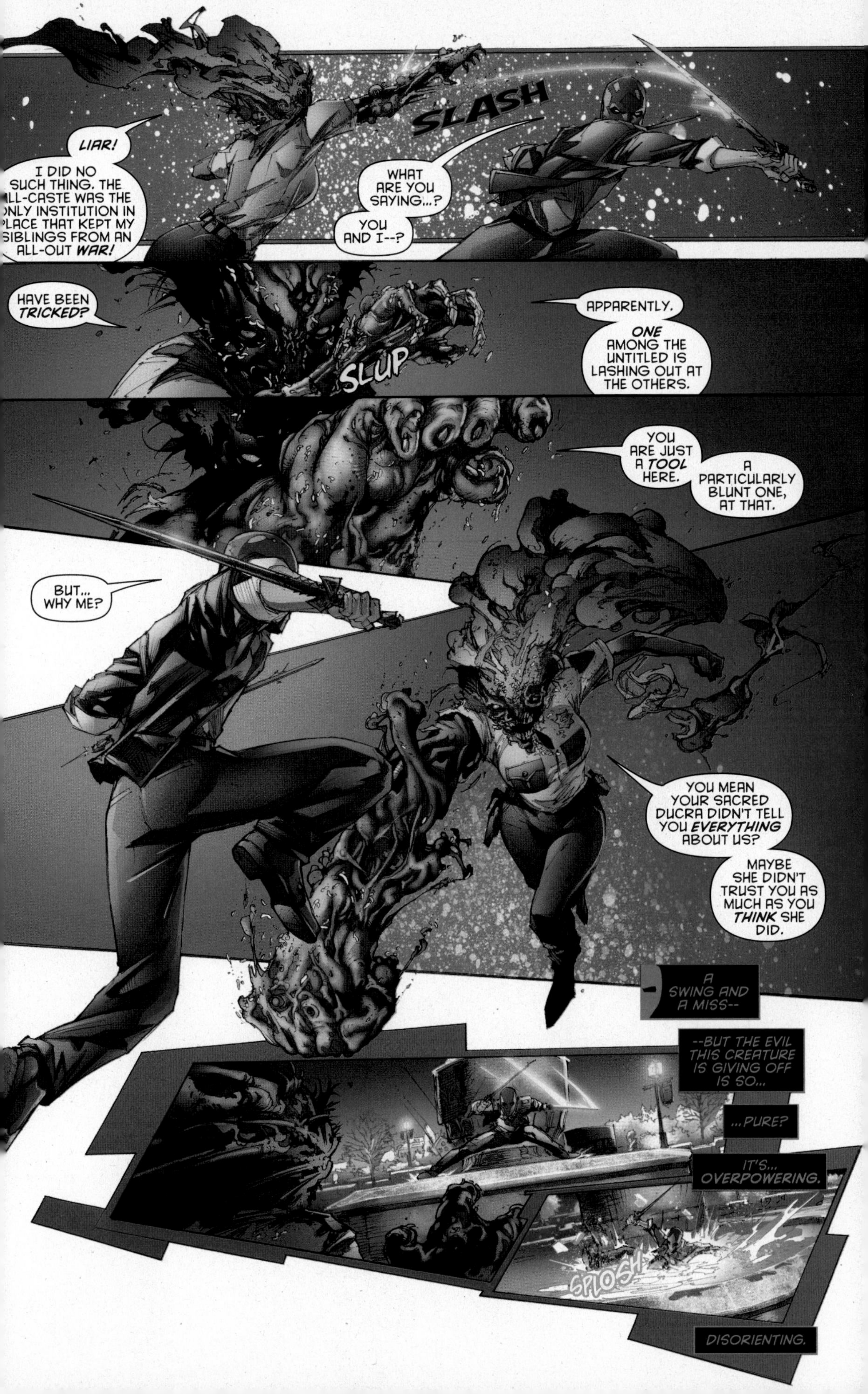
LIAR!
I DID NO SUCH THING. THE ALL-CASTE WAS THE ONLY INSTITUTION IN PLACE THAT KEPT MY SIBLINGS FROM AN ALL-OUT WAR!
SLASH
WHAT ARE YOU SAYING...?
YOU AND I--?
HAVE BEEN TRICKED?
SLUP
APPARENTLY.
ONE AMONG THE UNTITLED IS LASHING OUT AT THE OTHERS.
YOU ARE JUST A TOOL HERE.
A PARTICULARLY BLUNT ONE, AT THAT.
BUT... WHY ME?
YOU MEAN YOUR SACRED DUCRA DIDN'T TELL YOU EVERYTHING ABOUT US?
MAYBE SHE DIDN'T TRUST YOU AS MUCH AS YOU THINK SHE DID.
A SWING AND A MISS--
--BUT THE EVIL THIS CREATURE IS GIVING OFF IS SO...
...PURE?
IT'S... OVERPOWERING.
SPLOSH
DISORIENTING.

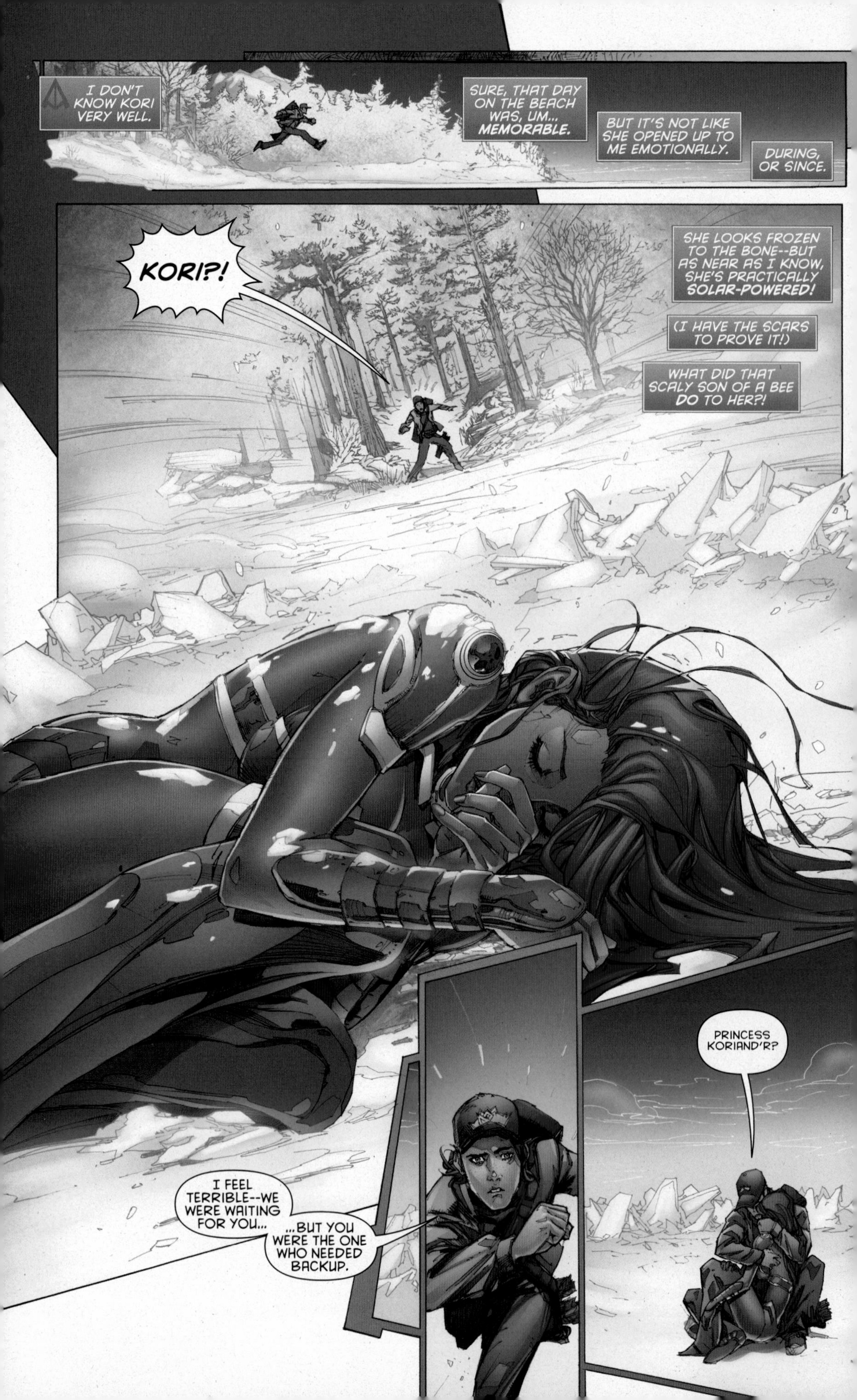
I DON'T KNOW KORI VERY WELL.
SURE, THAT DAY ON THE BEACH WAS, UM... MEMORABLE.
BUT IT'S NOT LIKE SHE OPENED UP TO ME EMOTIONALLY.
DURING, OR SINCE.
KORI?!
SHE LOOKS FROZEN TO THE BONE--BUT AS NEAR AS I KNOW, SHE'S PRACTICALLY SOLAR-POWERED!
(I HAVE THE SCARS TO PROVE IT!)
WHAT DID THAT SCALY SON OF A BEE DO TO HER?!
PRINCESS KORIAND'R?
I FEEL TERRIBLE--WE WERE WAITING FOR YOU...
...BUT YOU WERE THE ONE WHO NEEDED BACKUP.

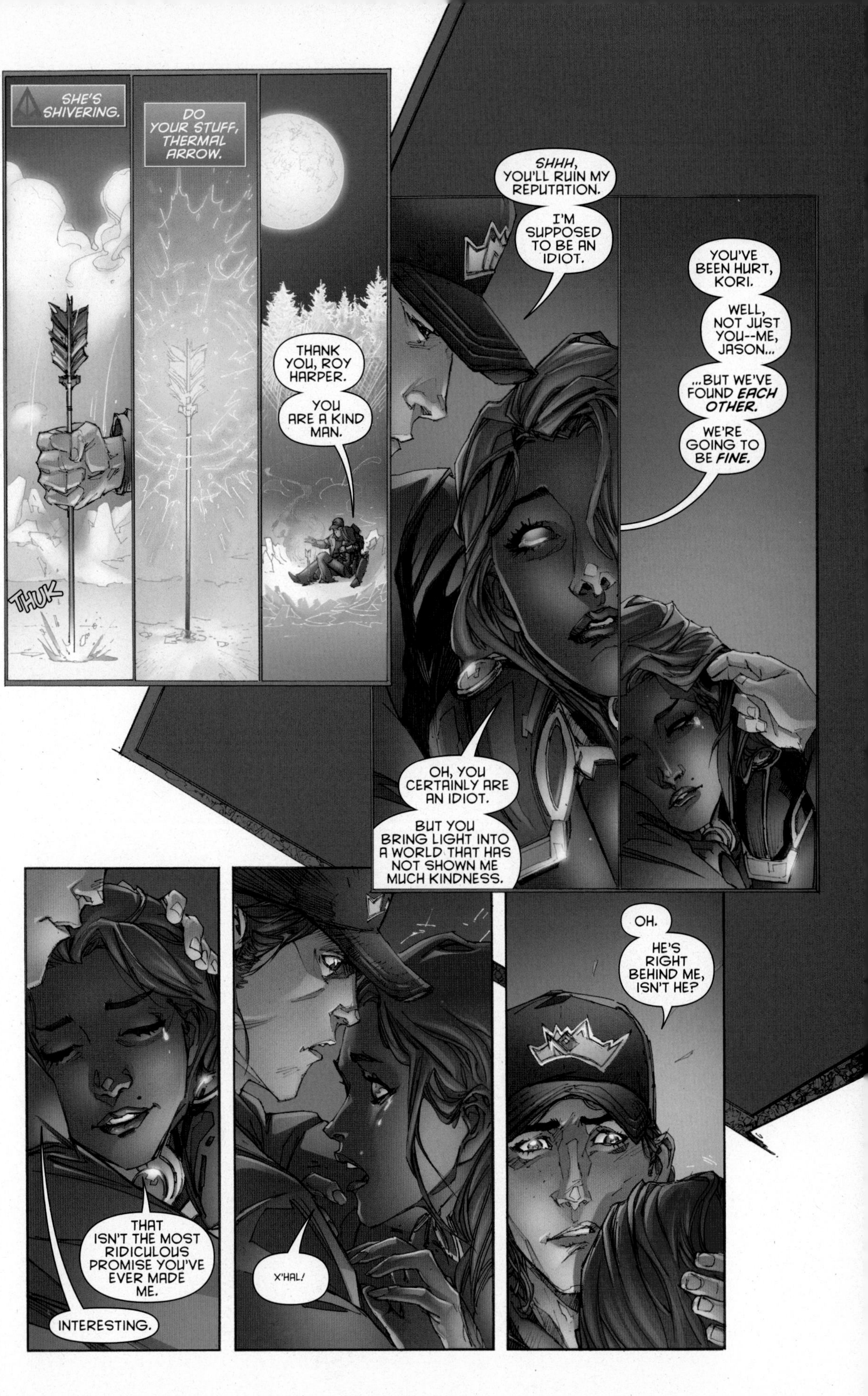
SHE'S SHIVERING.
THUK
DO YOUR STUFF, THERMAL ARROW.
THANK YOU, ROY HARPER.
YOU ARE A KIND MAN.
SHHH, YOU'LL RUIN MY REPUTATION.
I'M SUPPOSED TO BE AN IDIOT.
OH, YOU CERTAINLY ARE AN IDIOT.
BUT YOU BRING LIGHT INTO A WORLD THAT HAS NOT SHOWN ME MUCH KINDNESS.
YOU'VE BEEN HURT, KORI.
WELL, NOT JUST YOU--ME, JASON...
...BUT WE'VE FOUND EACH OTHER.
WE'RE GOING TO BE FINE.
THAT ISN'T THE MOST RIDICULOUS PROMISE YOU'VE EVER MADE ME.
INTERESTING.
X'HAL!
OH.
HE'S RIGHT BEHIND ME, ISN'T HE?

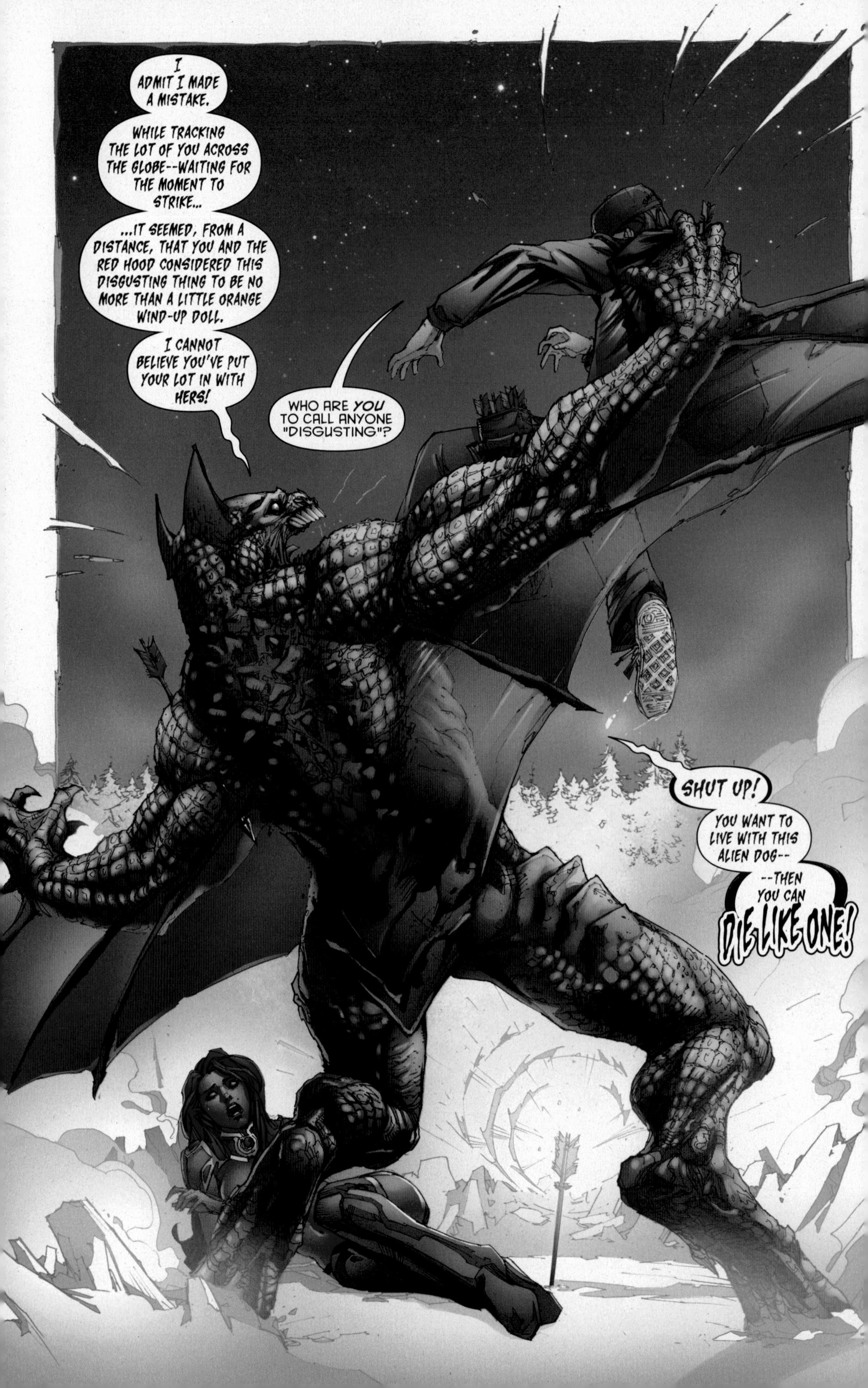
I ADMIT I MADE A MISTAKE.
WHILE TRACKING THE LOT OF YOU ACROSS THE GLOBE--WAITING FOR THE MOMENT TO STRIKE...
...IT SEEMED, FROM A DISTANCE, THAT YOU AND THE RED HOOD CONSIDERED THIS DISGUSTING THING TO BE NO MORE THAN A LITTLE ORANGE WIND-UP DOLL.
I CANNOT BELIEVE YOU'VE PUT YOUR LOT IN WITH HERS!
WHO ARE *YOU* TO CALL ANYONE "DISGUSTING"?
SHUT UP!
YOU WANT TO LIVE WITH THIS ALIEN DOG--
--THEN YOU CAN
DIE LIKE ONE!

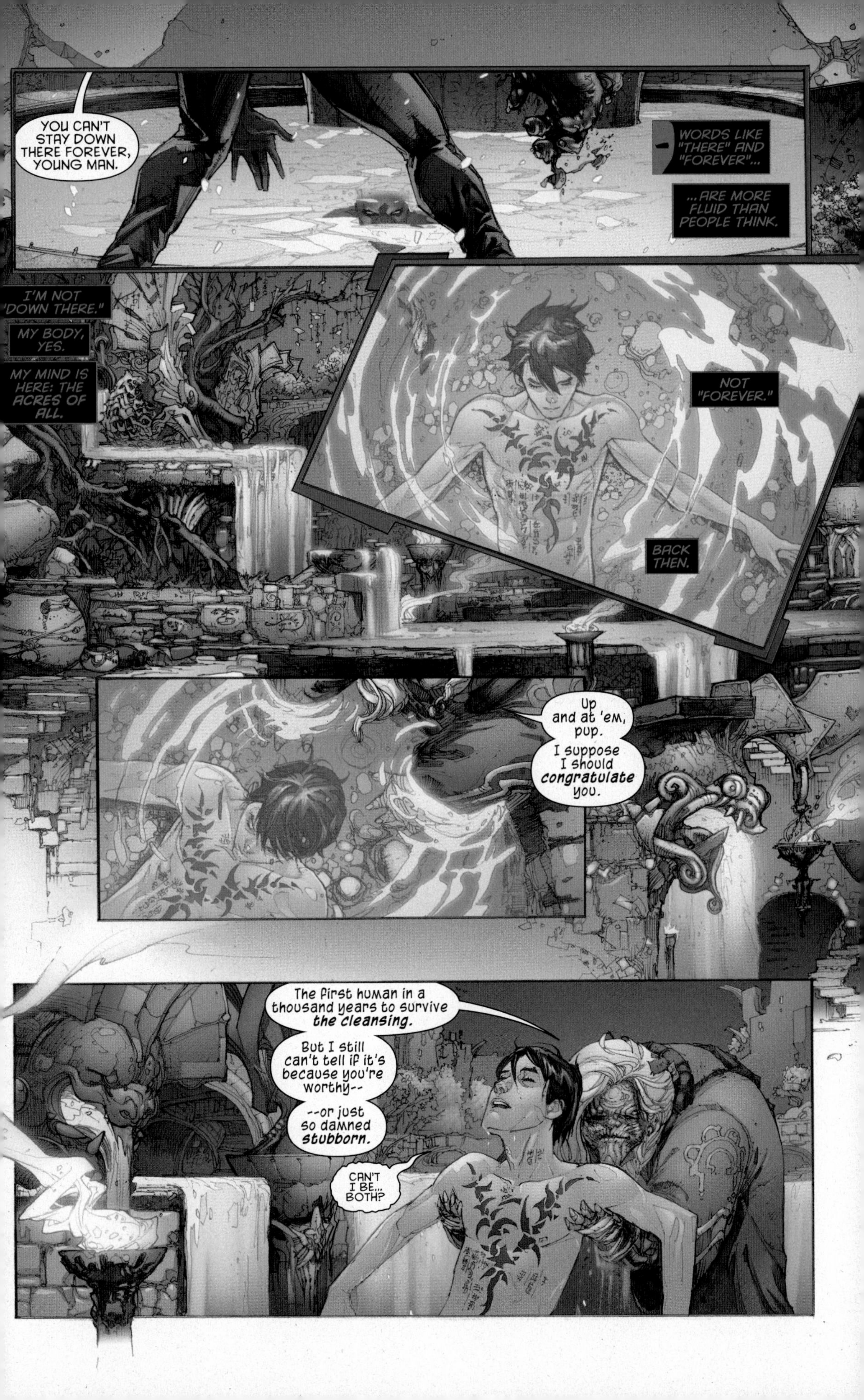
YOU CAN'T STAY DOWN THERE FOREVER, YOUNG MAN.
WORDS LIKE "THERE" AND "FOREVER"...
...ARE MORE FLUID THAN PEOPLE THINK.
I'M NOT "DOWN THERE."
MY BODY, YES.
MY MIND IS HERE: THE ACRES OF ALL.
NOT "FOREVER."
BACK THEN.
Up and at 'em, pup.
I suppose I should congratulate you.
The first human in a thousand years to survive the cleansing.
But I still can't tell if it's because you're worthy--
--or just so damned stubborn.
CAN'T I BE... BOTH?

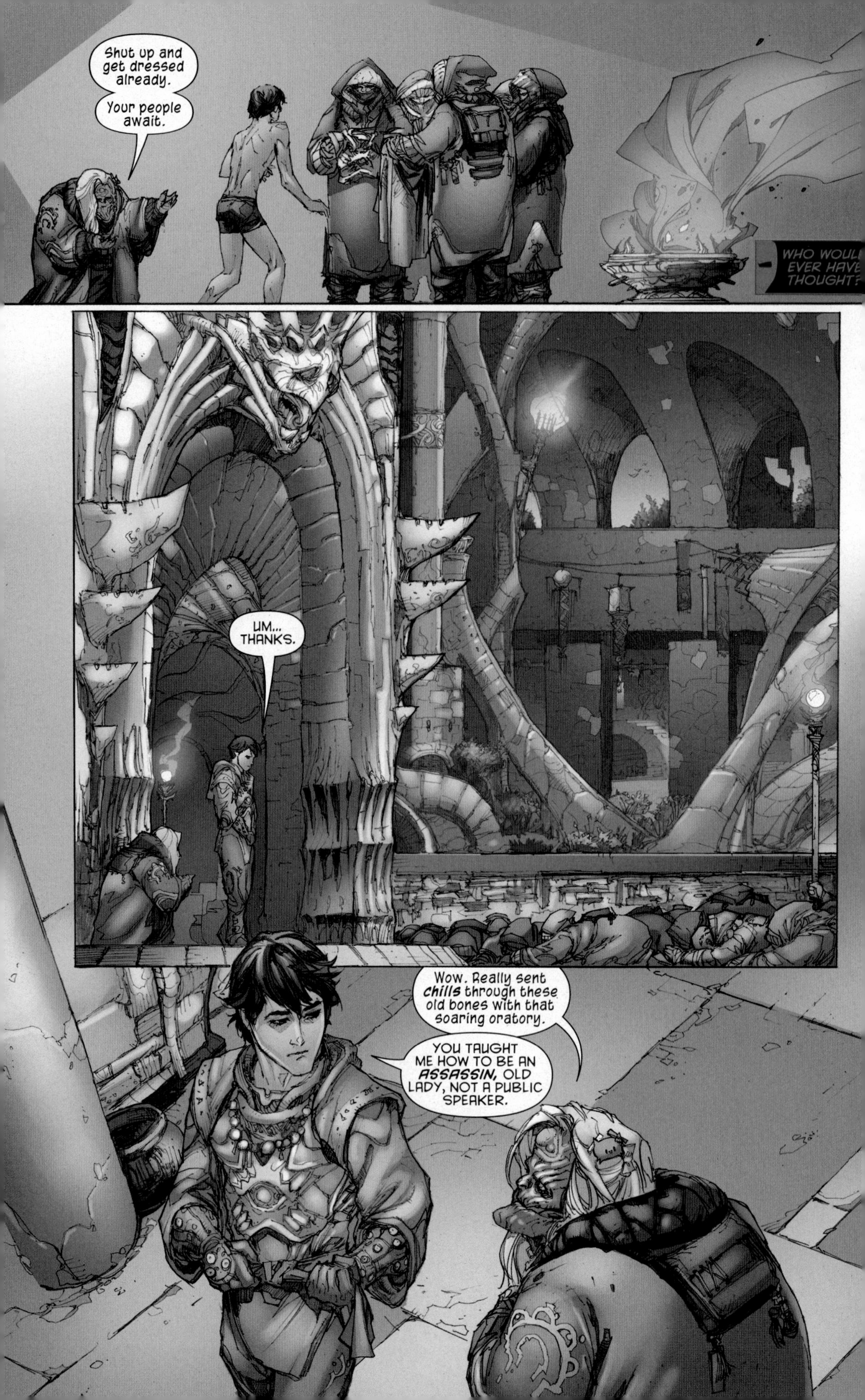
Shut up and get dressed already.
Your people await.
WHO WOUL
EVER HAVE
THOUGHT?
UM... THANKS.
Wow. Really sent *chills* through these old bones with that soaring oratory.
YOU TAUGHT ME HOW TO BE AN *ASSASSIN,* OLD LADY, NOT A PUBLIC SPEAKER.

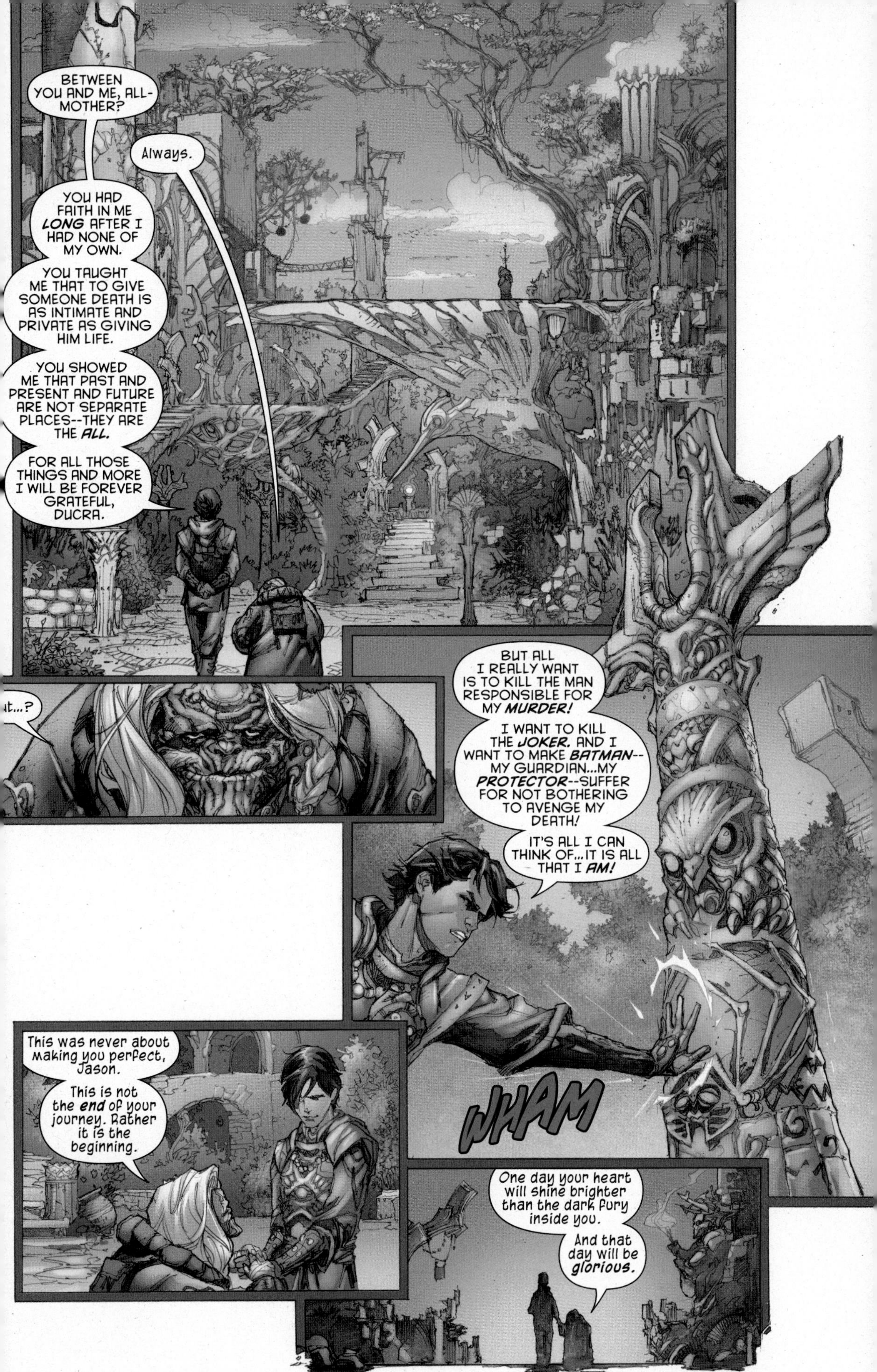

BETWEEN YOU AND ME, ALL-MOTHER?
Always.
YOU HAD FAITH IN ME LONG AFTER I HAD NONE OF MY OWN.
YOU TAUGHT ME THAT TO GIVE SOMEONE DEATH IS AS INTIMATE AND PRIVATE AS GIVING HIM LIFE.
YOU SHOWED ME THAT PAST AND PRESENT AND FUTURE ARE NOT SEPARATE PLACES--THEY ARE THE ALL.
FOR ALL THOSE THINGS AND MORE I WILL BE FOREVER GRATEFUL, DUCRA.
BUT ALL I REALLY WANT IS TO KILL THE MAN RESPONSIBLE FOR MY MURDER!
I WANT TO KILL THE JOKER. AND I WANT TO MAKE BATMAN--MY GUARDIAN...MY PROTECTOR--SUFFER FOR NOT BOTHERING TO AVENGE MY DEATH!
IT'S ALL I CAN THINK OF...IT IS ALL THAT I AM!
WHAM
This was never about making you perfect, Jason.
This is not the end of your journey. Rather it is the beginning.
One day your heart will shine brighter than the dark fury inside you.
And that day will be glorious.

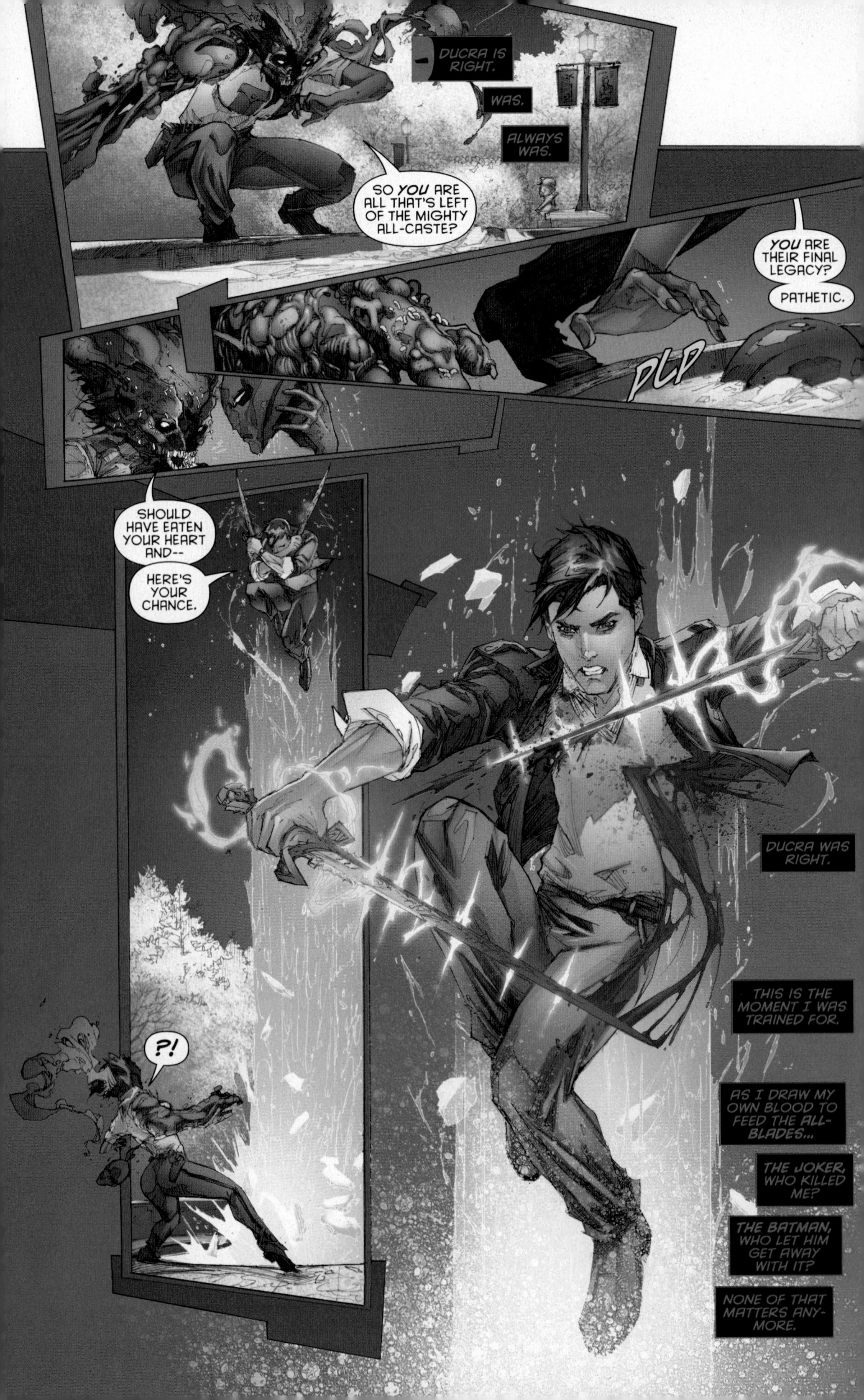

DUCRA IS RIGHT.
WAS.
ALWAYS WAS.
SO YOU ARE ALL THAT'S LEFT OF THE MIGHTY ALL-CASTE?
YOU ARE THEIR FINAL LEGACY?
PATHETIC.
PLP
SHOULD HAVE EATEN YOUR HEART AND--
HERE'S YOUR CHANCE.
?!
DUCRA WAS RIGHT.
THIS IS THE MOMENT I WAS TRAINED FOR.
AS I DRAW MY OWN BLOOD TO FEED THE ALL-BLADES...
THE JOKER, WHO KILLED ME?
THE BATMAN, WHO LET HIM GET AWAY WITH IT?
NONE OF THAT MATTERS ANY-MORE.

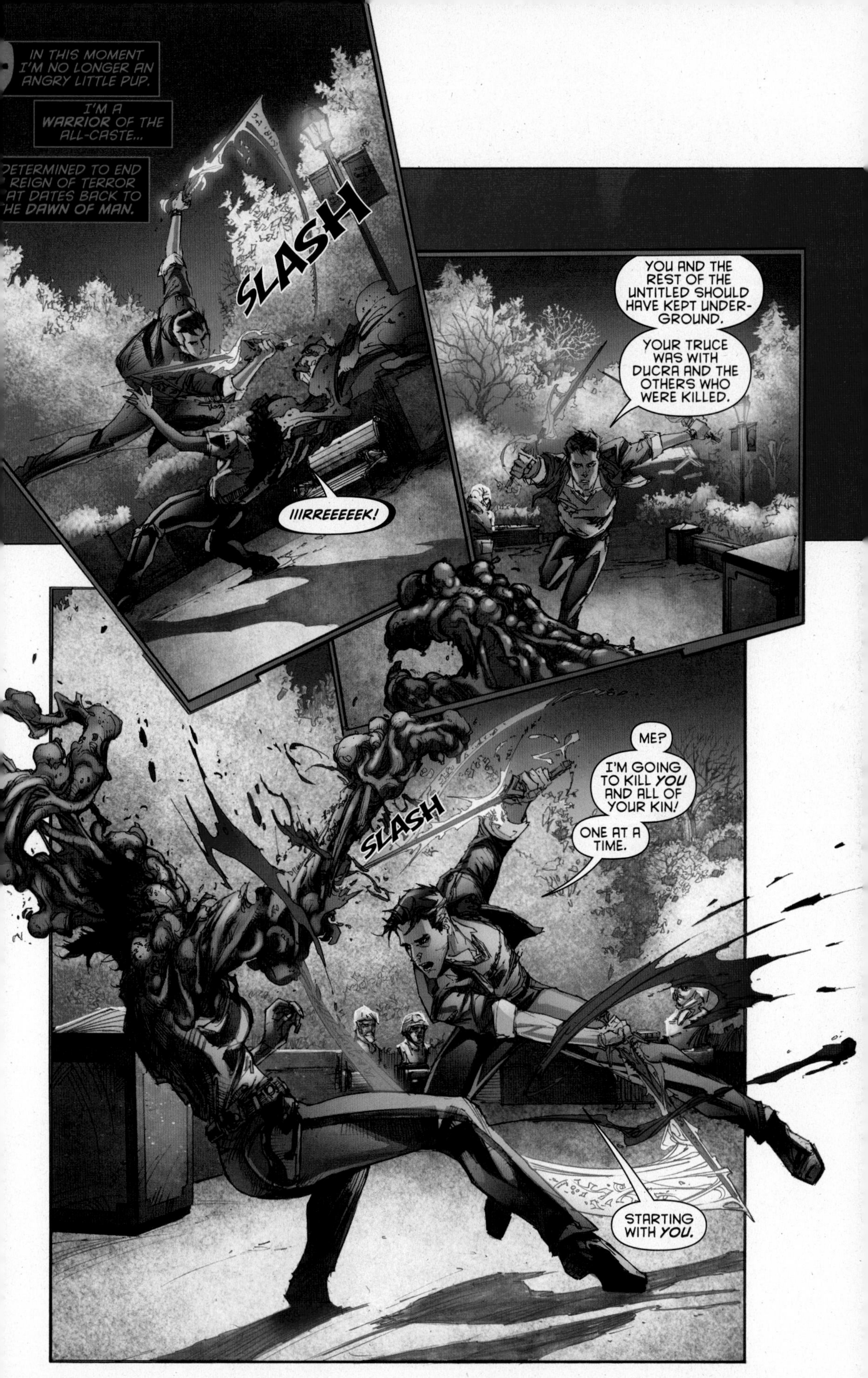
IN THIS MOMENT I'M NO LONGER AN ANGRY LITTLE PUP.
I'M A WARRIOR OF THE ALL-CASTE...
DETERMINED TO END REIGN OF TERROR AT DATES BACK TO HE DAWN OF MAN.
SLASH
IIIRREEEEEK!
YOU AND THE REST OF THE UNTITLED SHOULD HAVE KEPT UNDER-GROUND.
YOUR TRUCE WAS WITH DUCRA AND THE OTHERS WHO WERE KILLED.
ME?
I'M GOING TO KILL YOU AND ALL OF YOUR KIN!
ONE AT A TIME.
SLASH
STARTING WITH YOU.

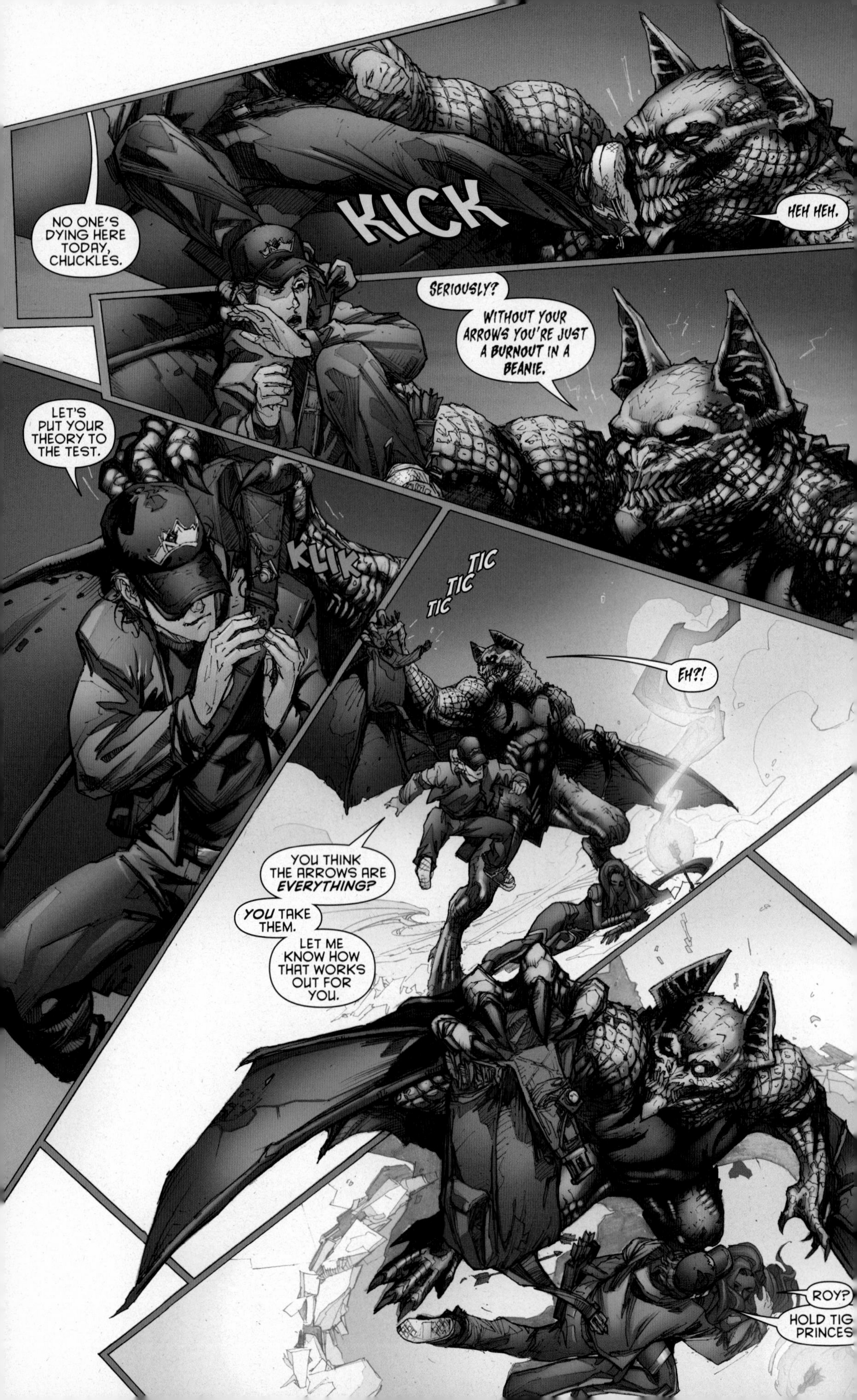
NO ONE'S DYING HERE TODAY, CHUCKLES.
KICK
HEH HEH.
SERIOUSLY?
WITHOUT YOUR ARROWS YOU'RE JUST A BURNOUT IN A BEANIE.
LET'S PUT YOUR THEORY TO THE TEST.
KLIK
TIC TIC TIC
EH?!
YOU THINK THE ARROWS ARE *EVERYTHING?*
YOU TAKE THEM.
LET ME KNOW HOW THAT WORKS OUT FOR YOU.
ROY?
HOLD TIG
PRINCES

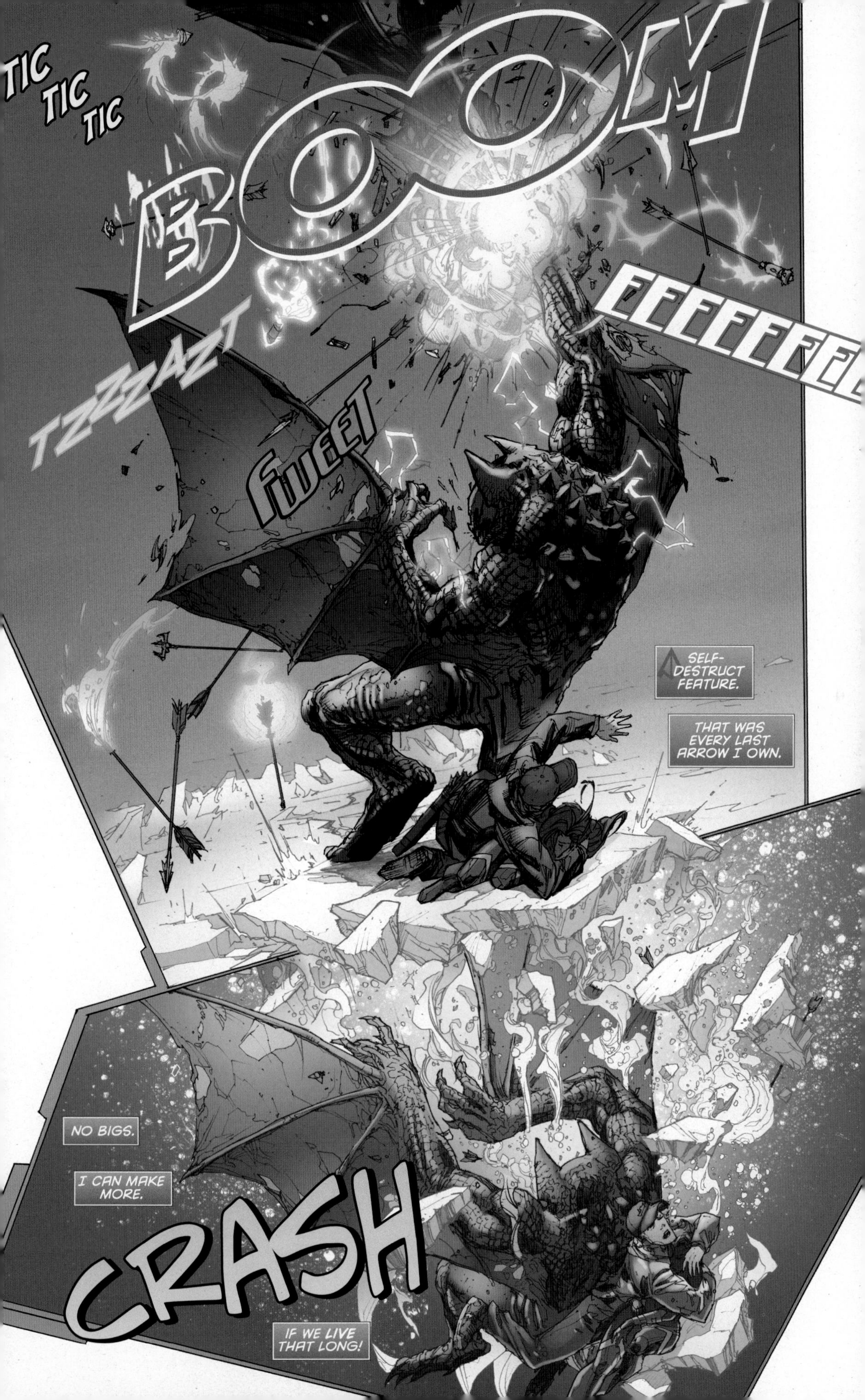
TIC
TIC
TIC
BOOM
EEEEEEEEE
TZZZAZT
FWEET
SELF-DESTRUCT FEATURE.
THAT WAS EVERY LAST ARROW I OWN.
NO BIGS.
I CAN MAKE MORE.
CRASH
IF WE LIVE THAT LONG!

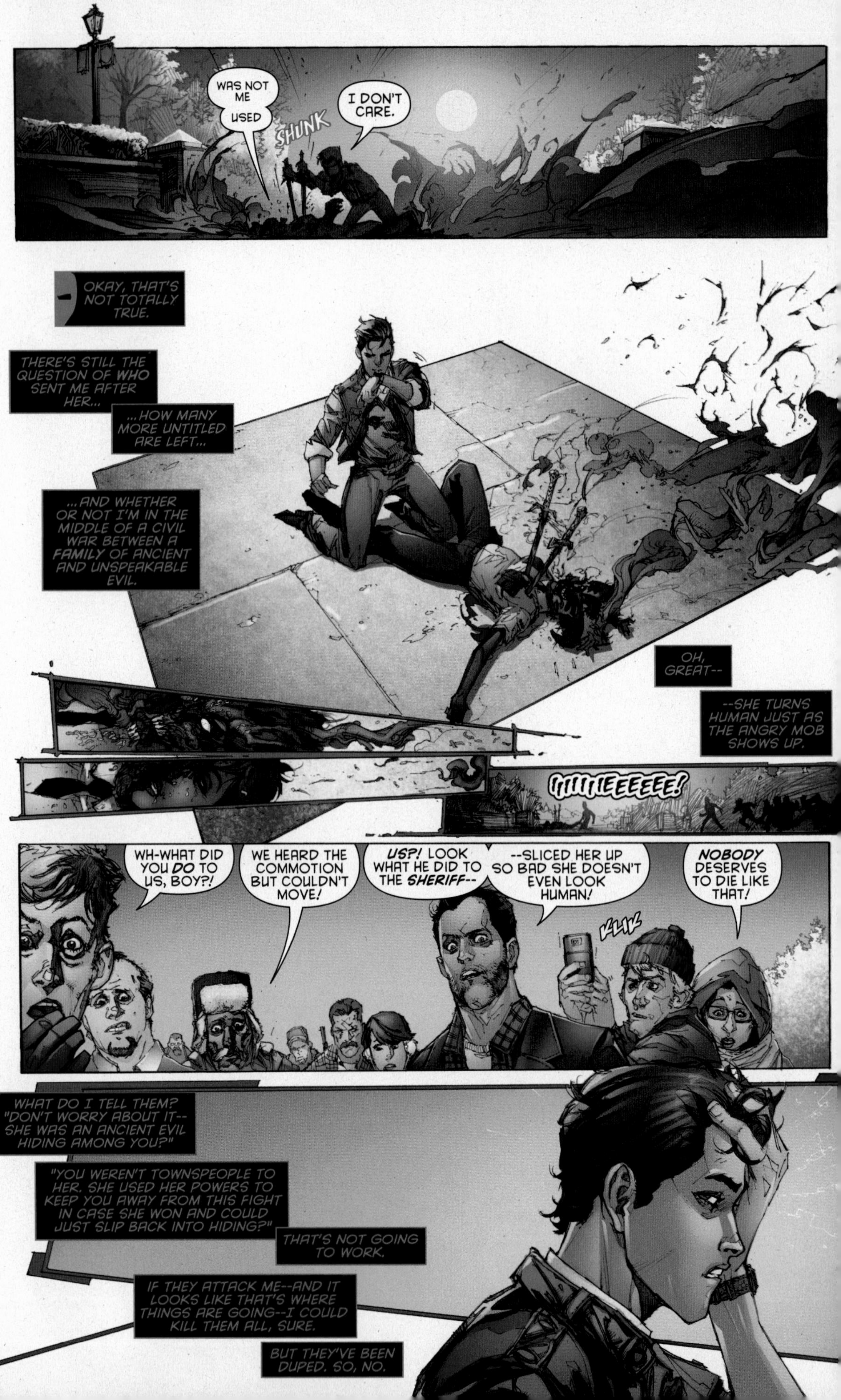
WAS NOT ME
USED
SHUNK
I DON'T CARE.
OKAY, THAT'S NOT TOTALLY TRUE.
THERE'S STILL THE QUESTION OF WHO SENT ME AFTER HER...
...HOW MANY MORE UNTITLED ARE LEFT...
...AND WHETHER OR NOT I'M IN THE MIDDLE OF A CIVIL WAR BETWEEN A FAMILY OF ANCIENT AND UNSPEAKABLE EVIL.
OH, GREAT--
--SHE TURNS HUMAN JUST AS THE ANGRY MOB SHOWS UP.
IIIIIIEEEEEE!
WH-WHAT DID YOU DO TO US, BOY?!
WE HEARD THE COMMOTION BUT COULDN'T MOVE!
US?! LOOK WHAT HE DID TO THE SHERIFF--
--SLICED HER UP SO BAD SHE DOESN'T EVEN LOOK HUMAN!
KLIK
NOBODY DESERVES TO DIE LIKE THAT!
WHAT DO I TELL THEM? "DON'T WORRY ABOUT IT--SHE WAS AN ANCIENT EVIL HIDING AMONG YOU?"
"YOU WEREN'T TOWNSPEOPLE TO HER. SHE USED HER POWERS TO KEEP YOU AWAY FROM THIS FIGHT IN CASE SHE WON AND COULD JUST SLIP BACK INTO HIDING?"
THAT'S NOT GOING TO WORK.
IF THEY ATTACK ME--AND IT LOOKS LIKE THAT'S WHERE THINGS ARE GOING--I COULD KILL THEM ALL, SURE.
BUT THEY'VE BEEN DUPED. SO, NO.

PENCILLER KENNETH ROCAFORT INKER PAGE# COVER
TITLE RED HOOD AND THE OUTLAWS ISSUE # 7 MONTH INTERIORS

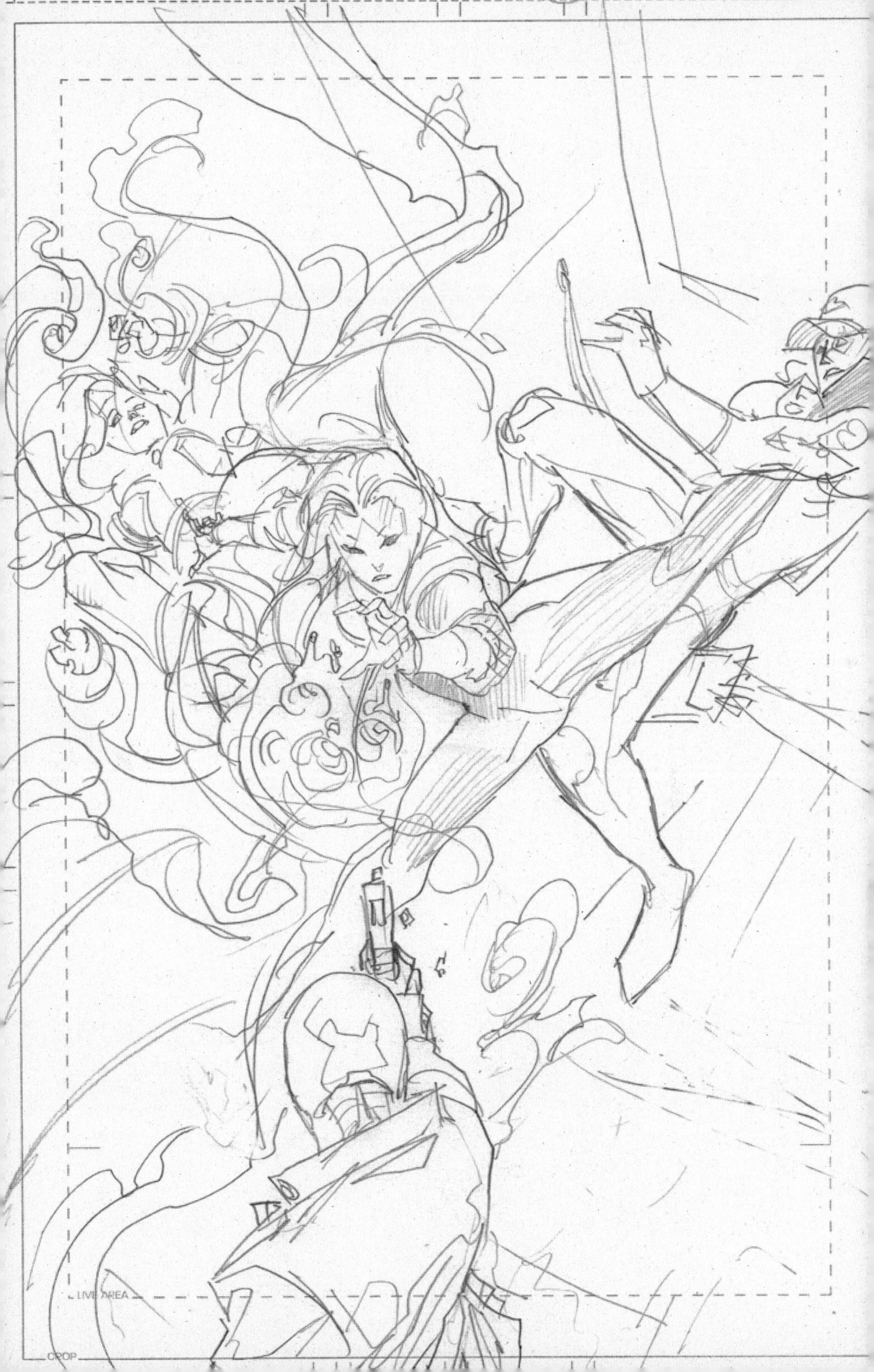

LIVE AREA
CROP

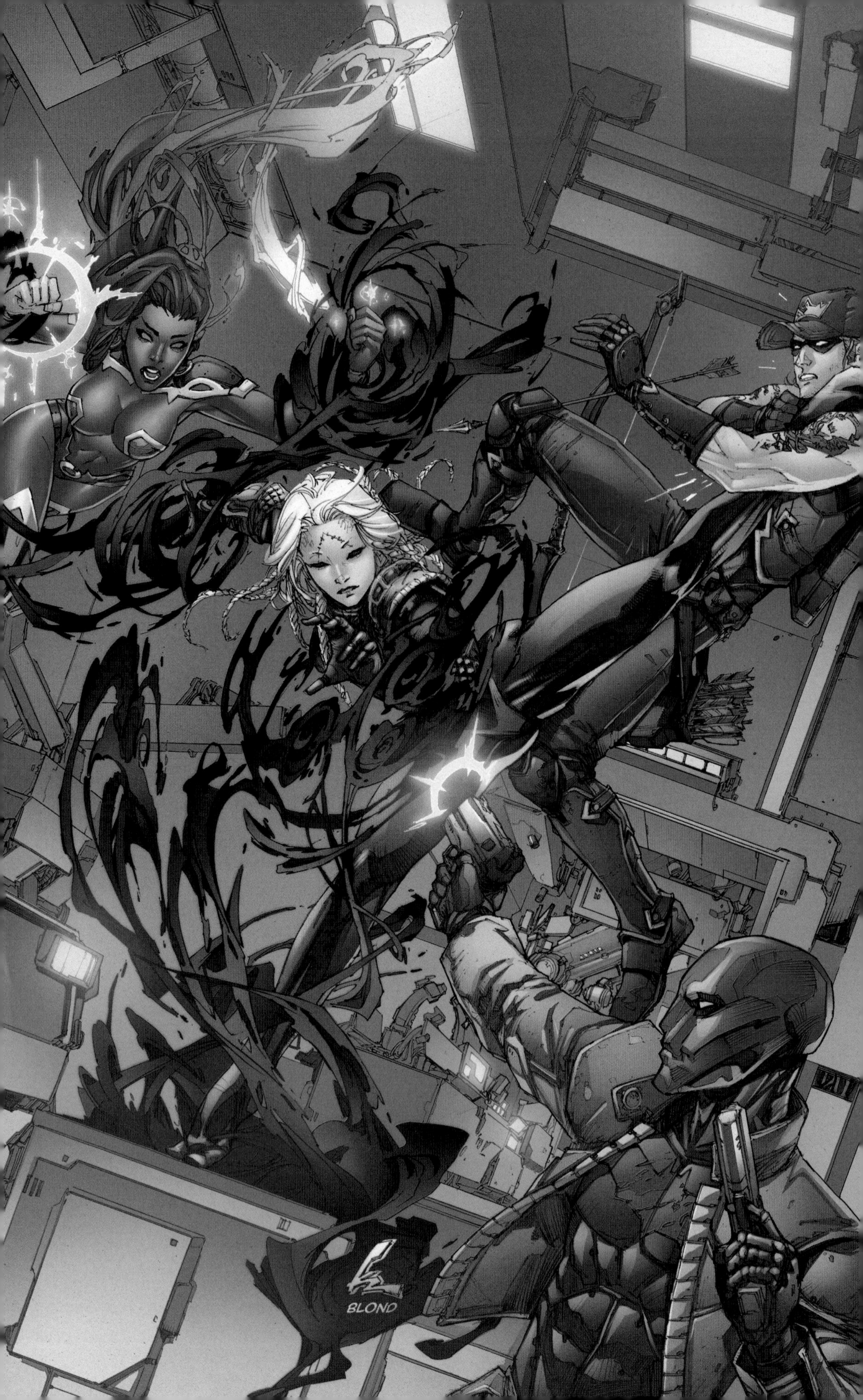
BLOND

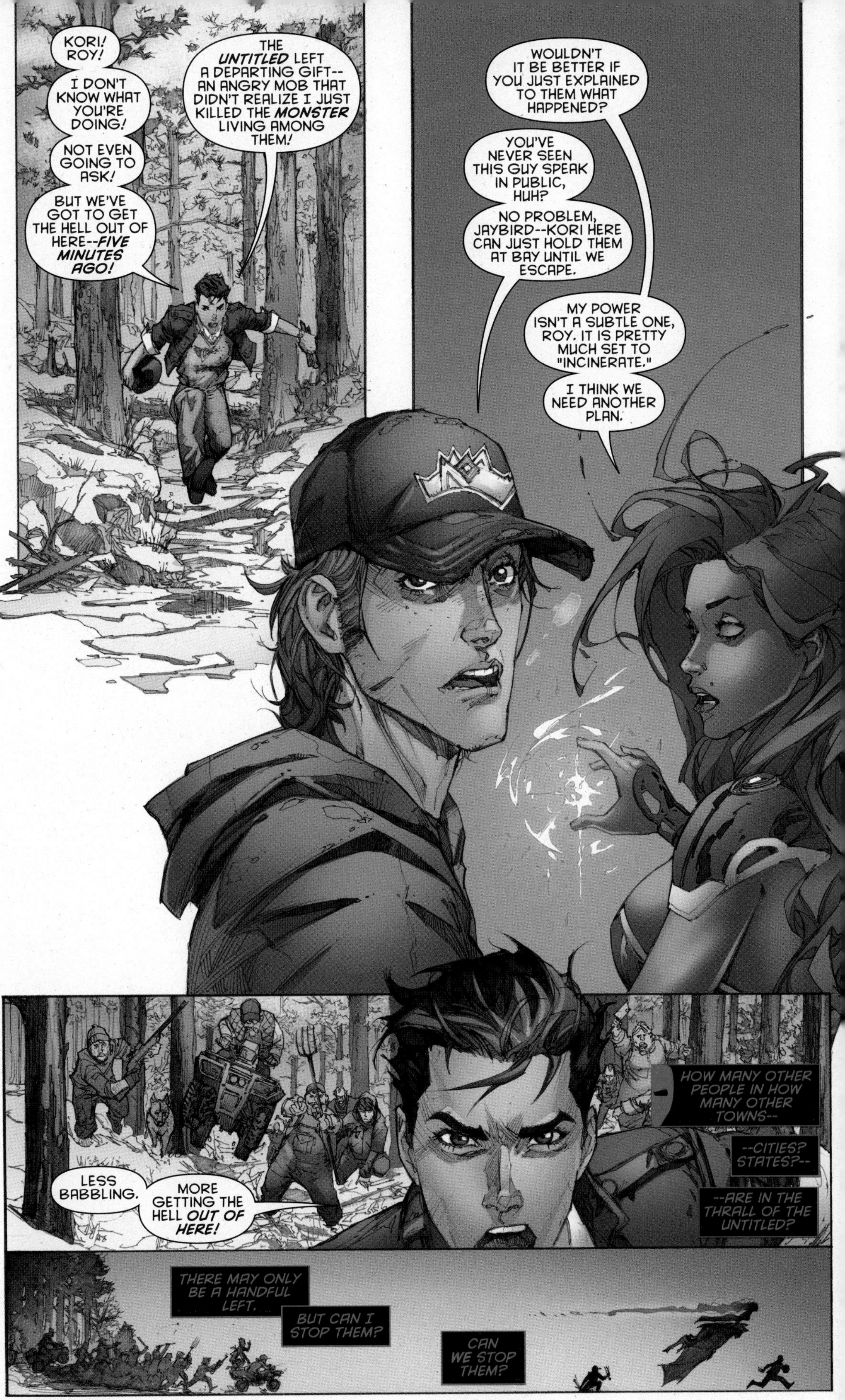

KORI! ROY!
I DON'T KNOW WHAT YOU'RE DOING!
NOT EVEN GOING TO ASK!
BUT WE'VE GOT TO GET THE HELL OUT OF HERE--FIVE MINUTES AGO!
THE UNTITLED LEFT A DEPARTING GIFT--AN ANGRY MOB THAT DIDN'T REALIZE I JUST KILLED THE MONSTER LIVING AMONG THEM!
WOULDN'T IT BE BETTER IF YOU JUST EXPLAINED TO THEM WHAT HAPPENED?
YOU'VE NEVER SEEN THIS GUY SPEAK IN PUBLIC, HUH?
NO PROBLEM, JAYBIRD--KORI HERE CAN JUST HOLD THEM AT BAY UNTIL WE ESCAPE.
MY POWER ISN'T A SUBTLE ONE, ROY. IT IS PRETTY MUCH SET TO "INCINERATE."
I THINK WE NEED ANOTHER PLAN.
HOW MANY OTHER PEOPLE IN HOW MANY OTHER TOWNS--
--CITIES? STATES?--
--ARE IN THE THRALL OF THE UNTITLED?
LESS BABBLING.
MORE GETTING THE HELL OUT OF HERE!
THERE MAY ONLY BE A HANDFUL LEFT.
BUT CAN I STOP THEM?
CAN WE STOP THEM?

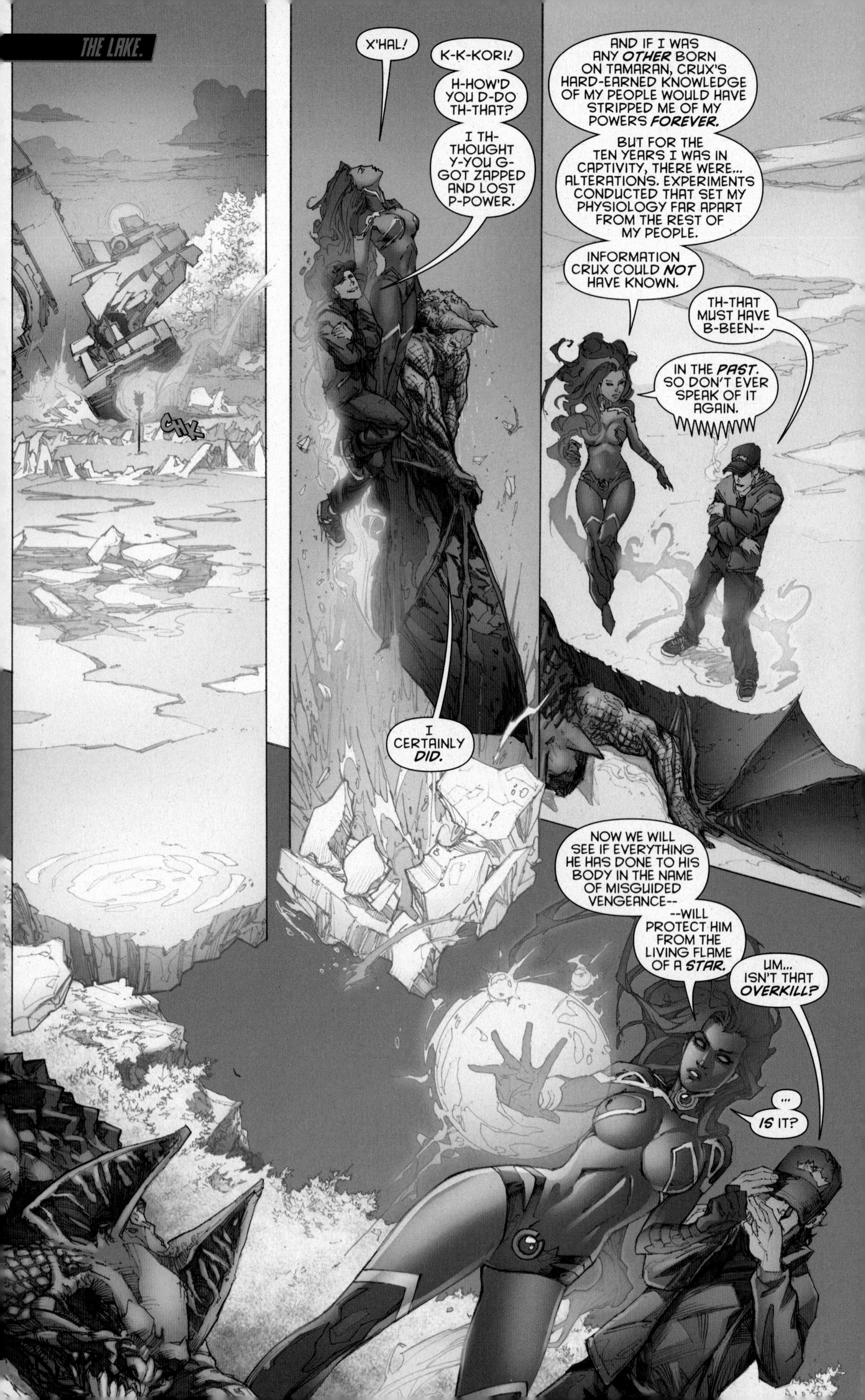
THE LAKE.
CHK
X'HAL!
K-K-KORI!
H-HOW'D YOU D-DO TH-THAT?
I TH-THOUGHT Y-YOU G-GOT ZAPPED AND LOST P-POWER.
I CERTAINLY DID.
AND IF I WAS ANY OTHER BORN ON TAMARAN, CRUX'S HARD-EARNED KNOWLEDGE OF MY PEOPLE WOULD HAVE STRIPPED ME OF MY POWERS FOREVER.
BUT FOR THE TEN YEARS I WAS IN CAPTIVITY, THERE WERE... ALTERATIONS. EXPERIMENTS CONDUCTED THAT SET MY PHYSIOLOGY FAR APART FROM THE REST OF MY PEOPLE.
INFORMATION CRUX COULD NOT HAVE KNOWN.
TH-THAT MUST HAVE B-BEEN--
IN THE PAST. SO DON'T EVER SPEAK OF IT AGAIN.
NOW WE WILL SEE IF EVERYTHING HE HAS DONE TO HIS BODY IN THE NAME OF MISGUIDED VENGEANCE--
--WILL PROTECT HIM FROM THE LIVING FLAME OF A STAR.
UM... ISN'T THAT OVERKILL?
... IS IT?

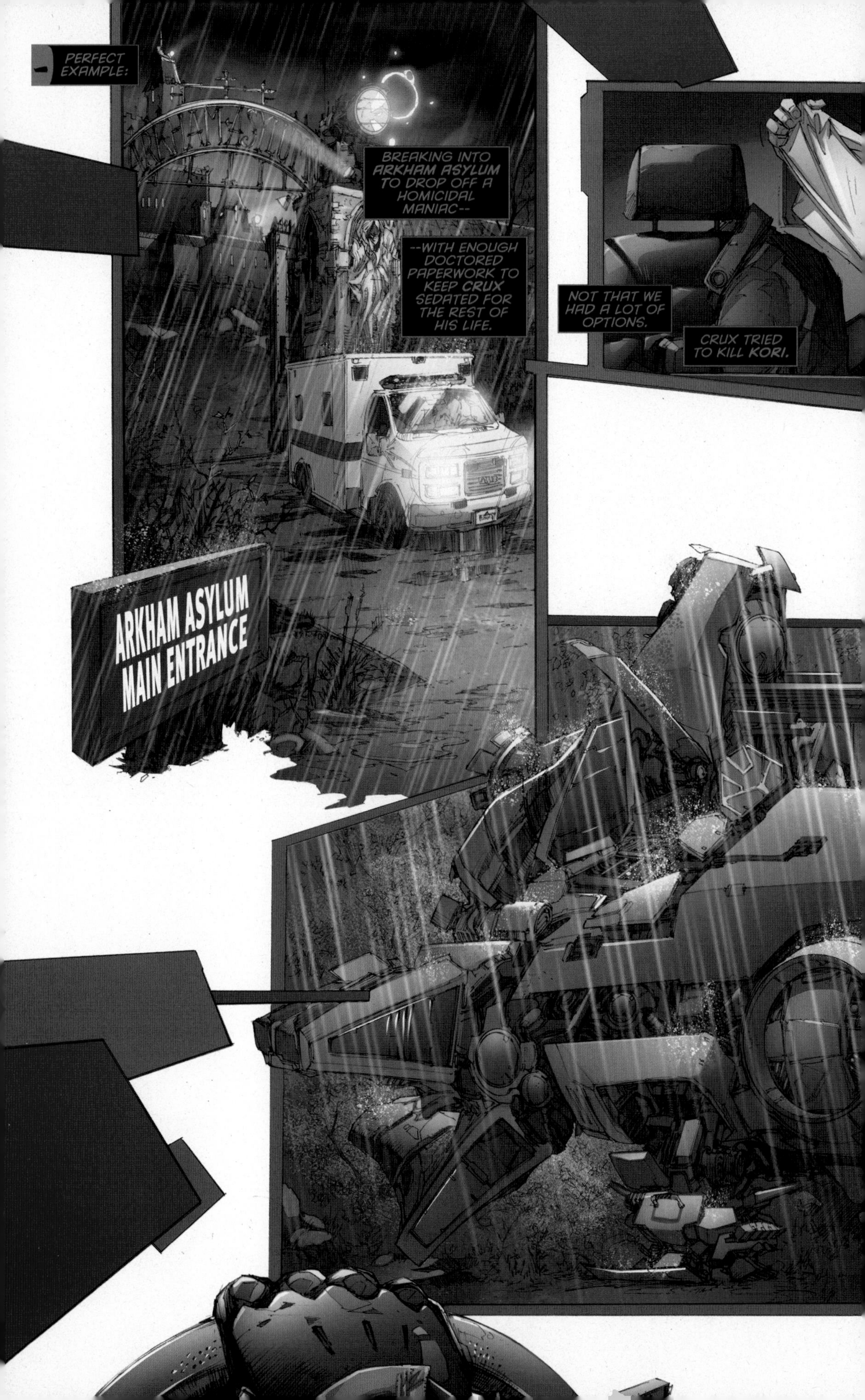
PERFECT EXAMPLE:
BREAKING INTO ARKHAM ASYLUM TO DROP OFF A HOMICIDAL MANIAC--
--WITH ENOUGH DOCTORED PAPERWORK TO KEEP CRUX SEDATED FOR THE REST OF HIS LIFE.
ARKHAM ASYLUM
MAIN ENTRANCE
NOT THAT WE HAD A LOT OF OPTIONS.
CRUX TRIED TO KILL KORI.

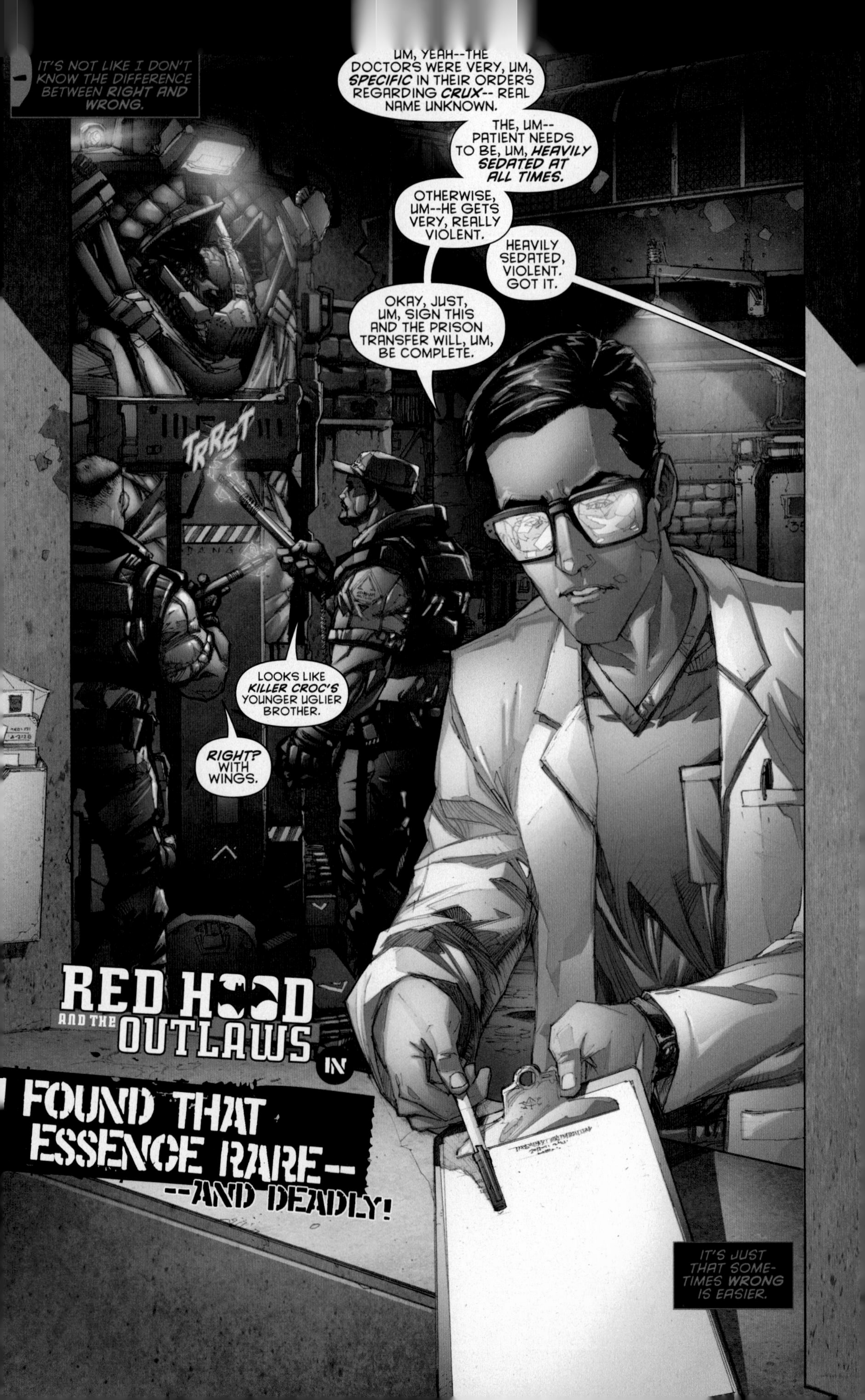
IT'S NOT LIKE I DON'T KNOW THE DIFFERENCE BETWEEN RIGHT AND WRONG.
UM, YEAH--THE DOCTORS WERE VERY, UM, SPECIFIC IN THEIR ORDERS REGARDING CRUX-- REAL NAME UNKNOWN.
THE, UM-- PATIENT NEEDS TO BE, UM, HEAVILY SEDATED AT ALL TIMES.
OTHERWISE, UM--HE GETS VERY, REALLY VIOLENT.
HEAVILY SEDATED, VIOLENT. GOT IT.
OKAY, JUST, UM, SIGN THIS AND THE PRISON TRANSFER WILL, UM, BE COMPLETE.
TRRST
LOOKS LIKE KILLER CROC'S YOUNGER UGLIER BROTHER.
RIGHT? WITH WINGS.
RED HOOD AND THE OUTLAWS
IN
I FOUND THAT ESSENCE RARE--
--AND DEADLY!
IT'S JUST THAT SOMETIMES WRONG IS EASIER.

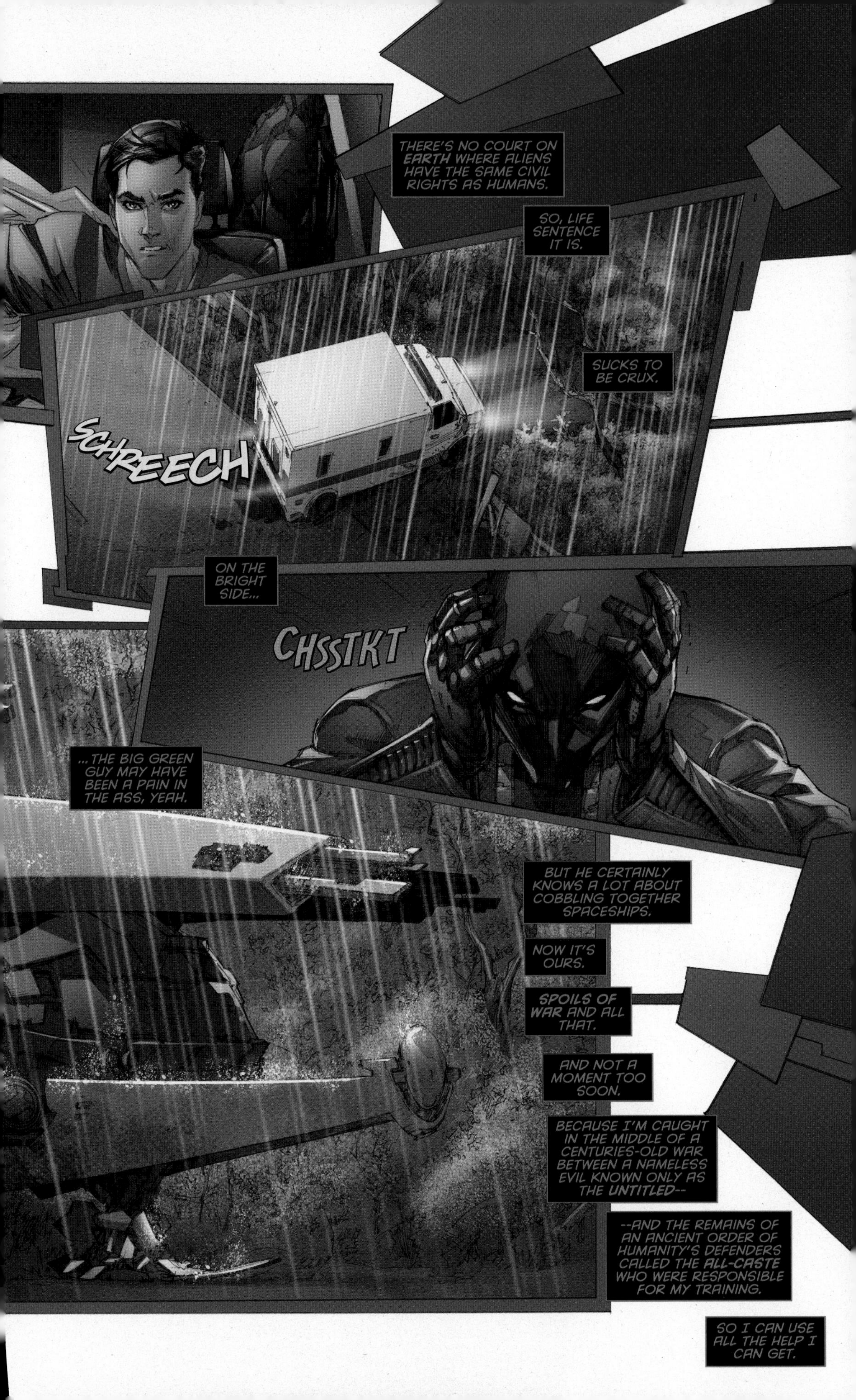
THERE'S NO COURT ON EARTH WHERE ALIENS HAVE THE SAME CIVIL RIGHTS AS HUMANS.
SO, LIFE SENTENCE IT IS.
SUCKS TO BE CRUX.
SCHREECH
ON THE BRIGHT SIDE...
CHSSTKT
...THE BIG GREEN GUY MAY HAVE BEEN A PAIN IN THE ASS, YEAH.
BUT HE CERTAINLY KNOWS A LOT ABOUT COBBLING TOGETHER SPACESHIPS.
NOW IT'S OURS.
SPOILS OF WAR AND ALL THAT.
AND NOT A MOMENT TOO SOON.
BECAUSE I'M CAUGHT IN THE MIDDLE OF A CENTURIES-OLD WAR BETWEEN A NAMELESS EVIL KNOWN ONLY AS THE UNTITLED--
--AND THE REMAINS OF AN ANCIENT ORDER OF HUMANITY'S DEFENDERS CALLED THE ALL-CASTE WHO WERE RESPONSIBLE FOR MY TRAINING.
SO I CAN USE ALL THE HELP I CAN GET.

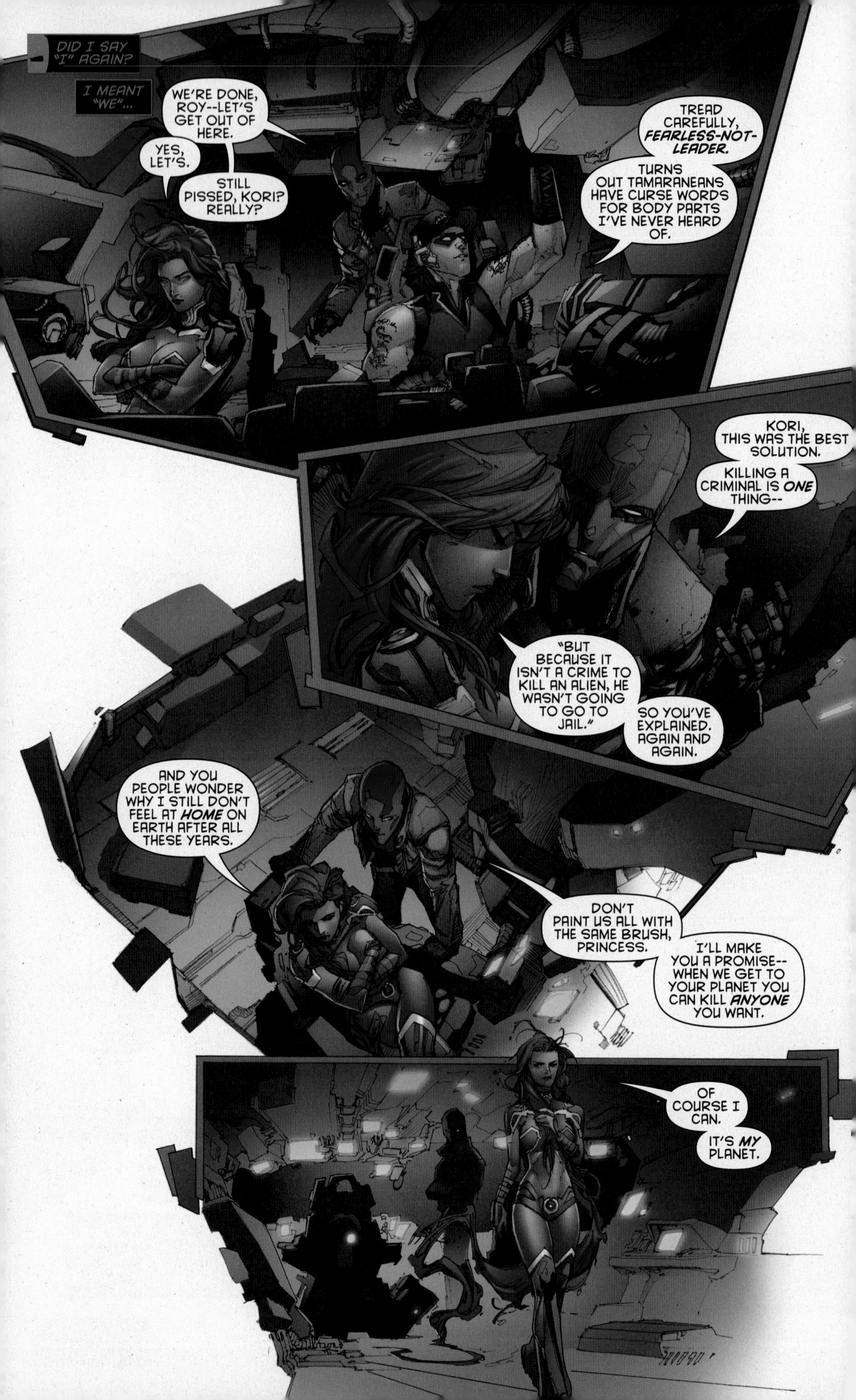
DID I SAY "I" AGAIN?
I MEANT "WE"...
WE'RE DONE, ROY--LET'S GET OUT OF HERE.
YES, LET'S.
STILL PISSED, KORI? REALLY?
TREAD CAREFULLY, FEARLESS-NOT-LEADER.
TURNS OUT TAMARANEANS HAVE CURSE WORDS FOR BODY PARTS I'VE NEVER HEARD OF.
KORI, THIS WAS THE BEST SOLUTION.
KILLING A CRIMINAL IS ONE THING--
"BUT BECAUSE IT ISN'T A CRIME TO KILL AN ALIEN, HE WASN'T GOING TO GO TO JAIL."
SO YOU'VE EXPLAINED. AGAIN AND AGAIN.
AND YOU PEOPLE WONDER WHY I STILL DON'T FEEL AT HOME ON EARTH AFTER ALL THESE YEARS.
DON'T PAINT US ALL WITH THE SAME BRUSH, PRINCESS.
I'LL MAKE YOU A PROMISE-- WHEN WE GET TO YOUR PLANET YOU CAN KILL ANYONE YOU WANT.
OF COURSE I CAN.
IT'S MY PLANET.

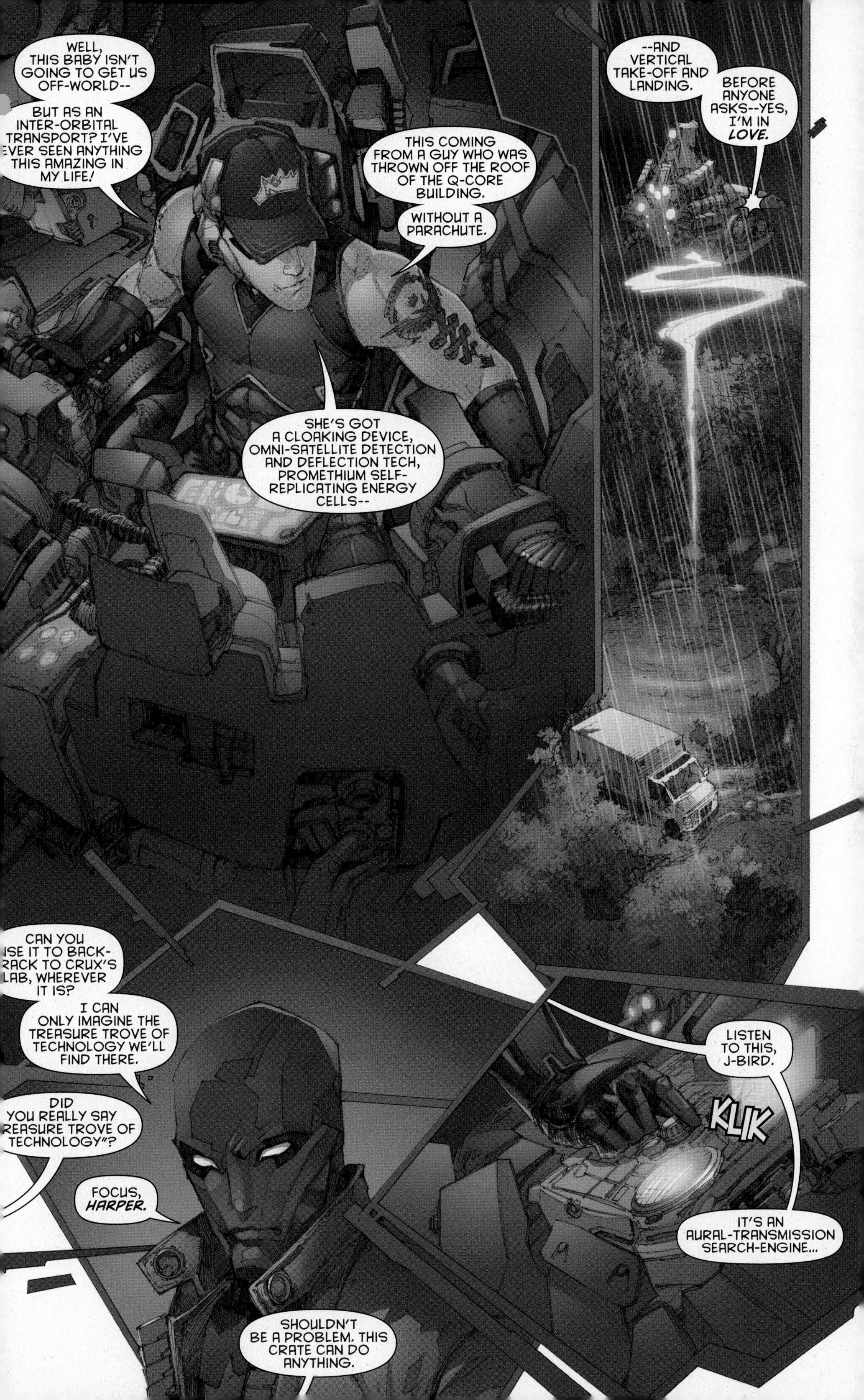

WELL, THIS BABY ISN'T GOING TO GET US OFF-WORLD--
BUT AS AN INTER-ORBITAL TRANSPORT? I'VE EVER SEEN ANYTHING THIS AMAZING IN MY LIFE!
THIS COMING FROM A GUY WHO WAS THROWN OFF THE ROOF OF THE Q-CORE BUILDING.
WITHOUT A PARACHUTE.
SHE'S GOT A CLOAKING DEVICE, OMNI-SATELLITE DETECTION AND DEFLECTION TECH, PROMETHIUM SELF-REPLICATING ENERGY CELLS--
--AND VERTICAL TAKE-OFF AND LANDING.
BEFORE ANYONE ASKS--YES, I'M IN *LOVE.*
CAN YOU USE IT TO BACK-TRACK TO CRUX'S LAB, WHEREVER IT IS?
I CAN ONLY IMAGINE THE TREASURE TROVE OF TECHNOLOGY WE'LL FIND THERE.
DID YOU REALLY SAY "TREASURE TROVE OF TECHNOLOGY"?
FOCUS, *HARPER.*
SHOULDN'T BE A PROBLEM. THIS CRATE CAN DO ANYTHING.
LISTEN TO THIS, J-BIRD.
KLIK
IT'S AN AURAL-TRANSMISSION SEARCH-ENGINE...

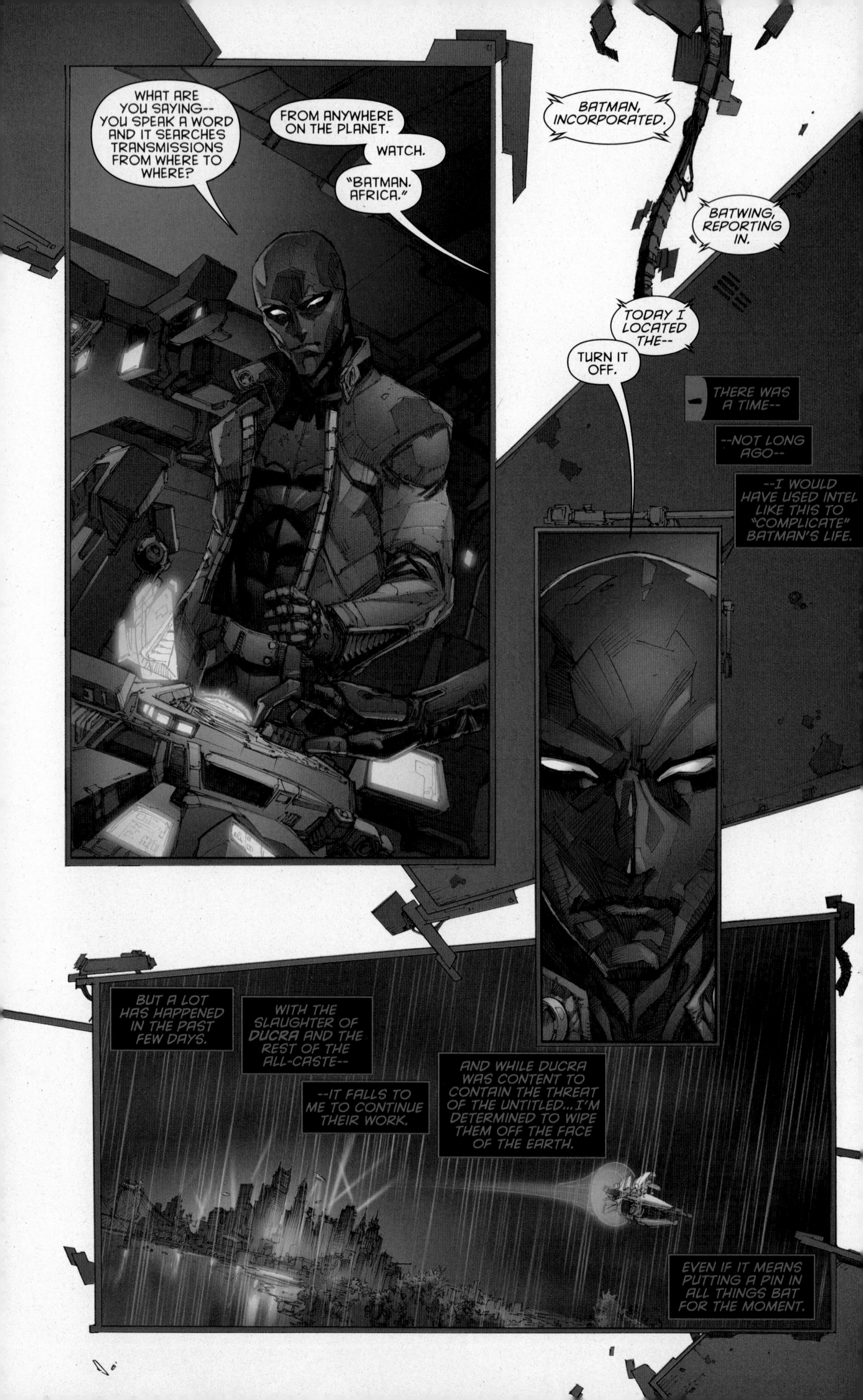
WHAT ARE YOU SAYING-- YOU SPEAK A WORD AND IT SEARCHES TRANSMISSIONS FROM WHERE TO WHERE?
FROM ANYWHERE ON THE PLANET.
WATCH.
"BATMAN. AFRICA."
BATMAN, INCORPORATED.
BATWING, REPORTING IN.
TODAY I LOCATED THE--
TURN IT OFF.
THERE WAS A TIME--
--NOT LONG AGO--
--I WOULD HAVE USED INTEL LIKE THIS TO "COMPLICATE" BATMAN'S LIFE.
BUT A LOT HAS HAPPENED IN THE PAST FEW DAYS.
WITH THE SLAUGHTER OF DUCRA AND THE REST OF THE ALL-CASTE--
--IT FALLS TO ME TO CONTINUE THEIR WORK.
AND WHILE DUCRA WAS CONTENT TO CONTAIN THE THREAT OF THE UNTITLED...I'M DETERMINED TO WIPE THEM OFF THE FACE OF THE EARTH.
EVEN IF IT MEANS PUTTING A PIN IN ALL THINGS BAT FOR THE MOMENT.

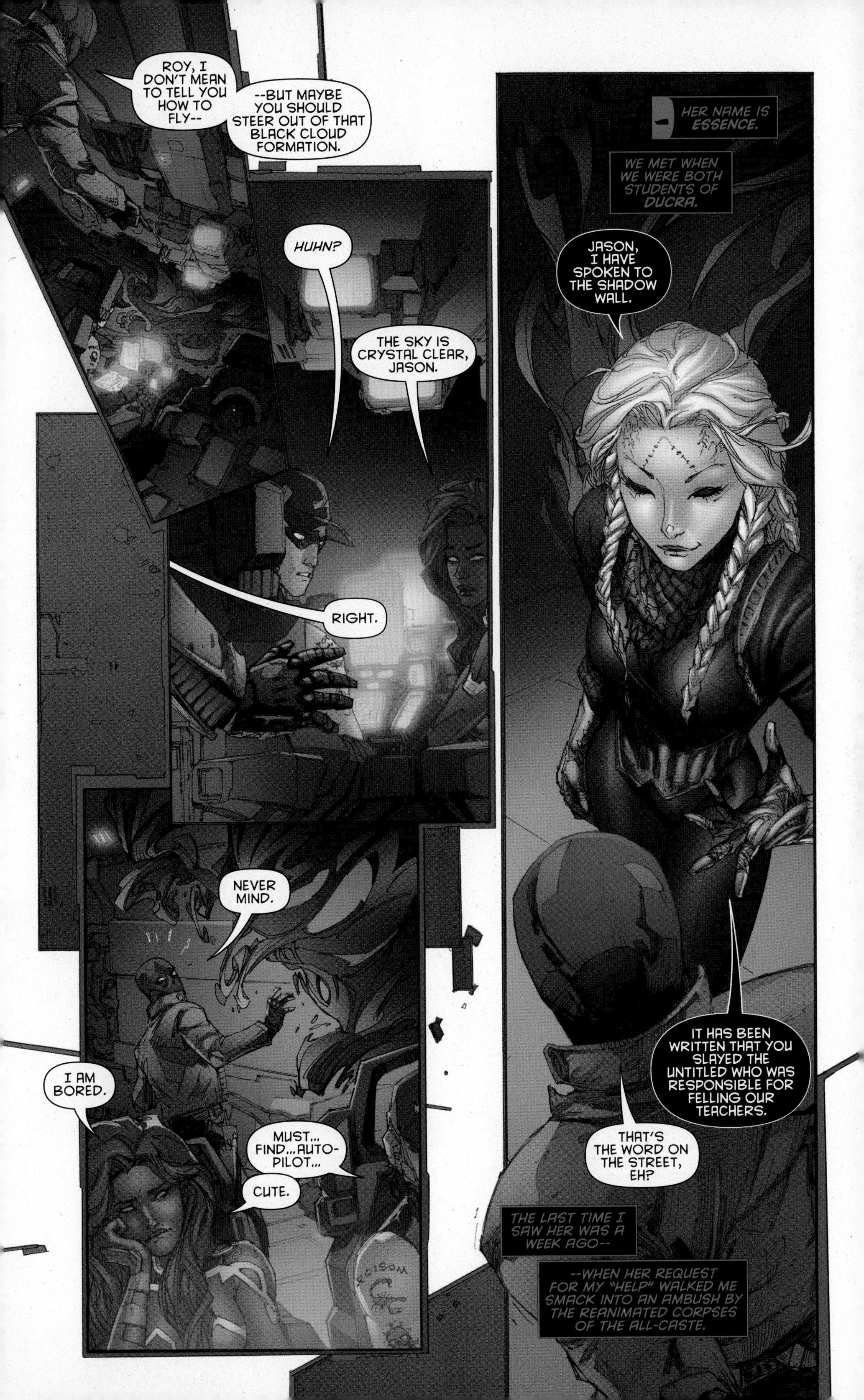
ROY, I DON'T MEAN TO TELL YOU HOW TO FLY--
--BUT MAYBE YOU SHOULD STEER OUT OF THAT BLACK CLOUD FORMATION.
HUHN?
THE SKY IS CRYSTAL CLEAR, JASON.
RIGHT.
NEVER MIND.
I AM BORED.
MUST... FIND... AUTO-PILOT...
CUTE.
HER NAME IS ESSENCE.
WE MET WHEN WE WERE BOTH STUDENTS OF DUCRA.
JASON, I HAVE SPOKEN TO THE SHADOW WALL.
IT HAS BEEN WRITTEN THAT YOU SLAYED THE UNTITLED WHO WAS RESPONSIBLE FOR FELLING OUR TEACHERS.
THAT'S THE WORD ON THE STREET, EH?
THE LAST TIME I SAW HER WAS A WEEK AGO--
--WHEN HER REQUEST FOR MY "HELP" WALKED ME SMACK INTO AN AMBUSH BY THE REANIMATED CORPSES OF THE ALL-CASTE.

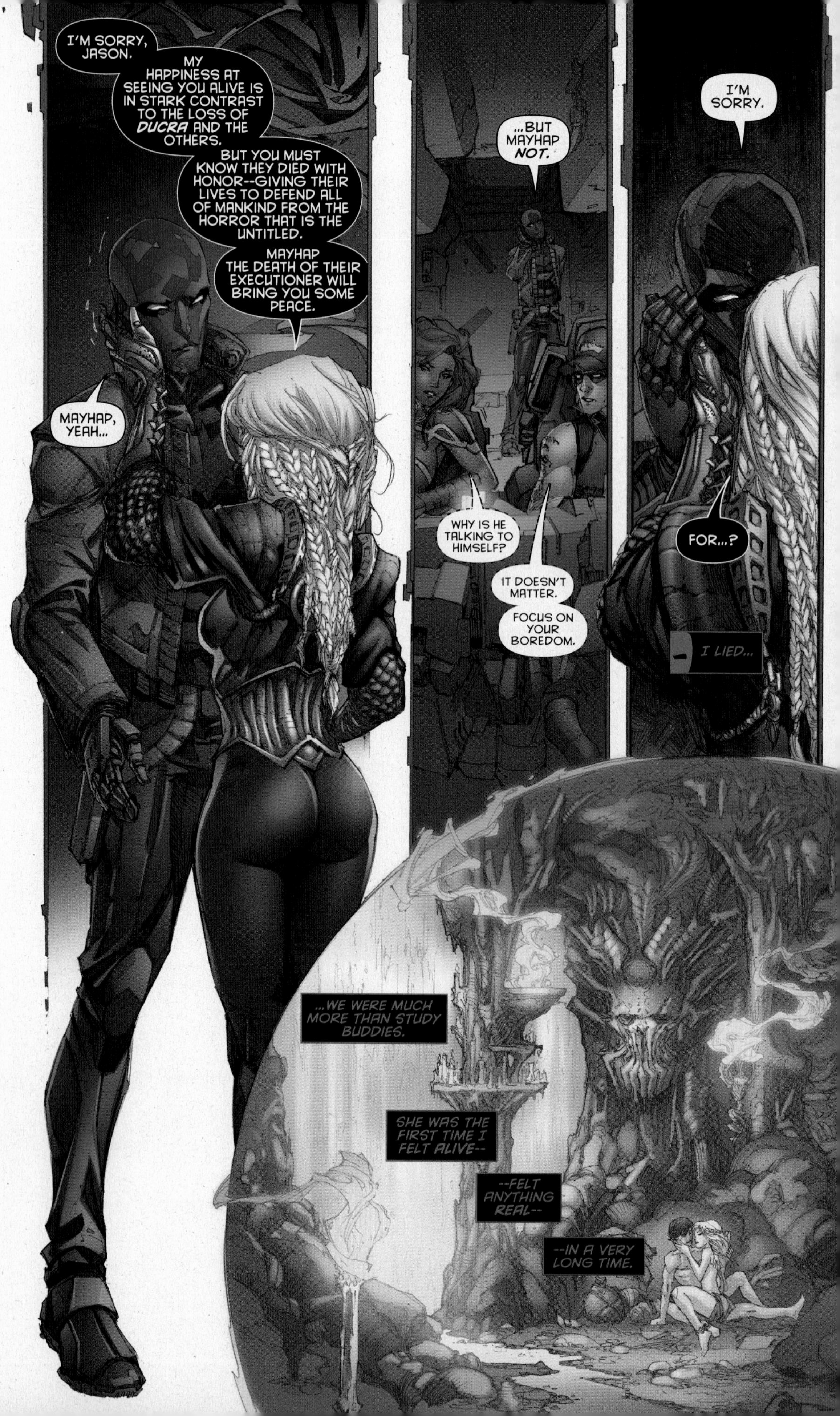
I'M SORRY, JASON.
MY HAPPINESS AT SEEING YOU ALIVE IS IN STARK CONTRAST TO THE LOSS OF DUCRA AND THE OTHERS.
BUT YOU MUST KNOW THEY DIED WITH HONOR--GIVING THEIR LIVES TO DEFEND ALL OF MANKIND FROM THE HORROR THAT IS THE UNTITLED.
MAYHAP THE DEATH OF THEIR EXECUTIONER WILL BRING YOU SOME PEACE.
MAYHAP, YEAH...
...BUT MAYHAP NOT.
WHY IS HE TALKING TO HIMSELF?
IT DOESN'T MATTER.
FOCUS ON YOUR BOREDOM.
I'M SORRY.
FOR...?
I LIED...
...WE WERE MUCH MORE THAN STUDY BUDDIES.
SHE WAS THE FIRST TIME I FELT ALIVE--
--FELT ANYTHING REAL--
--IN A VERY LONG TIME.

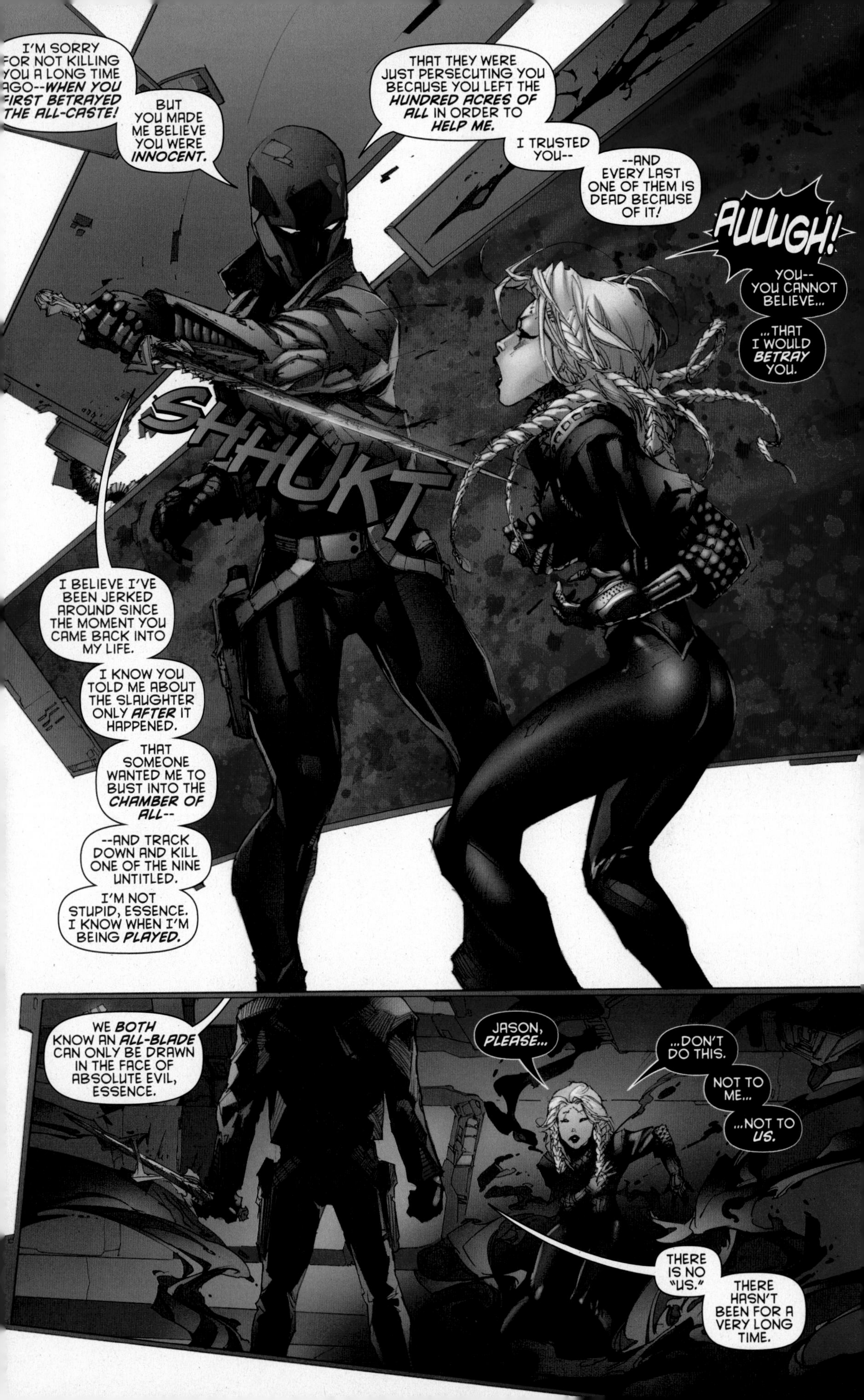
I'M SORRY FOR NOT KILLING YOU A LONG TIME AGO--WHEN YOU FIRST BETRAYED THE ALL-CASTE!
BUT YOU MADE ME BELIEVE YOU WERE INNOCENT.
THAT THEY WERE JUST PERSECUTING YOU BECAUSE YOU LEFT THE HUNDRED ACRES OF ALL IN ORDER TO HELP ME.
I TRUSTED YOU--
--AND EVERY LAST ONE OF THEM IS DEAD BECAUSE OF IT!
AUUUGH!
YOU-- YOU CANNOT BELIEVE...
...THAT I WOULD BETRAY YOU.
SHHUKT
I BELIEVE I'VE BEEN JERKED AROUND SINCE THE MOMENT YOU CAME BACK INTO MY LIFE.
I KNOW YOU TOLD ME ABOUT THE SLAUGHTER ONLY AFTER IT HAPPENED.
THAT SOMEONE WANTED ME TO BUST INTO THE CHAMBER OF ALL--
--AND TRACK DOWN AND KILL ONE OF THE NINE UNTITLED.
I'M NOT STUPID, ESSENCE. I KNOW WHEN I'M BEING PLAYED.
WE BOTH KNOW AN ALL-BLADE CAN ONLY BE DRAWN IN THE FACE OF ABSOLUTE EVIL, ESSENCE.
JASON, PLEASE...
...DON'T DO THIS.
NOT TO ME...
...NOT TO US.
THERE IS NO "US."
THERE HASN'T BEEN FOR A VERY LONG TIME.

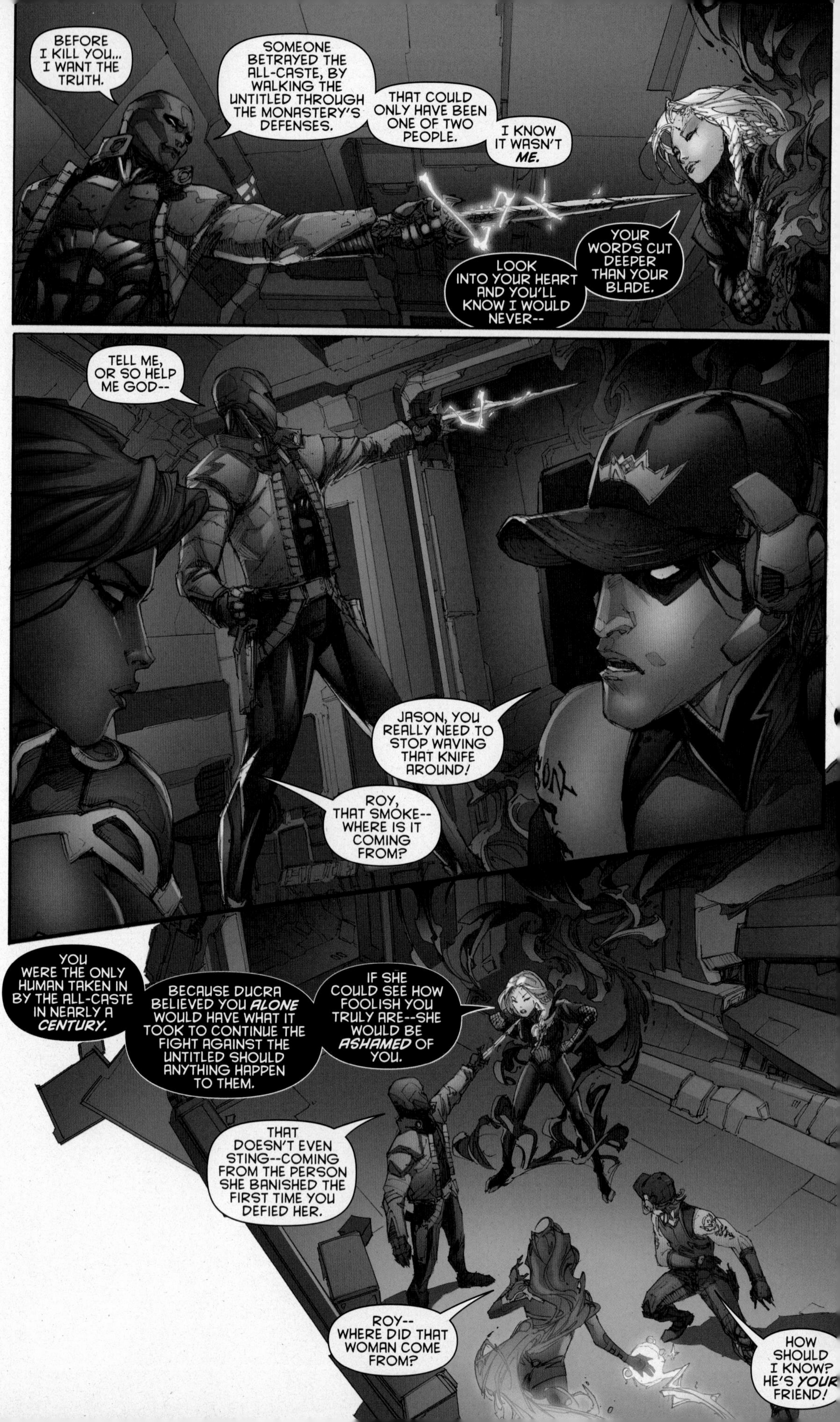
BEFORE I KILL YOU... I WANT THE TRUTH.
SOMEONE BETRAYED THE ALL-CASTE, BY WALKING THE UNTITLED THROUGH THE MONASTERY'S DEFENSES.
THAT COULD ONLY HAVE BEEN ONE OF TWO PEOPLE.
I KNOW IT WASN'T ME.
YOUR WORDS CUT DEEPER THAN YOUR BLADE.
LOOK INTO YOUR HEART AND YOU'LL KNOW I WOULD NEVER--
TELL ME, OR SO HELP ME GOD--
JASON, YOU REALLY NEED TO STOP WAVING THAT KNIFE AROUND!
ROY, THAT SMOKE-- WHERE IS IT COMING FROM?
YOU WERE THE ONLY HUMAN TAKEN IN BY THE ALL-CASTE IN NEARLY A CENTURY.
BECAUSE DUCRA BELIEVED YOU ALONE WOULD HAVE WHAT IT TOOK TO CONTINUE THE FIGHT AGAINST THE UNTITLED SHOULD ANYTHING HAPPEN TO THEM.
IF SHE COULD SEE HOW FOOLISH YOU TRULY ARE--SHE WOULD BE ASHAMED OF YOU.
THAT DOESN'T EVEN STING--COMING FROM THE PERSON SHE BANISHED THE FIRST TIME YOU DEFIED HER.
ROY-- WHERE DID THAT WOMAN COME FROM?
HOW SHOULD I KNOW? HE'S YOUR FRIEND!

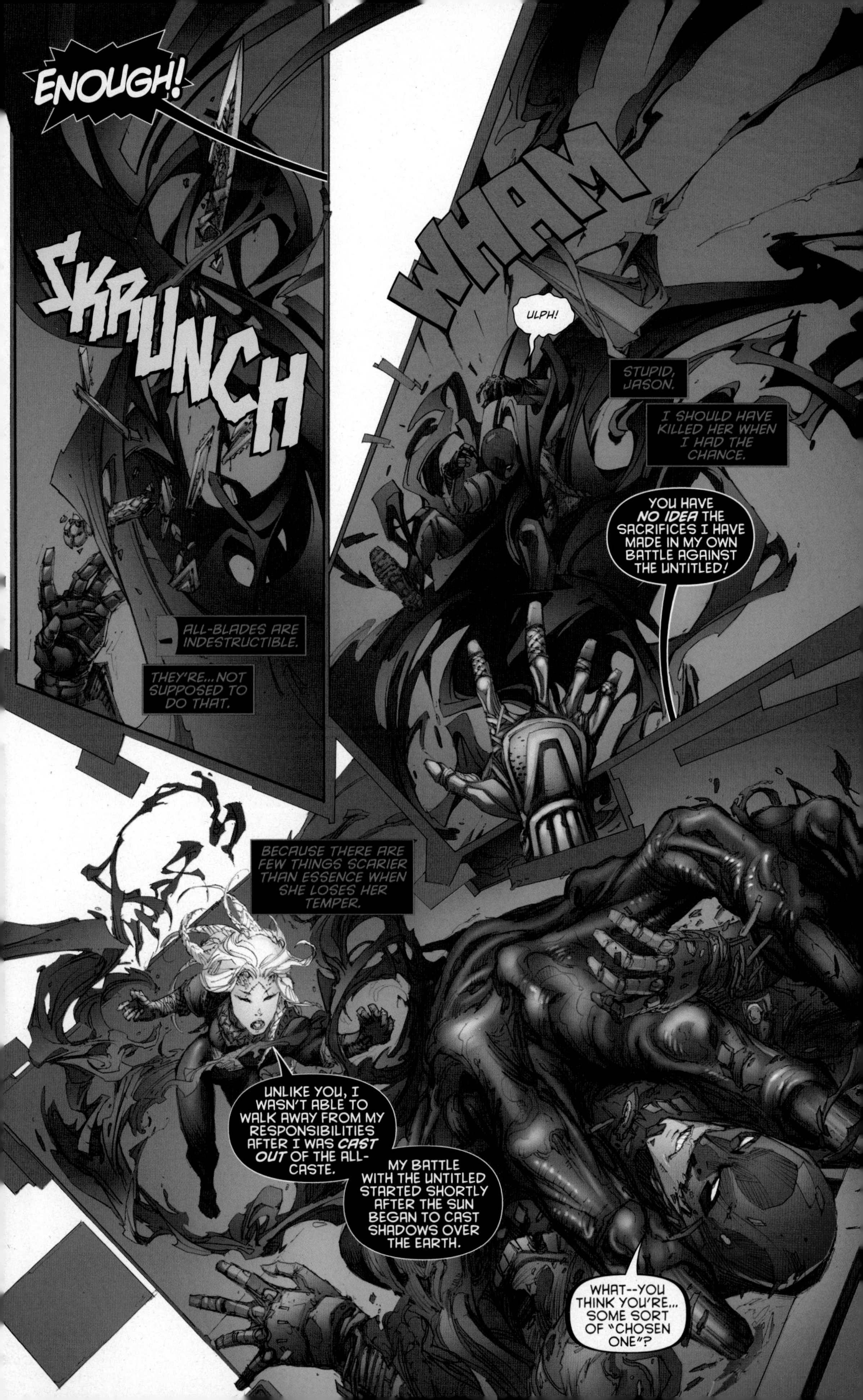
ENOUGH!
SKRUNCH
ALL-BLADES ARE INDESTRUCTIBLE.
THEY'RE...NOT SUPPOSED TO DO THAT.
WHAM
ULPH!
STUPID, JASON.
I SHOULD HAVE KILLED HER WHEN I HAD THE CHANCE.
YOU HAVE NO IDEA THE SACRIFICES I HAVE MADE IN MY OWN BATTLE AGAINST THE UNTITLED!
BECAUSE THERE ARE FEW THINGS SCARIER THAN ESSENCE WHEN SHE LOSES HER TEMPER.
UNLIKE YOU, I WASN'T ABLE TO WALK AWAY FROM MY RESPONSIBILITIES AFTER I WAS CAST OUT OF THE ALL-CASTE.
MY BATTLE WITH THE UNTITLED STARTED SHORTLY AFTER THE SUN BEGAN TO CAST SHADOWS OVER THE EARTH.
WHAT--YOU THINK YOU'RE... SOME SORT OF "CHOSEN ONE"?

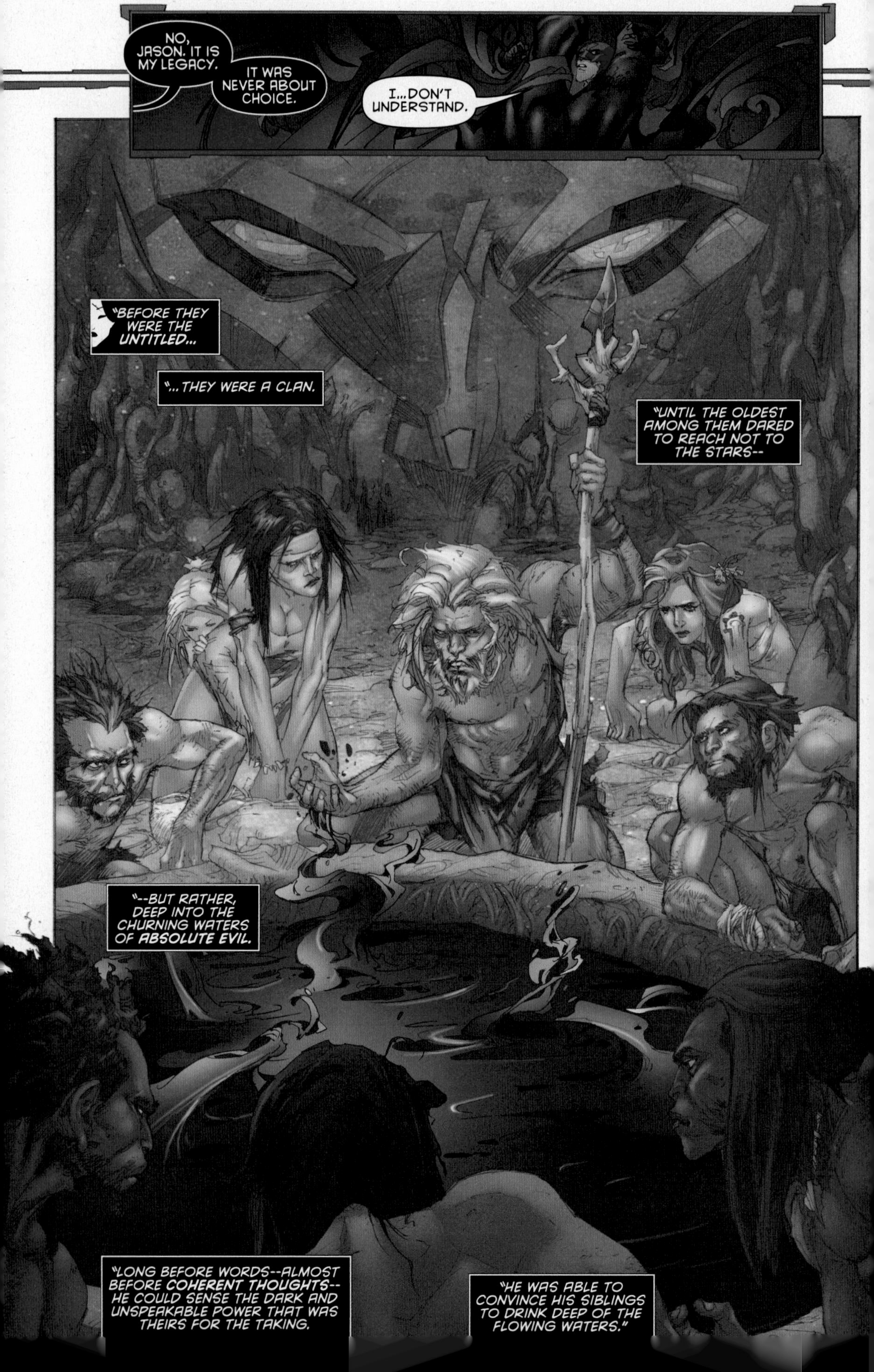
NO, JASON. IT IS MY LEGACY.
IT WAS NEVER ABOUT CHOICE.
I...DON'T UNDERSTAND.
"BEFORE THEY WERE THE UNTITLED...
"...THEY WERE A CLAN.
"UNTIL THE OLDEST AMONG THEM DARED TO REACH NOT TO THE STARS--
"--BUT RATHER, DEEP INTO THE CHURNING WATERS OF ABSOLUTE EVIL.
"LONG BEFORE WORDS--ALMOST BEFORE COHERENT THOUGHTS--HE COULD SENSE THE DARK AND UNSPEAKABLE POWER THAT WAS THEIRS FOR THE TAKING.
"HE WAS ABLE TO CONVINCE HIS SIBLINGS TO DRINK DEEP OF THE FLOWING WATERS."

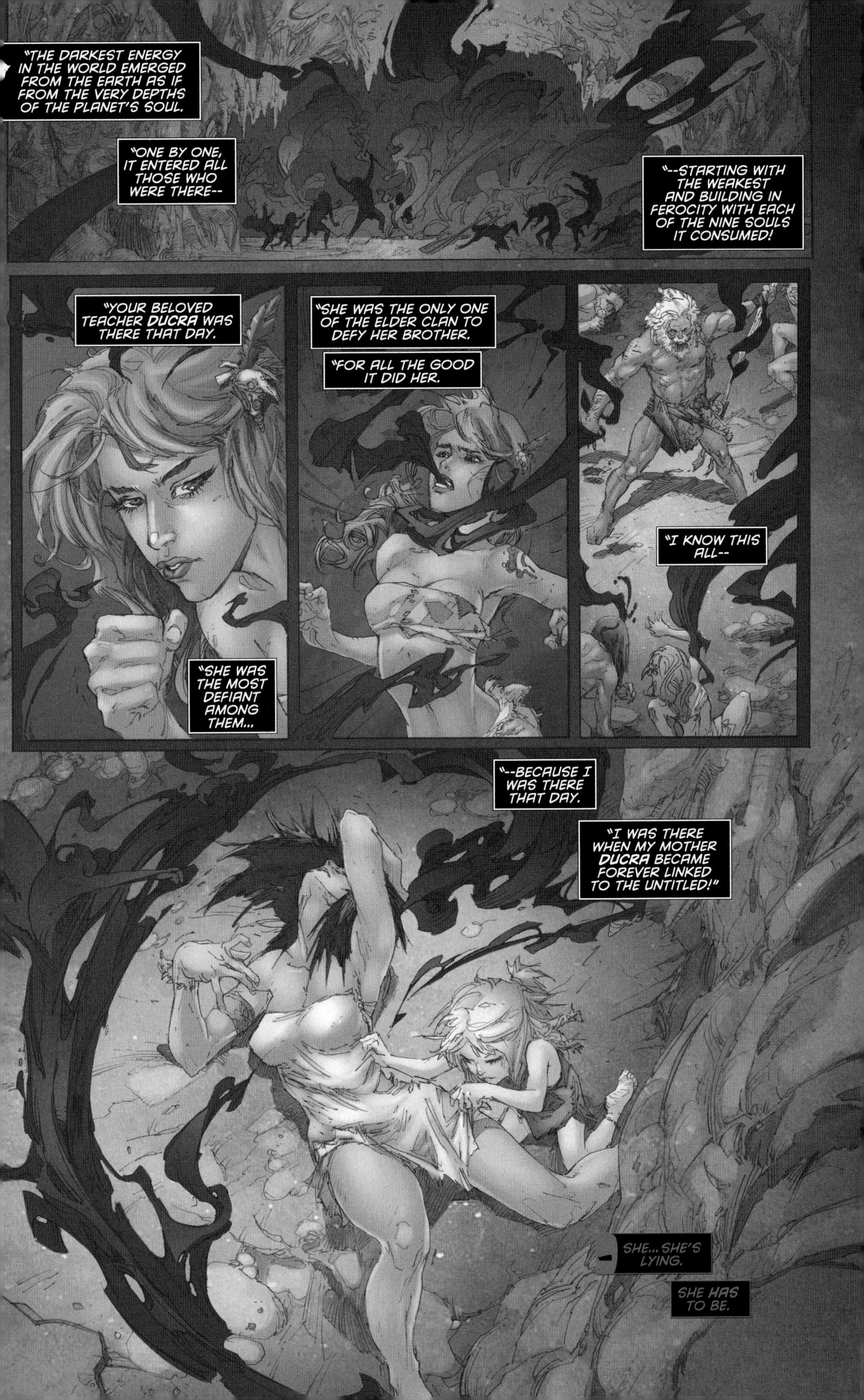
"THE DARKEST ENERGY IN THE WORLD EMERGED FROM THE EARTH AS IF FROM THE VERY DEPTHS OF THE PLANET'S SOUL.
"ONE BY ONE, IT ENTERED ALL THOSE WHO WERE THERE--
"--STARTING WITH THE WEAKEST AND BUILDING IN FEROCITY WITH EACH OF THE NINE SOULS IT CONSUMED!
"YOUR BELOVED TEACHER DUCRA WAS THERE THAT DAY.
"SHE WAS THE MOST DEFIANT AMONG THEM...
"SHE WAS THE ONLY ONE OF THE ELDER CLAN TO DEFY HER BROTHER.
"FOR ALL THE GOOD IT DID HER.
"I KNOW THIS ALL--
"--BECAUSE I WAS THERE THAT DAY.
"I WAS THERE WHEN MY MOTHER DUCRA BECAME FOREVER LINKED TO THE UNTITLED!"
SHE... SHE'S LYING.
SHE HAS TO BE.

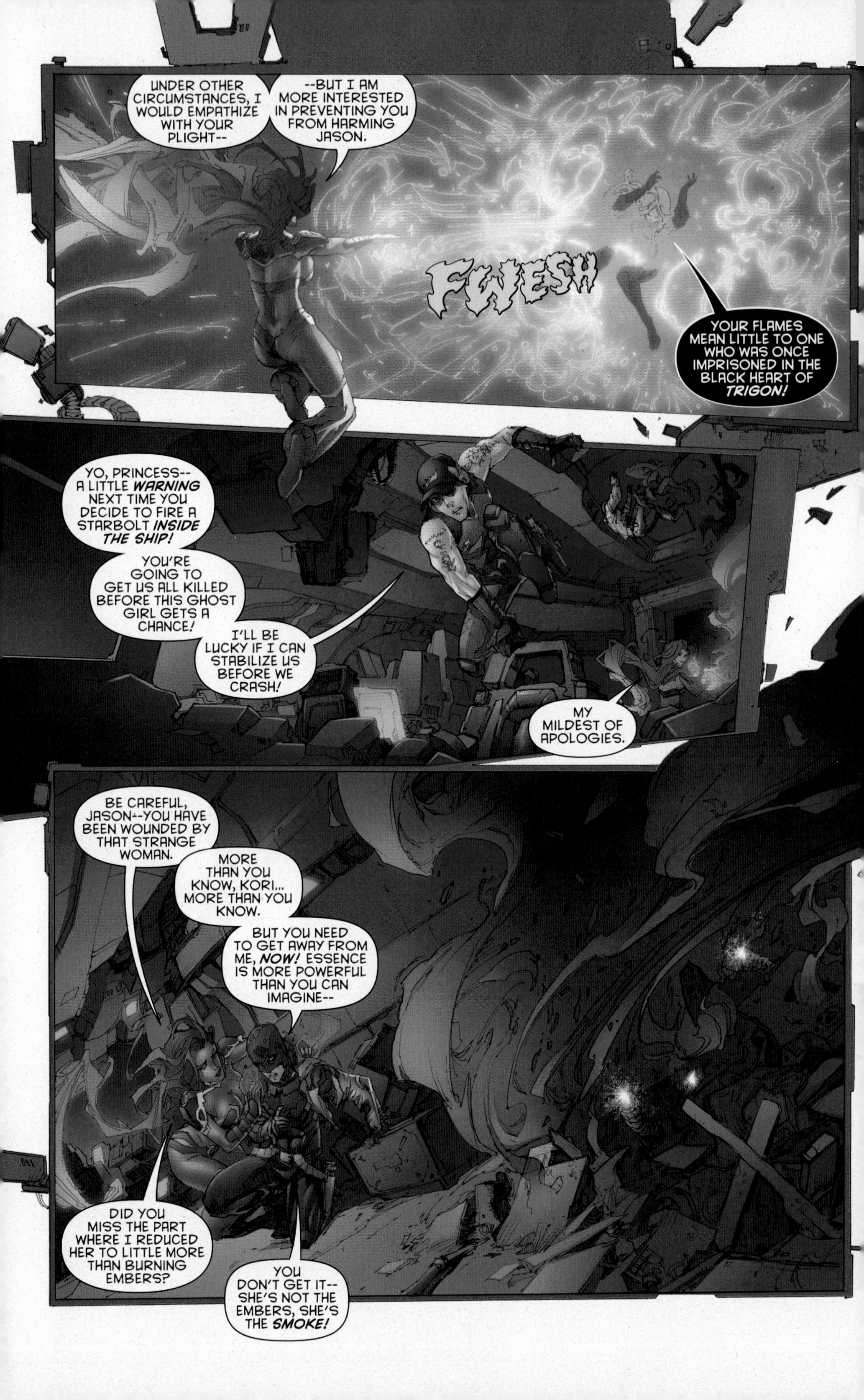
UNDER OTHER CIRCUMSTANCES, I WOULD EMPATHIZE WITH YOUR PLIGHT--
--BUT I AM MORE INTERESTED IN PREVENTING YOU FROM HARMING JASON.
FWESH
YOUR FLAMES MEAN LITTLE TO ONE WHO WAS ONCE IMPRISONED IN THE BLACK HEART OF TRIGON!
YO, PRINCESS-- A LITTLE WARNING NEXT TIME YOU DECIDE TO FIRE A STARBOLT INSIDE THE SHIP!
YOU'RE GOING TO GET US ALL KILLED BEFORE THIS GHOST GIRL GETS A CHANCE!
I'LL BE LUCKY IF I CAN STABILIZE US BEFORE WE CRASH!
MY MILDEST OF APOLOGIES.
BE CAREFUL, JASON--YOU HAVE BEEN WOUNDED BY THAT STRANGE WOMAN.
MORE THAN YOU KNOW, KORI... MORE THAN YOU KNOW.
BUT YOU NEED TO GET AWAY FROM ME, NOW! ESSENCE IS MORE POWERFUL THAN YOU CAN IMAGINE--
DID YOU MISS THE PART WHERE I REDUCED HER TO LITTLE MORE THAN BURNING EMBERS?
YOU DON'T GET IT-- SHE'S NOT THE EMBERS, SHE'S THE SMOKE!

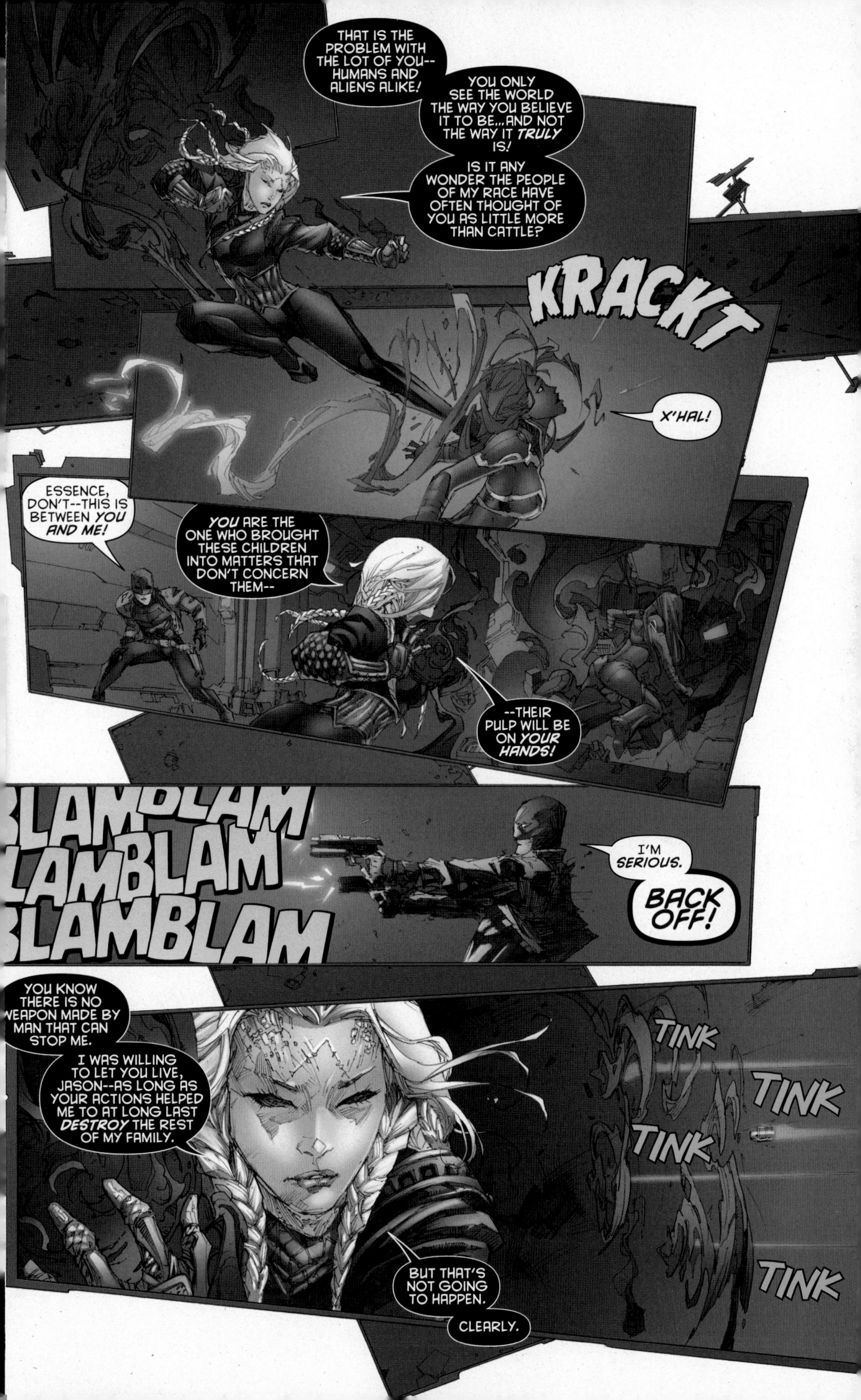
THAT IS THE PROBLEM WITH THE LOT OF YOU-- HUMANS AND ALIENS ALIKE!
YOU ONLY SEE THE WORLD THE WAY YOU BELIEVE IT TO BE...AND NOT THE WAY IT *TRULY* IS!
IS IT ANY WONDER THE PEOPLE OF MY RACE HAVE OFTEN THOUGHT OF YOU AS LITTLE MORE THAN CATTLE?
KRACKT
X'HAL!
ESSENCE, DON'T--THIS IS BETWEEN *YOU AND ME!*
YOU ARE THE ONE WHO BROUGHT THESE CHILDREN INTO MATTERS THAT DON'T CONCERN THEM--
--THEIR PULP WILL BE ON *YOUR HANDS!*
BLAMBLAM
BLAMBLAM
BLAMBLAM
I'M *SERIOUS.*
BACK OFF!
YOU KNOW THERE IS NO WEAPON MADE BY MAN THAT CAN STOP ME.
I WAS WILLING TO LET YOU LIVE, JASON--AS LONG AS YOUR ACTIONS HELPED ME TO AT LONG LAST *DESTROY* THE REST OF MY FAMILY.
TINK
TINK
TINK
TINK
BUT THAT'S NOT GOING TO HAPPEN.
CLEARLY.

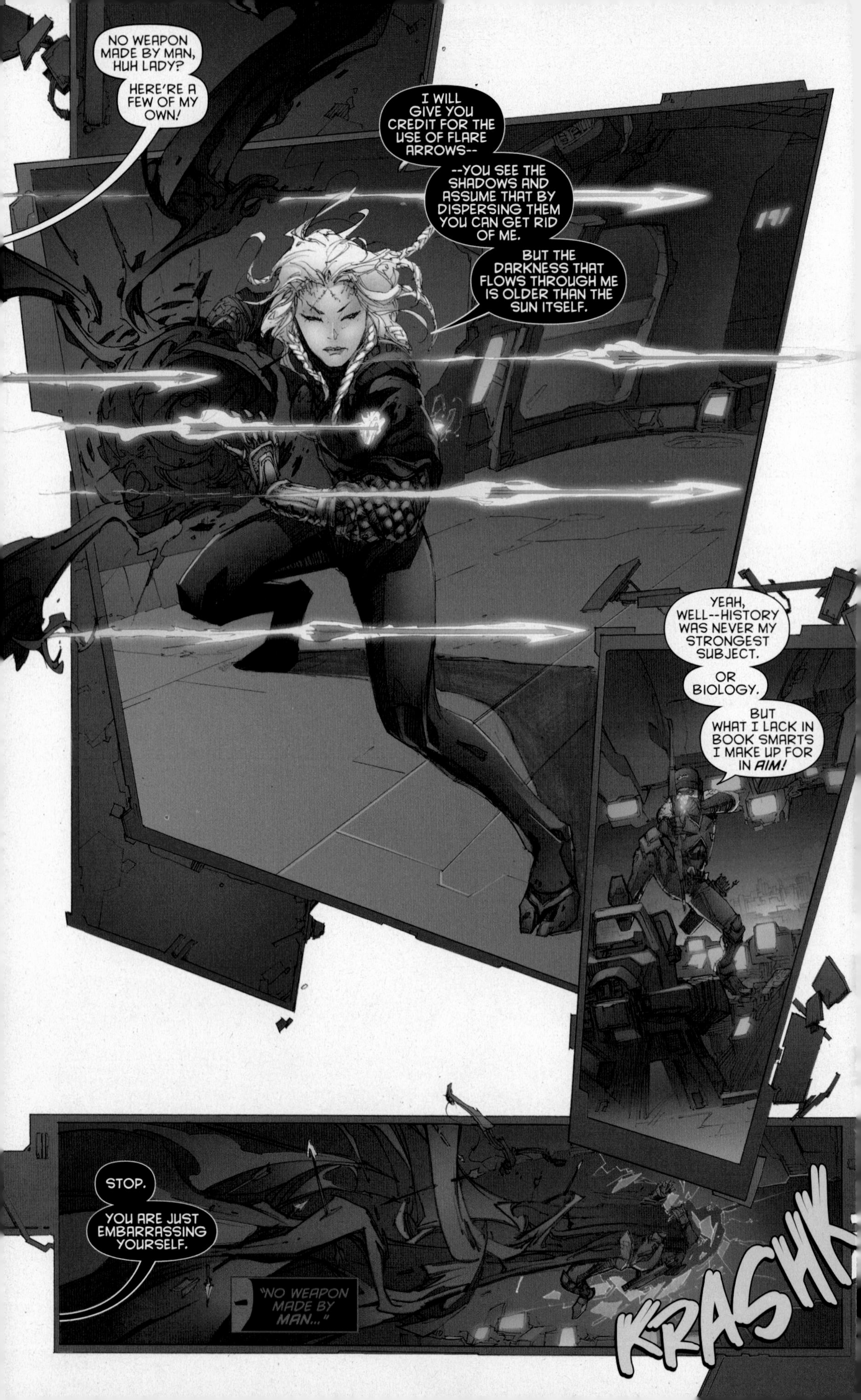
NO WEAPON MADE BY MAN, HUH LADY?
HERE'RE A FEW OF MY OWN!
I WILL GIVE YOU CREDIT FOR THE USE OF FLARE ARROWS--
--YOU SEE THE SHADOWS AND ASSUME THAT BY DISPERSING THEM YOU CAN GET RID OF ME.
BUT THE DARKNESS THAT FLOWS THROUGH ME IS OLDER THAN THE SUN ITSELF.
YEAH, WELL--HISTORY WAS NEVER MY STRONGEST SUBJECT.
OR BIOLOGY.
BUT WHAT I LACK IN BOOK SMARTS I MAKE UP FOR IN *AIM!*
STOP.
YOU ARE JUST EMBARRASSING YOURSELF.
"NO WEAPON MADE BY MAN..."
KRASHK

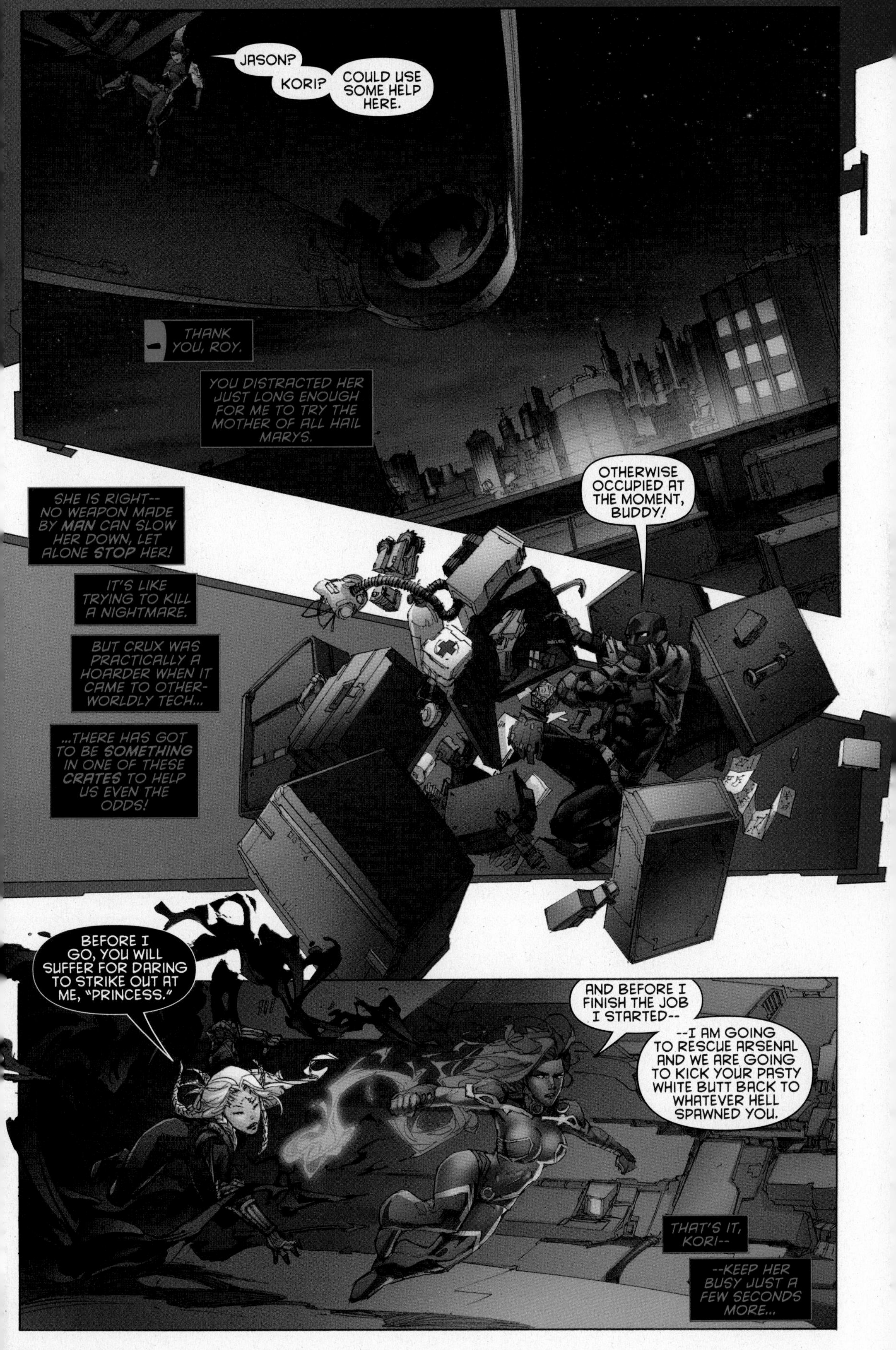
JASON?
KORI?
COULD USE SOME HELP HERE.
THANK YOU, ROY.
YOU DISTRACTED HER JUST LONG ENOUGH FOR ME TO TRY THE MOTHER OF ALL HAIL MARYS.
SHE IS RIGHT-- NO WEAPON MADE BY MAN CAN SLOW HER DOWN, LET ALONE STOP HER!
IT'S LIKE TRYING TO KILL A NIGHTMARE.
BUT CRUX WAS PRACTICALLY A HOARDER WHEN IT CAME TO OTHER-WORLDLY TECH...
...THERE HAS GOT TO BE SOMETHING IN ONE OF THESE CRATES TO HELP US EVEN THE ODDS!
OTHERWISE OCCUPIED AT THE MOMENT, BUDDY!
BEFORE I GO, YOU WILL SUFFER FOR DARING TO STRIKE OUT AT ME, "PRINCESS."
AND BEFORE I FINISH THE JOB I STARTED--
--I AM GOING TO RESCUE ARSENAL AND WE ARE GOING TO KICK YOUR PASTY WHITE BUTT BACK TO WHATEVER HELL SPAWNED YOU.
THAT'S IT, KORI--
--KEEP HER BUSY JUST A FEW SECONDS MORE...

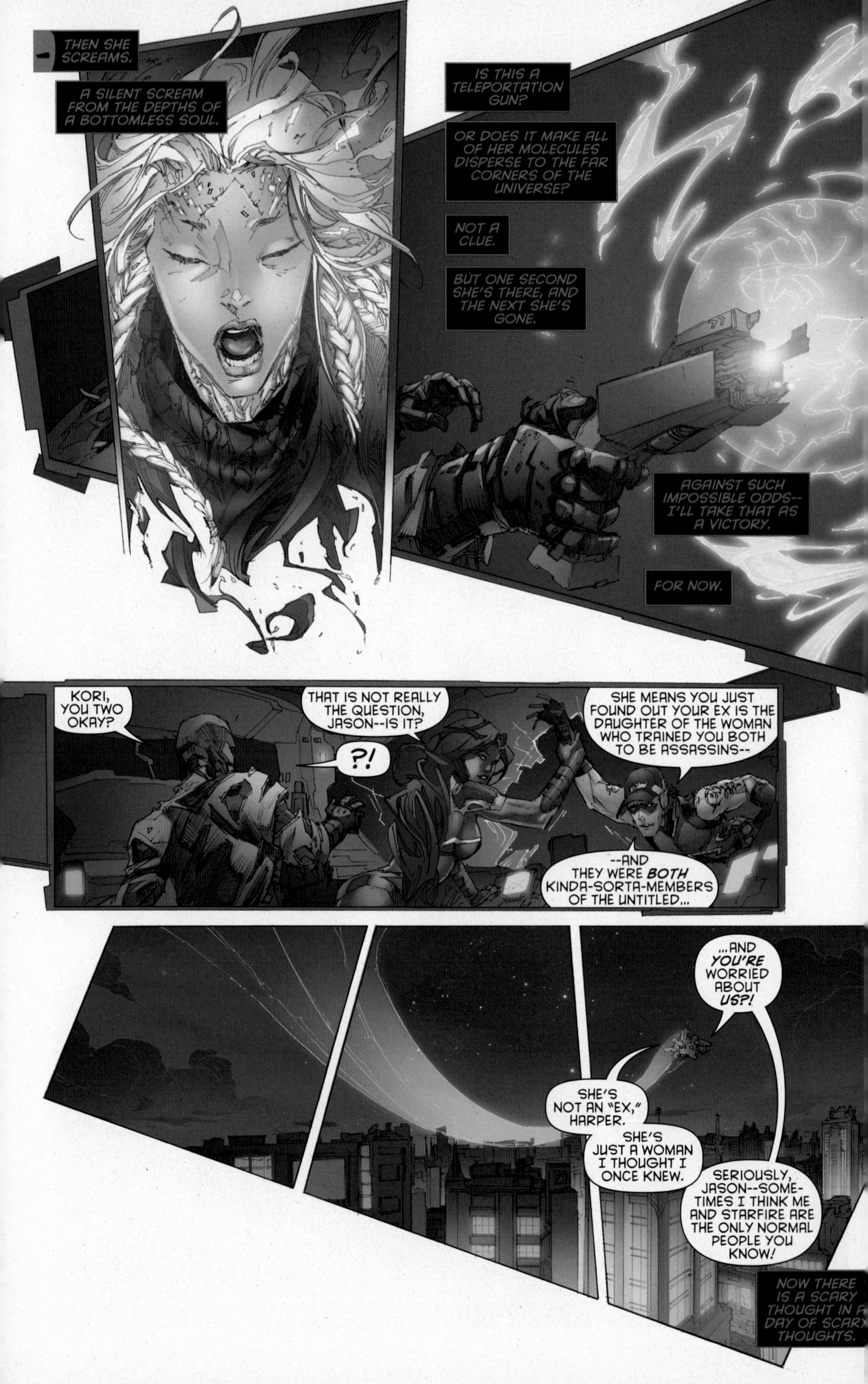
THEN SHE SCREAMS.
A SILENT SCREAM FROM THE DEPTHS OF A BOTTOMLESS SOUL.
IS THIS A TELEPORTATION GUN?
OR DOES IT MAKE ALL OF HER MOLECULES DISPERSE TO THE FAR CORNERS OF THE UNIVERSE?
NOT A CLUE.
BUT ONE SECOND SHE'S THERE, AND THE NEXT SHE'S GONE.
AGAINST SUCH IMPOSSIBLE ODDS-- I'LL TAKE THAT AS A VICTORY.
FOR NOW.
KORI, YOU TWO OKAY?
THAT IS NOT REALLY THE QUESTION, JASON--IS IT?
?!
SHE MEANS YOU JUST FOUND OUT YOUR EX IS THE DAUGHTER OF THE WOMAN WHO TRAINED YOU BOTH TO BE ASSASSINS--
--AND THEY WERE *BOTH* KINDA-SORTA-MEMBERS OF THE UNTITLED...
...AND *YOU'RE* WORRIED ABOUT *US?!*
SHE'S NOT AN "EX," HARPER.
SHE'S JUST A WOMAN I THOUGHT I ONCE KNEW.
SERIOUSLY, JASON--SOME-TIMES I THINK ME AND STARFIRE ARE THE ONLY NORMAL PEOPLE YOU KNOW!
NOW THERE IS A SCARY THOUGHT IN A DAY OF SCARY THOUGHTS.

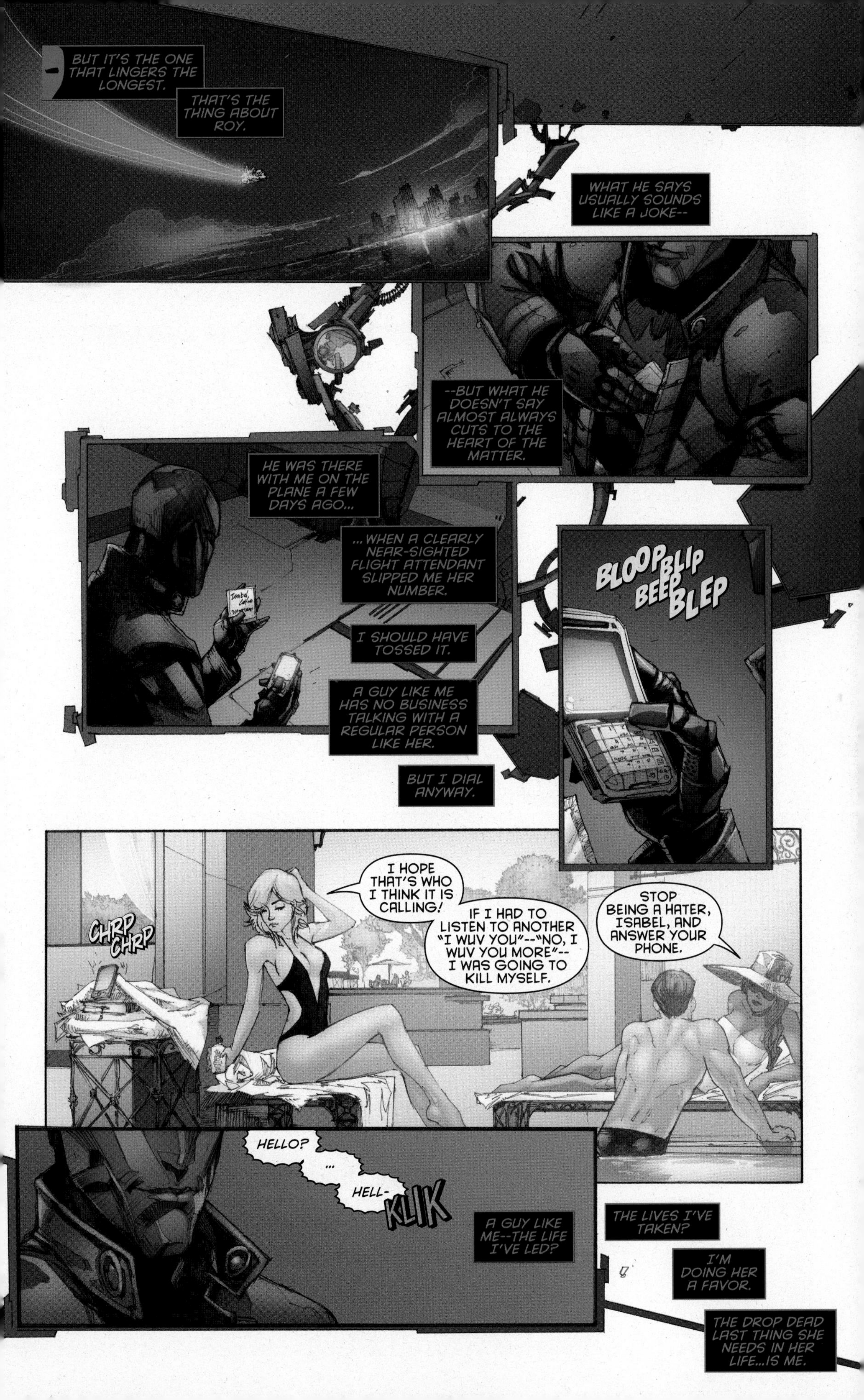
BUT IT'S THE ONE THAT LINGERS THE LONGEST.
THAT'S THE THING ABOUT ROY.
WHAT HE SAYS USUALLY SOUNDS LIKE A JOKE--
--BUT WHAT HE DOESN'T SAY ALMOST ALWAYS CUTS TO THE HEART OF THE MATTER.
HE WAS THERE WITH ME ON THE PLANE A FEW DAYS AGO...
...WHEN A CLEARLY NEAR-SIGHTED FLIGHT ATTENDANT SLIPPED ME HER NUMBER.
I SHOULD HAVE TOSSED IT.
A GUY LIKE ME HAS NO BUSINESS TALKING WITH A REGULAR PERSON LIKE HER.
BUT I DIAL ANYWAY.
BLOOP BLIP BEEP BLEP
CHRP CHRP
I HOPE THAT'S WHO I THINK IT IS CALLING!
IF I HAD TO LISTEN TO ANOTHER "I WUV YOU"--"NO, I WUV YOU MORE"--I WAS GOING TO KILL MYSELF.
STOP BEING A HATER, ISABEL, AND ANSWER YOUR PHONE.
HELLO?
...
HELL-
KLIK
A GUY LIKE ME--THE LIFE I'VE LED?
THE LIVES I'VE TAKEN?
I'M DOING HER A FAVOR.
THE DROP DEAD LAST THING SHE NEEDS IN HER LIFE...IS ME.

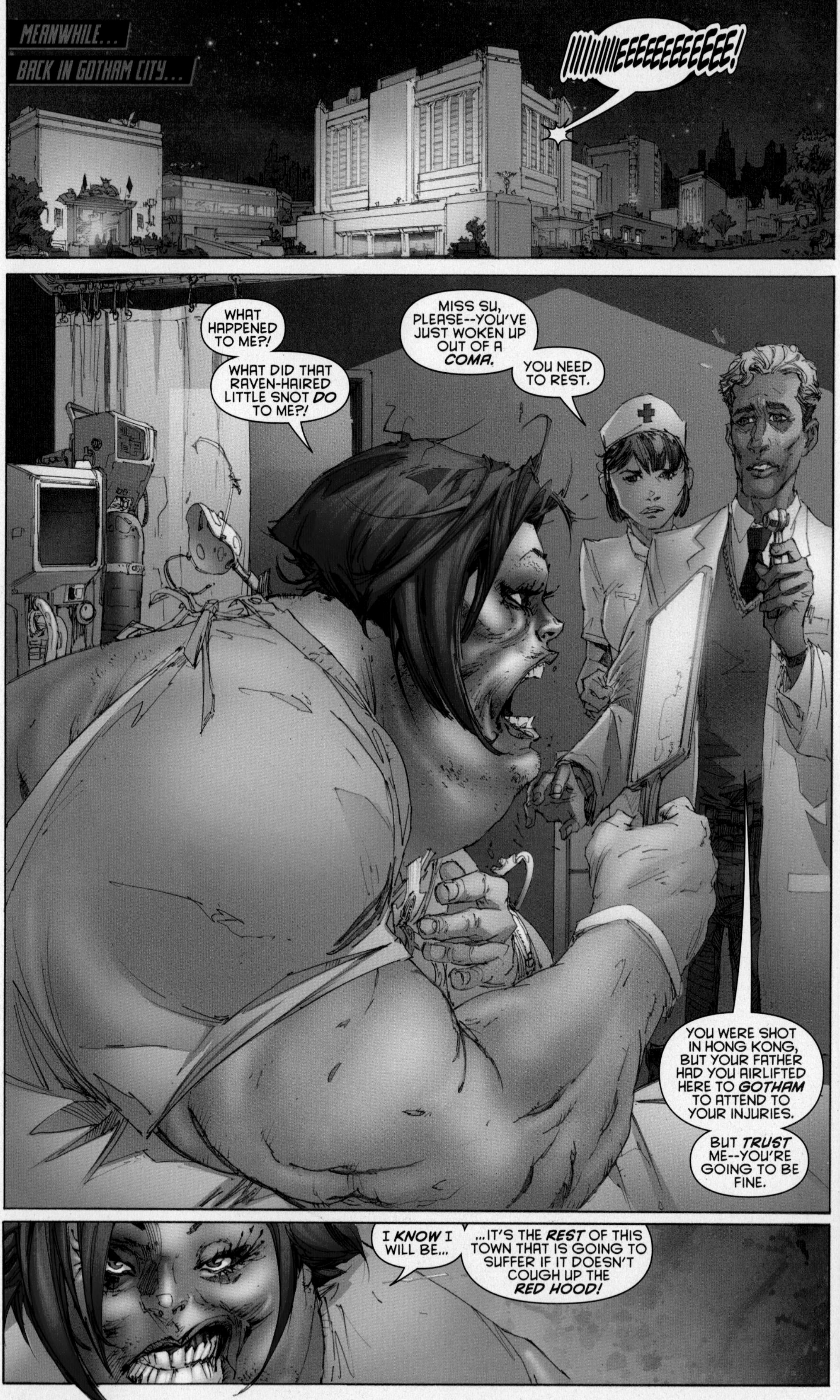
MEANWHILE...
BACK IN GOTHAM CITY...
IIIIIIIIIIIEEEEEEEEEEEE!
WHAT HAPPENED TO ME?!
WHAT DID THAT RAVEN-HAIRED LITTLE SNOT DO TO ME?!
MISS SU, PLEASE--YOU'VE JUST WOKEN UP OUT OF A COMA.
YOU NEED TO REST.
YOU WERE SHOT IN HONG KONG, BUT YOUR FATHER HAD YOU AIRLIFTED HERE TO GOTHAM TO ATTEND TO YOUR INJURIES.
BUT TRUST ME--YOU'RE GOING TO BE FINE.
I KNOW I WILL BE...
...IT'S THE REST OF THIS TOWN THAT IS GOING TO SUFFER IF IT DOESN'T COUGH UP THE RED HOOD!

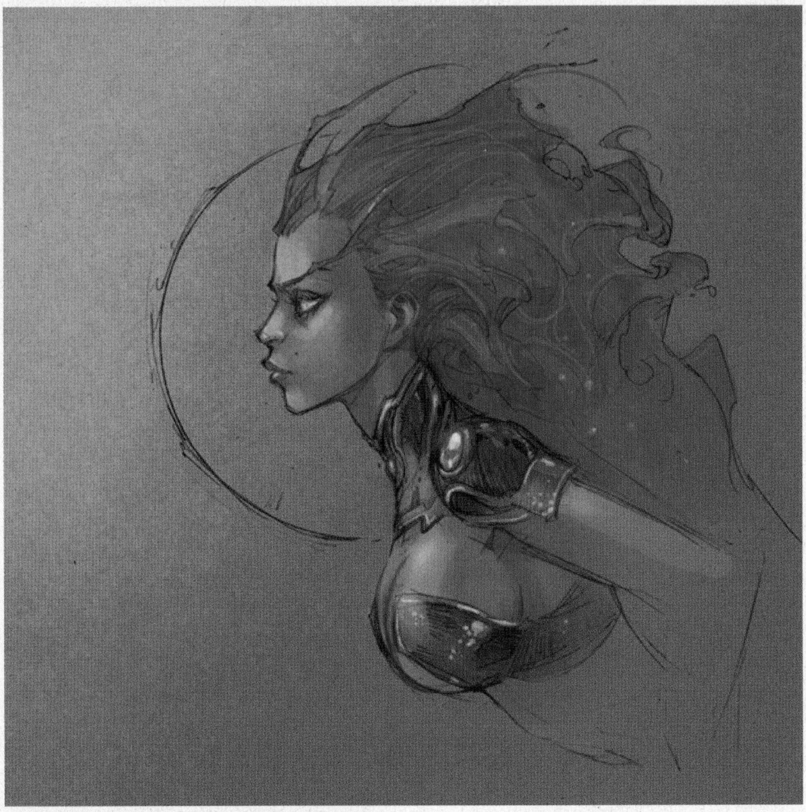

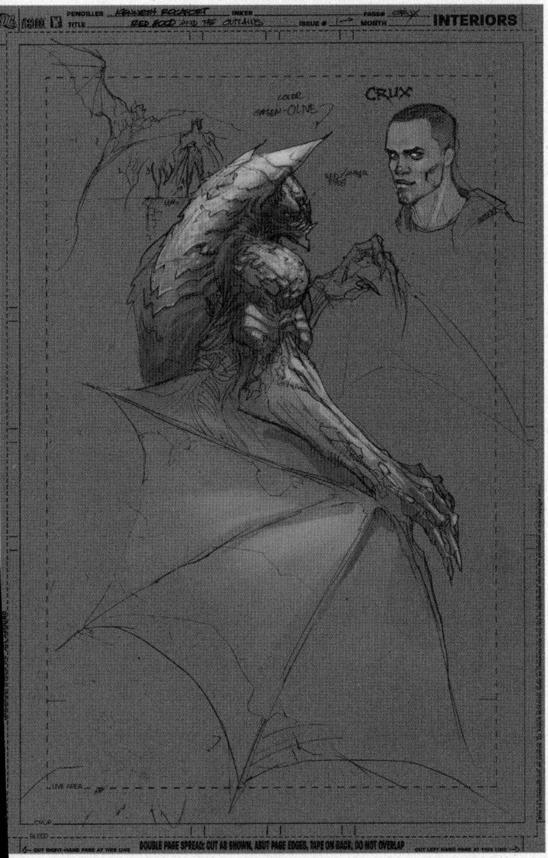
PENCILLER KENNETH ROCAFORT
INKER
PAGE# CRUX
TITLE RED HOOD AND THE OUTLAWS
ISSUE #
MONTH
INTERIORS
CRUX
COLOR
GREEN-OLIVE
LIVE AREA
CROP
BLEED
CUT RIGHT-HAND PAGE AT THIS LINE
DOUBLE PAGE SPREAD: CUT AS SHOWN, ABUT PAGE EDGES, TAPE ON BACK, DO NOT OVERLAP
CUT LEFT HAND PAGE AT THIS LINE

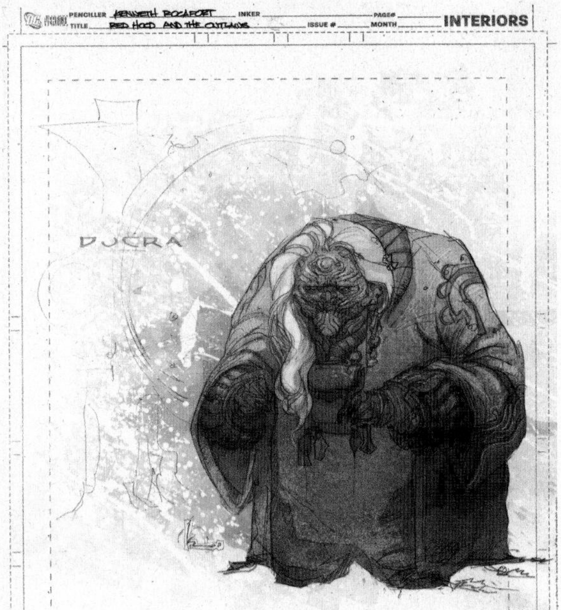
PENCILLER KENNETH ROCAFORT
INKER
PAGE#
TITLE RED HOOD AND THE OUTLAWS
ISSUE #
MONTH
INTERIORS
DUCRA
LIVE AREA
CROP
BLEED
CUT RIGHT-HAND PAGE AT THIS LINE
DOUBLE PAGE SPREAD: CUT AS SHOWN, ABUT PAGE EDGES, TAPE ON BACK, DO NOT OVERLAP
CUT LEFT HAND PAGE AT THIS LINE

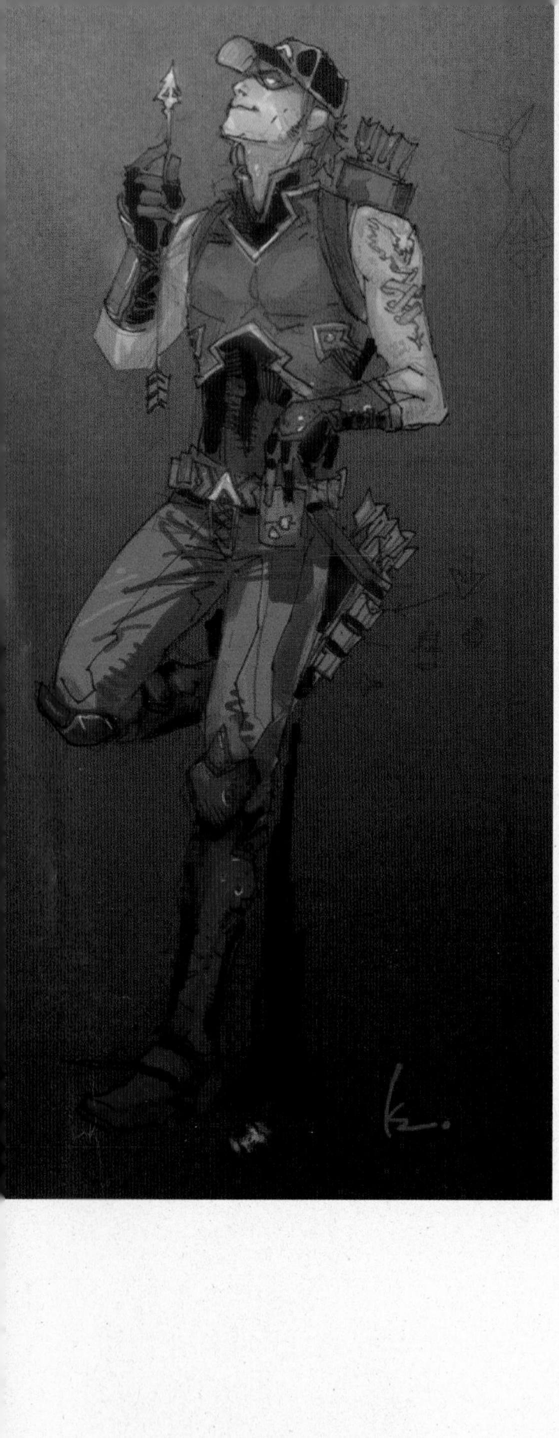

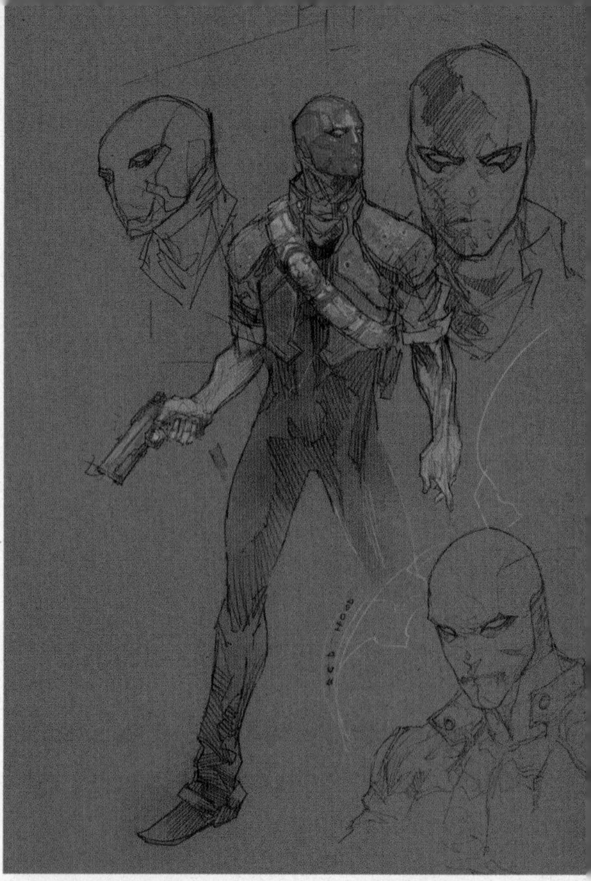

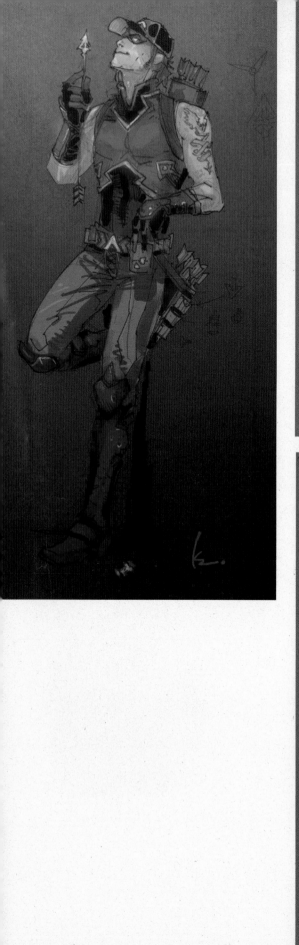

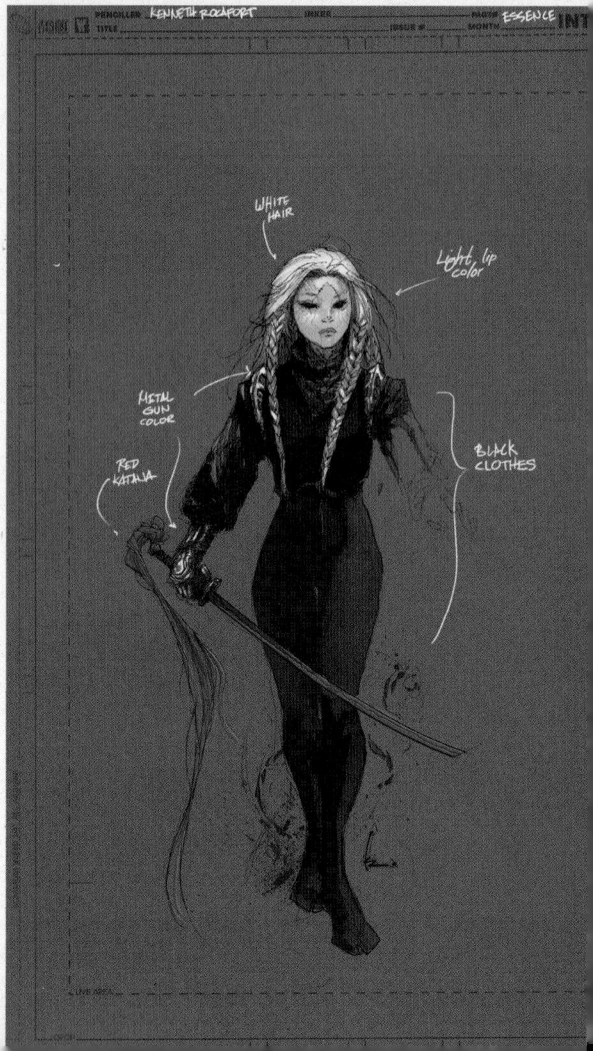
PENCILLER KENNETH ROCAFORT
INKER
PAGE# ESSENCE
TITLE
ISSUE #
MONTH
WHITE HAIR
Light lip color
METAL GUN COLOR
RED KATANA
BLACK CLOTHES
LIVE AREA